A New Nation
of Goods

oct. 10

EARLY AMERICAN STUDIES

SERIES EDITORS

Daniel K. Richter, Kathleen M. Brown, and David Waldstreicher

Exploring neglected aspects of our colonial, revolutionary, and early national
history and culture, Early American Studies reinterprets familiar themes
and events in fresh ways. Interdisciplinary in character, and with a special
emphasis on the period from about 1600 to 1850, the series is published
in partnership with the McNeil Center for Early American Studies.

A complete list of books in the series is available from the publisher.

A New Nation of Goods

The Material Culture of Early America

David Jaffee

PENN

University of Pennsylvania Press

Philadelphia · Oxford

Published by
University of Pennsylvania Press
Philadelphia, Pennsylvania 19104-4112

Printed in the United States of America on acid-free paper
10 9 8 7 6 5 4 3 2 1

Library of Congress Cataloging-in-Publication Data
Jaffee, David.
    A new nation of goods : the material culture of early America / David Jaffee.
        p.   cm.— (Early American studies)
    Includes bibliographical references and index.
    ISBN 978-0-8122-4257-7 (hardcover : acid-free paper)
    1. Connecticut River Valley—Social life and customs—19th century.   2. Connecticut River Valley—Social conditions—19th century.   3. Material culture—Connecticut River Valley—History—19th century.   4. Artisans—Connecticut River Valley—History—19th century.   5. Villages—Connecticut River Valley—History—19th century.   6. Social change—Connecticut River Valley—History—19th century.   7. Community life—Connecticut River Valley—History—19th century.   8. Industrialization—Connecticut River Valley—History—19th century.   9. Middle class—Connecticut River Valley—History—19th century.   10. Consumption (Economics)—Connecticut River Valley—History—19th century.   I. Title.
F12.C7J34 2010
974—dc22
                                                                          2010008850

To Barbara, Isadora, and Oscar

Contents

Plates follow page 192

Preface

Middle-class Americans embraced a new culture of domestic consumption in the mid-nineteenth century that centered on chairs and clocks as well as family portraits and books. How did that new world of goods, with its overstuffed furniture and profusion of daguerreotypes, come into being? *A New Nation of Goods: Material Culture in Early America* highlights the significant role of provincial artisans in four crafts—chairmaking, clockmaking, portrait painting, and book publishing—to explain the shift from pre-industrial society to an entirely new configuration of work, commodities, and culture. As a whole, the book proposes an innovative analysis of early nineteenth-century industrialization and the development of a middle-class consumer culture by using the types of objects that intrigue decorative arts scholars and fans of the PBS series *Antiques Roadshow* to tell about the vitality of village craft production and culture in the decades after the War for Independence.

The familiar tale of how industrialization came to North America features textile factories, surmounted by clock towers and filled with long rows of machines tended by toiling women operators in Lowell, Massachusetts, and surrounding towns. At the same time, the exquisite "folk" portraits of brightly clad children and colorfully stenciled rocking chairs attract admiration; collectors and museum visitors cherish these antiques for their remoteness from the emerging industrial colossus. These two seemingly separate moments, one featuring all the essential elements of industrial society and the other achieving its renown as a vision of a pre-industrial critique of that society, are actually intimately connected. *A New Nation of Goods* focuses on the artisan entrepreneurs who came of age during the Revolutionary era in a world of "small things" and imported luxuries. This generation refashioned large luxury goods such as tall clocks and weighty imported literary tomes into cheap shelf clocks (Eli Terry, shelf clock) and popular biographies (Mason Weems, *Life of Washington*) in the early nineteenth century. The relatively stable colonial world of goods with its restricted range of consumers gave way in the decades after the War for Independence to a new and decentralized world of workshop manufacture and "fancy" goods. These provincial producers took the lesser known route: itinerant portrait makers and inventive clock makers toiled in rural villages, using skilled workers like themselves and serving consumers whom they knew. That era of flux at the provincial grassroots slowly ended at midcentury as a newly emergent group of industrialists and middle-class consumers consolidated their position around the commodities and codes of the Victorian parlor—a new vocabulary of goods. While the endpoints may be well known, this book focuses on the intervening place and time.

We begin with Reverend Ebenezer Devotion, a stern minister of the "old school," sitting for a portrait in his Woodstock, Connecticut, study that his wife, Martha, commissioned in 1770 from the decorative painter and occasional portraitist Winthrop Chandler. Ebenezer sternly sits on a fashionable but restrained Chippendale chair (with a tack missing on the seat), amidst his well-thumbed book collection, culled from throughout the Atlantic world, with the bindings depicted in such detail that we can make out the titles. While the Atlantic world did swirl with the circulation of fashionable objects such as books and tea sets that reached a wider portion of the population, much of that production remained in the hands of overseas importers or urban artisans and was dominated by the patronage of merchants or magistrates like the Devotions in the Revolutionary era. By the time his son Ebenezer, Jr., is portrayed by Chandler with his books—merchant's account books, not literary or theological texts—and furniture, we can see the emergence of village artisans who could meet the provincial gentry's demand for fashionable domestic furnishings in the last quarter of the eighteenth century.

With the opening of the nineteenth century a proliferation of print came from village printshops and entered rural farmhouses, giving young men and women the means to promote new identities that brought together commercialization and knowledge (Chapters 2 and 3). Rural readers such as Silas Felton and female academy students such as Orra White looked for their destiny in the increasingly available precepts of print rather than the ways of their parents. Painters such as Ralph Earl no longer served as isolated local pioneers of domestic cultural production but took to the road to portray the new patrons of the emerging commercial villages. The Village Enlightenment, as I call this cultural movement, did not just involve print but extended to a wide range of domestic goods. I offer a case study of the cosmopolitan commodities and communities of the upper Connecticut River Valley that became a center of American cartography and boasted a bevy of cosmopolitan chair and cabinet makers with their up-to-date designs. City-trained artisans set up village shops until a network of information and commodities crisscrossed the provincial northeastern United States. The growing availability of fashionable furnishings across the United States was based upon no mere diffusion of high-style items, but rather a hybrid creation of cosmopolitan and vernacular design. A popular new form such as a sideboard, for example, when made for a Windsor, Vermont, residence looked different than than one intended for a New York City townhouse.

In the decades of the 1820s and 1830s, enterprising artisans reworked production in their small workshops and reconfigured familiar commodities such as clocks, chairs, and family portraits (Chapters 4, 5, 6). Their itinerancy and inveterate tinkering gave them familiarity with popular tastes and the potential market for cheaper versions of desired household goods. Middling families took advantage of the products that spilled out of provincial workshops, such as painted Windsor chairs with their stenciled seats and wooden shelf clocks with exuberant cornucopia designs. These commodities promoted their claims for inclusion in a village society based upon parlors that represented provincial versions of a refined vision. These producers and consumers entered an era of social and cultural fluidity in the 1820s and 1830s as mass marketed consumer goods became the means by which new entrants competed for social and cultural authority. In this decentralized cultural moment, "fancy" designs brought a look to the provincial family's domestic interior.[1]

Grassroots innovation was soon superseded by industrialization, though not with the suddenness that characterized the birth of Lowell, whose factory system blossomed directly from the entrepreneurial efforts of the Boston Associates. By the 1840s urban manufacturers seized upon new economies of scale and consolidated their position atop the new industrial structure in chairmaking and brass clockmaking, book publishing, and family daguerreotype portraiture (Chapter 7). In many cases, the original industrialists were displaced by the very innovations they had fostered.

A New Nation of Goods grounds its broad narrative of cultural change in case studies of artisans, consumers, and specific artifacts. While the early American artisan has been the subject of a lengthy literature, those studies often focus on the political or economic roles of craftsmen rather than the meaning of their craft work. We are also fortunate to have a growing discussion of the consumerism of the "long eighteenth century," with a few expansive accounts of that process of refinement and democratization as it crossed the Atlantic and enveloped increasing number of colonial British Americans and new American citizens.[2] Many of those narratives, while taking a more cultural perspective, forsake a grassroots approach for a more top-down method of cultural diffusion led by urban taste makers, and do not fully account for how a pre-Revolutionary world of relative scarcity becomes a more abundant material one, and neglects the agency of makers and consumers. Finally, the world of Early American crafts has a noble lineage, with detailed studies of individual furniture makers and "folk" painters by specialists in a particular craft. These scholars and collectors have restored the details of artisans' work lives from account books and newspaper advertisements and collected their body of work through careful connoisseurship of extant objects in museum collections and private collections. However, we need to connect that actual research and hands-on analysis to broader historical questions to understand the nature of cultural change. When we do so, the early nineteenth-century countryside becomes a place of indigenous activity and great creativity.

A New Nation of Goods may start as a social history of makers and consumers, but I range across a variety of fields, including art history, material culture studies, the decorative arts, cultural anthropology, the history of technology, and literary studies. This multidisciplinary approach bridges the usual divisions between the visual arts, material culture, and the history of the book. While each of those literatures is immensely rich and sophisticated, bringing together these long separated fields of study helps us to better understand how the rural world of village artisans and itinerant innovators became a center of creative activity in the post-Revolutionary era and how provincial consumers created a new and colorful type of domestic interior.

Region is another factor in this study, with its primary focus on the villages of New England along with occasional forays into the Hudson River and Mohawk River valleys of New York and the rural counties outside Philadelphia. My argument is that these northeastern regions, first of provincial British North America and then the new United States, were critical for the development of an indigenous manufacturing movement, of artisans working in workshops, producing an ever mounting number of affordable goods for their neighbors, who desired fashionable domestic commodities at an affordable price.

A New Nation of Goods is a book not about the creation of the new United States occurring in political treatises or meeting chambers, but rather the cultural work of nation-building that occurred in towns across the northeast. Village artisans advanced this work by the manufacture of maps of the new states and new nation along with the production of chairs and clocks embellished with eagles and other republican symbols. The circulation of these cartographic and other kinds of objects and books promoted the cultural bonds that jointly contributed to a nationalism brought forth by the consumption of goods. From another angle this book offers a collective biography of the unique generation who came of age after the War for Independence.[3] Born into surroundings of scarcity, they created a new configuration of goods and culture in their roles as craftsmen and consumer. Looked at closely, several possible manufacturing or marketing methods may have coexisted for some time, even if later studies have foregrounded the successful passage to large scale entrepreneurial industry. The innovative techniques of entrepreneurs were often the result of a chance encounter on the road to meet the needs of earning a livelihood, rather than a part of a sustained plan for innovation. But viewed in the broadest perspective, artisan-entrepreneurs forged a culture of commerce, providing the link between provincial farmers and future manufacturers and consumers. They prepared the way for the production and consumption of household commodities. The flow and direction of cultural change shifted direction by mid century; the grassroots vitality of the village enlightenment with its local debating societies and its host of chair making shops scattered over the countryside dried up. Inveterate itinerants moved to the city.

The social and cultural fluidity of the early nineteenth century led to a return to a more hierarchical social structure, yet a very different configuration than the Devotions' pre-Revolutionary world. "The prosperous, upper-middling beneficiaries of New England's economic transformation in the early nineteenth century," Jack Larkin noted for portrait sitters, were not the isolated residents of the distant hinterlands, "but merchants, physicians, lawyers, clergymen, ship captains, manufacturers, the most successful farmers and artisan-proprietors, and their wives and children."[4] New household goods took their place in the codified parlor vocabulary that signified taste and refinement in the pages of *Godey's Lady's Book* and other printed tastemakers. The new middle class announced their arrival by display; fashionable clothes and elaborate furnishings set the middle class apart from their poorer neighbors. The widespread decentralization of the village "Franklins" like Silas Felton and the ranks of the numerous village entrepreneurs gave way to an increasing consolidation of cultural production and prestige, clustered around urban stations. For every local artisan who picked up a camera and successfully transformed himself from a village daguerreotypist to city businessman, many others did not make it. Rural families became dependent on advertisers, urban tastemakers, and other outside authorities for their design decisions. Ironically, the Victorian parlor with its urban manufactured goods and its codified cultural rules excluded many of the enterprising artisans and eager farmers who had participated in that rural revolution. Once-singular objects lost their stature and became mere elements of a standardized and commodified design vocabulary by mid-century.

Fundamentally, material culture matters in this book. Some scholars have hailed the arrival of a "pictorial turn" in the humanities, and historical studies of visual culture have moved forward; however, these approaches have remained at the periphery of the historical discipline. While scholars of material culture have embraced the study of the artifact along with the text in their recent contextual studies, social historical scholarship has paid little attention to the role of materiality in the past. Material culture has been far less prominent in what I and others have called a "visual turn" in this reconfiguration, but certainly vernacular architecture and more recently domestic textiles have been incorporated into the study of topics such as city life or war and identity in eighteenth-century North America.[5] Objects enable the social world to happen, and we need to pay attention to what objects do, and how they work.[6] I question, however, when many historians engage visual and material objects, whether those objects make a difference to the analysis or are they merely glosses on a narrative still based on textual evidence, with the artifacts tossed in just as illustrations? Long ago I was inspired by the writings of Michael Baxandall on the "period eye" regarding the painters and paintings of the Italian Renaissance, which he then extended to the Limewood carvers of Germany to explain the reciprocal relationship between artifacts and culture: "A society develops its distinctive skills and habits, which have a visual impact, since the visual sense is the main order of experience and these visual skills and habits become part of the medium of the painter: correspondingly, a pictorial style give access to the visual skills and habits and, though these, style gives access to the distinctive social experience."[7] And because materials matter, thinking about the tactile nature of a three-inch globe—a work of paper, wood, and metal—has shown us how such an object might appeal to users and viewers as a work of knowledge as well as an item of display and decoration. How can we best understand why a chest of drawers looks the way it does? We can scan patterns books or other contemporary pieces of furniture for clues, but to assess why certain designs are made, we need to think about the tools available on a cabinetmaker's shop bench that allow certain possibilities and not others and also be cognizant of the knowledge and experience embodied in the maker's contact with the wood.[8] These objects do not just exist as social markers but have material presences—that is why we have to "learn to look." The book shows readers how "learning to look" at the construction of a Windsor chair, for example, provides us insights about the changing division of labor as well as the rapid stylistic shifts taking place within the workshop model of rural production. Analyzing a "folk" portrait demonstrates that these paintings are hybrid creations, conforming to provincial tastes for "plain" and flat likenesses, but produced by artists with some academic training along with a keen sensitivity to price.

Finally, *A New Nation of Goods* is a work in the cultural history of taste. In addition to rethinking the direction and pace of social and cultural change, we need to go beyond models of social emulation and assumptions of fixed categories of culture. Instead, fluidity and flux are present in how consumers created domestic interiors and what they might mean, historians John Styles and Amanda Vickery have reminded us, "It is important to remember that as new types of objects moved through the social hierarchy, they changed." Commodities were fashioned from different materials and "they joined different assemblages of goods." They were used in different ways and most important, they acquired different meanings.[9] We need to be interested in the period eye and other ways of seeing objects to get at the big questions of cultural taste. We cannot assume continuities of taste across the Atlantic, from the urban centers to the village locale. Of course, such meanings are difficult to puzzle out from the evidence. While probate inventories and extant objects may tell us what sorts of commodities were available, the meaning of objects changed over time and across social and physical space. That is why we need to map out the many and overlapping communities of taste in the eighteenth and nineteenth century.

A New Nation of Goods weaves together case studies of producers and consumers who embraced these changes, who opposed them, or, most significantly, who fashioned the myriad of small changes that coalesced into a new Victorian cultural order that none of them had envisioned or entirely appreciated. The paths they took toward a capitalist reorganization of the labor process and the market were strewn with alternative models, including direct contacts between producers and consumers, decentralized modes of production within localities specializing in particular goods, and the fusion of design, engineering, and hand skills in a process of technological experimentation. Industrial alienation and commodity fetishism were not inevitable concomitants of the rise in productivity and the proliferation of goods, but rather the eventual result of competition among powerful interests that subordinated working people and subjected consumers to a flood of fashionable cheap goods. This book introduces another kind of "founding father," the inveterate tinkerers who started in small rural workshops or travelled along dusty turnpikes hawking their wares, but ended up, together with their customers, constructing a new kind of domestic culture centered around the middle-class parlor. *A New Nation of Goods* offers a new vision of the leading role of provincial craftsmen and village consumers in fashioning a new American industrial and cultural order.

CHAPTER ONE

Painters and Patrons

The Consumer Revolution

On 8 May 1770, Ebenezer Devotion, the longtime minister of Windham, Connecticut, celebrated his fifty-sixth birthday. Ebenezer and his wife, née Martha Lathrop, marked the occasion by commissioning matching portraits from local limner Winthrop Chandler, who inscribed the date on the reverse side of the two canvases. The patriarchal cleric is shown surrounded by his ample library, a testimony to his professional standing in the community; his unsmiling wife, seated on an expensive side chair and holding up a book for all to see, seems an appropriate consort for the well-read town minister (figs. 1 and 2). Just two years later, Chandler painted portraits of the Devotions' thirty-two-year-old son and daughter-in-law (figs. 3 and 4). Only an account book remains in the portraits of the later generation as Eunice Huntington and Judge Ebenezer Devotion parade their wealth more than their learning. Of course, it makes sense

Facing page, clockwise from top left: Fig. 1. Winthrop Chandler, *Reverend Ebenezer Devotion*, 1770. Oil on canvas. 55-1/4 × 44-1/4 in. Brookline Historical Society, Brookline, Massachusetts. Fig. 2. Winthrop Chandler, *Martha Lathrop Devotion*, 1770. Oil on canvas. 55-1/4 × 44-1/4 in. Brookline Historical Society, Brookline, Massachusetts. Fig. 3. Winthrop Chandler, *Judge Ebenezer Devotion*, 1772. Oil on canvas. 70 × 42 in. Scotland Historical Society, Scotland, Connecticut. Fig. 4. Winthrop Chandler, *Eunice Huntingdon Devotion and Her Daughter Eunice*, 1772. Oil on canvas. 53-1/4 × 37-1/2 in. From the permanent collection of the Lyman Allyn Art Museum, New London, Connecticut. Gift of Margaret Thomas Bower.

that Devotion Senior, a minister, and Devotion Junior, a merchant, would have chosen to be presented with the tools of their trades and to have their wives follow suit. The Reverend Ebenezer Devotion looks eastward in his portrait, toward a past largely dominated by British goods and ideas, even as he questions certain elements of that heritage, while his son, turning his gaze slightly toward the west, captures the energy of a political and consumer revolution that by century's end was centrally involved in shaping an American polity and culture.[1]

From its origins in the colonies' major ports, the American consumer revolution spread into the post-Revolutionary countryside, putting down roots and prompting extensive craft production along with widespread consumer demand. While commodities continued to stream west across the Atlantic, craftsmen, pressured to create a range of cheaper luxury goods for a burgeoning local market, used native materials and experimented with production techniques. At the same time, a growing and increasingly wealthy rural elite mediated local "plain" tastes and the cosmopolitan styles of London and Philadelphia. The dynamic reorientation of domestic production and consumption as well as of the patron-craftsman relationship in the later decades of the eighteenth century can be glimpsed in Winthrop Chandler's fascinating likenesses of Windham's proud father and son.[2] By examining in this chapter their portraits, the portraitist, and the goods the Devotions possessed and exchanged, we can appreciate the complexities of a process that gradually moved from the periphery of North America toward the center.

The concept of a consumer revolution requires qualification. In 1982, Neil McKendrick, one of the editors of *The Birth of a Consumer Society*, hailed the discovery of a consumer revolution that spilled across the Atlantic from Great Britain to encompass the British North American colonies. The revolution he described was not the familiar, production-driven, industrial one attributed to the textile barons of northern England, with its export-driven economy, but rather one fueled by domestic demand awakened by market-oriented entrepreneurs. Historian T. H. Breen, claiming McKendrick's eighteenth-century English consumer revolution for America, then championed the vision of "an empire of goods" in the colonies.[3]

In recent years, new research has brought nuance to this story of cultural innovation, in which a previous material world seemed to be replaced with one strangely like our own. Some scholars, carefully accounting for actual consumers, have examined households in various regions and studied the production and consumption of particular products. Others, fashioning broad historical narratives of Anglo-American material life over several centuries, have made us more aware of the evolutionary, halting character of the construction of a new middle-class world.[4] Although I have opened with a focused study of a pair of

CHAPTER ONE

consumers, I am mindful of the larger context in which such an examination must take place. Recent historians of eighteenth-century Britain have cautioned against assuming a sweeping transformation defined by a consumer revolution and mass-produced goods, terms long associated with the Fordist system of mass production and consumption of the early twentieth century, and have argued for a long transition from an aristocratic system in which goods, often imported, confirmed the authority of their elite owners to a bourgeois, capitalist exchange system in which consumers made claims for social power by means of their purchases and possessions. These historians have pointed to a "product revolution" marked by new innovative manufacturing techniques of novel high-design products, such as china teaware or Birmingham steel buckles, for the "ornament and pleasure of life for a newly emergent middle class in the eighteenth century."[5]

The emerging North American gentry's system of goods—with their expensive cost and occasional use for a genteel performance—did not make for a life dominated by consumption or transform the social or economic structure of agrarian life. The consumer revolution of the British colonies did have limits. The tall clocks and teasets that graced gentry parlors were imported or of urban origin, as the local agrarian economy did not experience a significant structural transformation. Rural craft production came from farmer-craftsmen still tied to the agricultural economy, which made limited numbers of such household commodities as clocks and chests designed to circulate via predominantly local exchange. Rural portrait makers were few and far between in time and place, composed of artisan-artists such as Winthrop Chandler, whose clientele was limited to the elite of New England society. For these families, such luxury goods as family portraits only confirmed a status that was based on the prominent roles they played in the colonies' social, political, economic, and educational life. Finally, these domestic goods took pride of place in a colonial consumption regime dominated by rural elite households that still featured a spare and sparse design aesthetic. However, in the Revolutionary era and beyond, Devotion's son Judge Ebenezer Devotion sought out local craftsmen, part of the growing number of chairmakers and clockmakers who found a niche in the commercializing hinterlands. The post-Revolutionary countryside was the site of innovation and expansion.[6]

The Sitter

When, in 1735, Yale-educated Ebenezer Devotion assumed the pulpit of Windham's Third Society, located in the parish of Scotland (which become a town only in 1857), the Congregational church was in turmoil. Steeped in Enlightenment ideas, Devotion turned away from the harsh Calvinism of his seventeenth-century forebears to portray a loving God who delighted in a humankind that, through its own agency and with the help of divine grace, pursued a moral agenda. The twenty-one-year-old Ebenezer had come to the frontier parish of Windham armed with the collegiate curriculum of classics and theology that served as the base for his later intellectual development and book collecting. This hilly region of northeastern Connecticut was opened up for colonization in the late seventeenth century after the expulsion of the Nipmuc Indians in King Philip's War. Windham quickly filled up with settlers clustered in three villages, each with its own religious establishment. Ebenezer soon married Martha Lathrop, the daughter of a prominent local family; the marriage reinforced his influence in the community and connected him to a thick web of interwoven and important families in the region.[7]

Poised at the apex of the local social hierarchy, ministers were key cultural mediators who managed the flow of information from the larger world to their rural parishioners. "Public news from outside the village was usually disseminated hierarchically," historian Christopher Grasso writes in his study of eighteenth-century Connecticut, "from state proclamations to colonial subjects, from pulpits to congregations, from networks of elite gentlemen to the general populace." The Federalist politician David Daggett nostalgically recalled after the Revolution that colonial Connecticut was "a most perfect aristocracy," with the minister and "two or three principal characters" reigning "supreme in each town," while the entire colony was ruled by the "body of the clergy" in alliance with "a few families of distinction." Books were expensive, often reserved for scholarly purposes, and other information was scarce. In Massachusetts, 70 percent of the learned professionals in 1740 were ministers. Men of authority—those with religious, military, or political stature—commanded the respect of their neighbors when they spoke at church or town meetings in this deferential society. The promulgations of the clergy from the pulpit were the most frequent form of public communication in a world where print was far less important than personal exchanges.[8]

Ministerial authority faced challenges in the second quarter of the eighteenth century. In 1735, Devotion's fellow Yale graduate Jonathan Edwards sparked a revival in Northampton, Massachusetts. Spread by George Whitefield and other itinerant ministers, the Great Awakening produced discord between ministers and the laity. Many established ministers, such as Ebenezer Parkman, had initially lauded the infusion of religious enthusiasm. But the itinerant revivalists who followed Whitefield threatened to shatter the fixed, organic relationship between the established minister and his people that lay at the center of the orthodox system. New Lights, as they were called, challenged a ministry disposed toward reason and routine instead of inspiration and enthusiasm. The cultural landscape for which Devotion had been trained was irrevocably changed. A clerical counteroffensive soon followed. In 1742, the Connecticut Assembly banned itinerant preaching. Two years later, Devotion and his Old Light colleagues in Windham County signed a declaration against itinerants, who "have for some time past & in diverse places in this country gone about recently Publicly preaching the Gospel . . . having no better warrant than a profession of an inward call & motion of the Holy Ghost." Not among the signatories were Devotion's New Light peers in the First and Second Societies of Windham, who had been caught up, along with the majority of eastern Connecticut residents, in the enthusiasm incited by the traveling revivalists.[9]

Itinerants, such as the Reverend James Davenport, fanned the flames of religious enthusiasm, even though the colonists' fervent desire for consumer goods limited their commitment to austerity. When Davenport traveled to New London in 1743, one observer noted:

> I went home att 6 o'clock, and Deacon Green's son came to see me. He entertained me with the history of the behaviour of one Davenport, a fanatick preacher there who told his flock in one of his enthusiastic rhapsodies that in order to be saved they ought to burn all their idols. They began this conflagration with a pile of books in the public street, among which were Tillotson's Sermons, Beveridge's Thoughts, Drillincourt on Death, Sherlock and many other excellent authors, and sung psalms and hymns over the pile while it was a burning. They did not stop here, but the women made up a lofty pile of hoop petticoats, silk gowns, short cloaks, cambrick caps, red heeld shoes, fans, necklaces, gloves and other such aparrell, and what was merry enough, Davenport's own idol with which he topped the pile, was a pair of old, wore out, plush breaches. But this bone fire was happily prevented by one more moderate than the rest, who found means to perswade them that making such a sacrifice was not necessary for their salvation, and so every one carried of[f] their idols again, which was lucky for Davenport who, had fire been put to the pile, would have been obliged to strut about bare-arsed, for the devil another pair of breeches had he but these same old plush ones which were going to be offered up as an expiatory sacrifise. Mr. Green took his leave of me att 10 o'clock, and I went to bed.[10]

Latitudinarian sermons and silk petticoats—all saved from the conflagration by colonists' reluctant to part with some of their prized possessions.

Ebenezer Devotion staunchly rejected the Great Awakening's espousal of a fervent personal relationship with God along with its "horrid Outcries." The Brunswick Separate Church of Scotland publicized its twelve grievances against the established church throughout the town. In their response, "the Pastor & Brethren of the Third Church in Windham" denied that "the present Work in the land" was the "work of God's SPIRIT." When some of Devotion's parishioners removed from his church and charged him with "Preaching Up Works Before faith, and his setting poor Blind Sinners to Work [in] order to Obtain Salvation" in 1746, the church sanctioned the separating members with a formal order of noncommunion.[11]

There was no middle ground in Scotland. Each Sunday, Devotion sent his slave Dick to the separatist meetinghouse to read a proclamation denouncing the schism. In his 1750 sermon "The Mutual Obligation upon Ministers, and People, to Hear, and Speak the Word of God," Devotion, distressed over the dissolution of authority, wondered what might happen if "the Honour, and Obedience which is due to Magistrates, to Parents, and Masters be denied," assuming the undermining of one form would lead to the loss of all. Rhetorically, he answered, "What a doleful Habitation must this be." The revivalists had decried the established clergy's learning and proclaimed it an impediment to a direct experience of the Spirit. Addressing the point, Devotion vehemently defended a decades-old hierarchy in which "the duty of one to Speak, and of the other to Hear the Word of the Lord, will remain in force to Ministers and People respectively throughout all Ages." The Word of God was revealed, Devotion went on, through "hard Study" rather than "immediate Inspiration." "*The Matter must be well Studied*," he insisted, and its spiritual message delivered in a dignified manner. Ministers were obligated to display "all that Authority, Gravity, and Seriousness that becomes their Employment" and to avoid a "Theatrical" approach.[12]

The Great Awakening had been sparked by powerful orators who linked local communities as they traveled from town to village. The subsequent controversy over its social consequences was marked by an unprecedented flurry of print, as clergymen sought to proclaim their authoritative judgments beyond the confines of their local congregations. Promoters and opponents of the revivals each claimed a larger sphere of publicity and authority. The controversy was not just the expression of different interpretative opinions; it was a struggle over which reading of recent events would be legitimized and enforced by the powers of church and state.[13]

During the Stamp Act crisis of 1765, Windham County, a center of protest against the abominable tax levied in violation of the colonists' cherished rights, approved of Devotion's serious defense of the established order, and the town made the uncustomary decision of choosing him to be its representative to the

Connecticut General Assembly. It was unusual for a clergyman to serve in the legislature and even more unusual for a New Light town to elect an Old Light minister to the post. Devotion, however, who saw the church as the moral center of an orderly society, asserted that that society must be free from not only internal revolution but external oppression as well. In his 1766 pamphlet *The Examiner Examined,* he summoned the Whig rhetoric of slavery, tyranny, and rights along with the concept of covenant, in this case shorn of the spiritual dimension that he had previously invoked to uphold the Standing Order. Like God's covenant with man, England's charters with the colonies were "sacred," the source of "the liberties and immunities of natural and free-born subjects."[14]

Both the Great Awakening and the War for Independence offered ordinary parishioners and citizens opportunities to challenge the deference and hierarchy Devotion held sacrosanct and to dispute his pastoral claim to an exclusive authority in all matters social and religious. Although he found himself on different sides of those two great social upheavals of his lifetime, as a religious conservative and a political revolutionary, Devotion's legalistic understanding of the covenant, deepened through his reading in Enlightenment thought, lent intellectual consistency to his arguments.

The Possessions

Books were the tools of a clergyman's trade, a fact that is made visible in Winthrop Chandler's portrait of the Reverend Ebenezer Devotion. In the portrait, his collection of over fifty volumes displays the minister's Enlightened erudition: two volumes of Locke's *Works* face out along with Newton's *Opticks,* while a Puritan tome, William Ames's *Medulla Theologie,* rests upside down. A few volumes can still be found in the family collection, such as Thomas Prince's *Chronology* (*A Chronological History of New-England*), lying on its side on the top shelf, and Robert Jenkins's *The Reasonableness and Certainty of the Christian Religion.* The works so exhibited, which demonstrate Devotion's wide learning in religion, history, law, and philosophy and his mastery of Latin, Greek, and Hebrew, are, we know from the inventory of his estate, a mere selection from his immense library, which contained 123 books and 230 pamphlets worth more than £39. Viewers of Devotion's portrait have the sense that we are interrupting his reading, for his index finger temporarily marks his place in the book he holds in his hand; the disarray of other printed materials in the scene, either upside down or otherwise askew, suggests their ongoing use. Given the genres issuing from eighteenth-century printing presses as well as Devotion's own professional and educational needs, the collection's composition is not surprising: about 33 percent theology, 14 percent classics, and 11 percent history, with a generous sprinkling of schoolbooks, philosophy, law, science, literature, and periodicals. By any measure, his library was magnificent, and it far outstripped other contemporary libraries of the gentry in northeastern Connecticut.[15]

Provincial book collections granted access to metropolitan culture. Such leaders as Devotion went on occasional shopping trips and to ministers' meetings in New Haven and Boston, which gave him an opportunity to replenish his bookshelf. He gathered with his learned colleagues at election days, college commencements, and ministerial conventions. The Worcester County clergyman Ebenezer Parkman returned inland from his visits to relatives in Boston and commencements in Cambridge with books purchased from the port city's booksellers and merchants. Aside from aiding in a minister's pastoral functions, those volumes helped him prepare youngsters for college. Samuel Huntington, later his son-in-law and governor of Connecticut, remembers reading extensively in Devotion's library. Another Connecticut youth recalled Parkman's conversation and collection: "I enjoy not only the Advantage of his most Learned as well as Christian Conversation; but also the pleasure & profit of perusing a Collection of Books not inferior to the best in the hands of Any Country Minister nor do I imagine my priviledges less noble than those to be enjoyed at College." Reference materials also came in handy; Devotion drafted land deeds, wills, and business documents as well as supplied medical advice for his neighbors, since Scotland had no lawyer, doctor, or other learned professional in residence.[16]

Ebenezer Devotion's library signaled his status within an Anglo-American consumer network, as his most prized possessions had made the long journey across the Atlantic. Well over half of his collection was published in London; Geneva and Edinburgh were also represented. Given the provincial state of the colonial book trade and London's secure position as the center of English-language prints, it is hardly surprising that Devotion would have looked east toward the metropolis.

Along with imported books, Devotion's library contained numerous mezzotints, maps, and pictures. The room was furnished with a desk, a square table, and some chairs. Most of the furniture had been ordered from Boston and, like the pastor's portrait, was of the plain style. New London County seating furniture—Chippendale or rococo joined chairs—lacked elaborate carved ornamentation and was made from cherry rather than imported mahogany, but it still possessed a formal complexity and decorative nuances. In his portrait, Devotion sits on the most expensive of such chairs, one with a leather-covered seat. Desks were becoming more popular, and Devotion's, at which he may have written his weekly sermon, has a family history dating to the turn of the eighteenth century. A more elaborate mahogany desk and bookcase also associated with the family originated in Boston.[17]

In the dining room were a large round table, several smaller tables, and eight brown (probably Windsor) chairs. For the kitchen, the inventory listed more chairs as well as cooking and eating utensils. The chambers held various beds and bed hangings along with chests, trunks, and case drawers. A "case draws," the second most expensive item enumerated in the inventory, suggests a high chest of drawers, probably one manufactured in Connecticut that descended through the family.

The fashionable parlor likely contained the family portraits and framed prints, a few leather-bottomed chairs, tea equipment, and an expensive, imported, eight-day London tall clock—all listed in his room-by-room inventory. The clock's brass works had been fashioned by the London clockmaker Henton Brown, and its oak case was ornamented with japanning, a decorative application that imitated Chinese lacquerware. The piece was the most valuable item listed in Devotion's probate inventory (fig. 5). Three small prints that remain in the family, still in their original frames, depict Queen Charlotte, wife of King George III; the king of Prussia; and Sir William Johnson, the British Superintendent of Indian Affairs in the 1750s and 1760s. Robert Trent has written in his study of eastern Connecticut probate inventories that Devotion "possessed most of the prerequisites of elite status."[18]

Tea, an exotic commodity initially esteemed for its medicinal purposes, came to be valued as a mark of gentility, and its use spread through all ranks of society, including the ministry. The preparation, service, and consumption of tea required an entirely new panoply of goods: the teapot, sugar bowl, imported cups and saucers, and even a new furniture form, the tea table, "one of the most culturally charged furniture forms in eighteenth-century Anglo-America," according to Ann Smart Martin, because of its associations with gentility, luxury, and performance. Ebenezer Devotion owned a tea table, along with "3 Setts China Teacups & Sawrs [saucers]," as well as several silver teapots, tea tongs, and spoons. In addition to equipment, tea drinking required mastery of a special kind of knowledge dictating how to hold a teacup, as well as how to prepare and pour tea. The successful performance of the genteel ritual of tea taking eased one's inclusion into the ranks of the refined and excluded those unwilling or unable to participate. A new beverage, featuring exotic imports from the Orient, signaled the new commodity culture of the British Atlantic world.[19]

The Portraitist

Winthrop Chandler found his clients among the aspiring gentry of northeastern Connecticut and, just over the border, in southern Worcester County, Massa-

Fig. 5. Brass-clock movement made by Henton Brown, working 1726–66, in London. Oak case with japanning on red ground, 102 in. This tall clock was the most expensive object in the Devotion home. Brookline Historical Society, Brookline, Massachusetts.

chusetts. He had been born on Chandler Hill, a high ridge of land in Woodstock, Connecticut, with its fine views of the surrounding landscape that had
been home to three generations of Chandlers. His great-grandfather John Chandler thought the eastern town of Roxbury too crowded and, like many other
New Englanders, had ventured off to new lands and new opportunities further
inland; he eventually participated in the founding of Woodstock, Connecticut.
Both Winthrop's grandfather and father had been surveyors as well as farmers
and had accumulated substantial acreage in Woodstock.[20]

William and Jemima Bradbury Chandler, who had given birth to ten children, named their youngest after Governor John Winthrop, one of Jemima's
ancestors. The family lived in what one local historian referred to as "a colonial
mansion," but after her husband's death in 1754, Jemima faced the daunting
task of placing each son in an occupation. When Winthrop came of age in 1762,
his brother-in-law, who also served as his guardian, apprenticed him to a portrait painter in Boston, according to Worcester's nineteenth-century local historian. No other documentation exists for this statement; however, it seems that
Chandler entered the circle of coach, sign, and fancy painters in Boston, one of
British North America's centers of craft production.

In the port city's cosmopolitan culture, artisans moved adroitly from decorating furniture to painting portraits. Several practitioners of the urban painting
trade—John and Samuel Gore and Thomas Craft—had been Chandler's neighbors in Woodstock, and they would have been well known to Jemima Chandler
as she searched for an appropriate position for her son. Once in Boston, it
appears likely that Winthrop made the acquaintance of America's premier portrait painter, John Singleton Copley, who painted the boy's cousin, Mrs. Lucretia Chandler Murray, circa 1763.

Chandler's work achieves its power from his keen sense of observation and
precise description of what lies before him. His large and imposing portraits of
the Reverend Ebenezer Devotion and his wife compel our attention by means
of what art historian Nina Little has called the artisan-artist's stark realism. The
leather binding on one volume is torn and peeling, while the chair Devotion
sits on is missing a brass tack (see fig. 1). Chandler's direct, somber likenesses of
Windham and Worcester County notables feature individual characterization, a
penchant for detail, tight linearity, and sophisticated but hard modeling. His
skills were not always adequate for rendering the complexities of anatomy and
foreshortening, and he blocked out color in a basic way. No classical allusions,
such as columns or vases, clutter the scene. Instead, Martha holds a single book,
perhaps the devotional tract *A Saving Interest in Christ* (a book in the Devotion
family collection inscribed "Martha Lathrop"), and a fan (see fig. 2). The only
decorative flourish in the painting is the drapery hung above her head.[21]

How different from the work of his contemporary, John Singleton Copley. The first great American-born painter, Copley (1738–1815) grew up in Boston. His stepfather, the engraver Peter Pelham, died in Copley's youth. The largely self-taught young Copley took advantage of the available resources: immigrant portraitists, mezzotints, and picture galleries. His rapid progress in graphic designs and rich color schemes made him the portraitist of choice for the colonial merchant princes of Boston beginning in the 1760s; later he visited New York and Philadelphia. He distanced himself from his artisanal activities, lamenting in a famous letter, possibly written to his fellow artist Benjamin West, in 1767: "A taste of painting is too much Wanting to affoard me any kind of helps; and was it not for preserving the resembla[n]ce of perticular persons, painting would not be known in the plac[e]. The people generally regard it no more than any other useful trade, as they sometimes term it, like that of a Carpenter tailor or shew maker, not as one of the most noble Arts in the World." Copley displayed his fluency with metropolitan conventions in his pastel self-portrait of 1769, clad in a gold-trimmed waistcoat, covered by green silk banyan, a high-style dressing robe, looking every bit the English aristocrat. He painted the elite of Boston society, men such as the merchant Nicholas Boylston, the very "Prince" whose home so dazzled John Adams. In his diary, Adams described a 1766 visit with Boylston: "Went over the House to view the Furniture, which alone cost a thousand Pounds sterling. A seat it is for a noble Man, a Prince. The Turkey Carpets, the painted Hangings, the Marble Tables, the rich Beds with crimson Damask Curtains and Counterpins, the beautiful Chimny Clock, the Spacious Garden, are the most magnificent of any Thing I have ever seen."[22] Certainly, Copley's portrait must have been the centerpiece of that consumer palace, with its owner's refined taste and extraordinary wealth declared by his banyan made of expensive English silk damask and by his turban, the picture of luxury, "looking more like a sultan than a businessman," art historian Paul Staiti has written (fig. 6).[23] Finally, the sheen and sensuality of Copley's portraits would have been quite out of place in Woodstock, Connecticut. Chandler's depiction achieves its declarative power from its subject's direct connection to his audience and working mode. This was the face of provincial aristocracy.

Patron and Craftsman in the Hinterland

Ebenezer Devotion helped suppress a revolutionary challenge to the established religion and was on the leading edge of the American Revolution. Yet there was also a third revolution looming in the late eighteenth century. While he followed colonial patterns of consumption, he witnessed the onset of a consumer revolution that, as it gradually washed over the countryside after the War for

Fig. 6. John Singleton Copley, *Nicholas Boylston* (1716–71), 1767. Oil on canvas. 50-1/4 × 47-1/4 in. Harvard Art Museum, Fogg Art Museum, Harvard University Portrait Collection, Bequest of Ward Nicholas Boylston to Harvard College, 1828, H90. Cambridge, Massachusetts. Katya Kallsen © President and Fellows of Harvard College.

Independence, transformed American culture. For a conservative rural resident like the Reverend Ebenezer Devotion, the luxury goods he possessed—family portraits, a tea service, and an imported clock—were only one marker of a status that derived from multiple, mutually reinforcing sources: social, political, economic, religious, and educational. In the aftermath of war, Americans found themselves increasingly on the move. "Migrants and travelers needed a standardized system of social communications," Cary Carson has noted for early modern Europe, a system by means of which they could signify their status no matter how far they journeyed from home. Gentry in urban areas initiated the system of universal and portable goods, such as fancy clothes or teaware, but rural buyers began following suit by the takeoff point for the consumer revolution of the second quarter of the eighteenth century.[24]

The material world of seventeenth-century colonists had been rough, even by comparison to the English peasantry. By the end of the century, a creole, or American-born, aristocracy composed of merchants and planters in the north and southern colonies began to coalesce. They accumulated a more abundant array of household objects to set themselves off from their rude origins and plebeian neighbors, yet there were limits to that distinction. In 1704, William Brinton, a second-generation descendant of English immigrants to Delaware County, Pennsylvania, built his "Great House," as it was known, a two-story stone house to supplant his immigrant father's simple frame house (fig. 7). The building stood without decoration, its low ceilings, absence of paint, and narrow stairs connecting it to a barebones past as well as to contemporary building stock in southeastern Pennsylvania and the rest of the British colonies.[25]

By the 1720s, that material world changed. The emerging gentry began to assume a provincial high style, historian Kevin Sweeney has written, constructing a qualitatively different way of life intended to differentiate and distance themselves from their social inferiors. Local patrons and craftsmen turned to the William and Mary style, an early Baroque form marked by motifs derived from the Orient, with a new emphasis on smooth surfaces for tea tables, and providing new forms, such as dressing tables, for refined activities. Even poorer families entered into the world of goods through the acquisition of inexpensive bits of clothing and decoration. For example, shortly before Christmas 1721, William Moore, described as "a Pedler or Petty Chapman" in the court records, journeyed to the remote frontier town of Berwick, Maine. Berwick villagers consumed his pack of manufactured goods from Boston. Daniel Goodwin bought "a yard and halfe of Stuff for handcarchiefs." His daughter Sarah Goodwin purchased "three quarters of a yeard of muslin," fine thread, and black silk, along with enough "Lase for a Cap." Sarah Stone obtained some "smole trifeles."[26] Berwick's local authorities were quick to confiscate Moore's "bagg or pack of goods," armed with provincial legislation that cited the "great hurt to and decay of trade" that was occasioned by the "hawkers and pedlars passing through the country." The magistrates' investigations proved that Moore had come north with "sundry goods and Merchandizes for Saile & that he had Travelled from town to town Exposeing said Goods to Sale and has Sold to

Figs. 7 and 8. William Corbit built his Georgian mansion house, known today as the Corbit-Sharp House (*bottom*) in Odessa, Delaware (1772–74) with ample decoration, inside and out. The exterior featured a pedimented doorway and carved window lintels. Much had changed since his grandfather William Brinton's far plainer 1704 house (*top*) in West Chester, Pennsylvania, that stood with about half the Corbit footprint and little of its decoration. William Brinton House, 1704. West Chester, Pennsylvania. Historic American Building Survey, Library of Congress, Washington, D.C. William Corbit (Corbit-Sharp) House. 1772–74. Odessa, Delaware, National Park Service.

Sundry persons." Moore was taken into custody and his wares left in a neighbor's charge. Upon his return, he found that the greater part of those eagerly sought-after goods were missing.[27]

The revolution becomes most obvious to later-day observers with less portable goods. By midcentury, mansions were reorienting space and status in urban centers. Many middle-class gentry built anew or rebuilt their existing houses, turning small and cramped dwellings into stately homes with symmetrical Georgian facades and fashionable central halls that introduced the elements of formality and separation. West of the town of Dover, Delaware, Nicholas Ridgely in 1749 incorporated an adjoining older structure; while the outside did not have a uniform exterior, on the inside he was able to provide the necessary center passage and staircase. His death only a few years later revealed his middle-class status by his income and furnishings: a sparse domestic interior, with no curtains and carpet to cover the floor and windows. Even his best room, the parlor, contained "old and broken" china, according to the assessors. A tea table and two other tables stood in the parlor, along with eight chairs, the necessary equipment for genteel entertaining, even if a few rough edges remained in his interior decoration owing to his limited means and restrained aspirations.[28]

As one moved across the colonial cultural landscape, the language of goods became the lingua franca. Alexander Hamilton, a Scottish physician traveling through the colonies in 1744, met three strangers at an inn outside Philadelphia. Morison, "a very rough spun" and "clownish blade," was much "desirous to pass for a gentleman," constantly apologizing for his "misbehavior," which he characterized as frankness. However, their landlady, seeing his dirty cap, greasy clothes, and clownish air, took him for "some ploughman or carman." Presented with "some scraps of cold veal" for breakfast, Morison flew into a rage, threatening the innkeeper with violence except for the presence of his genteel companions. To prove the mistaken social identification, he replaced his worsted night cap with a linen one from his pocket. He informed his company that although he might appear a plain fellow, "he was able to afford better than many that went finer: he had good linen in his bags, a pair of silver buckles, silver clasps, and gold sleeve buttons, two Holland shirts, and some neat night caps; and that his little woman att home drank tea twice a day." The traveler was sure that his host and all the audience would negotiate his passage by reference to the commonly understood language of goods, his ownership of buckles and consumption of tea clinching his claims to gentility.[29]

Colonial wars and the economic boom in British North America at midcentury quickened the competition for display and decoration. In the 1760s and 1770s, splendid carriages appeared in the streets, and Copley portraits graced patricians' houses in Boston and New York. Even among the rural gentry, the scale of country seats increased. When William Corbit built his new house in the small village of Cantwell's Bridge, Delaware, in the spring of 1772, he chose an imposing structure of two stories, four rooms on each floor, separated by a hall and central passage for domestic privacy along with public display (see fig. 8). The Georgian-style house, with its clear Philadelphia patterns, stood apart from neighbors' dwellings in the small community of just fourteen families—by its commanding size and decorated details along with unusual innovations, such as its broad staircase and social spaces for entertainment—as well as being removed from his own grandfather "William Brinton's Great House" of 1704.[30]

By the 1770s, goods previously considered luxury items, such as tableware, were appearing in humble households as well. Almost half of Massachusetts inventories of those at or below the median in personal wealth listed tea equipment and wares, and almost 40 percent owned knives and forks. The likelihood that rural-gentry households would have family portraits was also increasing. Devotion and his fellows did not slavishly follow the latest fashions or display their most opulent forms, however. Patrons navigated amidst the proliferation of consumer choices in the third quarter of the eighteenth century, mediating between cosmopolitan British trends and local community preferences. That mediation is evident in the intriguing negotiations that took place between craftsmen and consumers in the American hinterland.[31]

In the bustling port cities of British North America, the numbers of craftsmen rose rapidly. Forty furniture makers worked in Boston in the first decade of the eighteenth century; that number had tripled one decade later. As communities of artisans grew denser, they in turn created a complex infrastructure of related tradesmen. In portraiture, for example, relatively stable communities of artists and patrons were well served by vendors offering artists' supplies, books, and lessons in painting. When Charles Willson Peale left Annapolis on a visit to Philadelphia in 1763, he was able to view the work of James Claypoole, Jr., visit the painter Christopher Steele, and go to a bookstore and color shop: "Rivington who then kept a Bookstore at the Corner of Market & front street in who's store Mr. Steele was often seated. At this store I bought the hand maid to the arts, it was the only Book he had on colours or painting; this I began to study art at my lodgings in order to enable me to form some judgment on what Colours I ought to purchase also the quantity. Mr. Marshall in Chestnut Street, the only colour shop in the City, obligingly gave me a list of what colours he had and the prices annexed."[32] Craftsmen were irrevocably linked to the urban mercantile economy and faced the competition of a bustling marketplace. In response, they perfected a year-round specialization, as well as stockpiling products with access to long-distance trade networks. As townspeople walked along seventeenth-century Boston's crowded lanes, they encountered the shops of joiners, turners, upholsterers, cabinetmakers, and chairmakers; by the eighteenth century, carvers, japanners, chair caners, Windsor chairmakers, picture-frame carvers, and looking-glass makers had joined the ranks of those artisans.[33]

The same networks of trade and communication that carried goods to America from Europe brought artisans and ideas across the Atlantic, mostly to the port cities; these artisans were armed with new designs from London and Edinburgh. Port cities were centers of government as well as commerce, with clusters of merchants, magistrates, and other professionals for patrons. Design books, such as Thomas Chippendale's *The Gentleman and Cabinet-Maker's Director*, provided information about the most up-to-date furniture forms. The first colonial clockmakers boasted metropolitan British training; James Batterson, maker of the earliest known dated American clock, had arrived in August 1707 in Philadelphia and moved to Boston that fall, advertising "lately from London"; he then worked in New York City and Charleston, South Carolina. Boston and Philadelphia developed clockmaking clusters with urban-trained artisans fanning out along coastal New England, New Jersey, and New York. Printers remained rare in colonial British North America and were confined to cities; twelve towns in the colonies had printers in 1760, but two-thirds of the total number of printers was concentrated in Boston, New York, and Philadelphia. The twelve artists fashioning portraits in 1750 had doubled by 1776. Some portraitists took up residence in smaller commercial centers in New England, such as Portsmouth and Salem, and others began to travel from Boston and New York to inland communities in search of commissions. Connecticut even produced some native-born portraitists, such as Ralph Earl and Winthrop Chandler, by the 1770s to paint the emerging regional gentry.[34]

As more and more artisans set up shop in Boston, the economic prospects of the class diminished. At the same time, rural communities were becoming socially more sophisticated. Conditions were ripe for skilled craftsmen to chase better opportunities outside of urban centers. As they did so, they brought new modes of work to the agrarian economy. As Robert St. George has detailed them, those practices included "a strategic knowledge of wage labor and quantity production based on the stockpiling of premade parts for later assembly, the journeyman's strategy of moving from job to job for work, and the workshop whose efficiency relied on the carefully monitored orchestration of several workers."[35]

As these craftsmen integrated their urban trades into the rhythms of the agrarian economy, they affected the plain taste of the rural gentry. William Manley had left the Massachusetts Bay area around 1730 for the prosperous Connecticut River Valley region, where he introduced the new Queen Anne style to his Wethersfield, Connecticut, customers. At the same time, fathers faced a declining stock of land to pass on to their sons, and farmers intensified their labors in the field throughout the year; the rural economy accelerated the movement from agriculture into manufacturing. More precisely, the economic sectors of agriculture and industry, farming and manufacturing, as well as urban and rural had never been entirely distinct; and the cultural categories of sophistication and naïveté were not rigid or clearly demarcated, but rather represented behavior along a spectrum that offered possibilities for creative adaptation all along the way. Once in the countryside, eighteenth-century craftsmen were often forced to become farmers, too, in order to support themselves and their families. And handy farmers, accustomed to making their own furniture and tools during the long winter months, began to devote more time and energy to craft production. Indeed, boundaries were quite fluid between production taking place within farm households by family labor, production for local exchange by farmers swapping work or goods, and production by skilled craftsmen in shops with the assistance of journeymen and apprentices. Women manufactured textiles and made cloth; many households listed a spinning wheel or loom for making yarn or weaving. In Brookfield, Massachusetts, one quarter of the farmers owned carpentry tools, and several combined farming with coopering, blacksmithing, and shoemaking. In all the Brookfield inventories or land deeds, only four men designated themselves as artisans: one hatter, one cooper, one cordwainer (shoemaker), and one watchmaker.[36]

Both craftsmen and farmers labored in a pre-industrial agricultural economy marked by a division of time—the seasons—rather than a division of labor. The rural economy was closely bound to the rhythms of agrarian life. Farmers and artisans worked by the same calendar; a part-time farmer made chairs in the slow winter months, and a craftsman took time to plant crops in the spring and harvest them in the fall. The Scots-Irish New Hampshire furniture maker Major John Dunlap did most of his furniture making in the winter; shop productivity dropped sharply in April as he and his employees probably turned to preparing the fields. In May, house joinery began; it continued over the next few months, along with mowing and reaping and the sales of furniture from the shop. Farmers must have been ready to make purchases in the expectation of harvest. In the fall, the making of such simple furniture forms as tables and chairs continued along with house joinery; more complex case pieces were reserved for the winter months. The Ipswich turner John Gaines II and his son Thomas displayed an urban degree of specialization, with over 60 percent of their income coming from furniture production, mostly chairs. However, only a mere tenth of their furniture was sold during the fertile months of June through September when Gaines and his neighbors were busy with farming. Even as a

Fig. 9. Side chair attributed to John Gaines II or Thomas Gaines, Ipswich, Massachusetts, 1720–45. Maple and white pine. 46 × 18-1/4 in. Photograph courtesy of Ipswich Museum, Ipswich, Massachusetts.

part-time chairmaker, John Gaines II made almost 1,200 chairs in the first half of the eighteenth century. The Gaines family of turners and chairmakers produced large numbers of banister-back chairs like the side chair with its numerous turned parts (fig. 9). Only the carved crest was not turned, and it supplied a crown for the person sitting in the chair.[37]

The agrarian economy was embedded in a social network of kin and neighbors. Farmers and craftsmen kept track of this intricate web of exchanges and mutual obligations in their account books, the most common surviving records of rural residents of pre-industrial communities. Farm families grew crops and made things for their own use and to sell to neighbors; a few goods went to wider markets outside the town. Before 1800, according to one historian of the rural economy, most products "were consumed in the households producing them or entered a thriving, complex, and predominantly cashless network of local exchange in which agricultural goods, farm labor services, and the work and products of generally part-time craftsmen were traded between households."[38] The cultural values of interdependence and the goal of securing a "competency" for the family induced farmers to look to the market, trading their small surpluses to obtain things that were not available from their holdings.[39] Long-distance trade dealt primarily in the few "necessities" not available in town and the limited "luxuries" that rural residents could afford. Storekeepers were important middlemen between the rural world of local exchange and the broader trading networks of the cities and the Atlantic world. Those exchanges took place in a very different economic system, requiring cash payments, long-distance trading, and promptness in reckonings.

Account books are single-entry ledgers, which usually have opposing pages devoted to debit and credit transactions, more often than not with the debits complete, the goods made, or the labor provided. This system was not the double-entry bookkeeping of great merchants with calculations of profit and loss; it recorded a set of reciprocal obligations between households, revealing the interdependence of members. These accounts reveal that face-to-face relationships were not simple or direct exchanges, but established a complex web of obligations satisfied by exchanges of goods and services, third-party credits, or infrequently by cash. Rural craftsmen were versatile. On the eastern tip of Long Island, the remarkable clan of Dominys carried on several crafts simultaneously. According to Charles Hummel's examination of their account books, they were "clockmakers, watch and clock repairers, cabinetmakers, house and mill carpenters, wheelwrights, turners, toolmakers, gun repairers, metalworkers, and surveyors"; each family member was trained in and pursued this variety of trades. Indeed, as with many other rural craftsmen, each object they made involved more than one craft. Although in England or a bustling provincial city the labor would be divided among several specialists, in rural regions, craftsmen needed to be jacks of all trades.[40] Rural clockmakers performed a variety of other metalworking tasks. With limited demand for portraits of the rural gentry, an artisan-artist, such as Winthrop Chandler, provided gilding, likenesses on canvas, landscapes on fireplace mantels, and decorative painting on various surfaces.

The typical craftsman in a colonial rural community worked with wood, the plastic of the pre-industrial world, found in great variety and abundance all around him. Artisans arriving from Europe moved from a continent where forests had been cut down for fuel to a place where a wide variety of native woods grew in great abundance. Cherry was used in Connecticut and along the Connecticut River, for it was easily worked and finished to an attractive red color. Birch and maple were plentiful throughout New England and were versatile, attractive, tightly grained, and easy to work, while red and white oak, along with poplar, were lightweight. The ubiquitous eastern white pine was the most popular secondary wood for drawers and other pieces not on display. Rare and exotic woods, such as imported mahogany from the West Indies and black walnut from the southern colonies, were durable with a dark finish. Clockmakers and other metalworkers used far more expensive materials, most of them imported. Craftsmen required plenty of tools, and many of their metal tools were imported.[41]

Craftsmen toiled in a handmade and burdensome world—if not a handcrafted one. When we look back at colonial life from the post-industrial age, we discard some of our culture's cherished nostalgia for the pre-industrial world of work. Humans, through burdensome and repetitive labor over time, supplied the basic power source. Nonhuman effort could be used early in the labor process. For example, water-powered sawmills, established early in the seventeenth century, provided sawn lumber for the shops of chairmakers and clockmakers. But the extensive use of waterpower for shop production lay ahead in the nineteenth century. Furniture makers could rely on apprentices to turn great lathes, foot power to turn smaller pole lathes, mallets to drive chisels, and plenty of muscle to perform the other necessary tasks. Printers required young, nimble eyes and fingers to set type and backbreaking toil to operate the wooden press. The operation of a printing press required the heavy labor of pulling a level that made an impression on each sheet of paper—perhaps up to five hundred pulls an hour—while an assistant fed each sheet onto the form, removed it after it was printed, and in between those operations inked the form by beating it with two inked leather balls.[42]

Woodworkers in particular moved easily and frequently among such tasks as building houses, repairing sashes, and making furniture. Not all woodworking was conducted in the shop or performed by skilled craftsmen. Many rural residents had a rough acquaintance with woodworking, and furniture makers often turned to these "unskilled" workers to supply chair legs and spindles. In mid-eighteenth-century Windsor, Connecticut, Timothy Loomis III demonstrated the versatility of a local artisan working in wood. By the close of the seventeenth century, the Loomises had turned to the trades of weaving, blacksmithing, and joinery. Timothy Loomis, Sr., was the first of four generations of joiners who dominated the local craft, following architectural methods of construction and ornament rather than newer cabinetmakers' methods. Joiners built furniture far thicker than necessary, reinforcing joints with numerous pins, and did minimal carving, which was more likely to appear on a cupboard than a drawer front. Both grandfather and father married into well-established clans of joiners locally and in Hartford. When Timothy's father died, the sixteen-year-old was well placed with a large inheritance, craft training already in progress, his father's ample account book of debts, and a practice book filled with instructions for measuring and cutting the parts for such forms as a chest of drawers, a dressing table, and a clock case. He continued his father's occupational versatility, settling into a seasonal rhythm of tending the farm during the spring planting and fall harvest while pursuing furniture making in the quieter times of the agricultural calendar.

We learn from his ledger that Timothy Loomis III was a professional craftsman but not a specialist. He made cabinet furniture, but was not a "cabinetmaker." Most of his time was spent building and repairing houses and barns. He constructed Windsor's first "Connecticut Valley doorway," the highly decorative baroque doorways that graced the homes of the valley's merchants and ministers, key elements in the regional high style formulated by the housewrights and joiners. His ledger listed about forty furniture forms. The occasional elaborate "case of draws," the most expensive item, probably required about twenty-two days to complete and cost one hundred and ten shillings in 1783. But Loomis also made coffins and window frames, much less elaborate forms. He fashioned the stylish clock case to house the clock movement made by his neighbor Seth Youngs, the valley's first clockmaker. Most of Loomis's accounts were fulfilled by labor exchanges that stretched over many years. His woodworking was enmeshed in the local community; 93 percent of his 108 patrons lived in Windsor, while those beyond the town were either fellow joiners or relatives. Most customers were rooted in the agricultural world, landowners with conservative tastes who preferred the forms that Loomis made; while almost half owned a piece of cabinetwork valued at a pound or more, only a few owned two or more such luxuries. Even among Windsor's affluent residents, simple turned chairs were the norm rather than joined or upholstered ones. The local community sustained the artisan by its web of training and by patronage of provincial style goods fashioned and marketed in familiar ways.[43]

Shops were small places, perhaps holding a bench or two at most. A print shop might hold a printing press or, in larger establishments, two presses. The Dominy House, a two-and-a-half-story frame house built in 1715 at the north end of East Hampton's Main Street, had two attached shops: a woodworking shop on its northeast corner (fig. 10) and a clock shop. At first clockmaking went on in the house in a space no larger than seven feet by eight feet and eight inches. Nathaniel Dominy IV built and then improved the clock shop seen in the photograph of its interior, a simple structure of vertical planks with a wood shingle roof. A brick forge enabled the Dominys to shoe horses, work metal, and make wheels. In photographs of the clock-shop interior taken in 1940 when the shop had long ceased its active function, one can see the workbenches, original lathes, tools, and drawers beneath the benches, along with the gear-

Fig. 10. Northeast corner of Dominy House in East Hampton, New York, built in 1715, with woodworking shop on the right and extending around the rear of the house, possibly added about 1745–50. The house was destroyed in 1946. Photograph by Stanley Mixon, 1940. Historic American Building Survey, Library of Congress, Washington, D.C.

cutting engine (used to cut teeth for clock gears) under the benches in the corner (fig. 11).[44]

Apprenticeship was the most reliable pathway to a craft. In time, as daughters tended to marry their father's apprentices or other youths who worked in the same trade, interlocking clans of artisans arose, such as the Loomises; Timothy Sr.'s father-in-law and several first cousins were joiners along with three of his brothers.[45] Such alliances ensured a shop would endure and its craft processes would pass to a subsequent generation. In the close confines of a rural shop, through the casual interactions between apprentice, journeyman, master, and anyone else who worked there, the apprentice would observe and imitate the master in this handiwork world, learning his solutions to problems of design and construction. This collective education, which connoisseurs and historians of decorative arts identify as a shop tradition, helps us attribute unsigned pieces to specific workshops, as well as understand the transmission of skill and style in the countryside. The Dunlap family supplied New Hampshire's Scotch-Irish residents with distinctive furniture. Their unique decorative motifs, such as the flowered ogee, the signature S-shaped molding that graced the top, or "gallery,"

Fig. 11. East and south interior of the Dominy Clock Shop, built in 1798, with work-benches, lathe, and tools; a gear-cutting engine sits below the right bench. 1940. Historic American Building Survey, Library of Congress, Washington, D.C.

of this high chest (fig. 12), was passed on by family and apprentices throughout southern New Hampshire, and indicated the presence of an ethnic design tradition as well as a consumer preference in a region mostly settled by Scotch-Irish. The towering case piece had all the trimmings, with two courses of flowered ogee molding, a basket-weave motif in the gallery, sunburst shells in the skirts, and dramatic cabriole legs. The local maple wood for this chest was originally stained a dark red to simulate mahogany, and the top level of molding was painted green along with gilded rosettes: it would have stood out in Jane Walker's house for all these reasons, not just for its towering verticality.[46]

But despite the cost, the Dunlaps and their customers wanted their furniture to look quite different from the work of urban cabinetmaking shops. Their chests were made of maple and pine rather than mahogany; and featured distinctive modes of adornment and ornament despite their access to cosmopolitan centers and formal traditions. The similarity of the clocks of the Blasdel family of northern New England over three generations shows that artisan families in the hinterlands perpetuated specific designs. The heavy iron movements indicate their familiarity with traditional English clockmaking, and the thirty-hour posted frame mechanisms are reminiscent of seventeenth-century house clocks and eighteenth-century tall clocks.[47]

Fig. 12. John Dunlap, high chest of drawers, 1782. Maple, 83-1/2 × 40-1/2 × 20 in. This high chest made for Jane Walker in 1782 was the most expensive item listed in Major John Dunlap's account book. New Hampshire Historical Society, Concord.

As the furniture scholar David Pye points out, "Design proposes, workmanship disposes." The quality of workmanship influences the outcome with the transformation from design to object. Pye identifies two approaches: the workmanship of risk and the workmanship of certainty. In workmanship of risk, which we overvalue today in our post-industrial world, "the quality of the result is continually at risk during the process of making." Elaborate hand carving is a good example, for the outcome is continually at risk by a slip of the tool. Workmanship of certainty, by contrast, is when "the quality of the result is exactly predetermined." Pye points to modern printing, where "the newspapers come pouring out in an absolutely predetermined form with no possibility of variation between them" by virtue of all the exacting work before on toolmaking and preparing the plant. While there are examples of reduction of risk in colonial craftwork by using templates, molds, and stencils, when we look at numerous early American artifacts, there is greater evidence of regularity than Pye recognizes. Furniture scholar Benno Forman has suggested a third category: a workmanship of habit such as displayed in the turnings on colonial chairs, a result of a template of action lodged in the mind of the worker. How deep each cut goes is the result of turning hundreds of stretchers in a few days or the need to make the same kind of chair foot so often that there is little difference among his handmade products. "In a time of human power and relatively low technology, a reliance on internalized solutions to structural problems, systematic and habitual motions, and familiar sequences helped to ensure efficient, satisfactory work," writes historian Edward Cooke; "this workmanship of habit made craftwork economically viable," becoming part of their chest of tools.[48] The mid-eighteenth-century Philadelphia turned chairs that Benno Forman and Philip Zimmerman have so carefully examined point to the inventive techniques to speed production and ensure regularity in appearance: standardized parts, the stockpiling of furniture parts, and the outsourcing of production. "In the eighteenth and early nineteenth century," Zimmerman writes, "these ubiquitous turned chairs were products of workmanship of habit. Later, they were factory-made products of sophisticated woodworking tools and other means of workmanship of certainty." From price lists such as those kept by Timothy Loomis IV and the careful analysis of actual artifacts, we can see how a clockmaker or chairmaker might have his basic model of a tall case clock or Chippendale chair and then offer a wide variety of embellishments—a lunar dial or a carved splat—to customers who desired a more expensive and elaborate possession. Still, most of the parts in those various models, the cabriole leg or clock wheels, would be the same, but a more elaborate version could be made and substituted to satisfy the customer.

The versatility required of a rural clockmaker or cabinetmaker could give rise to innovative and resourceful experiments at the shop bench or lathe. Even the "plain style" preferred by rural customers could prompt interesting and striking solutions in the use of decoration and design, as evidenced by Winthrop Chandler's family portraits, which incorporated intriguing elaborations within artisanal and plain traditions. Sophisticated work emerged from the workshops of craftsmen throughout the northern colonies, not just the urban ones, and unsophisticated products just as readily tumbled out of urban shops.[49]

Making clocks was a relatively new branch of manufacture in Connecticut. Immigrant clockmakers first set up shop in the early eighteenth century in Boston and Philadelphia, bringing the latest style—a tall cased clock—with them. Seth Youngs, who settled in Windsor, was one of a new generation of specialized clockmakers in the eighteenth-century Connecticut River Valley. Clocks were rarely found in valley households. One study of residents before 1750 found few mechanical timepieces; the most common device for telling time was a sand glass. Youngs produced eight-day brass clock movements for his customers of substantial means while offering a thirty-hour timepiece with fewer gears at lower cost. That timepiece indicated time by only an hour hand, which suggests the characteristic rhythms of the countryside.[50]

Cost drove innovation in the hinterlands. The brass tall clocks made by Gawen Brown and other Boston clockmakers required large amounts of pricey imported metals. In the lower Connecticut River Valley, the Cheney brothers embarked upon a different path to solve the problem of satisfying, indeed, increasing demand for timepieces. Sons of a cabinetmaker, they constructed their clock movements entirely out of wood—oak or chestnut plates, cherry wheels, and maple arbors—with the sole exception of a brass escape wheel. Cheney clocks, which ran for thirty hours, were wound by pulling on the roped weights behind the waist door, but their heavy movements were hidden behind brass-covered wooden dials, on some of which were painted false winding holes to mimic the appearance of their eight-day cousins. A less expensive housing was fashioned from native pine and stained to imitate more expensive hardwoods, such as mahogany, walnut, or cherry. From across the room, wooden clocks were indistinguishable from brass ones; only the true connoisseur could identify a wooden movement because of its considerably deeper hood (fig. 13). Soon the number of clocks appearing in rural inventories climbed appreciably, and rural Connecticut clockmaking was launched in earnest.[51]

Craftsmen worked within a dynamic tradition. A craftsman was not condemned to follow his master's work slavishly, and travel, design books, and products from other shops suggested new approaches. Colonial artists absorbed the implicit rubrics of English mezzotints to pose their customers correctly. When John Singleton Copley painted Mrs. Jerathmael Bowers, circa 1763, he drew heavily upon the engraving of Sir Joshua Reynolds's portrait of Lady Caroline Russell, an image circulating in the colonies. The demands of clients or regional tastes could push a craftsman to change his techniques or adopt new styles. Eliphalet Chapin, after being trained as a cabinetmaker in Windsor, Connecticut, set off in the late 1760s for Philadelphia, where he worked as a journey-

Fig. 13. Benjamin Cheney innovated by making this thirty-hour clock movement, ca. 1770, which was made of cheaper wood (oak, cherry, and maple) rather than expensive imported brass. The thicker wooden plates would be hidden within the tall clock hood. Butler-McCook House and Garden, Connecticut Landmarks, Hartford, Connecticut.

man. When he returned to the Windsor area about a decade later, he displayed his familiarity with various principles of Philadelphia construction.[52]

The circulation of ideas and goods in the eighteenth century influenced the opinions of consumers about both style and cost. John Chester of Wethersfield wrote to his brother-in-law and fellow merchant, Joshua Huntington, in Norwich in 1782 about his keen interest in securing some Norwich cabinet furniture, perhaps from Joshua's relative, Felix (and Ebenezer Devotion's wife Martha's second cousin), but only if a satisfactory price could be found:

> Was in hopes to have procured those articles at least some cheaper. They still appear to me to be very unreasonably high considering the scarcity of hard Cash. The Chairs we will have, but as for the other articles it will make no material difference whether we answer you now or by next opportunity which cannot be long first. If we can procure them *Cheaper* we *shall,* and I think we *can,* unless Mahogany is much dearer than I am aware. [Felix] Huntington [of Norwich] has rather raised the price of Bureaus. I understand you he asked £7 for one swell'd and trimmed [serpentine front with brass pulls]. £6 is certainly higher for a plain one without trimmings.[53]

Community norms shaped a craftsman's repertoire, and the newest fashions were not always those most desired in the hinterland. A John Singleton Copley portrait, with its shimmering and satin surface, would not have been appropriate for Ebenezer Devotion's Scotland parsonage; much more suitable were Winthrop Chandler's steady line and broad expanses of solid color. Even among the urban patriciate, the plain mode became popular in the pre-Revolutionary era. Philip Livingston of New York counseled Stephen Van Rensselaer, his son-in-law, against stucco work on his hall ceiling, for "a Plain Ceiling is now Esteemed the most Genteel." And when Charleston's Peter Manigault sent his order of furniture to England, he noted that he preferred "the plainer the better so that they are fashionable."[54]

The Atlantic World of Print

Reverend Devotion's engagement with consumer goods placed him firmly within the Atlantic world. His most direct connections with metropolitan culture came through his books, largely from London, the center of the English-language printing trade, which reminds us of the provincial position of the colonial gentry and colonial craftsmen. The Revolution provided new opportunities for local producers, but the greatest changes came after the Revolution. For colonial printers, the long struggle for independence from the yoke of English suppliers and sources paralleled the broader political struggles of the patriots in the late eighteenth century.

Imports of British books, like those of other manufactured goods, soared during the eighteenth century, but domestic production remained limited because of high costs, the confined geographical scope of print shops, and the limited range of products. Colonial printers had to maintain diverse enterprises because of the modest size of the trade, while in London, bookstores had separated from print shops. Colonial printers could not deal only in books; they sold writing paper along with patent medicines, spectacles, and mathematical instruments, and even such sundries as "whalebones, live goosefeathers, pick[l]ed sturgeon, chocolate, Spanish snuff, &c," according to printer and historian Isaiah Thomas.[55] The printer often assumed the office of postmaster, as with that most famous of colonial postmasters, Benjamin Franklin.

Printers struggled with a chronic shortage of printing materials, as well as with their high cost and insecure supply. Presses and type made up about 90 percent of the capital required. Even with adequate capital secured from family and friends, the budding entrepreneur had to face the problem of obtaining a press and type; new equipment had to come across the Atlantic, while local competitors might try to sell off antiquated presses. The greatest cost was paper. Colonial newspapers appeared at irregular intervals or in odd sizes because of the haphazard availability of paper supplies. A few experiments were made with domestic manufacture of the low-grade paper suitable for newspapers or almanacs.[56]

Few provincial booksellers could challenge "the oligopolistic dominance of London," according to British historian James Raven. Imports rose sharply in the third quarter of the century. Even if one discounts the metropole's economies of scale and control of distribution networks, colonial printers were closed out of the production of significant titles, such as Bibles or law books, because of British copyright restrictions. Most colonial books were a "dingy lot," Hugh Amory remarks, "confined to a smaller, narrower range of types, papers and formats than that of the metropolis." "The significant numbers were Almanacks, Psalters, Psalm and Spelling Books, and Primers," Thomas remembered. "Of these 5,000, 10,000, 15,000 & 20,000 were not uncommon." Newspapers were the mainstay of most successful colonial printing establishments, but some survived on government-related printing, with sermons and almanacs rounding out the fare. A typical newspaper's circulation in Boston at midcentury was about six hundred, according to Isaiah Thomas, with a few exceeding that minimum; Franklin's *Pennsylvania Gazette* reached two thousand weekly.[57]

The book trade boomed in the 1760s. Domestic production increased, especially in such cities as Philadelphia, with its well-known competition among printers. Print shops proliferated along the coast, to Providence in 1762, and inland along major river routes, to Hartford in 1764. Franklin advised Hall not to worry "at the Number of Printing Offices setting up. . . . The Country is increasing and Business must increase with it." But the largest beneficiaries were the booksellers who took advantage of the burgeoning Atlantic trade to bypass the port-city merchants and establish direct ties with London and Edinburgh. Jeremy Condy left the pulpit of Boston's Baptist Church for a bookstore in the market district. The successful entrepreneur made excellent use of his overseas connections from his days in the dissenting communities of England and of his ties to local coreligionists. In 1771, Boston boasted eight bookbinders, seven importing booksellers, two stationers, ten printer-booksellers, four printers, and seven firms in the printing trade. To the south in Philadelphia, British transplants brought new, aggressive business tactics. James Rivington fled the monopoly of London's publishers for a chain of bookstores in Philadelphia, New York, and then Boston, where he offered prices nearly as low as in London. Robert Bell abandoned Dublin because of book-pirating activities for a new career as a Philadelphia book auctioneer. His extravagant sales catalogs promised sentimental fiction and other "modern, Instructive, and entertaining books." Bell anticipated new markets and the practice of extensive reading, which flowered only after the Revolutionary era.[58]

The colonial book trade remained the province of refined readers. Those who entered Jeremy Condy's Boston bookstore were men like Ebenezer Devotion, who could afford and appreciate the imported, expensive, and limited quantities of his stock. The reverend purchased Lord Chesterfield's *Letters to His Son* to send to his own son, who was away at school; he also bought other books, the kind that historian Richard Bushman has argued were instrumental in bringing new ideas of refinement and gentility to the provincial elite of British North America. Condy's records trace six hundred patrons in the 1750s and 1760s, scattered over 134 towns in the four New England colonies. These were educated men—and a handful of women; a quarter were Harvard students, another two hundred had graduated from the College, and almost half were ministers. Looking at the world of books through the account book of Jeremy Condy "reveals a tightly knit, well-educated, and financially stable, even comfortable, network of readers that extended from Boston out into the New England countryside." Dispersed as the members of that community might be, they were connected by their membership in the republic of letters. Although literacy rates in the colonies were high and the volume of printed materials rose over the century, for most colonists, devotional tracts and almanacs remained the staple of their libraries. Few people had libraries of any size; the exceptions were such learned men as Ebenezer Devotion.[59]

The Revolutionary crisis did offer opportunities for new entrants into the trade. Printers fled inland when the British occupied the ports; the new state and national governments provided patronage. The number of newspapers doubled between 1763 and 1775, and then doubled again by 1790, beneficiaries of the political partisanship of those tumultuous years. By 1778, the *Connecticut*

Courant claimed a circulation of over eight thousand and "became of much consequence," in the words of Isaiah Thomas: "Its circulation rapidly increased; and, for some time, the number of copies printed weekly was equal to, if not greater, than that of any other paper then printed on the Continent." The number of extant American imprints, mostly broadsides and pamphlets, peaked at about a thousand in 1774–76. *Common Sense*, Thomas Paine's scathing attack on George III's claim to authority, quickly became the first American bestseller, as well as the purveyor of a new kind of direct and powerful language.

That most celebrated printer of the Revolutionary era, Isaiah Thomas, faced severe challenges to his resourcefulness, for bottlenecks remained in the domestic print trade. The fatherless Isaiah was fortunate enough to be apprenticed at age six to the printer Zechariah Fowle. He took full advantage of the opportunity, despite his master's eccentricities, teaching himself to read by setting type. After a "serious fracas," he fled his bonds and toured the various printing establishments of the British Atlantic world, enjoying stints in London, Halifax, and Bermuda, among other ports. The perpetual obstacles faced by colonial entrepreneurs—the chronic credit crunch and tight supply of printing equipment—tested his resolve before he returned to Boston in 1770 to start the *Massachusetts Spy*. He abandoned his dreams of political neutrality and economic independence, a victim of the polarizing politics of the time, ending up firmly in the service of the Patriots. His published invectives and the arrival of British troops led to his midnight removal some fifty miles west of Boston to Worcester in April 1775. Despite John Hancock's encouragement, his paper's circulation in Boston slipped, while others received Congress's custom. He launched an almanac in 1778 that achieved a modest rural circulation of a few thousand, hardly in the same league as Franklin or Nathaniel Ames. Thomas survived by reprinting British properties and the "steady sellers" of ballads, chapbooks, and children's books, the familiar stock in trade of his despised former master. Only in the post-Revolutionary era did Isaiah Thomas achieve the distinction of creating a flourishing national print market. Challenges also remained for other Revolutionary-era artisan-entrepreneurs, including those in the printing field and beyond.[60]

Ebenezer Devotion, Jr.: Merchant, Judge, and Patron

Ebenezer Devotion died in 1771, remembered by Ezra Stiles in his diary as a "Gentleman of solid Understanding, extensive Reading, and eminent for every kind of Merit. A great Divine, a pious Man, an able Politician." To mark his consequent ascension to the regional elite, his son commissioned a portrait from his father's limner, Winthrop Chandler (see figs. 3–4). Ebenezer the younger, born in Windham in 1740, had followed his father to Yale. Returning in 1764 to marry Eunice Huntington, the third marriage between the two families in two generations, he established himself as father, farmer, and merchant.

As agriculture commercialized during the decade and a half before the War for Independence, Windham became a rural entrepôt. For a half-century, Ebenezer Devotion recorded transactions in his account book that detail how he collected his neighbors' farm surpluses, transported them to markets as far away as Providence and New York, and exchanged those rural products for imported goods. Devotion also provided significant financial services to his neighbors in Windham and surrounding towns.[61]

Although the Revolutionary crisis disrupted local economic life, it also presented entrepreneurial and political opportunities for the merchants of Windham County. Like his father, Ebenezer Devotion, Jr., became a local leader in the patriot cause. He was involved in Windham's nonimportation movement to protest parliamentary duties in 1767. He joined the Sons of Liberty, and his neighbors elected him a member of the town's Committee of Correspondence in 1774. That same year, he became a justice of the peace, an office his father-in-law, Jonathan Huntington, had held; Ebenezer remained in that office for forty-four years. He followed in Jonathan's footsteps the next year when he was appointed to the county court as Justice of the Quorum for Windham County, a Superior Court. He served as Windham's representative to the state assembly in 1775 when war broke out.

Given its established commercial character, Windham became an important supply center during the war. Devotion, who owned shares in a privateer and several other vessels, held various contracts to furnish food and supplies to the Connecticut militia and, working with his kinsman Joshua Huntington, quartermaster for the War Department, to the Continental Army as well. His relationship with another brother-in-law, Samuel Huntington, a member of the Continental Congress and president of Congress from 1780 to 1788, brought him into the center of national politics and to Philadelphia to see Martha and Samuel. Travels for business and politics during the conflict sent Ebenezer Devotion to Hartford, New Haven, and other Connecticut ports, so he became an important source of information for his neighbors. The war's many hardships did little to diminish his patriotic fervor. Devotion wrote to a friend about the cry of lost virtue that went up amidst the "depreciation of our currency" as some sought profit during the distress. But he was confident that these economic calamities would not diminish the integrity of the people because the "honest merchant and farmer have acted on the same principle as ever before—in open market to sell their merchandize or produce at as high a price as the purchaser was willing to give."[62]

The formation of the new republic served to perpetuate Judge Devotion's political career. Indeed, he sat on the county court until 1811, through much of the political turmoil of the post-Revolutionary decades. To keep informed, Devotion read at least four newspapers, and he added American imprints, such as Tom Paine's *Common Sense* and the *American Museum*, to the family book collection, along with Enlightenment works, such as John Locke's *Some Thoughts Concerning Education*. When Connecticut's Federalists and Congregationalists faced challenges in the tumultuous 1790s, Ebenezer backed the established order. He enjoyed the support of Windham's townspeople, who elected him to the assembly several times between 1788 and 1801. Still, in the new century, Devotion began to move some distance from his familial affiliations. He was attracted to the Jeffersonian cause and was elected to represent it in 1801. He diversified his investments by speculating in Western Reserve lands as many Connecticut residents headed west.

Ebenezer and Eunice Devotion had a large family. Winthrop Chandler had painted four of the children in 1772; another four were born later. One son, Jonathan, followed Ebenezer as a merchant, justice of the peace, and assembly representative for Scotland and Norwich, while daughter Eunice, who was depicted on her mother's lap in the Chandler portrait, remained in rural Scotland. Younger Devotions launched their lives further afield, in Boston or New Orleans. Eunice died in 1827 at the age of eighty-four, and Ebenezer died in 1829 at eighty-nine, the last surviving member of his Yale class.[63]

The Portrait, the Possessions, and the Transactions

Ebenezer Devotion, Jr., chose to be portrayed at work, standing at his high, slant-top desk, his right arm resting on his open account book, his right hand holding a quill pen, poised to make an entry. The painting is full-sized, almost six feet high, and blocked out with broad expanses of somber colors. Its striking resemblance to a 1757 Copley painting of James Tilley, the ropemaker, with its similar pose and props, reinforces the assumption that Chandler had seen the portraitist's work when he apprenticed in Boston. Eunice Huntington Devotion, seated on a Chippendale side chair and wearing her best dress, an elaborate cap trimmed with pink ribbon, and black gloves, is very much the prosperous merchant's wife, proud of her expensive furniture and clothing. Family tradition maintains that Eunice wore the peach-colored, imported silk dress to a state dinner in Philadelphia—a fragment has survived, preserved as a memento—and Chandler renders it carefully, concentrating on such decorative details as its gathered stitched ruffles and expensive lace adornments. In addition to the two generations of Devotion men and their wives whom Chandler painted in the early 1770s, he was commissioned to produce separate portraits of Ebenezer and Eunice's three sons, Ebenezer, John, and Jonathan. The judge acknowledged the valuable portraits in his will, where he instructed, "The seven *Family Pictures* painted by Chandler must be divided as justly as possible among my four surviving children."[64]

In their household furnishings, as with their portraits, the Devotions exhibited sophisticated but provincial tastes. The family was blessed with comfortable but not unlimited means and was fashionable but not flamboyant, able to mount a convincing, if not quite urbane, display for their neighbors. According to family tradition, Ebenezer gave Eunice a mid-eighteenth-century dressing table of maple and pine, listed in the probate inventory, when he married her. The unusual heart-shaped cutout decoration, a "folk" motif, has been integrated into a very sophisticated design, according to Lance Mayer and Gay Myers, "which successfully balances the overhang of the top, the curves of the legs, and the strong movement of the skirt."[65] Growing in popularity after 1750, dressing tables tended to appear only in the inventories of the top fifth of the economic hierarchy.

The Reverend Ebenezer Devotion had looked to London and Boston artisans for his consumer goods, but his merchant son was able to find local suppliers for furnishings. In his account books, he listed a variety of transactions with a number of local furniture makers. The family purchased some of its most expensive items from Martha's kinsman Felix Huntington, a cabinetmaker in Norwich, the town nearest to Windham. A pair of Chippendale side chairs attributed to Huntington has been handed down through the Devotion family. These chairs were among the more elaborate products issuing from Huntington's shop, compared to seats with plainer splats or horizontal cross plats, but they were not the fanciest line he produced (see fig. 14). Made of cherry, not mahogany, the Devotions' chairs are not draped with carving on the ears or crest like those owned by General Jabez Huntington, Devotion's superior in organizing Connecticut's wartime distribution network. From the 1770s through the 1790s, Devotion purchased a raft of fashionable furniture—mahogany bureaus, a half-dozen chairs, and Pembroke tables; later he ordered sideboards and bedsteads. A restrained but high-style chest of drawers would have been recognized by Devotion and his neighbors, who understood the design vocabulary, as a first-rate status commodity.[66]

Devotion patronized other craftsmen closer to home, and as he did so, he cemented relations with the local community. A number of chairmakers settled in Windham during the last decades of the eighteenth century, and they brought with them a new style—the Windsor chair—that originated in England and was developed for the American market in Philadelphia. In 1784, Theophilus Parsons sold Devotion an armchair and a half-dozen Windsor chairs. Artisans such as Parsons and Beriah Green traded furniture for other commodities and services available at Devotion's store. Such transactions could prove risky, however. Huntington, the best cabinetmaker in the region and Devotion's second cousin, ran up substantial bills at the Scotland store—a powerful reminder that craftsmen and consumers were bound together in the welter of exchanges that defined economic life in the agrarian world of the eighteenth century.[67]

High-style products were no longer exclusively fashioned in Boston and Philadelphia shops. Clockmakers, chairmakers, and other artisans who established themselves in inland commercial centers looked to new regional elites like Judge Devotion and his peers for patronage. The economic uncertainty of Revolutionary Boston prompted Thomas Harland, "Watch and Clock-maker from London," to relocate almost immediately to Norwich, Connecticut, a town of about 7,500 inhabitants with a budding cluster of craftsmen. Introducing the latest design in British clocks, Harland trained a generation of Connecticut clockmakers. The variety and increasing elaborateness of goods available to rural patrons like Devotion offered unprecedented choice. European rococo—today referred to as Chippendale—was applied to chairs; furniture and silver were festooned with such rococo motifs as shells and leaves; and later even "gothick" and "Chinese" decorative motifs graced local products.[68]

Still, Connecticut furniture often betrayed a mix of urban styles and rural standards. Eliphalet Chapin of Windsor, Connecticut, offered his customers the sculptural Georgian look of English Chippendale designs and the construction details of Philadelphia craftsmanship in the 1770s and 1780s. Chapin has stood first among eighteenth-century provincial cabinetmakers since the discovery of a set of splendid chairs over a century ago. Born in Enfield in 1741, Chapin was propelled by a series of unfortunate but fortuitous events into the ranks of innovative artisans. When his father who operated a modest farm died prematurely with several young children, his mother's brother, a member of a dynasty of joiners and turners, was selected as his guardian. After completing his apprenticeship with one of those woodworking relatives, Chapin went off to try his fortune as a journeyman in the larger community of East Windsor. He fled town after fathering an illegitimate child with Hannah Bartlett and the ensuing paternity suit, going to the flourishing high-style furniture center of Philadelphia. He returned to the Connecticut River Valley around 1770 and "set up his trade of a joyner in this town." After completing his child-maintenance payments to Hannah and accumulating enough capital to purchase a lot for his shop on East Windsor's Main Street, he introduced the rich carved detail and sinewy scroll design of Georgian furniture into the region. The rococo style, an international style that reached North America in the 1750s, departed from clas-

Clockwise from top left: Fig. 14. Side chair attributed to Felix Huntington, 1770–85. Norwich, Connecticut. Cherry. 35-7/8 × 21 × 17 in. Brookline Historical Society, Brookline, Massachusetts. Fig. 15. Side chair attributed to Thomas Affleck, ca. 1770. Philadelphia. Mahogany and northern white cedar. 37 × 22-1/2 × 23 in. Metropolitan Museum of Art, New York. Purchase, Sansbury-Mills and Rogers Fund, Emily C. Chadbourne Gift, Virginia Groomes Gift, in memory of Mary W. Groomes, Mr. and Mrs. Marshall P. Blankarn Gift; John Bierwith and Robert G. Goelet Gifts, The Sylmaris Collection, Gift of George Coe Graves, Gift of Mrs. Russell Sage, by exchange, and funds from various donors, 1974 (1974.325). Image copyright © The Metropolitan Museum of Art / Art Resource, NY. Fig. 16. Eliphalet Chapin, side chairs with cabriole legs for Alexander King, 1781. Cherry and white pine. 38-9/16 × 20-1/2 × 16-11/16 in. Yale University Art Gallery, New Haven. Mabel Brady Garvan Collection. Fig. 17. Eliphalet Chapin, diamond-splat side chair, 1775. Cherry and pine. 38 × 21-3/4 × 16-11/16 in. Connecticut Historical Society, Hartford. Gift of Frederick K. and Margaret R. Barbour.

sical order in favor of embellishment. The emphasis was on naturalistic ornament with shells and leaves, along with other flora and fauna often arranged in
symmetrical compositions. The rococo style crossed the Atlantic via pattern
books, imported objects, and immigrant artisans. Philadelphia, the largest colonial city, attracted a wave of highly skilled and ambitious artisans, carvers, and
upholsterers, who enthusiastically applied the latest designs to architectural
interiors, engravings, silver, and furniture alike. Thomas Affleck, Scottish-
trained and fresh from London, arrived in 1763, a copy of Chippendale's *Director*
under his arm, soon to become the most successful of these woodworking artisans. Affleck drew upon many of those carvers and upholsterers when he made
a parlor suite (including three sofas and twenty chairs) for Philadelphia's leading patron of the rococo style, with a side chair dripping with rich decoration
in wood and silk (fig. 15).[69]

How do we know that these Connecticut chairs are products of rural sophistication rather than urban imports when most furniture bears neither stamp
nor paper label of its maker? Recent scholarship uses a combination of connoisseurship—the examination of the details of construction—and the archival documentary record of family papers and business records. Chapin's identity
surfaced when pioneer furniture scholar Irving Lyon purchased two striking
chairs in 1877 (fig. 16) and was shown the bill of sale from Chapin to Alexander
King of South Windsor, Connecticut, dated 1781. Lyon bought the two chairs
from King's daughter, so the direct line of inheritance gave a clear provenance.
Sixty chairs have been attributed to Chapin, all without direct documentation,
but related to the original pair by their distinctive Philadelphia stylistic and

Facing page, clockwise from top left: Figs. 14–17. Rococo side chairs had a variety of
decorative elements and design choices with prices to match. Thomas Affleck's side
chair featured a collaboration with a cluster of European-trained craftsmen-cabinet-
makers and carvers and upholsterers—and one of Philadelphia's wealthiest families.
This chair featured elaborate naturalistic and expensive carving that required tremendous skill and added greatly to the cost on every surface. Eliphalet Chapin
brought back from Philadelphia patterns and templates for rococo standards, such
as ball-and-claw feet, cabriole legs, and intricate pierced splats, while also making
concessions to his central Connecticut customers' pocketbooks and tastes. Interlaced
splats such as those on this side chair made for Alexander King did not have carved
volutes and were among the less expensive items in the order. The diamond-splat
chairs were from the more expensive of the "Claw Foot Cherry Chairs" with their
more intricate pattern and additional carving. A neighbor and relative of the Devotions, Felix Huntington also made rococo side chairs; this chair sat between his
fancier and more modest offerings, with its pierced splat and Chinese bracket below
the seat but with a straight leg and no carved decoration.

construction details. Later genealogical research connected Eliphalet to a clan of furniture craftsmen who worked in Chapin's shop. In addition, the extensive fieldwork for a groundbreaking 1985 exhibition, *The Great River: Art and Society of the Connecticut River*, brought to light the cultural subregion of the Connecticut River Valley—extending from Connecticut through Massachusetts into Vermont and New Hampshire—and expanded the Chapin corpus beyond chairs to include dressing tables and chest-on-chests, along with the craftsmen inspired by Eliphalet Chapin's work who produced similar commodities. According to furniture scholars Robert Trent and Joseph Lionetti, "the conservative farmer-merchants of the Connecticut Valley created a market for furniture of restrained design and urban associations that illustrated their worldliness." Winterthur's Nancy Evans brought together seventeen Chapin chairs and examined their most distinctive features—their interlaced splat pattern, the carved shells on the crest rails at the top, and their stubby claw feet—to reveal "the basic features and subtle variations" of the Chapin workshop, the vocabulary that Chapin worked in. Finally, three independent scholars conducted fourteen years of field work, examining five hundred pieces, one a week, to systematically classify the body of Chapin's work and his workshop, by identifying four major local "style centers" in work published in 2005.[70] Chapin did not sign or mark any of his furniture, but we know a lot about his work and the world of Connecticut cabinetmaking.

Chapin chairs are noted for their elaborate scrolled ears, squared ball-and-claw feet, and strapwork splat—all characteristic of the Philadelphia manner. In addition, the side-rail tenons go completely through the back posts of the chair, where they are exposed to view, a rare construction practice in New England. Chapin adapted to local conditions, however. He used cherrywood rather than the more expensive mahogany, and he introduced construction features that sped the mass production of the multiple sets of chairs his patrons ordered. He stockpiled chair parts and could offer customers distinctive designs, at varying cost, by changing the splats on the back of the chair or its legs. Although the basic chair form remained Chippendale, it could have curved legs or straight, claw feet or not, diamond patterns or Gothic ones. The Lyon or King chairs had cabriole legs but lacked the four carved volutes on the scrolls of the banister of other chairs with this pattern—"claw feet cherry chairs." A more intricate and expensive splat pattern, the diamond banister, also appears in a set sold to Ebenezer Grant in 1775 for the dowry of his daughter Ann, who married the Reverend John Marsh of Wethersfield; Chapin earned the enormous sum of £41, twice the cost of his shop lot, for this commission of thirty-one pieces, including six tables and twenty chairs (fig. 17). Another set of chairs with simpler Marlborough legs was as expensive as the diamond pattern because of the added cost of the stretchers, carved knee brackets, and extra carving of the crest rails. When Roswell Grant married Flavia Wolcott in 1783, they purchased yet another variation, with two cross slats and a top rail with various piercings. Flavia's parents had purchased a clock case by Timothy Loomis III that she inherited, but she and Roswell turned to Chapin for their stylish furniture.[71] Chapin provided high-style provincial furniture in a range of prices and stimulated interest with a changing repertoire for those regional gentry aspiring to emulate the urban mercantile elite.

The Portraitist and His Patrons

Like other craftsmen, Winthrop Chandler was trying to make a living by creatively applying his skills and talents to a range of patrons' design requests. In 1772, he married Mary Gleason, accumulating real estate and raising a family of five sons and two daughters. Two of Chandler's portraits circa 1780 offer a dramatic view of the patriot side of a family that, like so many others, was divided by the Revolutionary conflict. With the large battle scene viewed through the window beside him, Captain Samuel Chandler, Winthrop's brother, commands the canvas just as decisively as he commanded a Connecticut militia company in 1776. The battle scene, which commemorates Chandler's commission, probably represents one of his successful engagements. In his portraits of Captain and Mrs. Anna Paine Chandler, Winthrop again worked in a firm linear style and paid close attention to detail (figs. 18 and 19). Dressed in his uniform, his left elbow resting on a mahogany drop-leaf table on which his tricorn hat has been placed, his right hand steadying his sword topped with a silver hilt of the type fashioned by Boston craftsman Jacob Hurd, Samuel is portrayed as a member of the gentry. Indeed, he lived on a three-hundred-acre farm near his and Winthrop's father. His wife, too, is a gentlewoman of note, wearing her best dress, which follows Paris fashion. Winthrop later added remarkable detail to his sister-in-law's costume to heighten its fashionable appearance. Anna sits with her hands resting in her lap holding a half-open fan. Family possessions, such as the oval mahogany table and the substantial shelves of books, as well as the dramatic drapery behind her, reinforce her genteel stature.[72]

In 1785, perhaps in search of new opportunities, Winthrop Chandler moved his family to Worcester. As early as 1775, he had experienced a series of financial difficulties that continued to plague him until his death. He diversified his occupation with over-mantel landscapes, house painting, and gilding. Still, his additional craft production did not keep him from plunging further into debt. In fact, no portraits can be definitively traced to the Worcester period, although, from its characteristics, a self-portrait appears to date from the later years of his

Fig. 18. Winthrop Chandler, *Captain Samuel Chandler*, ca. 1780. Oil on canvas. 54-3/4 × 47-7/8 in. Gift of Edgar William and Bernice Chrysler Garbisch. Image courtesy of the Board of Trustees, National Gallery of Art, Washington, D.C.

life (fig. 20). In 1789, Mary Chandler fell ill and died; just one year later, Winthrop died in Woodstock at the age of forty-three. The *Massachusetts Spy* took note of his station in the community, although his skills in brightening the exterior walls of inland towns were of more obvious, or at least more universal, import than his portraits: "Died at Woodstock, Connecticut, Winthrop Chandler of this town, a man whose native genius has been serviceable to the community in which he resided. In profession he was a house painter, but many likenesses on canvas shew he could guide the pencil of a limner."[73]

Fig. 19. Winthrop Chandler, *Mrs. Samuel Chandler*, ca. 1780. Oil on canvas. 54-3/4 × 47-7/8 in. Gift of Edgar William and Bernice Chrysler Garbisch, Image courtesy of the Board of Trustees, National Gallery of Art, Washington, D.C.

"In rural New England, as elsewhere in the American colonies," historian Kevin Sweeney reminds us, "the embrace of genteel culture helped create a conscious class of gentlemen united by common standards across colony lines." Winthrop Chandler had never traveled very far from his village, and he painted only relatives and family friends. Those he did paint, like his brother Samuel and the Devotions, were members of the rural elite of northeastern Connecticut and central Massachusetts. However, more than mere economic standing or availability of goods determined a family's patterns of consumption and partici-

Fig. 20. Winthrop Chandler, *Self-Portrait*. c. 1789. Oil on canvas. 26-1/8 × 23-3/8 in. Courtesy of American Antiquarian Society, Worcester, Massachusetts.

pation in a particular way of life. Beverly Johnson's imaginative comparison of Chandler's sitters with other members of the elite in northeastern Connecticut without portraits reveals the different modes of household decoration and consumer practice that existed in the countryside. Winthrop's sitters were more likely to be college educated, to be high-ranking military officers, and to have distinguished political careers. Chandler used aristocratic conventions to suggest his patrons were well-educated professionals; their books were laid open on tables, were held in hand, or provided the background, while merchants had account books at the ready or quill pens in hand. Their household furnishings extended those demonstrations of genteel living, providing the stage upon which the display of new ideas could take place. Sitters owned 20 percent more chairs, and almost twice as many tables. Chairs were more likely to be of the more expensive types, with flag bottoms or crooked backs. The most costly had slip seats, either rare leather-bottom ones such as the fifteen that Levi Willard owned, or worked-bottom ones that portrait sitters' inventories contained. Only sitters owned tea tables, for this form was rarely found in rural homes, even among the wealthy; those who patronized Chandler also possessed more tea-wares to be prominently displayed on those tables. Another means of showing wealth was the type of wood employed. Only two inventories, both of portrait owners, mentioned the particular woods as a way of noting their expensive taste; Charles Church Chandler and Rufus Lathrop owned "8 mahog chairs" and 8 separate "mahogy" forms, respectively, setting them off from their neighbors with cherry or maple. Both groups were building large, two-story, double-pile houses with a central hall; but when one entered those elite houses, the furnishings around the room and on the walls would have varied. There were competing styles even within the elite. The growing availability of commodities was no mere proliferation, but a subtler mode of differentiation crafted by artisan and customer, both within and between social groups in colonial society.[74]

Before the Revolution, patrons like the Reverend Ebenezer and Martha Lathrop Devotion had begun to seek out local craftsmen and to foster the production of cultural commodities in the hinterlands that combined cosmopolitan and plain styles. In the wake of the Revolution's destruction of the aristocratic and hierarchical colonial regime, the new middle ranks, eager to advance their social claims in the bustling, mobile, commercial society of late eighteenth-century America, allowed their pretensions to swell. They wanted objects to signify their cultural authority, and a host of artisan-entrepreneurs were only too happy to oblige by creating new forms at increasingly affordable prices. Thus did a consumer revolution at first propel and then help stabilize America's political revolution, as the dynamic enterprise of self-fashioning and social differentiation necessary to establish the new republic brought about a new cultural order in the nineteenth century that looked considerably different from any world the Reverend Ebenezer Devotion or Judge Ebenezer Devotion had ever imagined.

The

Life

or

Biography

of

Silas Felton

written by

himself.

So retain the Casualties of Life,
Is the happiness of contented Man.

Marlborough, Massachusetts

CHAPTER TWO

The Village Enlightenment

Silas Felton and the Young Ladies' Literary Society

When we peruse Silas Felton's manuscript autobiography, *The Life or Biography of Silas Felton Written by Himself,* we can see how this twenty-five-year-old resident of an inland Massachusetts town constructed a self, eager to keep up with literary fashion but writing in a "plain" style (fig. 21). Silas Felton aspired to see the new American nation become a republic of letters whose citizens not only were literate—that is, truly civilized and capable of being republican—but also who would employ their literacy to improve their minds and lives. Felton lived in a rural village, remote from the cosmopolitan centers of culture; yet, as his autobiography relates, such exemplary texts as Benjamin Franklin's "life and writings" fell into his hands, and he modeled himself on America's first great man of letters. His life was crafted by print, by the consumption of entertaining stories and Franklin's writings, along with conversations with like-minded young men nearby about the "improvement" of self, community, and country. The manuscript minutes of Marlborough's Society of Social Enquirers, or Deerfield's Young Ladies' Literary Society, record that young men and women debated the great issues of the time, such as the nature of the French Revolution and "can a state of Equality exist in society," and mulled over such mundane

Facing page: Fig. 21. Silas Felton, *The Life or Biography of Silas Felton written by himself, 1800,* Marlborough, Massachusetts. Manuscripts and Archives Division, The New York Public Library, Astor, Lenox and Tilden Foundations, New York City.

matters as the best way to stack a dunghill. All these conversations connect to the Enlightenment's search for reason and system.[1]

Felton began his education as an ordinary consumer of print and moved on to contribute to the enlightenment of his neighbors by serving as a village schoolmaster. As a youth, he sought to escape from the tedium of farm work and the authority of his father by devouring the printer's products in which he searched for alternatives to the constricted horizons of Marlborough, Massachusetts. Felton's reading inspired habits of reflective writing and systematic thinking. He was not a passive consumer of print, but wrote his life as a blueprint for action. Felton's papers include a variety of forms: his "Biography," a journal of his reading extracts, his accounts, a listing of "Authors, I have Read," and a "Table of Scholars" he had taught. When at age twenty-six he found his vocation as a merchant and closed his autobiography, he still carried with him his ciphering and account books and "Extracts of Various Authors," all records of a countryside in the throes of economic and cultural change.[2] Felton's autobiography, with its many erasures and slightly convoluted narrative, was probably never intended to appear in print. It would never be confused with Franklin's *Life*, and the Marlborough Social Enquirers bear only a faint resemblance to the Junto in Philadelphia.

Felton's manuscripts are critical documents in a process of transformation that I call the Village Enlightenment. This term embraces the formation of a market for cultural commodities in printed form; it signifies the erosion of a hierarchical structure of authority, in which local culture was controlled by a clerical or college-trained elite; and it points to the emergence of a social organization of knowledge suitable to the requirements of rural folk in the rising republic. This complex development can best be understood by looking at agents of the ideology of practical reason and at the institutions they created. Print provides the model for us to understand the extensive cultural movement composed of numerous village Franklins, living in many towns in the hinterlands where knowledge became an engine of both personal and social change. New ideas took hold within the rural educational settings of craft shop and district school. But this cultural movement in which ordinary Americans promoted commercialization through their thirst for new cultural knowledge extended far beyond printed matter and is the subject of this chapter and Chapter 3.

Young men and women like Felton contributed to the rise of a broad market for print and other cultural goods; in turn, those goods facilitated the active construction of new identities in the new nation. Individuals forged careers pioneering a rural form of the "business" of Enlightenment. The circulation of ideas in the hinterlands intensified the transmission of knowledge and challenged the older arbiters of rural culture. Finally, local institutions took root all over New England, created as exercises of Franklinesque self-improvement. Libraries, schools, print shops, stores for selling printed wares, literary and debating societies—all were vehicles of cultural improvement.

Print culture initiated the Village Enlightenment, but other cultural commodities soon extended the scope of the movement. Clockmakers set up shop with such mechanical marvels as the movement of the planets or the tides that miniaturized the working of the world by measuring tides and phases of the moon all in one mechanism. Portraitists allowed village gentry the means to represent their newfound status in grand family portraits, formerly the exclusive reserve of aristocrats and the urban mercantile elite. Americans were interested enough in mechanical marvels and in the shape and extent of their new nation to spend scarce funds on such devices as musical clocks and globes. Craftsmen applied Enlightenment notions in the form of neoclassical designs to country newspapers and provincial furniture, vastly expanding the reach of the European Enlightenment into backwoods areas of North America, such as the upper Connecticut River Valley (Chapter 3). Clocks and globes, offering consumers visual control over time and space, satisfied the quest for knowledge while fulfilling the refined person's desire to exhibit symbols of gentility.

The agrarian world of the late eighteenth and early nineteenth centuries provided many opportunities besides farming. In the postwar years, many rural residents took up merchandising or manufacturing. Together, new notions of personhood and structural changes in society initiated a dramatic transformation in the northern countryside. Novel cultural authorities replaced or at least contested such established figures as ministers. These voices, as well as the commodities they crafted, came dressed in vernacular garb, combining provincial and cosmopolitan sources. They did more than purvey materials trickling down from London or New York; rather, they constructed something different. New designs emerged alongside old favorites in forms as diverse as sideboards and schoolbooks. Neoclassical motifs—whether decorative or literary—carried nationalist messages that promoted the democratization of knowledge and the commercialization of the countryside.[3]

There were many paths to the Village Enlightenment. Rural style did not evolve in a vacuum. We can map provincial design as a wagon wheel with an urban hub, with vernacular production located deep on the outer rim: but as Philip Zea has reminded us, the spokes are linked—along the rim and often with the presence of separate traditions. "Fashion rode on the back of commerce," a hybrid creation in the back of the beyond or far hinterlands. This matrix of production and consumption contradicts popular notions about the post-Revolutionary countryside. Too often, we still cling to the mystique of rural isolation. But when we document rural culture, we find cosmopolitan influences and expectations as well as plain products. But *plain* did not mean naïve or unconscious; it, too, was a deliberate style. Rural craftsmen had links far beyond local boundaries. The cultural complexity of these provincial forms married skills, materials, and intent that hybridized all that had gone before to create something new as craftsmen provided a vital place for Felton and his colleagues.[4]

Print Culture

> *I was born on the 24th Feb. 1776 and named Silas after my uncle of that name. . . . When arrived to an age sufficient for Labour I followed working with my father upon the farm, except such times as we had a School kept near us, which I generally attended. . . . Being more fond of School than of work I generally had more praises bestowed upon me at school than at home. . . . Becoming more fond of books, I used at every convenient opportunity to take my book and step ought [sic] of sight; by often repeating this and being out of the way when wanted caused the people often to bestow the name of Lazy upon me, which I acknowledge was not altogether misplaced.*[5]

Local folks were not appreciative of the value of reading books, Silas Felton discovered, as they saw bookishness as an avoidance of the hard work needed on the farm. But, like other country boys, he was not satisfied with watching his social betters or following his father's choices. Silas's grandfather, a third-generation New Englander, had come to Marlborough, a central Massachusetts town, when it was resettled after King Philip's War. His father, Stephen, was a prosperous farmer, standing out from his peers by his accumulation of considerable properties in town and beyond its borders in order to provide settlements for his eight children. Stephen had "followed farming [just like his father] and brought his Children up to it, giving them common school Education," Silas recounted. Stephen inherited the family farm and energetically added parcels of land to his holdings—along with cherry chests of drawers, fashionable Windsor chairs, and light stands to the farmhouse decor. Born in 1775, Silas was the oldest child. Paternal control had lessened, and individual choices expanded in the post-Revolutionary countryside. The rising generation not only left town in search of new farmland but also sought new opportunities in local villages. Silas was not content to follow his father into farming; he objected to the dull and narrow round of rural labor. His books enabled him to imagine alternatives, offering a powerful mix of Franklinesque improvement and ambition. Inspiration for crafting a new identity could come from reading or gathering with like-minded souls, as Silas Felton and his circle of "Social Enquirers" did in Marlborough.[6]

Felton always felt unsuited to be a farmer: "I frequently met with some accidents such as cutting my finger and once broke my left leg by a Wheel falling on it and which caused me often to say that Nature never formed me to follow an Agricultural Life, for my mind was never content when about it; but learning was my greatest delight." He faced the dilemma of children whose bodies seemed unsuited for the labor expected of them. His favorite occasions were evenings and "Stormy Days" when he read "all the boy books within my reach." The titles available to him expanded in 1792, when he urged his reluctant father to join sixty other inhabitants of Marlborough to form the Marlboro Library. Social libraries were voluntary associations where individuals contributed money (in Marlborough the initial fee was $2.50 and annual dues 25 cents) toward a common fund for the purchase of books. For a long time, Silas had little choice but to prepare to take over the farm, as his father intended. When he looked back on that period of his life, he issued the post-Revolutionary generation's challenge to patriarchal authority in the all-important matter of finding one's calling: "Experience has since taught me that people do not pay attention enough to the Inclinations of their children, but commonly put them to the same kind of business, which they themselves follow, and when they find them not attentive to those particular occupations, accuse them of being idle, (although diligently employed in forming something, which their different fancies or inclinations lead them.) . . . Whereas if the leading inclinations of the children were sought after, and when found, permitted to follow them, [it] might often prove highly advantageous to themselves, their parents and Society."[7] Silas was determined to find his own path by following his "inclinations" and actively sought his opportunities through a program of reading that relied upon "fancy work" or the workings of the imagination.

Books, besides being a retreat from unpleasant realities, provided guidance at critical moments in Felton's development. He was thrown into the gravest of spiritual crises when, at about age sixteen, some books with "dark and mysterious passages" caused him to doubt Scripture. When Thomas Paine's *Age of Reason* appeared, he witnessed vitriolic debates between deists and clergymen in Marlborough; each side, he thought, "advanced" its case "beyond the truth." The flood of print that had plunged him into this crisis also furnished the means of resolving it: "At this time (viz. about 18) Doct. Franklins life and writings fell into my hands." Felton found in that text the Enlightenment principle of reason necessary for making his way through the thicket of theories. "From that time I determined to *adhere strictly to Reason, Industry, and good Economy, to Always examine both sides, to keep my mind free from prejudice of any kind whatever, always to practice reason and truth.*"[8] Reading became a form of cultural rebellion and was understood as such by those who favored a more traditional path: "[My bookish ways] caused me to be the subject of some conversation, especially among those, who had never ventured to think of [for] themselves, but had taken the opinions of their fathers as handed down to them, without enquiring why they did so." Silas faced opposition to his habits of rational inquiry, not just from his father but also from others in the community who were suspicious of any viewpoint that made its proponents impatient with accustomed ways, more individualistic than inclined to mutuality and community, "ambitious to excel," and eager to engage in a wider public world of distinction and knowledge.[9]

Reading had always been important to the New England way of life. The intensive study of texts, authorized by the monitors of right thinking, had marked regional culture from the beginning. One scholar of the "reading revolution" notes that "the local minister not only served as God's anointed spokesperson" but also was often the only resident with a college education. "As expert witness to the world and the Word, the minister interpreted science, philosophy, and other forms of learning as well as religion for his congregation/audience." Felton's grandmother Hezediah, who lived with the family, had given the family's "greate Bible" to her son Stephen as a source of guidance and a symbol of continuity. But during the Village Enlightenment, cultural mediators of received and divinely sanctioned wisdom were supplanted by printed sources of practical information and personal insight. Literate townspeople sifted through a variety of new ideas and incorporated some of them into their everyday beliefs. Reading became less a conservator of convention and more a force for change. In Franklin's *Life* and other entertaining narratives, Silas Fenton found a discursive world in which he could inscribe his own life story, which he did literally seven years later and metaphorically in his career as a commercial entrepreneur in Marlborough. Franklin became Felton's "virtual patron," as historian Jason Opal has written.[10]

Silas Felton's reading contributed to a rapid progression of ideas. He read voraciously and wrote copiously in his "reading book." He closed his autobiography in 1802, at the age of twenty-six, with a list of "AUTHORS, I HAVE READ": 106 titles arranged in ten "Professions or Arts." The first and largest category was "Religion or Morality," with history and novels in close succession and about equal in number. Under religion, Felton included the "Christian Bible" as well as the "Mahometan Bible or Alcoran." He read ancient and modern historians and English and American novelists. Law, geography, and travel rounded out the roll. Such omnivorous consumers of print vastly expanded the bounds of inquiry in village life. Felton actively confronted each book with the critical view that no one author could hold the entire truth in one volume. This extensive mode of reading carried rural folk beyond a reliance on devotional tracts and the sermons of a ministerial elite. The rise of such genres as the novel marked not just new forms, new authors, and a new audience, but also "a new contract between the producers and consumers of print." Reading fiction empowers readers in ways inherently inimical to social authority, some scholars assert. Felton's list of reading, which included over twenty titles of fiction, shows a move from devotional to informational texts.[11]

Felton's penchant for system gave him a jump over other young men in Marlborough; his systematic approach to self-education made up for the lack of continuity in his formal schooling. He not only made out his own accounts in great detail, but also wrote letters and other important legal and commercial documents for his neighbors. He noted that unfortunates who spent their time "roging or gaming," who may have been among those who disparaged Silas's "bookish ways," were forced to call upon him to transact their business, such as "writing notes" or "casting interest," perhaps to cover the debts incurred by their roguish ways. He had attended the district schools only occasionally from the age of fourteen to nineteen. It was his five years of schoolteaching, above all, that enabled him to avoid farming and opened the door to further self-education. Schoolteaching, while unremunerative—after three years Felton found that his wages barely met his expenses—provided a stepping-stone to a career in business. After the Revolution, the opening of academies, private institutions of higher education in the hinterlands, offered more avenues from the farm toward new commercial pursuits. These academies offered an "English" curriculum with such practical subjects as bookkeeping, an alternative to the classical curriculum that prepared students for the ministry. In 1799, Felton pooled his small capital with that of Joel Cranston, a tavernkeeper and surveyor, to open a store in Marlborough. The same rationality that informed his reading served him as a merchant. In 1801, a busy Silas Felton closed his autobiography, reflecting on the "pleasure I now derive, by looking back, and contemplating the time I have spent in studying." His written account of the "transactions which have occurd in my past life" confirmed the principles of *"Reason, Industry, and good Economy."*[12]

Young women in the post-Revolutionary provinces also found reading enlightening. Many personal accounts stress how a daughter's reading began in the family circle. Catharine Maria Sedgwick, growing up in Stockbridge, Massachusetts, remembered her father reading aloud to her family. Soon she was reading such massive tomes as Charles Rollin's *Ancient History* (Paris, 1730–38) on her own, hiding herself in the schoolhouse by creeping under her desk, where she "forgot myself in Cyrus's greatness."[13] Maria Campbell of Virginia reminded her younger cousin at the acclaimed Salem Academy in North Carolina that "in the days of our forefathers it was considered only necessary to learn a female to read the Bible." In a sharp departure from the colonial world, "post-revolutionary textual and visual portrayals limned a woman whose virtue was manifest in, and generated by, the cultivation of books," writes Mary Kelley. Teachers encouraged women students to become readers or to extend their habits of reading. Caroline Chester inscribed in her journal in 1816 the message that Litchfield's Sarah Pierce had drilled into her pupils: books inform "us of all important events which have taken place since the creation of the world" and serve as the means by which "our understandings are enlarged and our memories strengthened," reflecting the dual goals of faculty psychology.[14]

Whether taking place at home or in formal institutions, education promoted a lifelong immersion in a world of books. Books might offer comfort, as Margaret Bayard Smith wrote: "My books! When forsaken by other friends, they were with me still—when happy, they made me happier—when sad, they enlivened." Reading could also promote critical thinking. Charlotte Sheldon, another of Sarah Pierce's students, noted in her journal that Friedrich Schiller's *The Robbers* was an "excellent tragedy," but the character of Amelia was "rather inconsistent in my opinion." Reading was an active process of critical analysis and self-fashioning for young women, as for young men. Sedgwick advised her "young countrywomen" not to accept the views of others blindly: "Do not *take for granted*, believing, with ignorant credulity, whatever you see stated in a book. Remember an author is but one witness, and often a very fallible one. Pause in your reading, reflect, compare what the writer tells you with what you have learned from other sources on the subject, and above all, use your own judgment independently, not presumptuously."[15] Reading would only serve to begin a process of self-knowledge and growth.

Schoolgirls turned to biographies of women for models to live by. Julia Parker filled the pages of her journal in 1841 with the biographies of such learned women as Margaret Davidson, Madame de Staël, and Hannah More; the contemplation of "a mind like hers" moved Parker to consider consecrating her own life "to improvement," and she also shared those reflections with her students in her new position as a teacher.[16] Thoughts prompted by books could extend to the improvement of society. When Mrs. Rebecca Hammond Lord anonymously published her poems on "religious and moral subjects" in 1820, the provincial Vermonter echoed the learned women of her generation and used republican ideology to vindicate female reason. She affirmed her belief in the

Enlightenment's legacy for the rising American Republic in her poem "The Progress of Science," which sketched the path of science—imaginatively figured as feminine—in Western civilization from the ancient republics across the European continent to its present home:

> She cross'd the Atlantic main
> Till on Columbia's shores confess'd:
> Hail, blest Columbia! Happy land
> Fair science's tranquil seat,
> Virtue and freedom, hand in hand
> Here find a safe retreat.[17]

Rebecca Lord, like Silas Felton and their fellow readers and writers, anticipated a Village Enlightenment through the spread of knowledge and information through the countryside, but she also anticipated greater roles for educated women.

Many young men struggled over their choice of career and construction of self in the context of an emerging market society. All were more or less self-made, lacking influential patrons; they were also mostly self-educated. Reading served them instrumentally, as a way of learning commercial skills; internally, it was the means and measure of selfhood. The print-centered activities of these village enlighteners intensified the transmission of knowledge and challenged the hegemony of the old arbiters and custodians of rural culture, such as the Reverend Ebenezer Devotion.[18]

Growing up rural could now mean challenging the authority of patriarchs and ministers. The real American Revolution, as Gordon Wood has written, was not the political overthrow of British rule, but the late-eighteenth-century assault on aristocracy. New sources of information, close at hand, offered new models of living; learning about those lives enabled youths to imagine alternative futures for themselves. Cosmopolitan ideas entered villages along the turnpikes and through the printed word, along with printers, craftsmen, and teachers who embodied alternatives to farming.[19]

Hats and Chairs

Families and farms had long stood at the center of life in rural America. To find places for the next generation had always been the critical concern of families in an agrarian society. While the achievement of a "comfortable independence" remained the goal, the means of achieving that objective changed at the turn of the nineteenth century. Older rural communities saw their population rise dramatically, but the supply of available land did not. Young people and especially families with mature sons looked to new frontier farmlands to the north or west; others moved to burgeoning port cities or factory towns. Many, however, chose to remain closer to home. Seasonal and part-time artisans turned into full-time ones; agricultural by-occupations, such as hat or comb making, became manufacturing endeavors; more young men and women turned to commerce or craft work to secure a livelihood. For example, Solomon Sibley of Ward, Massachusetts, spent over a quarter of his time making furniture, according to his account book (1793–1823), but his furniture production was concentrated between December and April. In the fall and winter he also did carpentry, while during the warmer months he made farm implements for his neighbors. One of Sibley's products, a chest-on-chest, shows the kind of plain and sturdy products he made for his rural clientele (fig. 22). The originally red-stained chest has two bottom drawer fronts to conceal a single drawer, irregular dovetailing, and imperfect proportions between the upper and lower sections. Sibley was not able to practice his craft regularly, and his work shows his lack of habits of exactness.[20]

The term *market revolution* identifies the great transformation taking place in the northern countryside during the early nineteenth century. This "revolution" was a constellation of incremental changes occurring at different rates in different communities rather than a single cataclysmic event, but it entered into every facet of life. At its core was a thorough commercialization of economic life: a subsistence-oriented economy organized around local exchange, with small farms and tiny workshops, became reorganized so that farmers and manufacturers produced goods for distant markets where cash relations ruled. But this revolution was no imperial process or top-down imposition by a few large-scale capitalists; change occurred through the activities of a host of individuals and families on their farms and in their villages.[21]

The population continued to climb in the older areas of the rural northeast, such as southern New England and southeastern Pennsylvania. In western Massachusetts, Hampshire County had 6,500 inhabitants in 1765 and almost 25,000 in 1790. The price of land rose, and property became more unequally distributed. One third of Northampton's taxpayers owned no taxable real property, while the wealthiest 10 percent held half of all the taxable property in the town. Even among farmers, inequality became more pronounced: over half the town's farms contained fewer than fifty acres, making it difficult to conduct diversified operations and impossible to contemplate dividing the land among several sons. Once fathers could no longer provide their sons with a start in life, parental control over marriage declined sharply. Unmarried youth might set off for a period of work on someone else's farm or in a shop to accumulate the necessary

Fig. 22. Solomon Sibley, chest on chest, 1790–1810. Ward (Auburn), Massachusetts. Maple, chestnut, and white pine. 76-3/4 × 39-1/2 × 20 in. Collections of Old Sturbridge Village, Sturbridge, Massachusetts.

capital to enter the land market. Leaving home for employment became part of growing up. Parents watched their children move to increasingly distant settlements or pursue nonagricultural work. Those who stayed in the countryside could not follow their father's or mother's path. Instead, many young people forged—or backed into—new occupations made possible by the decline of patriarchy along with the expansion of commercial and cultural opportunities.[22]

The dynamic household economy facilitated the transformation of agriculture. Northern agriculturalists had always practiced mixed husbandry, cultivating crops and raising livestock. As agriculture commercialized, they grew new crops, grazed larger herds, and specialized in products with expanding urban markets. Farmers in long-settled regions moved away from raising crops for home consumption and relying on natural river meadows for feed toward plowing and seeding lands with cultivated grasses. Clearing and cultivating grasslands required more labor but supported more livestock. And livestock provided the best means for many farmers to increase their output and intensify their production, which represented a move away from the more extensive agricultural regime where farmers had saved on labor by exploiting land. Herds grew as country storekeepers collected cattle for market and drovers roamed the countryside. Production of butter and cheese increased markedly. All these efforts meant more work for farm families. Markets entailed considerable risk. New ventures often failed. The craze for merino sheep, a vast speculation in new breeds imported from Spain, receded just as quickly as it had begun, leaving many farmers stranded or broke. In one poignant example (perhaps apocryphal), Ben Hosmer set out from Concord, Massachusetts, in the 1790s for the Cambridge market with his wife's butter, eggs, and other goods. Realizing that his supplies of rum and other store-bought goods were low, he impulsively started off on a "hot dog-day morning in August." Without a wagon, he slung two baskets of butter and eggs across the "old mare's" back. He pushed the horse relentlessly toward Lexington, stopping for a brief rest at a brook in East Lexington. Hosmer only intended to take a quick drink, but the sweating horse, burdened down with panniers full of butter and eggs, decided upon a full bath and plunged into the water. The startled "Uncle" Ben was "dumb founded," unable to sputter anything out but "don't you know any better than to lie down in the brook with Dinah's butter and eggs on your condemned [damned] back?" When the horse did not reply, he began beating the unfortunate beast until a crowd gathered. When one onlooker asked him whether the horse had really wallowed in the water, Hosmer replied, "Don't you see the yolks running all down the ole mare's belly, and the butter fit for nothing more than grease!" The trip to market was a bumpy road in those days.[23]

Craft work provided a more promising avenue for young men and women. Farmers had long used the dull periods of winter or spring to make furniture or shoes, and artisans devoted to craft production still grew crops and raised stock. One Vermont local historian remembers, "The manufactures carried on in Vermont were, for many years, such only as the immediate wants of the people rendered indispensable, and in general each family were their own manufacturers." But the post-Revolutionary economic boom and the increasing pressure of population on the land changed manufacturing as surely as agriculture. Winter employment became ubiquitous, helping round out the vagaries of farming. The variety of village craftsmen, such as blacksmiths and shoemakers, was augmented by cabinetmakers and hatters. The shift toward more elaborate consumerism, which had been restricted to urban centers in the eighteenth century, accelerated in the post-Revolutionary countryside. "As the condition of the people improved, then by degrees, [they] extended their desires beyond the mere necessaries of life; first to its conveniences, and then to its elegancies," our Vermont local historian continued. "This produced new wants, and to supply them, mechanics more numerous and more skilful were required, til at length, the cabinet maker, the tailor, the jeweller, the milliner, and a host of others came to be regarded as indispensable."[24]

Young farm women who pursued employment opportunities were "a great help to many families," according to one New England chronicle, as well as adding to their own financial accounts. Straw braiding took a readily available agricultural by-product, rye straw, added value by the expert toil of women braiders, and turned it into salable bonnets, with piece-rate wages for the outworkers and profits for their employers. Stories from the beginning of the century illustrate how women learned this skill from one another. Sarah Anna Emery of West Newbury, Massachusetts, provoked by the excessive cost of a new bonnet, availed herself of her aunt's knowledge; she split or plaited the ripe straw, turned a grinding mortar upside down to use as a makeshift pattern, stitched the straw braid into a bonnet, and then trimmed it with white ribbon. Betsey Metcalf of Providence, Rhode Island, recalled that in 1798 she "learned them [locals] to braid from nearly all the towns around Providence" without asking for any compensation. She could easily earn a dollar a day, sometimes a dollar and a half, "for several weeks of a time," compensation equal to a skilled male laborer's wages. Soon storekeepers entered as middlemen to supply rye straw braid to the straw-hat industry: in 1809, two central Massachusetts storekeepers independently advertised for 20,000 yards of straw braid. Hardwick's Jason Mixter recorded credits for straw braid in his accounts by 1809; by 1818, he had 135 active straw-braiding households bringing him hats from a range of towns throughout the region. Palm-leaf hat makers faced low technological requirements to enter the trade; the only equipment needed was a splitter—a piece of wood with iron teeth at one end and a strip of tin or brass at the other—to make the splints or narrow pieces of straw used for braiding. Like other rural by-occupations, straw braiding was seasonal, taken up after the harvest and continued through the winter months. The ranks of braiders included poorer farming households with teenagers or young children available to do the work; the names of single women and widows were found in the accounts as well.[25]

As rural craftsmen looked beyond the local community and expanded their production in order to supply growing urban markets, the jack-of-all-trades gave way to a variety of specialized artisans. The bustling commercial center of Northampton, a town of sixteen hundred in 1790, attracted twenty furniture makers over the next few decades, eleven of whom made Windsor chairs. These cosmopolitan seating forms signified their owner's preference for the latest fashion, but also lent themselves to a division of labor. Windsor manufacturers, in contrast to Solomon Sibley, became full-time, year-round chairmakers. They clustered in an area called Shop Row rather than working in dispersed rural locations. The construction of the Tontine Building in 1786, with three stories of shops that craftsmen could buy or lease, testified to Northampton's status as an urban center of inland Massachusetts and to the distance between its residents and the routines of farm life.

Whenever Northampton chairmaker Ansel Goodrich finished one of his stylish but standardized Windsor chairs (fig. 23), he proudly pasted a label advertising his wares beneath the seat: "Ansel Goodrich Has on hand and keeps constantly for sale a quantity of warranted Chairs, a few rods North of the Court-House, Northampton." The construction of his chairs and his business records demonstrate that his manufactory sped up production. When Goodrich arrived in 1795, he advertised in the *Hampshire Gazette* that he had "on hand, and keeps constantly for sale all kinds of Windsor chairs, viz—Arm Chairs, Dining, do. Of all kinds, Fanback, do. Fanback Foretails, Rocking Chairs, Settees and Cannopies." Canopies had exotic French associations, which Goodrich enhanced by adding that he had "worked among the French" (which might mean that he had trained in New York City with such leading craftsmen as Charles-Honoré Lannuier). Below the chair seat, all the parts of Goodrich's chairs were interchangeable, regardless of whether the chair featured a fan back, bow back, side chair, or continuous bow or sack-back armchair: the details of Windsor style changed so rapidly as to baffle casual viewers. The chair's construction promoted the standardization of production. The thick, solid seats served as a platform to anchor turned legs and spindles; those parts could be made by different workers at separate locations and stockpiled for assembly. In the competitive climate of Northampton, Goodrich employed up to five journeymen and apprentices in his shop, but he also hired rural craftsmen to supply roughed-out chair parts. He probably produced about four to five sets of six chairs each week. Samuel Davison of Plainfield, a town west of Northampton, charged Goodrich for "hewing and dubbing 346 chair seats." When the chairmaker died in 1803 at the age of thirty, he left a great number of chairs in varying states of completion: "12 fanback chairs, primed . . . 14 do. not painted . . . 6 dozen chairs sets partly finished . . . 120 chair seats . . . Bunch of rods

Fig. 23. Ansel Goodrich, fan-back Windsor chair, 1795–1803. Northampton, Massachusetts. 1795–1803. Bass, maple; paint, paper, ink. Black and green paint over original red paints. 37-3/4 × 16-5/8 × 16-1/4 in. The chair's label advertises Goodrich's stock of chairs available at his shop "north of the Court-House Northampton." Courtesy of Historic Deerfield, Massachusetts. Photograph by Amanda Merullo.

about 400 . . . 150 bows"—mute evidence of the separation between production and assembly.[26]

Social relations were shifting inside farm families and country workshops. By-occupations, whereby members of farm households had produced and sold handmade goods, were replaced by outwork, whereby people toiled at home for piece-rate wages making products for merchant-manufacturers. Underemployed rural residents were drawn into networks of domestic production rather than clustered into factories.

Small shops were scattered throughout the northern countryside beyond New England. Southeastern Pennsylvania's Chester County, with its rich farmland and comfortable climate, was known as the "best poor man's country." Created by William Penn in 1682, the county attracted migrants throughout the eighteenth century. Rural residents could both feed their families and send goods to market. Chester County farmers increasingly looked to by-occupations, and by 1796, nearly 16 percent worked entirely outside agriculture. The county's population grew, and its economy diversified by expanding rural production; women wove cloth and men made furniture instead of migrating west or crowding into factory villages. Furniture making boomed, but continued to be decentralized. For every furniture maker in 1790, there were five in 1800, although the county's total population had increased only slightly. Historian Barry Kessler found these workshops widely dispersed throughout the townships rather than concentrated in urban centers and transportation hubs. Farmers throughout the region set up workshops on their properties, renting them out to artisans or making furniture themselves. These farm-based artisans probably sold most of their products directly to their neighbors rejecting the urban path of acquiring expensive equipment and using advertising.[27] Amos Darlington, Sr., was born in West Goshen, Chester County, in 1764. He appeared on several tax lists as a joiner or cabinetmaker, but his account book records only 173 pieces of furniture from 1791 to 1810. In the first five years he only made 11 pieces, but for the next seven years he averaged about 17. Darlington made mostly simple furniture; bedsteads and tables were the bulk of his output, with an occasional desk and chest of drawers. By contrast, his son Amos moved to a larger town and made almost 800 pieces of furniture during his fifteen-year career.[28]

Intensive production of Windsor chairs in the towns of Hampshire County, Massachusetts, and extensive production of furniture throughout Cheshire County, Pennsylvania, were the two faces of small-scale industry in the northern countryside.

Clockmaking

> *After your work is cast, first take your frame plates & hammer them hard (as you must all the rest of your work). After hammering they must be filed flat & then scraped till there is no filings to be seen. After that they are to be pinned together & filed square. After that take the wheels & find the center of them with the compasses & open a hole so that it will fit the wheel arbor . . .*
>
> Norwich, September ye 8th AD 1779
> Daniel Burnap, Memorandum Book

When Daniel Burnap wrote out his "Receipts" as well as "Directions for a Chime Clock," he recorded the fruits of his apprenticeship with the British clockmaker Thomas Harland. The "mysteries of the trade," as they were called, were passed down by a personal exchange between master and apprentice. New techniques and styles were imported from the metropole by men like Harland or invented by provincials like Benjamin Cheney, a Connecticut clockmaker who developed a cheaper wooden movement—innovations at the upper and lower ends of the clock trade.

Harland had come to Norwich in 1773, bringing with him the most advanced techniques of clockmaking then available in the colonies, and he passed on these methods to his numerous apprentices, leaving a legacy of instruction and innovation that bore fruit for decades. Books on clockmaking techniques were rare, as few masters were willing to commit the mysteries of the trade to print. When Daniel Burnap was about to set off on his own, he meticulously wrote down the results of his years of instruction—through observation, verbal directions, and supervised practice—in the intricate methods of working with metal, the composition of paints and alloys, the numbers of teeth in the wheels of clock movements, and the step-by-step procedures for making and polishing clock parts or silver spoons, all the standard work of a clockmaker.[29]

Gaining knowledge of the craft was sometimes difficult, even impossible. The Cheneys proved to be innovative artisans, but they were not generous teachers. John Fitch, born in 1744 in Windsor, Connecticut, to a hard-working but "penurious" farmer, went to school until he was eight or nine, when his father "set [him] to work" full-time with only a month of schooling in the "dead of winter." The ambitious young man was "desireous of learning some sort of business that I could make a living by when I came for myself." He informed his father he was "too small and weak" for farming and begged to be put to a trade or sent to sea. He had a chance meeting with "one Benjamin Cheany" who was looking for an apprentice to learn the clockmaking business—although Fitch suspected that the farmer-artisan wanted his labor in his fields more than in the shop. In 1762, he and his father signed indentures that specified the eighteen-year-old would spend seven months a year at clockmaking and the remaining five at farm labor until he turned twenty-one. Both Cheney and Fitch's father refused to supply the apprentice's clothing, but his older sister agreed to clothe him. So the indentures were finally executed.

Fitch found the Cheney household a strange one indeed. His master was "a pretty good sort of man but possessed with a great many oddities," including a physical deformity resulting from childhood rickets. His mistress was a poor housekeeper and spent money freely on liquor. The apprentice kept a strict accounting of his time. Toward the end of his indenture, he had only learned to make wooden clocks and had been kept busy with trifling brass work. When Benjamin Cheney found he could extract "no more benefit from me working his place," he worked out a plan with his brother Timothy, who made wooden and brass clocks and repaired watches. The new master agreed to take Fitch for a year, new indentures were executed, and the youth's "high sprites" rose once again in hopes "of getting a trade whereby might subsist myself in a genteel way when I came for myself." However, he was again put to small brass work for eight months. He never even saw a watch put together; when he tried to stand near Cheney to observe the mystery, he was ordered away. "It was but seldom that I could get to see any of his tooles for watchwork as he had a drawer where he was particularly cairful always to lock them up as if he was afraid I should know their use and by that means gain some information of the business." Shortly after reaching his majority, Fitch demanded that Cheney teach him watchwork, but the master refused and threatened blows. The Cheneys released Fitch four months early for eight pounds, totally ignorant of the business. "I sat out for home and cryed the whole distance," Fitch wrote.[30] This fruitless apprenticeship did not deter John Fitch from mechanical pursuits. After the Revolution, he experimented with building a steam-powered boat and inventing an automatic flour mill.

Burnap's master, in contrast to the Cheneys, was a generous teacher and undertook more modest innovations in brass clockmaking. Thomas Harland sped up production by making standardized parts for his tall clocks, and he served the clockmaking trade as well as retail customers. An advertisement in the Norwich *Packet* proclaimed: "Thomas Harland, Watch and Clock-maker from London, Begs leave to acquaint the public that he has opened a shop near the store of Christopher Leffingwell, in Norwich where he makes in the neatest manner and on the most approved principles, horizontal, repeating and plain watches in gold, silver, metal or covered cases. Spring, musical and plain clocks with the greatest care and dispatch, and upon reasonable terms. N.B. Clock faces engraved and finished for the trade. Watch wheels and fuzeees of all sorts and dimensions, cut and finished upon the shortest notice, neat as in London, and at the same price." Harland had brought gear-cutting machinery and other tools with him, which proved especially valuable when the Revolutionary War made it impossible to import tools and castings. Harland's dials, which he sold to other clockmakers, were finely engraved—a lucrative skill that he passed on to Burnap and other apprentices.[31]

By the 1790s, clockmakers could purchase gears and wheels as well as dials from a hardware merchant and specialize in assembly. In his "Memorandum Book," Burnap details the myriad steps to be taken in making an eight-day tall-clock movement, from finishing the cast parts so the wheels turned true to placing the Roman numerals properly on the dial. The instructions for hardening and tempering various small tools and for constructing a wheel-cutting engine were as important as those for assembly. Hammering, filing, drilling, turning, cutting, riveting, tempering, straightening, and polishing all had to be done accurately without measuring instruments. The book also details variations: recoil and dead-beat escapements, repeating work, moon-phase and calendar attachments, and the design and construction of a chime-clock movement. Burnap was freely taught what Fitch yearned to learn, including the art of regulating and repairing watches. The process of making silver, tea-, and tablespoons is outlined, along with chemical and metallurgical receipts for melting, refining, soldering, plating, and finishing gold and silver articles. Brief notes describe the fabrication of gold beads, sleeve buttons, stone buttons, and hairpins. A list of current prices for materials and shop work formed the foundation for Burnap's charges to his customers.[32]

Apprenticeship as a clockmaker resembled that in other crafts; apprentices provided labor for the master in exchange for instruction. A clockmaker would be hard pressed to run his shop without the labor of apprentices. Much of the work around the shop required little skill, though it was time-consuming and laborious; even a novice could fetch wood, run errands, make and blow the forge fire, and clean castings. The first task for an apprentice, one clockmaker related, was to cut hands out of a thin sheet of metal. The master inscribed the outlines of the hand, and the young boy cut out, filed, and polished them. After mastering that simple task, he moved on to making other small parts, filing and polishing hardware, turning the great wheel of the lathe, drawing wire, setting up molds, and making small brass castings. After three or four years, the apprentice was expected to have mastered all these skills, which he demonstrated by constructing a complete clock.[33] He was ready to move to a distant town to open his own shop and even start training his own apprentices. The system worked well for its participants. A family eager to secure mechanical training for one of its sons could do so at little cost, while the craftsman received much-needed unskilled or semiskilled labor without divesting scarce cash or capital. Mechanical training and marketing expertise were propagated within the tightly knit clockmaking community.[34]

Daniel Burnap, the most prolific clockmaker of the post-Revolutionary era, had served a traditional apprenticeship. He taught school for several winters and had returned to Harland's shop for a stint as a journeyman when he recorded his account of making clock wheels in his Memorandum Book. He removed to East Windsor, married Deliverance Kingsbury in 1782, acquired a dwelling house, and by the summer of 1786 had set up shop near Bissell's Tavern as clockmaker, watch repairer, instrument maker, silversmith, and brass founder. He hung out a painted sign that read "Daniel Burnaps Clock & Watch

Factory," prepared a copperplate engraving for a watch paper to advertise his business, and attracted his first apprentices to assist in his shop.

Burnap was well placed to take advantage of the growing demand for clocks, surveying instruments, and other brass goods that accompanied the postwar economic revival. He spent most of his time in those first years of independence—his own and the nation's—repairing watches and making brass hardware, with only the occasional clock or clock dial appearing in his account book. He made a small timepiece for Timothy Swan and traded hardware for Swan's hats. The hatter also was a musician and music publisher, so he occasionally printed watch papers for the clockmaker. Artisans commonly traded skilled work: Burnap recorded "Cutting Glass for grinding paint" for the miniaturist William Vestile. But Burnap spent much of his time mending teakettles and skillets. His most expensive account for a "Brass Wheel'd Clock" called forth his full training, and a *Connecticut Courant* ad in March of 1791 announced he "works in many other branches to those in the silversmith line," such as "Surveyor's Compasses, Watch repairing, &c." When Seth Pease set out from Suffield, Connecticut, to conduct surveys in "New Connecticut," which became known as the Western Reserve of Ohio, he carried one of Burnap's "Brass Compasses," bought in 1791. However, Burnap promoted clockmaking as "the governing business of his shops." His accounts recorded "chime clocks," "moon age clocks," "small clocks," "eight day timepieces," and even a "tower clock," or public clock, as his advertisement called it.

Burnap extended the lessons he had learned from Harland. He continued the traditional artisan's bespoke practice of waiting to make a clock until a customer came through the shop door, but he spent his slack time making parts in anticipation of future commissions. Harland's bequest included the division of labor and an increase in production. Fifty-one clocks and thirteen clock dials were recorded in Burnap's books. His clock production peaked at seven clocks a year between 1790 and 1795. Clocks sold for about ten pounds, such as the one that Elihu Colton, a resident of Longmeadow, Massachusetts, proudly engraved with his name on the brass cover of the pendulum bob (fig. 24). Burnap displayed his fullest powers in "chime," or musical, clocks, which sold for about twenty-two pounds. Customers for these luxury timepieces included East Hartford's Amherst Reynolds and Dr. Ashel Thomson of Farmington. Thomson's clock has a dial with elaborately engraved lettering, scalloping, and foliage, a flowering of rococo ornament in the hinterlands. Every three hours, the clock played a tune, one of six—"General Elliot's Minuet," "Banks of the Dee," "Hob or Nob," "Rakes of Rodney," "French King's Minuet," and "Rosey Wine"— selected by moving the hand in the dial arch.[35] Burnap's clocks show the proliferation of rococo ornamentation in rural Connecticut.

Fig. 24. Daniel Burnap of East Windsor, Connecticut, ornamented and silvered the brass dial of his eight-hour-day brass clock movement around 1785–90 with rococo raffles around the spandrels and intertwined leaves added to the naturalistic decoration. The clock's owner, Elihu Colton of Longmeadow, Massachusetts, proudly engraved his name on the back of the pendulum bob. 51 × 12 × 6-1/2 in. Courtesy of Winterthur Museum, Winterthur, Delaware.

The hinterlands were the site of experimentation and innovation that transformed the clockmaking industry. As settlement surged northward along the Connecticut River in the late eighteenth century, Burnap sold clock movements to cabinetmakers there, who constructed wooden cases and sold fashionably designed clocks to prominent men like Paul Brigham of Norwich, Vermont. Most clockmakers sold their clocks without cases; the consumer was responsible for obtaining a suitable enclosure, but sometimes just hung it up—"a wag on the wall." Burnap traded with such established cabinetmakers as Norwich's Hezekiah Kelly and Hartford's Samuel Kneeland before he brought case production inside his establishment and started to employ journeymen in 1794, obtaining his cases for about half as much. The entrepreneurial artisan made engraved clock dials for other less skillful clockmakers, an important part of his business. Watch repairing remained a lucrative business, and Burnap expanded watch manufacturing, starting a separate account book for his watch production in 1798. In 1795, Burnap acquired a farm in Coventry, selling his East Windsor home and shop. Two years later, he added a dam and water-powered sawmill, and lumber began to appear in his accounts as a major source of income. He built a substantial house between 1802 and 1805 and retired from the shop bench, occasionally cleaning a clock or making a set of spoons for his neighbors. Burnap took up a prominent place in Coventry town affairs, receiving his livelihood from his fields and sawmills and achieving distinction as the town's most prosperous citizen in 1810.

Daniel Burnap had retired from clockmaking just as one of his students, Eli Terry, was beginning the large-scale manufacture of clocks, a revolutionary development that consigned brass clockmakers such as Burnap to the sidelines.[36] Terry continued the Harland legacy into the third generation by increasing production, standardizing parts manufacture, and finding ways to expand the market for timepieces in American households. In the early nineteenth century, Terry extended those lessons into the Connecticut custom of working in wood, along with the notions of marketing prevalent in Connecticut commerce, to far outstrip his mentors; his wooden shelf clock literally "reinvent[ed] the notion of a clock."

Alternative sources of knowledge became available in the years after the War of Independence. No longer did apprenticeship or other household-based sources of authority remain the sole avenues to an occupation for young men and women intent on choosing their own careers or following their own inclinations rather than those of their parents or masters. Publication of craft secrets in such popular works as encyclopedias or recipe books devalued apprenticeship. According to William Rorabaugh, "If a youth wanted to learn a craft, he needed only a book and not a master." Although this statement exaggerates the change, the transmission of expertise through print subverted the master's authority. So, too, increasing reliance upon schooling diminished the force of a father's desires to have his sons follow him into farming, as Silas Felton's father discovered. Farmers continued to pass information down generation to generation, but such homespun authorities as *The Farmer's Almanac* or more patrician ones like the publications of the new agricultural societies exhorted agriculturalists to learn innovative methods. These printed avenues for the transmission of knowledge facilitated innovation.[37]

Schooling

New career paths developed after the Revolution with the expansion of formal schooling. A youth seeking to become a lawyer could attend Tapping Reeve's law school in Litchfield, Connecticut, while women aspiring to further education could attend Sarah Pierce's Female Academy in the thriving Litchfield County village. More widespread opportunities were offered by coeducational academies established in rural communities across New England. These new institutions enabled a broader group of young men and women to become consumers of the increasing variety of cultural commodities available during these decades.

The move toward more formal schooling was spurred both by the demand for commercial and scientific training and the national imperative of raising a new generation of virtuous republican citizens suited for a diverse and dynamic society. Public schooling expanded after the Revolution, as schools became more decentralized and mobile institutions. In "moving schools," a single teacher presided over brief sessions at several schoolhouses scattered around a town. Eventually, neighborhoods hired their own teachers, the sessions lengthened, and a district system came into existence. According to Carl Kaestle, "Long before the common-school reform movement and the creation of state free-school systems, beginning at least as early as the late eighteenth century, the proportion of children attending school each year was rising."[38] So did attendance at the village academies and country colleges that proliferated during the half-century after the Revolution. Young men and women in the countryside pursued protracted, though intermittent courses of study, often financing short periods of learning with stints of teaching. The higher schools served "as institutions for mobility for the poor but promising village scholars of rural New England." The sociable setting of academy promoted emulation, a powerful new way to stimulate "improvement" of all kinds, and facilitated the formation of peer groups that continued long after the students had scattered.

Academies were established in larger commercial villages, often by village leaders with translocal connections. Leicester Academy's founders pledged in 1784 to draw "a major part" of the trustees from beyond the town's borders; promoters included nearby Sturbridge's Ebenezer Crafts. Instruction began in the home of Aaron Lopez, a Providence merchant who had relocated to inland Massachusetts during the war. Village boosters took pride in erecting stately two-story academy buildings, distinguishing them from the unpainted structure of the common schools. Leicester Academy was housed in a village mansion with classical decoration, a magnificent new three-story structure opened in 1806. Cooperstown's academy, built in 1797, surpassed all the other structures in town. Deerfield Academy, probably designed by Asher Benjamin, had interior spaces suited for the many departments of the curriculum: "The Academy is an elegant Edifice, having, on the lower floor, four rooms, one for the English school, one for the Latin, Greek School, the Preceptor's room, and a room for the Museum and Library. The upper room, being all in one, is used for examinations, and exhibitions. . . . We had upwards of 20 in Latin and Greek, between 20 and 30 young Ladies studying English Grammar & Geography." Academies remained more local than colleges and served much larger numbers. They prepared students for a far wider range of occupations than the classical grammar schools, which prepared the select few for college and the learned professions. Students were quite heterogeneous in age, and school tuition was relatively affordable; as Felton found, many families allowed a student to attend for a season or two.[39]

Almost four hundred seminaries were established exclusively for women in the North and South between 1790 and 1830, before the first women's colleges were founded. A larger proportion of women than men attended academies during this period. Many institutions were coeducational.[40] The curricula were not sharply distinguished by sex, although female students might pay extra for lessons in ornamental needlework and French. English was the most common subject, followed by arithmetic and geography. A schoolgirl probably made this unusual watercolor and ink on silk panorama that shows the range of reading and sewing skills, along with painting, music, and geography, offered by female academies and seminaries (plate 1).

Litchfield emerged as an educational innovator in the Early Republic—for both men and women. Entry to the legal profession came after reading law over a period of time, an apprenticeship similar to craftsmen. Young men gathered around the charismatic figure of Tapping Reeve, who made Litchfield his home in 1772. When his household filled and his wife's health failed, he removed instruction to a small building in his backyard. There a new system emerged, "a paradigmatic alternative to the more customary and less systematic 'reading' of law in a lawyer's office." Reeve delivered 139 comprehensive lectures covering a wide range of topics. Here young men could obtain a legal education more easily and cheaply than anywhere else. Reeve's law school proved an enormous attraction, with over two hundred graduates by 1798.[41]

Litchfield supported an even more famous educational institution: Sarah Pierce's Litchfield Female Academy. Female seminaries "afforded young women unprecedented instruction in rhetoric, history, geography, philosophy, and the natural sciences," according to historian Catherine Kelly. Most of these schools also offered training in the feminine "accomplishments: drawing, painting, embroidery, music, and dancing. . . . Indeed, accomplishments and book learning were imagined as complementary parts of a single, unified project. Both were calculated to inculcate and demonstrate the virtuousness of American women, to provide proof of their sensibility." The opening of coeducational academies and female seminaries greatly expanded women's opportunities for learning. This prospect, which had become available to elite circles of women in the 1790s, was extended to urban and rural middling women in the 1820s, "consolidating and elaborating a social identity," writes Mary Kelley, that set them off from the lower orders.[42]

Sarah Pierce justified the expansion of women's educational opportunities through the notion of "Republican motherhood," the women's role in raising virtuous citizens. Like Felton and Thomas, her career in cultural advancement answered a personal need to earn her own livelihood. Pierce's mother died when she was very young, leaving Sarah and her brother and four older sisters; her father remarried, and he and his wife had three more girls, but he died in 1783. Sarah's older brother, John, sent the seventeen-year-old to New York for training as a teacher in 1784 in an effort to assume some financial responsibility for the family and free him to marry. He armed her with this injunction: "I hope you will not miss a single dancing school . . . to instruct you in every thing in walking standing and sitting, all the movements of which tho' they appear in a polite persons natural, are effects of art." Art aided in the creating the appearance of naturalness, and artifice served to demonstrate sincerity. John's death in 1792 left Sarah with the responsibility of supporting her three younger half-sisters and stepmother. First she opened a school for young women in the dining room of her home. Six years later, Reeve headed up a list of twenty-six of Litchfield's most prominent men supporting the project of "Building a House for a Female Academy."[43]

Pierce's curriculum was based on her belief in women's intellectual powers. Geography and history were as important as literature. Morse's texts appear in the letters and journals of student Lucy Sheldon in 1803: "Have for the past week been studying geography & Miss Pierce has been examining us every day." The study of geography demonstrated the breadth of God's plan, the superiority of Christian nations, the greatness of the United States' institutions and inhabitants, and finally, the superiority of New England to other regions. Instruction deepened as better geography texts appeared and globes were introduced to schools. Still, the ornamental arts of drawing, painting, and embroidery—even of maps and globes—supplemented academic lessons in geography and other subjects. Needlework with neoclassical themes and historical charts reinforced academic training and instruction in virtue and sensibility, while enhancing Pierce's profit margin since parents paid extra for this genteel instruction. The income generated from these classes kept many schools afloat and proved a crucial element in training young women as teachers. Sarah Pierce's Female Academy attracted such local students as Uriah Tracy, whose portrait was painted by Ralph Earl. Tracy's four daughters attended the academy. Soon young women from throughout the United States sought out Litchfield's famous seminary; all four of the Beecher sisters studied there, including Catharine, later to found a series of female seminaries and author texts on domestic economy, and Harriet, the author of *Uncle Tom's Cabin*. Its graduates dispersed nationwide, part of the vast corps of teachers that public schools required.[44]

Academies promoted the formation of formal organizations as well as informal ties among peers, which fostered the propagation of knowledge through the countryside. Edward Hitchcock, from a poor Deerfield family, recalled "a few companions . . . with whom I united in a society, which had a department for debate, and another for philosophical discussion." His sister Emilia and his future wife, Orra White, joined thirty-four other women in Deerfield's Young Ladies' Literary Society, another outgrowth of academy culture.[45]

Silas Felton's career as a student and teacher exemplifies the erratic paths traveled by many rural youths in search of an education. Silas had attended the local schools only occasionally from the age of fourteen to nineteen. His five years of teaching school enabled him to avoid farming and opened the door to further education. Felton accepted the Marlborough selectmen's 1795 offer to teach school only after his father and others assured him that his ignorance was no barrier. "When I entered the school-house, my heart almost leapt into my mouth for fear that I was not sufficient for the undertaking." He attended to "order and regulation" during school hours and spent his evenings and mornings looking over "sums or Lessons," which he barely understood. By these means he managed to keep ahead of his pupils and survive the seven-week term. But "ending the school [in July 1795] my father wanted me at home." Felton realized that pursing further schooling would require leaving town, so he pressed his father "and at length gained his consent to attend an Academy a few months." Upon arrival in Leicester, he found a young Harvard graduate, a banker's son who had been first in his class, in charge of scholars who were more like Silas. Ignorant of "the manners of the Cuntrypeople," he displayed his self-importance, and several students left. In ten weeks, Silas managed to pick up a "considerable Knowledge" of grammar, some of the "hardest sums" in arithmetic, and a smattering of geography before returning home to help get in his father's hay and go back to teaching school.[46]

The snobbishness that academies might inculcate in rural youth was a subject of frequent, often satirical, remark. School plays often caricatured these concerns about the difficulties haughty academy graduates faced in reentering local society, especially for women who might be scorned for too much education by their male counterparts. A play given at a Greenfield school in 1799 had one of the young female characters objecting to attending school, explaining that "Uncle Tristam says he hates to have girls go to school, it makes them so dam'd uppish & so deuced proud that they won't work. . . . How will the young fellows take it if we shine away & don't like their humdrum ways—Won't they be as mad as vengeance—& associate with the girls that don't go to school?"[47]

Felton returned to his district school with a newfangled spirit of emulation. He introduced "the art of oratory" by giving his pupils speeches to memorize and held "Exhibitions of scholars" for their parents and the townspeople. In the winter of 1797, he noted that most people who had crowded into the schoolhouse were quite gratified with the performance, "excepting a few superstitious bigots, who pretended they thought it was the work of the Devil."[48] Felton had been instrumental in greatly changing the local culture of education, a far cry from his early childhood days.

Printing

The story of the Village Enlightenment can be told most compellingly in the tales of printers and publishers, which combine knowledge and entrepreneurship. The print trade not only created informed rural consumers like Silas Felton but also served as a significant avenue of economic and cultural advancement for printers and publishers. These artisan-entrepreneurs fed the hunger for print by spreading over an ever-wider swath of the rural northeast, marking the leading edge of the extension of village manufacturing and the crafting of cultural identity. Isaiah Thomas, the publishing pioneer, led the way to the hinterlands. He moved his press from Boston to Worcester during the war and then created a northern outpost in the new community of Walpole, New Hampshire. In his *History of Printing,* Thomas noted that "after the establishment of our independence, by the peace of 1783, presses multiplied very fast, not only in seaports, but in all the principal inland towns and villages."[49]

The print trade captured the imagination of those toiling at its presses as well as those devouring its imprints. The stories of four print entrepreneurs outline how young men coming of age looked to make and sell cultural commodities to their neighbors. Robert Thomas, an almanac publisher, breathed new life and new ideas into an old genre. John Prentiss was captured by the power of print and the cosmopolitanism of the print shop at an early age; he moved around New England before settling on a long career as a newspaper publisher, a key product of the printing trade. The Merriam brothers were equally mobile, but their local newspaper was less successful; they became rural outwork suppliers for urban publishers. Elihu Phinney took a different route, becoming a pioneer publisher in Cooperstown, New York. Despite their varying journeys, all were captured by the post-Revolutionary generation's search for career and identity; all were linked by print's possibilities for personal advancement and cultural improvement.

The initial impetus for agricultural change in post-Revolutionary New England came in the guise of improvements to a staple of the farmer's bookshelf when the first issue of *The Farmer's Almanack* appeared in Sterling, Massachusetts, in 1792. Its publisher, Robert B. Thomas, advocated reading as a source of entertainment and edification as well as useful knowledge for rural folk. Born on a small farm in Sterling in 1766, Thomas was destined for college, but he refused to prepare for a ministerial career. Pursing an education on his own, he found in his father's ample library no more engrossing volume than Ferguson's *Astronomy*, from which he "first imbibed the idea of calculating an almanack."[50] Until the age of twenty-six, Thomas kept school, busied himself with bookbinding, and upon finding "but few books in the country," commenced bookselling. Finally, in 1792, he went to Boston to study with Osgood Carlton, "teacher of mathematics," and prepare the astronomical calculations for the almanac he was planning. Almanacs at that time concentrated on astrological details. Upon his return to Sterling, Thomas set out to produce a new kind of almanac. A cultural mediator who bridged the gap between cosmopolitan and rural cultures, he wished to do more than publish a mere guide to the stars. Knowing that an older generation set in its ways would resist the recommendations of gentlemen farmers, he realized that he could bring about change in the countryside only if new theories of agricultural "improvement" were consonant with farmers' beliefs. So he promoted the application of new methods through the results they yielded: "However prepossessed we may be in favor of old forms and customs, yet many deviations therefrom have proved beneficial to experimentalists." To succeed, farmers must pay attention to "order and system." To drive home his plea for progress on the farm, Thomas peopled his calendar with stock village types, such as Tom Bluenose and publican Toddy Stick, to serve up a message of temperance.

Each year, Thomas gradually replaced astrological signs and weather predictions with advice about imbuing children with book knowledge and school learning (fig. 25). Thomas's first almanac in 1793 featured only text on its title page. Two years later, he had added among his "New, Useful, and Entertaining Matter," an illustration of an industrious farmer plowing his field with a sturdy farmhouse in the background, while a cornucopia adorned the top of the picture. He criticized "the heedless man who can just write his name and pick out a chapter in his Bible, and perhaps find the changes of the moon in his almanac" and who "thinks that his children and his children's children are to go on in the same way with himself, and so is regardless of their education." To such a man—or at least to his children—Thomas offered "new, useful, and entertaining matter." His first issue closed with this recommendation: "Now comes on

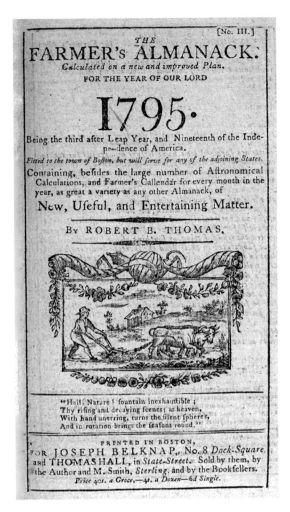

Fig. 25. Robert Thomas, title page of *The Farmer's Almanack. Calculated on a new and improved plan. For the year of our Lord, 1795* [1794]. With its industrious farmer woodcut. Courtesy of American Antiquarian Society, Worcester, Massachusetts.

the long and social evenings, when the farmer may enjoy himself, and instruct and entertain his family by reading some useful books, of which he will do well in preparing a select number. The following I should recommend as books worthy of perusal by every American: Ramsay's *History of the American Revolution*; Morse's *Geography*; and Belknap's *History of New Hampshire*."[51] Men like Robert Thomas mediated shifts in the organization of knowledge, personalized the changes in the expanding print industry, and localized them within familiar village bounds. Thomas fostered the connection of commerce with culture in the countryside. The knowledge he promoted was preeminently practical, but nonetheless directed toward entry into the market. Thomas remained in Sterling until his death in 1846, but his almanacs went far afield. In his hands, the promotion of learning and commerce were conjoined.[52]

Demand for American schoolbooks took off after the Revolution, fueled by nationalist sentiments and the expansion of education. One popular text, Jedidiah Morse's *Geography Made Easy* (1784), captured the imagination of young readers. One entrant to the print trade, John Prentiss, third son of a Reading, Massachusetts, minister, fondly recalled in his manuscript autobiography the textbooks of his youth. New authors came forward to define American books: "Webster's Spelling Book when published [1783] took the place of Perry's. Our principal reading was Webster's 3rd part; which had a comprehensive history of the Revolutionary War with other reading. . . . In Geography, Dr. [Jedidiah] Morse had furnished the New Republic with his first 12 mo. Edition [1789] with two or three maps cut on a leaden block and printed of the page size. That of the whole 13 United States most delighted, for at a glance was perceived the position and size of each, with the Rivers, bay, lakes and Mountains."[53] While his elder brother went off to Harvard, John's fascination with politics, especially the French Revolution, and with the cosmopolitanism of Boston's wharves and shops pointed him toward a desire "much to be a Printer." The office of his master Thomas Adams, publisher of the *Independent Chronicle*, proved to be a "political school" as well.[54]

After completing an apprenticeship, young men went in search of a place, but success was not assured; urban shops filled quickly, and the hinterlands did not always support their aspirations. The three Merriam brothers ventured to Brookfield, one of the oldest and largest towns of Worcester County. Local notables hoping to break out of Worcester's orbit wanted a newspaper as a source of commercial and other useful information. Ebenezer, fresh from his apprenticeship with Isaiah Thomas, took up a post that another Thomas trainee had given up. "The office consisted of an old press . . . a font of Long primer type and a small font of Pica, all worn down to the first nice, as the say[ing] is—cuts for John Rogers' Primer, one iron composing stick, two wooden ones made by one of our carpenters, a wooden composing stone, two letter racks, brass rules made of wood for column rules, two chases, and a few small galleys, all in honorable standing if age would make them so."[55] Debt weighed heavily on the Merriams, so they were constantly on the prowl for ways of turning a profit. In August 1798, they issued the *Political Repository; or Farmers Journal*. The next year Ebenezer and Dan brought out their first book, a primer. John Prentiss had also secured his first situation in central Massachusetts in 1798, but at a less advantageous site in Leominster. Hearing about an opening in Keene, New Hampshire, a county seat on the post road from Boston, John went off with the support of two of his father's Harvard classmates, gifts of cash from his father, and a keg of ink and font of type from his brother Charles. The *New Hampshire Sentinel* appeared on his twenty-first birthday, 23 March 1799.[56]

Town founders eagerly recruited printers to demonstrate their settlement's cosmopolitan character, even if their recruits remarked more on its provinciality. William Cooper, whom John Adams called "the great Pioneer," laid out an ambitious plan for a commercial village at the foot of Lake Otsego and set himself up as the patriarch of Cooperstown. His most important prize was the Yankee printer and publisher Elihu Phinney, who arrived in 1795. Printers followed the Yankee migration north up the Hudson River Valley and west along the Mohawk River; half the New York country printers whose origins can be traced came from New England. Phinney found "Cooperstown is about 75 pr cent below Proof—no life—no society," so he devoted himself to work. Subscriptions flooded into the shop. After just two months, circulation of the *Otsego Herald*, one of the earliest newspapers west of Hudson, New York, reached eight hundred. Its editor addressed "the enlightened citizens of the western counties" who were eager to transform the wilderness into a "fruitful field." As Levi Beardsley later recounted, "The *Otsego Herald* . . . was almost the only paper that any citizen in town had an opportunity of reading." Beardsley recalled the "scarcity of books" and the difficulty of locating any reading material except the "bible, psalm book, and a few other books" in his family's first years in Richfield, a remote village in the hardscrabble Southern Tier of counties. Residents hungry for news took turns going to Cooperstown to get the paper. His imagination caught by the exciting events of European war and politics, Beardsley would dash through the woods to a neighbor's house about a mile off, where the paper was left each Saturday afternoon by the post rider, "and I generally read the part containing the news, before reaching home."[57]

A strong subscriber base was only the first step to success; getting subscribers to pay up was an equally essential matter. Like most editors, John Prentiss kept busy reminding readers to send in the money they owed. Advertising proved more lucrative than subscriptions. As historian William Gilmore wrote, "The weekly newspaper, the fastest-expanding means of communication in the Early Republic, was crucial to the enlargement of commerce. It offered all businesses a brand new way of getting local feedback through direct appeals to consumers to reshape their personal consumption habits. The newspaper brought specific knowledge of goods and services to potential customers, and merchants learned quickly that advertising offered a potent alternative to neighborhood-based exchange relationships."[58] Whether or not a newspaper flourished, printers needed to keep their presses busy with schoolbooks, almanacs, and other steady sellers. The Merriams printed ten thousand copies of Isaac Watts's *Psalms and*

Hymns and sixteen thousand New Testaments before receiving the exciting news that the copyright had expired on Noah Webster's *American Spelling Book*. After rushing to print three thousand of that best seller, they heard that the copyright had been renewed and they were liable for infringement. Dan hastened to New Haven to pay Webster some of their scarce cash, and they consigned the rest of the print run to a South Carolina commission house, which later failed. John Prentiss and the Merriams realized that rural printing for urban markets was their ticket for success.

Problems loomed for even the most daring of businessmen during these years. With only incomplete information about the market, poor communication with suppliers, and weak to nonexistent credit networks, these "would-be printer-entrepreneurs," as historian Jack Larkin called them, attempted to expand. A nationwide system for book publication and distribution was still nascent. Ebenezer Merriam penned a hilarious but realistic description of the consequences of a project to print twelve thousand Bibles in 1815, with only vague commitments for financing from local investors and even sketchier ideas about the size of the market. As usual, the Merriams had signed notes, to be paid in books, to secure paper and type. Delays mounted, but the Merriams labored on, hearing nothing from their creditors and so believing that they were content to wait. Ebenezer went to bed on 15 May 1815, "somewhat elated with our prospects," only to be rudely awakened at one o'clock in the morning. Looking out the window, he saw twenty or thirty men, their creditors, dragging away their livestock, lumber, and a new chaise. "In the hopper was a fowl, who was expecting in a few days to be the mother of numerous offspring, and finding her repose broken at this unseasonable hour was venting her moans in most piteous accents." Making their way toward the shop, they found their path blocked by the tools of their livelihood, type cases and letter racks, strewn all over the yard. "The scene in fact was a lively representation of what I had fabled in my own mind of Hades." Even though the brothers' tools were returned, for the law forbade their attachment, "a great deal of other property," even "the old mansion," was gone forever, as the creditors gathered to secure their notes. Midnight raids by creditors and mortgage foreclosures were all too familiar to rural manufacturers and merchants.[59] Nonetheless, all three of these printers had solid and long-lasting careers. The Merriam brothers eventually found great success with their Merriam-Webster dictionary by relocating in urban Springfield; Elihu Phinney began a printing dynasty with his sons; and John Prentiss operated the *Sentinel* for forty-eight years.[60]

The modern model of an urban monopoly on curiosity and sophistication fails to capture the intellectual world of post-Revolutionary entrepreneurs like the Merriams, who took advantage of the curiosity fostered in schoolrooms and popular books and helped promote the democratization of knowledge and the commercialization of the countryside. While print served as a model of the extensive development of the Village Enlightenment, the cultural movement branched out to other crafts, such as portrait painting and clockmaking, all hastened by the travels of artisan-entrepreneurs and the tastes of provincial consumers.

Portrait Painting

> *To the patrons of the fine arts, the portrait painting by Mr. Earl, in this town, do him honor as an American and as an artist of great taste and ingenuity—Connoisseurs in this truly noble and refined art, pronounce several of his performances the most masterly ever exhibited in the U.S. Mr. Earl was pupil to the celebrated West; and acquired great reputation in London by his pencil; and possessing a lively imagination, and pure talent in the principles of his profession, we cannot double and hope, that in this age of refinement, the well-born and well-bred of his countryman will patronize him in the road to Fame. Some of his paintings are admirably finished; and display that similarity and expression as would seem to start them into life—though inanimate they speak.*
>
> Litchfield *Monitor*, 1790

In 1789, the merchant Elijah Boardman welcomed Ralph Earl to New Milford, a small but growing town in Litchfield County, Connecticut (plate 2). Earl advanced tastes in the countryside, using his British training in the eighteenth-century grand manner of portraiture while incorporating local tastes for direct pose and plain line. Boardman's illusionist likeness, where his left foot appears to step off the shop floor into the viewer's space, must have been quite a revelation to his neighbors in New Milford. Elijah's grandfather had come to northwestern Connecticut as the town's first minister and its largest landowner, but his grandson was a new kind of town founder, an agent of commercial capitalism taking root in once-isolated country places. The young merchant and itinerant artist collaborated on a powerful likeness of the new republic's entrepreneurial man. Merchants customarily had been portrayed as gentlemen in domestic settings; Boardman's more literal portrait displays him at work in his store, offering his merchandise to the viewer. But the simplicity of this image was carefully contrived. The seven-foot-tall painting with its double doors, a trompe l'oeil device, showed its subject's two sides: entrepreneurship and knowledge, commerce and culture. This was how the Village Enlightenment arrived in New Milford and many other communities, by dint of the efforts of itinerant portraitists and stationary merchants, and how it looked in the countryside, a vernacular that combined cosmopolitan examples and local tastes in the form of cultural commodities. Elijah was proud of his learning. In the library arrayed below his desk can be seen such current titles as *Guthrie's Geography*, *Cook's Voyages*, Shakespeare's plays, and Milton's *Paradise Lost*. His right arm gestures toward the open door of his storage room where his inventory of colorful textiles was stacked on their shelves.

The portrait stands as an advertisement for Elijah—his books, his cloth, and his imposing stature—and the painting offers his commanding presence in the world of commerce, his fashionable garb a "sartorial testimony to the fine fabrics on sale in his shop."[61] Boardman and Earl asserted his stance as an aristocrat in a new republican order. As he confided to his future father-in-law, "I confess my busy mind is anxiously employed in pursuit of wealth." A rural order of refinement was no simple collection of purchased commodities, however. Boardman's portrait constituted a statement of what that new cultural order might look like, made possible by the travels of Ralph Earl, the first portraitist to visit the northwestern corner of Connecticut, along with the success of Elijah Boardman and his fellows among New Milford's and Litchfield's newly arrived elite, "well-born and well-bred."[62]

Merchants connected town residents with the wider world, assembling local goods for distant markets while making the products of the wider world available to their customers. Storekeepers were crucial middlemen between the rural world of local exchange and the broader trading networks of cities and the Atlantic world. They received the hinterland's marketable produce and assembled it in wagonloads for transport to metropolitan markets, where they traded it for the small-scale manufactured and imported goods that rural residents desired. Merchants prompted significant change in the rural economy after the Revolution. Goods produced directly for a purchaser declined in proportion to goods made within the household economy for generalized exchange. Merchants functioned as third parties in local exchange networks, supplied credit, and promoted improvements in the transportation system. One study of late-eighteenth-century rural marketing emphasizes the central role of merchants in creating larger, more complex forms of enterprise. Some merchants entered into local production by organizing "putting-out" systems, employing farmers and their families in making brooms or palm-leaf hats. Rural households engaged in piece-rate labor in order to purchase more of what they needed in the market.[63]

Central Massachusetts proved a rocky soil for establishing an artistic career, as Winthrop Chandler had discovered. The coming of the Revolution offered an ambitious artist like Earl some opportunities, but the political crisis, coupled with personal indiscretions, eventually led him to flee abroad. Born in 1751 to a prosperous farming family, Ralph Earl turned his back on his family and community. An eldest son in line to receive substantial lands and status in Leicester, he left town with little more than a few years in local schools and the single-minded pursuit of an artistic career—along with the suspicions of the local Committee of Correspondence about his loyalties in the conflict that was brewing. Arriving in New Haven in 1774, he set up as "John Earll, Portrait Painter," the first of a series of identity shifts. He briefly revisited Leicester to marry his pregnant second cousin, Sarah Gates, and then returned alone to New Haven as Ralph Earl to begin his career. When Henry Pelham, John Singleton Copley's half-brother, visited New Haven to paint miniatures, Earl made sure to gain his acquaintance. He visited the artist's Boston studio, entered his circle of artist-friends, and had the opportunity to view Copley's work when the loyalist painter was already safely across the Atlantic. He emulated Copley's techniques of strong personal characterization and close attention to detail in his first few portrait commissions. He painted a large-scale portrait of Roger Sherman, whom John Adams characterized as "one of the soundest and strongest pillars of the Revolution." Earl depicted the self-educated surveyor and lawyer in a direct view, emphasizing his set expression and rough hands. The plain Philadelphia Windsor low-back chair on which he was seated linked him to his recent role in the Constitutional Convention (fig. 26). After fighting broke out at Lexington and Concord and the colonies plunged into war, the entrepreneurial artist maintained a neutral stance despite his Loyalist feelings. He took advantage of the opportunity to rush to the battlefield with his then-partner Amos Doolittle to produce four engravings of the battles. But fence-sitting could not be sustained for long. Denounced by a petition printed in the local newspaper as one of the "friends of George the third," Earl refused to take up arms and fled imminent imprisonment, disguised as a servant of Captain John Money, a British quartermaster. Renouncing his homeland, he sailed for London, the center of the art world.[64]

London boasted such luminaries as Sir Joshua Reynolds and Benjamin West and supported more than one hundred resident artists. For an artist from the colonies without formal training beyond his exposure to Pelham and Copley, the center of the art world was no place to set up shop. Earl removed to provincial Norwich, where Money's sponsorship gave him access to a lively set of local artists and potential patrons. His residence in East Anglia provided an important lesson: a regional clientele might demand very different likenesses, based

Fig. 26. Ralph Earl, *Roger Sherman*, M.A. (Hon.) 1768, ca. 1775. Oil on canvas. 64-5/8 × 49-5/8 in. Yale University Art Gallery, New Haven. Gift of Roger Sherman White, B.A. 1899, LL.B 1902.

on local tastes and social ranks. In his earliest English composition, a 1779 portrait of William and Mary Carpenter, Earl continued his use of strong lighting and detail, while adopting more elegant poses and adding such flourishes as a greater sense of color and texture. By 1784, Earl had removed to London to learn further elements of the grand style of portraiture. He gained access to

Benjamin West's studio and exhibition at the Royal Academy, though not into the transplanted American's inner circle. Earl practiced portraiture in a less flamboyant mode, emphasizing faithful likenesses and strong characterizations, but with freer brushwork and more relaxed poses, often set in lush landscapes or grand interiors. Earl did not attempt history painting, the pinnacle in the hierarchy of neoclassical art, because he lacked the necessary classical education. But he did add landscape painting to his repertoire. Elizabeth Kornhauser has noted that Earl's "English portraits have many skillfully executed backgrounds of loosely executed foliage, pastoral scenery, and pink and blue skies reminiscent of the works of Thomas Gainsborough." He did a series of formal military portraits, including one of the naval hero Admiral Richard Kempenfelt, around 1782. Soon he transferred this style to depictions of heroes across the Atlantic. His later English portraits reveal his mastery of the tenets of British neoclassical painting. Earl's portrait of his new wife, Ann Whiteside, had a brushy application of paint and subtle colors. (No record of a divorce from Sarah has ever turned up.) The painting featured a globe (one of the several geographical references in Earl's work) turned to display the North American continent, where the couple soon resided (fig. 27).[65]

After the cessation of hostilities between Britain and the new United States, Earl wasted no time in turning his London experience to good account, announcing the arrival of the "very capital Portrait Painter, Mr. Earl of Massachusetts" in the New York newspapers. He employed a dual appeal to the new citizens of the republic, proud of their independence but also eager for cosmopolitan products, by emphasizing his metropolitan training along with his American connections: "scholar of Copley, West, and Sir Joshua Reynolds." But Earl was perpetually dogged by money troubles. On the voyage across the Atlantic, he borrowed money from fellow passenger Levi Willard, whose father had sat for Winthrop Chandler, which set in motion a series of events that eventually landed him in jail. Earl was imprisoned for debt in the New York City Hall attic as the new U.S. Congress met below. Prominent New Yorkers and the Society for the Relief of Distressed Debtors took up his cause, sending friends and family to the "Gaol," allowing Earl to continue his profession. Among his visitors was Elizabeth Schuyler Hamilton, daughter of Philip Schuyler and Catherine Van Rensselaer Schuyler and wife of Alexander Hamilton. She "sat for the portrait there," and despite the dingy prison setting Earl painted her in a sensuous manner, dressed fashionably, hair piled high, sitting in an upholstered chair with gilt arms. Earl was released into the custody of another patron, Dr. Mason Fitch Cogswell, who introduced Earl to the gentry of provincial Connecticut.[66]

In the young republic, a rising class of village gentry embraced the project

Fig. 27. Ralph Earl, *Ann Whiteside Earl*, 1784. Oil on canvas. 46-5/8 × 38-1/8 in. Meade Art Museum, Amherst College, Amherst, Massachusetts. Gift of Herbert L. Pratt (Class of 1895). AC P. 1936.1.

of refinement, creating opportunities for cultural entrepreneurs who looked to support themselves in a commercializing countryside. Ralph Earl recognized this opportunity; indeed, he fostered this development by turning his back on the city and embarking on an itinerant career, boarding himself and often his family in the homes of the newly genteel in rural Connecticut and Vermont. Once again he remade himself, drawing on both his English experience and the traditional tastes of his country patrons to forge a distinctive vocabulary appropriate for the aristocrats of the new republican order. By 1788, he had focused his energies on the Litchfield County communities of New Milford and Litchfield and was warmly welcomed by its affluent citizens. Earl's Litchfield County portraits celebrated their status and possessions as emblems of gentility. Although he ventured back to New York and as far north as Bennington, Vermont, the bulk of his commissions came from inland commercial centers in northwestern Connecticut.[67]

Many artists pursuing a career as a professional portraitist could not easily follow Earl's path of a transatlantic education and peripatetic business travels. Mary Way, another pioneer Connecticut portraitist, blazed her way by drawing on her training in genteel women's accomplishments. Earl painted six members of the Shaw and Richards family, including Elizabeth Harris Richards, but her son and his family were "dressed" in miniature by Mary Way. Mary and her sister Betsey Way Champlain were born in New London, Connecticut, in 1769 and 1771, respectively. Mary and Betsey Way's father was a merchant, and their mother died when they were young. The two, along with Betsey's daughter Eliza Way Champlain, comprise a trio of miniature portraitists in the new nation. While Mary became the most famous of the three, moving to New York and becoming part of an artistic circle, the three stood between the artistic elite and the itinerant artisan-painters. Catherine Kelly notes, "the Way-Champlain women followed a different path, one that owed less to the various strategies pursued by male painters than to the expansion and transformation of women's education. The combination of delicately painted faces, appliqué, embroidery, and fine decorative sewing recall the elaborate needlework pictures produced by young ladies in the course of their education" (fig. 28).[68]

A group of "dressed miniatures," watercolor miniature portraits in profile decorated with painted paper or cloth scraps, most from the 1790s in the Norwich and New London region, have been attributed to Mary based on the "Rosetta Stone" of a signed example. Miniatures usually were done on ivory. Charles Holt, the young publisher of the New London, Connecticut, newspaper, the *Bee,* was Mary's cousin and helped promote her portrait business in his newspaper. The Jeffersonian editor faced the common commercial perils of all newspaper operators along with the additional burden of a successful prosecution against him and imprisonment for sedition in 1799. To create Holt's miniature Way used cutout paper profiles, as she carefully cut out Holt's nose along with the curl of his lips, chin, and brow. The features were carefully and dramatically delineated in watercolor with heavy shadowing around the mouth and sharp detailing of the eyes and brow; his curled sideburns and a queue tied down with a ribbon added a dramatic flourish. Then the cutout profile was attached to a brown fabric background, quite different from the miniaturist's thin ivory base.

Fig. 28. Mary Way, *Charles Holt*, portrait miniature, 1800. Watercolor and fabric on paper applied to brown fabric. 2-1/2 × 2 in. Nathan Liverant and Son Antiques. Colchester, Connecticut.

What made her work even more distinctive was Holt's military *chapeau-bras,* a tricornered hat made of black felt with a black silk-ribbon rosette sewn to the front. Other details are painted: Holt's blue coat, brass buttons, and waistcoat. We know this is Mary Way's work from her business card on the backing: "Mary Way fecit, New London Feb. 18th 1800." About forty of these tiny portraits have been found, with the face and hair painted on paper and the subject's clothing cut out from various materials, stitched and glued in place, and touched up with painted highlight or detail.[69]

Mary and her sister Betsey probably learned to paint at one of Connecticut's numerous female academies. Some of Mary's early decorative pieces, on such themes as "Friendship" and "Amabilité," were popular subjects for schoolgirls' needlework and verse exercises. Access to formal studio training was available only to the fortunate few, such as James Peale's daughters, Anna Claypoole and Sarah Miriam Peale. Anna demonstrated her earning ability along with her artistic talents. She specialized in portrait miniatures, a genre practiced by her

CHAPTER TWO

father and his brother Charles Willson Peale. Yet academic training was out of reach for Anna, and so was the possibility of working as an itinerant or maintaining a studio. The Ways pursued a different career, not offering expensive portrait miniatures on ivory, but instead unique, less expensive, yet finely crafted alternatives. Mary Way was very likely the first professional woman artist in the post-Revolutionary United States. She produced dozens of profile likenesses, charging between ten and twenty dollars to the residents of the New London and Norwich area, "using her conventional female training in sewing to create an original variation on the silhouette, the dressed miniature." One of the earliest was of the fifteen- or sixteen-year-old Polly Carew, who was finely dressed in cotton, linen, and silk. Profiles offered a likeness without foreshortening or shadowing, which proved easier for the self-trained artist and more affordable for the middle class. The inclusion of the fabric gave a feeling of depth, and the sitter was individualized by unique items of clothing. Jonathan Devotion, third son of Judge Ebenezer Devotion, who had been painted by Winthrop Chandler as a three-year-old, sat for Mary Way in the 1790s. The young merchant, working in Norwich, wore an elegant polka-dotted vest and ruffled shirt.[70]

In 1809, Mary Way advertised the opening of a school in New London where she taught "Painting, Tambour, Embroidery, Lace Work on Muslin, Reading, Writing, Plain Sewing &c." to young ladies. Mary moved on to a grander stage, reversing Ralph Earl's journey while Betsey stayed in New London, married George Champlain in 1794, and pursued a career over the next three decades as a provincial painter. By 1811, Mary, at the age of forty-two, had moved to New York and advertised in Charles Holt's *Columbian* newspaper: "Mary Way, portrait and miniature painter from New-London, Connecticut. Takes likenesses upon ivory or glass in colors or gold, landscapes or views of country seats." She had "painting rooms" in Greenwich Street. Her drawing school soon became a drawing academy. When Ethan Allen Greenwood, a central Massachusetts painter fresh from his education at Leicester Academy and Dartmouth College, came to New York to "examine everything related to the fine arts," he called on a series of the city's well-established painters such as John Vanderlyn, making his way finally to "Miss Way miniature painter." Way wrote a lengthy letter to her sister reporting on her progress and reminding her of the benefits of a provincial station: "There you are Painter General, and after you have taken a good likeness and are sure the outline is correct, the worst is over. You can sit down in peace and finish it as you please, in your own stile." In New York, it was far different, with the "dread of connoisseurs" who "flock'd in from all quarters" to examine her work and question her studies, talking of painting as a science and driving her to rely on William Joseph Williams and other experts in print to bolster her knowledge of the practice and especially the theory of art.[71]

While recognized by her peers, who loaned her paintings to copy and critiqued her work, Mary Way struggled financially her entire life and, as Earl had done in London, realized the limitations of her provincial education upon removal to a more cosmopolitan artistic center. Mary and her sister continued to rely upon the pictorial conventions of their training rather than adapting the newer styles of larger and rectangular ivories or a brighter palette with detailed backgrounds and props. She remained on the edge of the artistic community while securing a clientele from her Universalist church and New London ties. She exhibited two works on ivory in the American Academy of Fine Arts exhibition in 1818, but failing vision ended her career by 1820. Still, she hosted her niece Eliza in New York, taught her painting, and introduced her to the local artistic circle. Eliza attempted to support herself painting in New York City, writing to her brother in 1820 about her aunt's failing eyesight and her own difficulties. "This city is so overrun with artists that it is impossible that I should ever get business enough," as Eliza echoed Copley's earlier complaint, "American painters recieve [*sic*] so little encouragement. Anything which comes from abroad is all the rage, while native talent is supposed to live and die in obscurity."[72]

The careers of Mary Way and Ralph Earl illustrate the difference in the professional opportunities open to talented women and men in the New Republic. Both had advantages of birth and education; both showed extraordinary artistic abilities. They even moved in the same social circles. Yet, as artists, they took divergent paths marked out by gender. Struggling to support herself, Mary Way drew on her feminine skills in needlework to eke out a living as a teacher as well as a portraitist. Respectability, even if threadbare, was essential to attract students to her school and allow her entry into the homes of patrons. Earl worked full-time at his art, gaining commissions in the most respectable society despite his dubious political loyalties, irregular domestic arrangements, and financial embarrassments. While Way worked in miniature, Earl painted huge portraits of the new elite. Each managed a career in art in the new commercial society of post-Revolutionary America, but on very different scales and stages.

Members of southeastern Connecticut's gentry were eager for Ralph Earl's services in the late 1780s. He began with Litchfield's political and religious elite. Oliver Wolcott, Sr., was lieutenant governor of Connecticut and was known for his strong advocacy of federalism. He had been a signatory of the Declaration of Independence, a member of the Continental Congress along with Roger Sherman, and a participant in the state's convention to ratify the U.S. Constitution. Earl's formal portrait emphasizes that Federalist stance: Wolcott sits on a well-upholstered red chair, resting his hand on a copy of the Constitution, framed by a classical column that lends an air of gravity, while the Litchfield Hills appear through the window. Earl also painted Laura Wolcott equally formally, elegantly attired with a stylish French nightcap, flowing shawl, and elbow-length gloves, with a column and view of the Wolcott mansion in the distance. He gracefully posed the couple's youngest child, Mariann, in the Litchfield landscape, drawing on his English work.[73]

Litchfield was a shining example of the Village Enlightenment. "A delightful village, on a fruitful hill, richly endowed with schools, both professional and scientific, with a population enlightened and respectable," Daniel Huntington, its minister, remarked in 1798.[74] Upon his arrival from Yale College, Litchfield was the county seat and the fourth largest town in the state in 1810, with a population of 4,659. The community and its merchants had prospered during the war. Postwar economic turmoil left larger merchants who could command greater access to capital in control. This new generation of leaders was eager to demonstrate their cosmopolitanism. They constructed a commercial and communications infrastructure: five turnpikes crisscrossed the town and improved connections to other commercial centers; major stagecoach routes ran west to the Hudson River and south from New York to New Haven and then on to Massachusetts, Vermont, and Canada. Artisans and mechanics flowed into town—"a cabinetmaker from Boson, a clockmaker from London, a silversmith from New York," Ann Y. Smith has recently written, "and dozens of other craft specialists." Thomas Collier opened a print shop and began publishing the *Litchfield Monitor*, the town's first newspaper, in 1784. Books followed; he chose Jedidiah Morse's *Geography Made Easy* for one of his first imprints. Clock- and watchmakers, such as Timothy Barnes and Orange Hopkins, offered brass and wooden clocks along with silver objects. Fashionable furniture could be purchased close to home from Windsor chairmakers or case furniture craftsmen. The twenty-one-year-old Silas Cheney opened a "Joiner's Shop" in 1800, and, over the next two decades, he operated the largest workshop in the county, employing numerous workmen to manufacture a wide range of stylish furniture. By 1818 his advertisements boasted of a "Cabinet and Chair Factory."[75]

Cultural institutions in Litchfield promoted refinement and edification. As young men and women mixed sociability with their education, adults in the community were drawn into the search for culture and improvement as well as pleasure. A small ballroom opened in a local tavern in 1782; five years later, David Buell's tavern featured a ballroom extending across the entire second floor. The press of commercial business required a new county courthouse, a splendid new structure undertaken by merchant Julius Deming. Benjamin Tallmadge recalled his first trip to Litchfield in the 1780s: potholes marred the streets, livestock sauntered through the commons, and few trees shaded pedestrians. As village beautification became a new concern, Oliver Wolcott planted thirteen sycamores along South Street to commemorate the thirteen colonies.[76]

Litchfield's rapid rise to prominence and its collection of regional and national luminaries explain Ralph Earl's successful pursuit of commissions there. However, almost one-fifth of the hundred portraits he executed in Connecticut over the next decade were done in New Milford, a seemingly less promising place for a portrait painter to set up shop. Still, New Milford stood at the southwest section of the county as a trading center with a host of ambitious merchants. There Earl painted an extraordinary number of portraits of the lesser gentry of the rising commercial elite. In addition to Elijah, he painted five Boardmans; indeed, thirteen of his nineteen New Milford patrons came from the interwoven families of Boardmans and Taylors. The Reverend Nathaniel Taylor was Daniel Boardman's successor. Daniel's son Sherman had raised a large family on his substantial farm along the banks of the Housatonic River, and he sat atop the town's political ladder, serving continuously in town or state office from the age of twenty-one to sixty-eight. Four of his children and one daughter-in-law sat for Earl in 1789 and 1790. Elijah, Sarah Bostwick Boardman's third son, had studied with the Reverend Taylor. He served in the Revolutionary army, but his frail constitution broke down. He took up mercantile pursuits rather than entering the ministry, learning the trade in New Haven before returning inland in 1781 to open a store with his brother in half of a house on Town Street. Daniel and Elijah commissioned traditional full-length portraits rather than the more fashionable bust-length format Earl offered his English and New York patrons. Daniel posed gracefully in full length, leaning on an ivory-topped cane, before a landscape of the Housatonic River winding toward New Milford's town center, the site of significant Boardman landholdings (fig. 29). The two portraits complement each other, displaying two sides of the Boardmans' considerable wealth: inside was the mercantile establishment, and outside the speculative real estate. Daniel, the eldest son, had graduated from Yale College before the two unmarried brothers joined in their partnership. When Elijah married in 1792, they dissolved the partnership, and Daniel ran the store for two more years before moving to New York City to enter the wholesale dry-goods business. His pose and costume was one of "restrained Anglo-American elegance," of unostentatious wealth and established position, with one foot crossed in front of the other, the better to show off the fine cut-steel Artois buckles on his shoes.[77]

His services in demand, Ralph Earl traveled to other prospering Litchfield County towns. His exuberant 1790 advertisement in the Litchfield *Weekly Monitor* leaned heavily on the twin calls of patriotism and gentility. The ambitious artist claimed patronage as an American before boasting of his attendance

Fig. 29. Ralph Earl, *Daniel Boardman*, 1789. Oil on canvas. 81-11/16 × 55-1/4 in. Gift of Mrs. W. Murray Crane, Image courtesy of the Board of Trustees, National Gallery of Art, Washington, D.C.

among the celebrated circle of Benjamin West and acquisition of a "great reputation in London by his pencil." New Milford's celebrated son Roger Sherman had gone to New Haven to make his mark and be recognized; now Earl could minister to local demand for grand but realistic portraits. Earl added to his appeal to the new body of "well-born and well-bred" gentlemen in the provinces who desired his sumptuous paintings—"though inanimate they speak" —by saying that he could provide such examples of "this noble and refined art" in their very villages. Earl mustered more aristocratic images for Benjamin and Mary Floyd Tallmadge, newcomers to Litchfield. Benjamin sat for his monumental portrait on an upholstered chair, business paper in hand and library behind him; he wore his powdered wig and a splendid silk frock coat, "the epitome of ancien regime grandeur," with his badge of the Society of the Cincinnati, an emblem many of his neighbors chose not to display because of its elitist and unrepublican associations. Benjamin and his brother's mercantile firm had extensive ties to port cities and international trade, along with holdings in stocks, banking, and land speculation. Upon his brief excursions to Hartford or New York, where John Trumbull and Benjamin West had secured elite patronage, Earl reached back for an English style of more loosely executed brushwork.[78]

By 1795, Earl was offering landscape scenes showing the new mansions built by Litchfield County's merchants. Elijah Boardman wrote to Earl in April 1795 asking that he hasten to New Milford to fulfill his promise to "Mrs Boardman [of] having her Portrait taken by your inimitable hand—our little son too." But he warned the artist that he faced competition: "A Portrait Painter is here from Boston and has taken several persons and perhaps ma[n]y more unless they can depend on you." Richard and William Jennys painted sixteen portraits in New Milford in 1794 and 1795, which are much more modest in style and cost. Practicing a variety of trades, they looked back to Winthrop Chandler's artisanal roots. Their bust-length portraits had sharp contrasts of light and dark and looked far less refined than Earl's grand portraits. Boardman and Earl exchanged several letters before the promise of a horse and board for Earl and his wife brought the itinerant to town. He announced his arrival in far less grand terms than five years before, drawing a pointed contrast with his rivals: "Many gentlemen in this vicinity, having been disappointed of his services, and several of our friends being driven to accept the paultry *daubs* of assuming pretenders. Mr. Earl's price for a portrait of full length is *Sixty Dollars*, the small size *Thirty Dollars*, the painter finding his own support and materials."[79]

Elijah Boardman had been successful during the intervening years; with a growing family and other signs of his stature in town, he wanted his achievements memorialized on canvas. He had married Mary Anna Whiting in 1792 and built a splendid new house and adjoining shop; their first child, William, had been born the following year. If Elijah's 1789 portrait had represented the ambitious and enlightened village entrepreneur, the 1796 painting of Mary and William Boardman celebrated domestic bliss and commercial success. Mary Anna sat holding William in the elaborate household scene. The two life-sized portraits matched exactly; both sitters face right. Husband and wife are linked by the salmon shade, a popular eighteenth-century color, also present in Elijah's shelves of fabric. Mary Anna wore an elegant gown of coral-colored silk. Earl's familiar composition forms included a patterned carpet, red drapery, and the meandering Housatonic River, which ran behind their new Palladian house (fig. 30).

The Boardmans' house has been attributed to William Sprats. Trained in the English Georgian tradition, the Scottish architect devoted his American career to designing and building imposing homes in inland Connecticut for a rising commercial class. His buildings covered much the same terrain as Earl's canvases. Sprats boldly broke away from the plain structures of the pre-Revolutionary generation. His Litchfield County courthouse had four Ionic columns, a double pediment, and a cupola. The substantial house he designed for the Boardmans featured an imposing front entrance with a Palladian façade and pedimented pavilion; a wide hall opened into several rooms arranged for formal entertainment. Earl's landscape view captured the white fence with urn-shaped finials that surrounded the house, the driveway leading to Elijah's adjacent store, and the recently planted saplings that lined Town Street—while "the pink and blue sky and hazy sunlight" enveloped the scene with "an overall sense of well being" (fig. 31). Inside that house, Elijah and Mary furnished the house with costly carpets, mahogany furniture, including a piano and stool that were valued at $320. Elijah had assembled an ample library, well beyond what his portrait showed such as Adam Smith's *Wealth of Nations,* works on manufactures and agriculture and the laws of Ohio, along with maps and other publications.[80]

The Boardmans' neighbors, who also sat for portraits, actively pursued New Milford's beautification and refinement. Jared Lane and Apphia Ruggles Lane, who operated a farm and nursery, introduced the Lombardy poplar, a popular ornamental shade tree, along the main streets. The Lanes had purchased six portraits from the Jennyses, with their plain style and stark background. Earl's arrival gave them the chance to commission matching portraits along with a landscape view of their newly completed house. Lane's account book offers a glimpse into Earl's working style and personal life; he boarded the artist and his wife with his father-in-law for two weeks in June while Ralph painted Apphia. Lane returned for another eighteen days to paint Jared and the landscape. In

Fig. 30. Ralph Earl, *Mary Boardman and Son William*, 1796. Oil on canvas. 85-1/4 ×
56-1/4 in. Henry E. Huntington Library and Art Gallery, San Marino, California.
Virginia Steele Scott Collection, 1980.

addition to his payment of twenty-four pounds, well below his advertised prices,
the artist kept his patrons busy with "Washing for Mr. & Mrs. Earl"; they
supplied a pound of coffee along with several gallons of spirits and rum for
Ralph as he worked. Jared secured artists' supplies locally; he paid Elijah Boardman for varnish along with other entries for vermillion and Prussian blue pig-

Fig. 31. Ralph Earl, *Houses Fronting New Milford Green*, 1796. Detail of the Boardman house with its substantial front entrance, white fence, and adjacent store. Oil on canvas. 45 × 52-3/4 in. Wadsworth Atheneum Museum of Art, Hartford, Connecticut. The Dorothy Clark Archibald and Thomas L. Archibald Fund, The Ella Sumner and Mary Catlin Sumner Collection Fund, The Krieble Family Fund for American Art, The Gift of James Junius Goodwin and The Douglas Tracy Smith and Dorothy Potter Smith Fund.

ments for Apphia's portrait. Earl used a limited palette, employing the subtle coloring of neoclassical portraiture in accord with the patron's desire to contain cost and use locally available materials. Cabinetmaker Jonathan Mygatt made the frames and prepared the canvases. That year Earl painted sixteen portraits and three landscape views that offered Litchfield County's new merchant elite family portraits and paintings of their newly completed houses and landscaped grounds, executed after English models.[81]

Cosmopolitan culture moved ever more quickly in the 1790s to northern New England, western New York, and the Old Northwest, wherever New Englanders transplanted their culture of commerce. Elijah Boardman grew rich on mercantile activity and landholdings that reached well beyond Litchfield County with interests in Massachusetts, Vermont, and the Old Northwest. His final estate reached $94,000. A leader in the Connecticut Land Company, he gained by speculation; his store also outfitted emigrants. Some New Milford natives even settled in Boardman, Ohio, a town named after Elijah, who visited often and died there in 1823. By 1798, Ralph Earl had moved north into Vermont, finding clients in Bennington with ties to his Connecticut sitters and similar aspirations to gentility. He was the first to paint in Bennington, a town settled in the mid-eighteenth century, where market culture and taste for cultural commodities quickly appeared. His first and most ambitious painting there is a full-sized group portrait of Chloe Smith and her five children, relatives of the Boardmans. Son Daniel holds an atlas or schoolbook open to a map of the world, a spherical projection similar to those in map samplers. Husband Noah celebrated his reelection as a Vermont Supreme Court judge and was seated next to a table where a map of Bennington lay open and a globe sat below his shelves of books. Earl spent his last years in Northampton, Massachusetts, the rapidly growing commercial center of the upper Connecticut Valley, while undertaking an ambitious scheme to travel and prepare a panorama of that remarkable American natural wonder, Niagara Falls. He died penniless, of "intemperance," in 1801.[82]

The colonial elite of great landowners, merchants, and established ministers had given way to an entirely new group of lesser lights, the rising men and women of the post-Revolutionary gentry, eager to engage in the project of improving their persons, their houses, and their villages. An extensive market developed in the commerce of culture, and young men and women looking for a livelihood found the hinterlands hospitable places to peddle books and set up schools. Print entrepreneurs were early leaders in the Village Enlightenment. Men like Robert Thomas and Ralph Earl made a thriving business of advancing tastes in the countryside. Others made a good living by selling fashionable frocks and imported goods, as Elijah Boardman did. Training a new generation of republicans required self-education for such teachers as Silas Felton and Sarah Pierce. The leaders of the Village Enlightenment established formal and informal educational institutions, including libraries and academies. They cleared village greens and planted shade trees to signify their generation's coming of age, schooling their neighbors and customers in republican virtue through a refined material appearance.

Cultivation

Printers and publishers were significant forces in activating a market for knowledge, but it was the presence of rural consumers like Silas Felton and Orra White, with their immense hunger for print, that fueled the extensive base of support for the Village Enlightenment. A host of institutions—schools and academies, literary and debating societies, social libraries and lyceum lectures—rooted the circulation of print deep in rural communities. Early nineteenth-century Americans were joiners, as Alexis de Tocqueville observed. They formed a myriad of Masonic lodges, temperance societies, and other voluntary associations that combined sociability with cultural improvement.

Silas Felton, though preoccupied with trade, continued his self-education through books. In 1802, he joined with thirteen other men in Marlborough to found a Society of Social Enquirers. The Enquirers represented the stable and successful members of the community. Of the organizers for whom information is available, the average age was thirty-four, Felton being the youngest, and all but one came from long-settled families. The majority, like Felton himself, went on to hold important town and state offices. The society met weekly to discuss scientific topics, such as whether fire or water is the more powerful element, and to consider practical questions, such as the most profitable ways to run a farm. Felton composed the group's constitution and celebrated its first anniversary with a grand "Oration on the Happy Effects of Social Enquiries." He argued that such societies as the Social Enquirers were critical in this age of rapid progress "in agriculture, the Arts and Sciences," with its growing awareness of the "different Manners and Customs" brought about by reading geography and travel. He sprinkled his address with references to the Venetian republic and the Egyptian writing system. He stressed the young republic's role as a beacon of liberty to other nations and the village society's role in diffusing useful knowledge. Knowledge sustained liberty, and since knowledge was obtained in association, "then will not every true Republican encourage all sincere social enquirers, who form themselves into societies like this?" He reminded his listeners of the venerable origins of their association: "Doct. Franklin relates, in his life, that he received a considerable part of his information in this way." The social enquirer established local institutions to bring about enlightenment. Felton proposed an active creed to his neighbors: "To know that theoretic knowledge, without practice, is of little consequence to Society."[83]

About a decade later in Deerfield, Orra White, Emilia Hitchcock, and thirty-four young women, many former or present pupils or instructors at the Deerfield Academy, founded the Young Ladies Literary Society. Their charter stipulated that "any member shall have the liberty to make any original communication on any subject of science, literature or the domestic arts. . . . If approved by a committee to examine them." Groups like Marlborough's Social Enquirers and Deerfield's Literary Society brought young men and women together to promote Enlightenment beliefs about humans' ability to improve the world. The Literary Society's preamble mentioned the "pleasures of the intellect." These "enlightened friends of humanity" gathered fortnightly from 1813 until 1817 to promote the advancement of "rational beings." "To enlighten, expand and embellish the mind, to cultivate and purify the heart, are objects in the highest degree promotive of the happiness and dignity of man." Many women educated in academies also entered upon career as editors and writers. In so doing, Mary Kelley has noted, these women "were not only reproducing the knowledge in which they had been schooled at female academies and seminaries"; they were also exercising their influence in civil society.[84]

Orra White also promoted the interdisciplinary investigation of art and science as an assistant teacher at the Deerfield Academy as well as in her work as a scientific illustrator. The rise of academies and their need for scholarly texts provided a calling and a career for her. White, daughter of a prosperous Amherst farmer, had learned to draw at home and at a girl's school in Roxbury; her schoolbook demonstrates that she was performing astronomical calculations from the age of ten. She moved on to teaching the "exact sciences and fine arts" at Deerfield and Amherst Academies. While at Deerfield, she was credited as moving the curriculum away from embroidery toward a new emphasis on drawing and painting and map making. A scholar of classics and higher mathematics, she also was an experienced artist, probably the earliest published female scientific illustrator. Her first artistic work, a landscape of Turner's Falls on the Connecticut River, was published in the noted periodical *Port Folio* in 1818. When she married Edward Hitchcock, she rendered most of the plates and illustrations for his scientific publications, including his well-known report on the *Geology, Mineralology, Botany and Zoology of Massachusetts* (1833). The two shared excursions throughout the Connecticut River Valley for the study of geology and botany; during those travels, she drew numerous landscapes from life to be used later for study and publication (fig. 32). Edward later credited her with over 230 plates and well over 1,100 illustrations. She also produced botanical and other illustrations for use by her students. When Orra and her Deerfield colleagues gathered fortnightly for their discussions, they considered such questions as "What is the principal cause of evil in society?"—the answer was "Defective Education"—and "Ought ladies to endeavor to excell in the sciences?"—decided in the negative, even though some among their ranks, such as Orra White Hitchcock, were actively distinguishing themselves in the sciences. The final question for their deliberations—"Ought a female ever to rule a nation?"—did not receive a decision.[85]

Marlborough's Social Enquirers considered political and economic questions as well. While Felton praised the wonders of nature, he saved his warmest words for artisan-entrepreneurs who practiced "the art of working the natural productions of the earth into artificial commodities for our use, profit, conve-

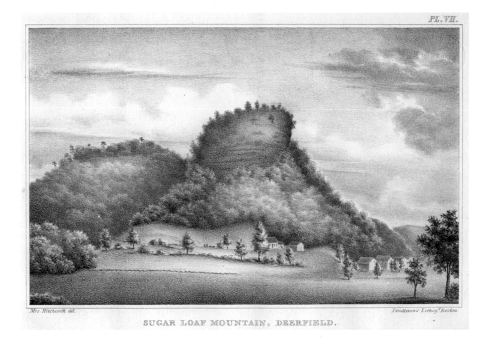

SUGAR LOAF MOUNTAIN, DEERFIELD.

Fig. 32. Orra White Hitchcock, *View of Sugarloaf Mountain, Deerfield*. Lithograph, paper, and ink. 9-1/4 × 10-3/4 in. One of the nine landscape plates drawn by Orra for Edward Hitchcock's massive geological survey of Massachusetts, *Report on the Geology, Mineralogy, Botany, and Zoology of Massachusetts*, first published in 1833, and signed "Mrs. Hitchcock del[ineavit]," Latin for "she drew it." The inclusion of a farm dwelling conveys scale. Butler Library, Columbia University in the City of New York.

nience and ornament." During an 1806 journey to visit his wife Lucretia's parents, he noted unfinished turnpikes and "Elegant" villages, such as Keene, New Hampshire, and the "new Village" of Bath at the falls of the Ammonnosiuc River "where they now have a grist mill, saw mill, fulling mill, forge where they make Iron, and a number of stores." The commercial activity of enterprising townspeople promoted the industrialization of the region.

Young middling men and women located themselves in the commercializing economy by using literacy and knowledge. For Felton, teaching school provided a stepping-stone to a career in business. During the first year that Felton and Cranston kept the store, he continued to teach. After the partners' decided to "sell very cheap for Cash in hand," their business slowly increased. The partners also engaged in smithing at the site, and their employees boarded in the household Felton had just established after his marriage. In the first year, Felton earned $58 from the store and $100 from teaching school; the following year the sums were reversed. Resolving to concentrate on commerce, he expanded the stock, "keeping a more general assortment" of goods, and sought customers from beyond the bounds of Marlborough.[86]

Just as Felton's commercial activities intensified his accumulation of capital and the pace of commercial change in town, the very landscape of New England experienced an increased concentration of population and shops. Village centers took hold at once diffuse crossroads, the physical manifestation of the Village Enlightenment bringing commercial and cultural change to provincial towns. In a pattern repeated all over New England, a commercial village developed around a commercial and industrial site in a corner of Marlborough, the only part of town to grow significantly in the nineteenth century. Boasting the town's only usable waterpower, it had long been the site of a sawmill; soon it became known as "the mills." Cranston and Felton chose this site, opening their "store of goods" from Boston with funds advanced by private individuals and banks; they encouraged artisans to set up shop in what they called "this village." Cranston, fourteen years older and Silas's surveying teacher, had greater access to credit because of his extensive landholdings. Felton obtained a loan from his father and relied upon his income from teaching. When their anxious Boston creditors, whom Felton called "cursed pests," called in their debts in 1803, the two men closed their partnership. Cranston fared better, building a "great house," while Silas fended off his creditors. The ample 1805 harvest renewed their partnership with the opening of a second store in nearby Boylston. Felton ran both stores and accumulated land along the Assabet River at the mills. By 1810, he had recorded a fortune of over $7,000 and entered into a partnership with Cranston and Elijah Hale. They sold off their landholdings and began small-scale manufacturing, buying a cider distillery, a carding machine, and a shoemaking shop near their original store: "Each of these afforded a little profit." By 1820, Feltonville, as the village came to be called, consisted of thirteen houses, two or three artisans' shops, the Felton and Cranston "English and West India" store, and a small cotton factory, a configuration similar to what Felton had observed in Bath. Well before the coming of the railroad or the steam engine, many small towns took on an industrial appearance from the activities of entrepreneurs like Felton. Before the establishment of such large-scale industrial communities as those at Lowell or Lawrence, New England became dotted with small-scale commercial enterprises initiated by local entrepreneurs.[87]

Marlborough's Society of Social Enquirers and its Social Library typified a host of local institutions that defined and diffused the Village Enlightenment. Well over five hundred New England towns founded libraries during the quarter-century from 1790 to 1815. These voluntary associations, in Robert Gross's words, served up useful information to folk who were "eager for fresh knowledge about the world in which they lived. The preference was for 'matters of fact': histories, biographies, travels, practical science, the latest knowledge of the past and the contemporary world." These societies gave collective expression to cosmopolitan aspirations prompted in no small part by the spread of the printed word in all its varied forms. They also enabled local custodians of culture like Silas Felton to set themselves above less enlightened neighbors. Not paradoxically, these agencies of the Village Enlightenment stood for the democratization of knowledge at the same time as they promoted an increasingly stratified community. Differential access and interest in new forms of knowledge fostered the emergence of new social rankings, which solidified by the second quarter of the nineteenth century.[88]

The careers of Silas Felton, Robert Thomas, and Orra White Hitchcock illustrate the impact of the Age of Enlightenment and the market revolution. Rural printers and promoters of knowledge may be seen as rural American counterparts to the hack writers and petty booksellers on London's Grub Street and in Paris who are vividly depicted by Robert Darnton. Yet the results of their aspirations were different. The ambitious youths from the French countryside who flooded Paris with the aim of becoming literati in the footsteps of Voltaire and Diderot found their way blocked by monopoly enterprises and were forced into demeaning subordination as spies for the police or peddlers of pornography. The barely suppressed rage of these "poor devils" against the *ancien régime* eventually erupted in an outpouring of Revolutionary pamphlets in 1789. In contrast, the American seekers of literary fame, when they rejected or were denied access to elite cultural status, turned instead to enlarging the democratic impulses of the American Revolution. They were able to activate a popular market for print because of the absence of privileged control of the press. Rather than becoming advocates of radical change, they launched Village Enlightenment in the wake of a successful popular Revolution.[89]

CHAPTER THREE

Cosmopolitan Communities

Encountering James Wilson in Vermont

Visiting the Bennington Museum a few summers ago, I not only made the acquaintance of James Wilson, the first American commercial globe maker, but I also discovered the unique power of objects to tell a story not available to us from the textual record (fig. 33). I had come to the museum to consult the curatorial records for an exhibit on Vermont furniture in the early Republic: a panoply of decorative sideboards, globes, and musical clocks that made many post-Revolutionary commercial villages into centers of fashionable consumption and profitable craft enterprises. Globes embody the story of making a business by enlightening one's neighbors, putting a vision of a rising nation and its constituent states taking its place among the nations of the world, standing in every schoolhouse and genteel dwelling.

In the sunlit main gallery where the museum's treasured objects from Vermont's early history are displayed, I saw things that helped me understand how artisans and consumers imagined their worlds. First my eye was caught by a large neoclassical sideboard, with a graceful bowfront and sleek lines, looking

Facing page: Fig. 33. Terrestrial globe made by James Wilson, ca. 1810. Bradford, Vermont. Paper-faced ash wood, brass quadrant, 18-3/4 × 18 in. Printed on globe: A NEW / TERRESTRIAL GLOBE,? On wich the/ TRACTS and NEW DISCOVERIES/ are laid down/ from the Accurate Observations/ made by / Cap.ˢ Cook, Furneaux, Phipps & C./ By J. WILSON, VERMONT. Courtesy of Vermont Historical Society, Montpelier.

Fig. 34. Musical tall clock made by Nichols Goddard, ca. 1805–10. Rutland, Vermont. Mahogany and white pine with mahogany veneer and light and dark wood inlays. Height 96-1/2 in. Bennington Museum, Bennington, Vermont.

for all the world like a sophisticated Boston product but made in Windsor, Vermont (see fig. 36). Then, at the other end of the room, I noticed a marvelous musical tall clock built by a Rutland clockmaking partnership. The timepiece boasted a calendar wheel and a moon dial, and it played seven tunes, one for each day of the week, with a psalm for Sunday (fig. 34). Between the globe and

Fig. 35. Desk-and-bookcase made possibly by James Wilson; he signed one of the drawer bottoms and designed the shelving for his prized *Encyclopedia Britannica*, the probable source of his geographical knowledge. Yellow birch and white pine. 83-1/2 × 40 × 21-3/4 in. Bennington Museum, Bennington, Vermont.

the clock, museum curators had hung a 1795 landscape of Bennington painted by Ralph Earl.

Suddenly I noticed a massive desk and encyclopedia-filled bookcase that dominated an entire corner of the room, where the museum staff had recreated the interior of an early nineteenth-century Vermont home (fig. 35). The desk, I learned, belonged to James Wilson of Bradford, Vermont, a town quite far north along the Connecticut River. The label states that Wilson was the United States' first globe maker, and one of Wilson's early globes sat in a Plexiglas case in front of the display (see fig. 33). It seemed strange that a man in such an out-of-the-way place had taken to making globes.[1]

Here, preserved and exhibited by the museum, is Vermont's contribution to the new nation's commercial and cultural history. The objects on display embody the intellectual curiosity and grand ambitions of men and women in rural New England. I left the Bennington Museum that day enthralled with

James Wilson, wondering how a globe maker could have worked in the upper Connecticut River Valley in the 1790s. As I later learned, others in the hinterlands also tried to make globes; New Hampshire shoemaker, surveyor, and farmer Samuel Lane, for example, made his own idiosyncratic version of a terrestrial globe around 1760. Lane turned a seven-inch oak sphere on his lathe, scored the painted surface, and cut degrees and continental boundaries into the painted surface, while pinning it onto a pine table made in the form of a milking stool so the globe could revolve.[2]

The four corners of that gallery of Vermont art and artisanry illustrate the dimensions of the Village Enlightenment.[3] Portraitist and cabinetmaker, globe maker and clockmaker, all were represented—making the upper Connecticut River into a region with a cluster of cosmopolitan towns, many only recently settled. Some entrepreneurs were local to the region and others migrated there to make their living, but all made careers out of producing and disseminating knowledge to their neighbors, promoting the Village Enlightenment, not just in books and newspapers but also in state maps and musical clocks. Enlightenment notions came in neoclassical forms, adding a decorative element to many a provincial household.

Globes

Globes captured James Wilson's imagination. Few eighteenth-century American households could boast ownership of a globe. Those who did likely purchased their globes from London manufacturers. When Benjamin Franklin, that inveterate scientist and homegrown *philosophe*, wanted to secure a pair of globes—a terrestrial and celestial set—he wrote to his frequent correspondent William Strahan, one of London's most important printers: "Please send me another of Popple's Maps of North America. . . . A Pair of Mrs. Senex's improved Globes . . . (or Neal's improv'd Globes, if thought better than Senex's) the best and largest that may be had for (not exceeding) eight Guineas."[4]

Instrument makers, engravers, and clockmakers all produced globes in Britain. Many considered cordwainer William Bardin the leading late eighteenth-century globe maker. Bardin and others relied on forms introduced with Martin Behaim's hollow wooden Nuremburg globe of 1492. Behaim's globe-making principles were codified and transmitted in print by Diderot's *Encyclopédie*, one of the major sources of globe-making information contained in Wilson's own set of the *Encyclopedia Britannica*. Globe makers who followed Behaim's example used a solid wooden mold with wire pivots at each end, which became the poles. The ball was covered with successive layers of damp papier-mâché or paper. When the paper dried, the shell was cut into two halves around the circumference of the equator, an axle shaft of wood was tacked at the poles, and the globe was put back together and sealed. Thin layers of plaster were applied and guidelines drawn so that printed gores could be attached. Breaking the map of the world into twelve sections, or gores, solved the problem of how to fit flat paper maps over spheres. In the early sixteenth century, engravers and printers began to produce gores for eager globe makers. Globe making thus sat at the intersection of woodworking, metalworking, printing, and mapmaking, as Wilson soon discovered.[5]

Globe making caught on in the eighteenth century. Interest was fueled by the expansion of geographical knowledge, thanks to imperial voyagers and traders, especially Captain James Cook. Cook's Pacific voyages rounded out European knowledge of the world. The information he brought back gave Enlightenment globes their marked "oceanic character," as geographer Denis Cosgrove has remarked. Cook's voyages and his death at the hands of resistant native Hawaiians captured Americans' imagination, too. There was a growing interest in popular science and geographic discoveries, along with a desire to display that newfound knowledge in homes and schools. Wilson shared this interest, but how did he come to make globes?[6]

Wilson was born in Londonderry, New Hampshire, in 1763. As a boy, he learned blacksmithing from his uncle. In 1795, the young man set out west across the Connecticut River to buy land in Bradford, Vermont, a town located at the scenic Coos Meadows where the Waits and Connecticut rivers meet. Along the way, he stopped in Hanover, New Hampshire, to see a friend at Dartmouth College. According to one family story, the young man, himself eager for knowledge but without the means for securing a formal education, saw a pair of globes when he peeked through the keyhole of a locked door in one of the college buildings. The college owned three sets of globes in the 1790s, but all were inaccessible to Wilson. Glimpsing the globes fired his curiosity and fortified his desire to construct one of these unusual objects, or so the story goes.

Wilson brought his wife and two sons to Bradford to develop his homestead and began making axes to help pay for his land purchases. While working as a smith, he did not forget his interest in making a map of the world. In 1796, he made his first globe, a large solid wooden ball covered with paper, with the continents and countries drawn in pen and ink. But Wilson intended to build and market a product that could compete with the European imports, thus making his mark and earning his living as an American globe maker. He faced formidable obstacles, starting with his lack of knowledge of geography, astronomy, and cartography. However, for a man gifted with Wilson's capacity for learning, the increasing variety of books and newspapers in the small towns of northern New England offered many sources of information. Wilson may not have had the advantages of his friend at Dartmouth, but he did have skills and products he could exchange for knowledge. He sold some of his farm produce and livestock and traveled the twenty miles to the Ryegate bookstore, where he purchased for the substantial sum of $130 the eighteen volumes of the *Encyclopaedia Britannica: Or a Dictionary of Arts, Sciences and Miscellaneous Literature*, the collection of books for which he built his imposing desk and bookcase.[7] Encyclopedias were the archetypal repository of the Enlightenment, with their compendia of all recognized knowledge; the third edition *Britannica* contained almost fifteen thousand pages and over five hundred plates, including substantial entries on globes and geography.

How could Wilson translate the information found in his encyclopedia onto his wooden spheres? His bookcase demonstrated his skills in woodworking, and as a trained blacksmith, he was a proficient metalworker. But he knew that hand-drawn globes could not compare with European imports. In order to move beyond shoemaker-surveyor Lane's effort and produce globes his neighbors would be proud to own, Wilson had to learn to engrave his maps on copperplates. Wilson had to find a teacher more skilled at engraving than his acquaintances in southern Vermont. His first trip to Boston and Newburyport brought disappointment when John Akin, a well-known engraver, asked a hundred dollars for tuition, a sum far beyond Wilson's purse. Later he went to New Haven to see Amos Doolittle, a silversmith turned engraver, who was celebrated for engraving the maps in Jedidiah Morse's *Geography Made Easy* (1784).

Wilson learned the basic principles of engraving during a brief stay in New Haven. But he still had much to learn about building globes. He began again with his original globe, covering it with papier-mâché, gluing several layers together, tracing continental outlines, cutting paper into hemispheres, and then gluing the hemispheres onto the sphere. He finished a hand-drawn globe, but then spent nearly a year engraving a world map on a large copperplate, only to discover that he did not know how to project the meridians of the map, a flat plane, in their true proportion onto a spherical surface.

Wilson took off once again in search of cosmopolitan training to suit his cosmopolitan imagination. This time he went to see the "Father of American Geography," Jedidiah Morse himself, in Charlestown, Massachusetts. Only two years older than Wilson, Morse already had five geography books in print. He told Wilson that the copperplate could not be salvaged. Wilson went back to Bradford, knowing he needed to obtain more copper but knowing too that his growing family needed the scarce resources he was spending learning to make globes. During the first years of the nineteenth century, balancing family demands and his map-making aspirations, Wilson worked on his globe making.

He built his own lathes and presses, mixed his inks, shaped the spheres, and printed all of his own maps, probably relying on the American atlases increasingly available in print shops. The Wilson Family Papers hold a small sheet printed with a gore; on the back of this scrap, Wilson wrote down a recipe for ink.[8] Around 1810 he produced his first globes of paper on a paper core suspended in a birch frame with turned legs. He opened a shop to manufacture these prized items and began to sell them to his neighbors in rural Vermont. Wilson charged around fifty dollars for a pair of globes: a terrestrial and a celestial one. His terrestrial globes measured thirteen inches in diameter, and each one was signed, "A NEW TERRESTRIAL GLOBE . . . By J. WILSON, VERMONT." Men like Wilson made a livelihood providing useful knowledge and genteel commodities. These material manifestations of the Village Enlightenment celebrated homegrown knowledge.

Wilson was part of a remarkable circle of Windsor County, Vermont, mapmakers and engravers whose products graced the walls of schoolhouses and homes in the new nation. Globes were prized as genteel objects and as means of education, where Cook's voyages could be traced or, in Wilson's words, the era's "TRACTS and NEW DISCOVERIES" could be displayed. Cartographic commodities made the nation into a materially tangible object to their users, often located quite far from urban print centers, along with adding decorative designs to a household. These consumers of globes and other cultural goods were linked together by a shared series of aspirations and an increasing means of transmitting them through schools and a web of print.[9]

Although the narrative of American globe making usually begins with James Wilson, the blacksmith-cartographer, or Samuel Lane, the idiosyncratic shoemaker-farmer, that story must now be revised. At exactly the same time that James Wilson was fashioning the first commercial globes, Ruth Wright of Exeter, a student in the Westtown Friends School, made a globe sampler of plain, woven light-blue silk covering a stuffed sphere. In fact, embroidered globes predate Wilson's first product. Map samplers were a significant means of learning geography as well as needlework, as advertisements for schools made clear; students progressed through alphabet samplers to map samplers fashioned of embroidered hemispheres, a design quite similar to the maps in the *Encyclopedia Britannica*, to the more elaborate embroidered globes.[10]

At the Westtown School, a coeducational Quaker academy founded in 1799 and located near Philadelphia in Chester County, Pennsylvania, a stronghold of Quaker culture, students made both celestial and terrestrial silk globes with needlework. The curriculum was similar for boys and girls, except the girls took sewing for two weeks out of six and the boys took more advanced mathematics and science. The globes were made to teach needlework as well as geography, astronomy, and mathematics; for the first fifty years of the school's existence, students made them along with other projects. In needlework, the students started with darning and then alphabet samplers; map samplers were not made at Westtown, but the girls did make conventional maps with pen and ink. While the school owned three globes, they were expensive items to purchase at this time. Judith Tyner has speculated that the globe's entry into the curriculum came as an economy measure, an advanced step in the progression in the needle-work arts: samplers, pincushions, and then globes. Also, three conventional globes would have been hardly sufficient for several hundred students to use to solve "the problems on the globes." Westtown's curriculum had significant influence in the region. Many former Westtown students were employed in Quaker schools throughout the Delaware Valley. Samuel Gummere, a Westtown teacher, must have drawn on his lessons for his popular textbook, *Definitions and Elementary Observations in Astronomy; also, Problems on the Globes* (1822). Gummere's text had detailed instructions for the construction of both terrestrial and celestial globes. The Westtown globes were quite unique: all highly similar, about five to six inches in diameter, with silk stitched over a canvas form stuffed with raw wool from the Westtown sheep. The form was made first, and then the silk gores stitched together, with one seam left open to insert the form. Sarah R. Sheppard fashioned a gold-colored terrestrial globe on a silk ground, with the longitude and latitude embroidered, the continents outlined in silk, the countries' borders in outline stitch, and the other elements, such as ships, people, and names, painted or inked.[11] The paired celestial globe sported color-fully painted signs of the zodiac (plate 3).

The globes were meant to be used, many mounted on stands or placed in cases. The explosion of academies for men and women, where geography and other cosmopolitan subjects were taught, offered instruction through books as well as objects. A Westtown student wrote of her globe work: "I expect to have a good deal of trouble in making them, yet I hope that they will recompense me for all my trouble, for they will certainly be a curiosity to you and of consid-erable use in instructing my brothers and sisters, and to strengthen my own memory, respecting the supposed shape of our earth, and the manner in which it moves (or is moved) on its axis, or the line drawn through it, round which it revolves every 24 hours." Wilson's printed and Sheppard's embroidered globes represented the nation in graphic form. Both the embroidered globes crafted by Westtown School's female students and those produced by Wilson's Bradford globe manufactory attest to the keen interest in imagining spatial relations in the new nation, just as the proliferation of clocks attests to the drive to master time.[12]

Maps and globes facilitated geographic and economic integration and helped people imagine their nation in the world. Maps have long aided political expansion and cultural consolidation. In the early Republic, cartography established an image of an authentically bounded nation. "After the Revolution many Americans self-consciously turned to the discourse of geography to negotiate and transform the representations of personal, regional, and political difference into material figures of national consent," literary scholar Martin Bruckner writes. Whenever they stitched a sampler of the United States or gazed on a state map that made their homes part of a larger whole, they "enacted the nation as a participatory model of coherence."[13]

Wilson belonged to a rising generation of men and women who left farm work for commercial pursuits but remained in the countryside. New men and women emerged in once out-of-the-way places, making provincial outposts into village commercial centers, ready and eager to support a bevy of cabinetmakers manufacturing neoclassical sideboards or even a group of cartographers fashioning decorative globes. Some were professionals and others were amateurs, but all promoted the refinement of village culture, creating an extensive base of communities linked together by cultural ideals in this post-Revolutionary generation. This was no mere modeling of metropolitan motifs but something different.

A Tale of Three Sideboards

In 1798, Elijah West, the owner of a dry-goods store and tavern in Windsor, Vermont, purchased a dramatic sideboard, possibly made by cabinetmaker Julius Barnard, as a wedding gift for his daughter Sophia and his business partner Allen Hayes (fig. 36). Hayes bought the Perez Jones house, most likely designed and built by Asher Benjamin, the town's resident neoclassical architect, where the sideboard took pride of place. West's ability to obtain such a sideboard locally tells us much about the presence of a cosmopolitan community of craftsmen and consumers in the upper Connecticut Valley. We can learn even more by comparing West's Windsor purchase with a New York City piece and another sideboard by a New Hampshire maker from across the river (figs. 37, 38). When we note their visual similarities of style and observe their modes of construction by peering inside, opening the drawers as well as ogling the ornamentation, we learn much about the rise of the neoclassical style and the proliferation of specialized forms in American furniture and the spread of such tastes and skills across the countryside. Rural cabinetmakers were not merely imitative; they introduced innovations in these fashionable forms, even in once-remote communities like Windsor and its neighbors.[14]

While Bradford, Vermont, honored James Wilson as its most distinguished

Fig. 36. Sideboards were imposing pieces of furniture that allowed owners to display their dining finery. Julius Barnard took his cosmopolitan training to Windsor, Vermont, where he might have made two of these sideboards. This sideboard has a simpler silhouette and less elegant construction compromises than the one made by Barnard for Mills Olcott, even while it continues the basic use of inlays and other intricate ornamentation. Sideboard made for Allen Hayes, possibly by Julius Barnard, Windsor, Vermont, 1798. Mahogany, pine, and cherry with mahogany and rosewood veneers. 40 × 62 × 28 in. Bennington Museum, Bennington, Vermont.

resident, Windsor, located just down the river, counted a remarkable range of cosmopolitan craftsmen and consumers among its residents. The town was known for the "elegance of the buildings, and the polished manner of the inhabitants," according to one visitor. As Timothy Dwight observed, it had more mercantile and mechanical businesses than any other town on the Connecticut River north of Massachusetts. The river offered speedy access to goods, services, and information. Seventy artisans in the woodworking trades alone appeared in the public records between 1795 and 1820, representing about half the total number of local woodworkers. The Tontine Building, a three-story brick structure, was built in 1805 by a subscription of the town's artisan-entrepreneurs. Architect Asher Benjamin, who came to town in 1797, was responsible for much of Windsor's elegance. Fresh from the publication of his *Country Builder's Assistant* (1797), he moved up the river from Greenfield, Massachusetts, to build sophisticated structures in the neoclassical style during his five-year stay. He designed

Fig. 37. Sideboard made by William Mills and Simeon Deming, New York, 1793–95. Mahogany, white pine, poplar, cherry, maple, ash, chestnut. 40-3/4 × 74-3/4 × 32-1/4 in. One of the grander urban workshop examples, with its mahogany wood, serpentine front, and elaborate decorative inlays on many visible surfaces. Private collection.

Fig. 38. Sideboard attributed to Julius Barnard, 1801. Windsor, Vermont. Mahogany and birch veneers on white pine and spruce, 40 × 74 × 27-1/2 in. Barnard's mahogany sideboard for Dartmouth treasurer Mills Olcott shares a serpentine front and draped inlays along the legs and other surfaces with the sideboard that Governor Oliver Wolcott purchased from New York's Mills and Deming shop. Hood Museum of Art, Dartmouth College, Hanover, New Hampshire; bequest of Philip H. Chase, Class of 1907.

the town's new meetinghouse and several private dwellings, including the 1801 Jonathan Hubbard house with its lavishly ornamented facades. Benjamin even operated a school of architecture to teach young men classical taste, which inspired the choice of clocks, furniture, and portraits for those homes.[15]

The neoclassical style, which was featured at scales ranging from house facades to clock cases, became known in America as the Federal style. After gaining popularity in England during the 1760s and 1770s, it provided Americans with an understated way to communicate status. "Because of the emphasis on plain and planar surfaces, rectilinear forms, and restrained use of carving," historian Kevin Sweeney writes, "neoclassical interiors, furniture and metalwares were invariably described as 'neat and plain.'" Furniture became lighter and rectilinear; ornamentation featured clean surfaces embellished with rich veneers and intricate inlays rather than heavy rococo carving. Neoclassicism with its reawakening of interest in antiquity appealed to the new nation's republicans looking to establish associations with the great republics of classical Greece and Rome. Still, Americans borrowed these stylistic associations from abroad.[16]

Sideboards with their undulating surfaces followed the aesthetic statements of Robert Adam, Scottish popularizer of neoclassicism:

> *Movement* is meant to express, the rise and fall, the advance and recess, with other diversity of form, in the different parts of a building, so as to add greatly to the picturesque of the composition. For the rising and falling, advancing and receding, with the convexity and concavity, and other forms of the great parts, have the same effect in architecture, that hill and dale, fore-ground and distance, swelling and sinking have in landscape: That is, they serve to produce an agreeable and diversified contour, that groups and contrasts like a picture, and creates a variety of light and shade, which gives great spirit, beauty, and effect to the Composition.[17]

Furniture, like landscape, would inculcate an appreciation for dynamism that drew from the Greek and Roman worlds.

The sideboard, a dramatic surface to display a family's household treasures, was a large and imposing new furniture form. First developed in the 1770s in England, it appeared in George Hepplewhite's *The Cabinetmaker and Upholsterer's Guide* (1778) and made its way across the Atlantic by the 1790s. New York City shops manufactured grand examples, such as the sideboard made for Oliver Wolcott, Connecticut's first governor, who sat for Ralph Earl in 1789 when living in Litchfield. This most elaborately decorated American sideboard was commissioned from "Mills & Deming" (fig. 37). Transplanted Connecticut craftsmen ran many of the successful New York firms; Simeon Deming of Wethersfield had come to New York in 1793. While many sideboards feature rare woods, such as mahogany and satinwood, fashioned into nicely tapered legs, the expressive inlays that drape the serpentine front set Wolcott's piece apart, demonstrating the financial resources and aspiring tastes of its owner. The cupboard doors are inlaid with drapery and swag urns; the central drawer has a drapery chain of inlaid bellflowers; drawers and cupboard doors are bordered by green tinted cross-banding with fan inlaid quadrants in the corners; the legs have tinted bellflowers and interlaced loops. As new furniture forms were introduced during the last decade of the eighteenth century—Pembroke tables and dining tables, as well as sideboards—more specialized forms appeared in the dining rooms of the provincial elite. The sideboard, used for serving at the side of the room, could provide storage for flatware and linens, but its primary purpose was to provide a shining surface to display glass, silver, and ceramics.[18]

Hayes's sideboard illustrates the innovative compromises inland villagers sought when they purchased refined furniture. Its simpler bow front, with fewer undulating surfaces than Wolcott's, still offers a compelling silhouette that was derived from Boston furniture styles. But the secondary wood was very thick cherry, and the maker used several drawer divides. The inlays were sophisticated in concept and execution, but applied with three of four shells facing left and one right. Finally, the banding round the top edge continues only two-thirds of the way around the sides, a gesture toward frugality in an otherwise sophisticated piece.[19] A sideboard's simplicity of outline might suggest an equally simple construction, but nothing could be further from the truth, as furniture scholars suggest: the great size and sweeping shape made possible by refinements in sawing technology, with joined glued sandwiches of many types of wood, permitted a freedom of geometry, forms, and ornament not previously possible; the thin layering of decorative and exotic woods with banding upon the supporting substructure was common practice.[20]

Village cabinetmakers combined London designs and sophisticated urban techniques with rural tastes and modest prices. Sometimes they suggested inventive solutions to construction issues within the price constraints of their clients; at other times they offered exuberant answers as well. Silas Cheney offered to his Litchfield customers some of the most ambitious pieces of furniture made by a rural cabinetmaker at the time. The sideboards with their expensive mahogany wood, shimmering curved fronts, and extensive use of inlaid decoration must have satisfied the tastes of Tapping Reeve, the eminent lawyer and teacher, or Colonel Benjamin Tallmadge. He also made fancy chairs, the light and painted chairs produced in the style of the English neoclassical taste-makers Robert Adam and George Hepplewhite; Tapping Reeve ordered his in the popular New York bamboo style.[21] Sometimes ambitious craftsmen from the hinterlands, such as Simeon Deming, chose metropolitan careers, but increasingly, artisans, fresh from their training in the major urban centers, established large workshops in the countryside. They retailed a wide range of elegant and sophisticated commodities across northern New England and beyond.

Julius Barnard, a former native of Northampton who had received some of his training in New York City, set up shop in Windsor in 1802 and produced sideboards, possibly the Hayes sideboard (see fig. 36) as well as this imposing sideboard for Mills Olcott, the treasurer of Dartmouth College and a prominent businessman and lawyer (fig. 38). The elegant and expensive mahogany sideboard, with its serpentine surfaces and protruding drawers similar to Wolcott's New York City piece, demonstrates not only his expert craftsmanship but also his familiarity with the high style, while the innovative, indeed exuberant variety of inlays, dramatically festooned with bellflowers, some applied upside down, speaks to the rural tastes of valley residents. The road to placing this rare piece in the upper Connecticut River was a long and winding one. It was long believed to be a Baltimore piece, for the conventional wisdom was that only an urban cabinetmaking center could have produced such a bold item. But the Hood Museum's curator, Margaret Moody, combined documentary evidence and construction details to locate it in the Connecticut Valley. The papers of its original owner, Mills Olcott, identified its maker as Julius Barnard. While Barnard was working in his Hanover, New Hampshire, shop in 1801, he and Olcott exchanged several letters. Barnard was busy securing cherrywood and awaiting orders, but he warned Olcott that "if there is any Mahogany furniture wanted, will need time to get it from Boston." Barnard crossed the river to Windsor the next year. He purchased land and a share in a "new brick building" from Nathan Hale, a local clockmaker, and advertised more frequently than any other furniture maker. His workshop was the largest in Vermont at the time, with six to eight apprentices and journeymen turning out a wealth of fashionable furniture. One detailed advertisement listed twenty-five separate forms of furniture available at his shop, including a variety of sideboards: "Sash-corned, commode, & strait front Sideboards," along with such other stylish items as "Secretaries and Bookcases—Ladies Writing desks . . . Card and Pembrome [sic] Tables . . . Sofas, Easy and Lolling Chairs," and even clock cases.[22]

Ethan Allen Greenwood, a central Massachusetts portraitist, traveled through Walpole and Windsor in search of commissions in 1809 at the end of a lengthy process of self-discovery. He had started portrait making while teaching at the Leicester Academy and attending Dartmouth College. After graduation, he pursued a desultory legal training, tended his father's store, and started several business ventures, but painting, which he studied in New York City with Edward Savage, was his chosen vocation. Before setting off on his journey north, he visited "the old mansion house of Gov. Gill" and "Viewed some of Copley's paintings etc."[23] In Windsor, he was "Treated with much civility by the gentlemen of the place," as he began "painting Mrs. Tileston." In October, he "packed up [his] dudds," settled his accounts, and noted "how pleasant his situation had been—8 portraits here another five in Rockingham." By 1811, Greenwood had painted sixty-six portraits, and the next year he moved to Boston. Greenwood's decade as an itinerant artist was fertile training ground for his appearance as an academic figure in the Boston art world.[24]

Those living along the Connecticut River benefited greatly from the movement of stylish goods and well-trained artisans. The firm of Kneeland and Adams advertised in the *Vermont Journal* in 1794, over 150 miles upriver from their Hartford shop, "that they can furnish them with every kind of Cabinet Work, made in the newest and most approved fashion from Europe . . . cased and delivered at the water side Hartford." When Paul Brigham, a prominent Norwich, Vermont, citizen, located upriver from Windsor, wanted a clock, he was able to obtain the latest Connecticut design, an uncased Burnap movement with its engraved dial, originally silvered; the case was probably made by Hezekiah Kelly, a Vermont cabinetmaker with whom Burnap traded movements for cases. At the same time, Windsor's own Nathan Hale made a tall clock with a cherry and white-pine case. The two clocks' cases were similar in their fretwork and shape, differing only in details. But Hale, who had obtained all his training in his hometown of Rindge, New Hampshire, before locating in Windsor, adopted a different method of manufacture. Instead of casting his own parts, he purchased parts from Boston, obtained clocks and clock faces from local suppliers, and got his cases from local cabinetmakers. Weathersfield saddler Barnabas Ellis purchased a Hale clock with decorative scalloping around its base and the Vermont State Seal ornamenting its dial. The two Vermonters—clockmaker and client—collaborated in this celebration of Vermont identity and artisanal pride.[25]

Connecticut clockmaker Benjamin Cheney's three sons, who moved up the river in the 1790s, developed a market for more cosmopolitan and costly designs. Ashael and Martin Cheney in Putney, Vermont, manufactured an engraved brass-dial clock with a lion in its tympanum. After the brothers parted company, Martin moved to Windsor where he continued to make elegant musical tall clocks and Massachusetts-style shelf clocks with kidney-shaped dials, a design pioneered by the Willard family of Massachusetts clockmakers. Martin Cheney's clock came with an engraved brass dial rather than a painted one. The clock's two-part mahogany case, possibly by Julius Barnard, with its veneered and inlaid panels on French feet, clearly indicated affluence and eastern Massachusetts ties.[26]

The bustling commercial centers of the region supported numerous rural craftsmen, financially and civically. Jedediah Baldwin's copious accounts record the life and livelihood of a rural clockmaker around the close of the eighteenth and opening of the nineteenth century. Baldwin, fresh from his own Harland training in southern New England, searched for a community to sustain his craft; first, he tried Northampton, certainly thriving but also filled with competition, then Hanover, New Hampshire, where the mix of Dartmouth College faculty and students, a printing center, and over thirteen thousand living within fifteen miles kept him busy for almost two decades. He sold fifty-five clocks at about fifty dollars apiece between 1793 and 1808 in his busy shop, mostly in the winter months. In a good year he earned over seven hundred dollars, half from his sales of clock silver and jewelry, the rest coming from repair work and his job as postmaster. He, too, could avail himself of a ready supply of clock parts from his Boston suppliers along with trading parts with other nearby clockmakers in New Hampshire and Vermont; and he had little trouble securing cases for his customers from local cabinetmakers. These were prosperous years for Baldwin. By 1811, amid the economic distress of the embargo years, his finished products dwindled to only 16 percent of his accounts, selling only one clock and a few silver spoons, while his repair and postmaster work made up the rest. It was time to move on, and Jedediah Baldwin tried his luck in the newer settled areas of western New York.[27]

According to Philip Zea, "The human proportions and animation of tall clocks appealed to the Enlightenment mind, interested in harnessing nature and valuable time." More intricate clocks appealed to the Enlightenment fascination with mechanism along with a clear nationalist message to their new American owners. By the 1790s, clocks told the tides of the oceans and played patriotic tunes. These elaborate products had dials with animated displays and were housed in highly styled neoclassical cases strewn with inlaid eagles. Few clocks were more mechanically complex and visually stunning than the musical clock made by Nichols Goddard about 1805–10 in Rutland, up the road from Windsor (see fig. 34). Goddard's career exemplifies the transmission of skill and styles into northern New England, along with the patterns of itinerancy and migration that characterized the clockmaking trade. He was born in Shrewsbury, Massachusetts; his cousin, Luther Goddard, was probably trained by Simon Willard. Goddard's 1795 diary demonstrates how a country journeyman served as the catalyst of change: he worked on clocks in four shops during the few months detailed in the account book. First, with his cousin in Westborough, he assembled precast stock and cut the wheels himself. Then he moved on to cast a clock for Northampton's Isaac Gere. By 1797, he had advanced north into a Rutland partnership with Benjamin Lord, a silversmith; their ad prominently featured "MUSICAL CLOCKS" along with other kinds of clocks—one featuring a rocking ship! The painted dials featured American shields in its spandrels, and the clock played seven tunes, including such patriotic songs as "Virginia" and "Yankee Doodle" along with such British favorites as the country dance "Careless Sally" and the military tune "The Marquis of Granby." The timepiece boasted a calendar wheel and moon dial, and the case contained a striking sequence of matched mahogany veneers, derived from New York City work. Eventually Lord concentrated on selling gold and silverwork, while Goddard made at least 150 clocks.[28]

Clockmakers, who fabricated expensive objects, were scarcer than cabinetmakers, in both the cities and the countryside. In Charlestown, New Hampshire, furniture maker Thomas Bliss set up a partnership with John Horswill in 1797. Their labels and advertisements boasted of being "Cabinet and Chair Makers from Boston"; their furniture displayed their familiarity with metropolitan design and construction, older rococo favorites as well as the newer neoclassical forms. A cherry chest of drawers with a plain front followed eastern Massachusetts practice, its deeply overhanging top attached directly to the sides of the case (fig. 39). Its façade borrowed from Boston serpentine forms, such as a chest from 1770–95 with an oxbow form and ogee bracket feet, or "swelled brackets," and the well-known George Bright chest of 1770, a rounded Boston block front with a carved fan glued to the front base; this more modest product of the best-known Boston shop of its day moved with its owner Jonathan Bowman to the hinterlands of Pownalborough, Maine, where Bowman was to look over his uncle Thomas Hancock's mercantile interests that same year, the young merchant being well equipped with a house and furnishings also sent from Boston.[29]

In New Hampshire, Bliss and Horswill followed the valley practice of fluted quarter columns along the sides of their chest, similar to a 1793 Kneeland and Adams chest from Hartford, Connecticut (fig. 40). The Hartford entrepreneurs' may have introduced stylish neoclassical furniture to the Connecticut River Valley, but this chest had more traditional roots, with its serpentine front, a design popular for much of the late eighteenth century and still seen in the 1794 plate from the English Hepplewhite pattern book. The Connecticut product also had ogee bracket feet on the rear (but fancier cabriole feet for the front) similar to the New Hampshire chest, but its columns were made from brass and

Fig. 39. Chest of drawers made by Bliss and Horswill, Walpole, New Hampshire, 1798. Cherry with pine. 35 × 41-1/8 × 21 in. Bliss and Horswill announced in their advertisements and the paper label attached to this chest that they were from Boston; the construction of this piece, for example, its overhanging lid, reveals their familiarity with the region's construction practices. Private collection. Photograph courtesy of New Hampshire Historical Society, Concord.

adapted from clock parts, a rare touch. A plainer relative is the cherry and pine Amos Denison Allen chest, from the Tracy family, with a plain front but a serpentine top and fluted chamfered corners.[30]

Bliss and Horswill advertised "Easy Chairs, Lolling Chairs, Sofas and stuff the same"; they did their own upholstering. Their labeled upholstered easy chair of mahogany with whitewood inlay had a serpentine crest, high flared wings on horizontally rolled arms (a newer fashion than the rounded cylinders of a Martha Washington–style lolling chair), and front legs featuring double stringing with light wood. The handwritten label on the bottom of the chair reads "price $16." Bliss and Horswill operated a branch in Woodstock, Vermont, with two other partners; their March 1798 ad had extended their wares with a desk, bookcases, sideboard, and clock cases, adding "work done with as much neatness as at Philadelphia, Newyork, Boston or any other Sea port." Other attributed

Fig. 40. Chest of drawers made by Samuel Kneeland and Lemuel Adams, Hartford, Connecticut, 1793. Cherry. 35-1/2 × 46-1/2 × 20-3/4 in. This chest bears a close resemblance to the serpentine-front chest that appeared in their first advertisement from 1792 in the *Connecticut Courant* that boasted "all kinds of Cabinet Work of Mahogany, And Cherry-tree, in the newest fashions" along with looking glasses. Courtesy of Winterthur Museum, Winterthur, Delaware.

pieces include a mahogany inlaid, veneered card table and two upholstered armchairs with shaped crest and concave arms. Bliss and Horswill offered a mix of the old and the new, making much of their metropolitan training to their New Hampshire customers but careful to fashion in forms modest enough for local custom. In other inland locations, such as Sturbridge, Massachusetts, upholstered furniture and sideboards still remained rare, even among the affluent residents, around the turn of the century. The wealthy Bullock family owned mahogany tables and bureaus, a sideboard and secretary, along with a clock and card table; but these fashionable forms, new to town, were most likely brought when they arrived from Salem in 1805. In other Sturbridge homes, chairs and chests increased in frequency, and an occasional desk or clock made its appearance. When gentry father Josiah Walker "fit out" his daughters at marriage between 1803 and 1811, he made sure that local cabinetmakers supplied fancy chairs, a "swell front" bureau, and card tables, with many items of cherrywood. Still, the average household did not experience a great change in its domestic goods.[31]

When Julius Barnard left Windsor to continue his northern perambulations in 1809, Thomas Boynton took over as the region's leading cabinetmaker. Born in Hartland, Vermont, he had gone for training to Boston, where his copious business records begin in 1811. Returning home in 1812, Boynton promoted himself and his metropolitan designs to his northern New England neighbors through the Windsor newspaper. He recorded his feverish activity that spring in obtaining supplies and labor for the opening of his new "Manufactory." That summer he proudly announced the opening of his "Japanned Furniture Manufactory," located a half mile from the village of Windsor, where he offered a wide variety of "CHAIRS," "Fancy and Single Top, dining or Childrens, Bamboo or Windsor," as well as tables and bureaus and clock cases, all done "in a style superior to any in the state." His accounts list the fashionable imitation bamboo work for "gilt fancy bamboo chairs." Frederick Pettes ordered a half-dozen chairs from Boynton in 1815 at a cost of three dollars apiece for his Windsor coffeehouse, which one traveler recalled as "the best Public House in Vermont." Boynton kept busy during those years, expanding his workshop, building another lathe, and adding more workbenches. By 1815, he likely employed at least a dozen workmen in the allied branches of cabinetwork, chair-making, and painting and ornamenting. The ambitious entrepreneur integrated several types of furniture production. In addition to regular employees, he secured labor for the manufactory through a network of pieceworkers and by exchanging services. Boynton did well; he reckoned at the close of his 1816 accounts that his income that year had been $1,234 and his expenses $806, leaving him a "net gain" of $428. When he subtracted clothing, debts, and other expenses, his profit was over $100.[32]

Such obvious success highlighted Windsor's economic promise and attracted competitors. In 1815, Boynton boasted that his Windsor manufactory featured experienced workmen, some with "many years of Boston and New-York" experience, making sure that the shop could "furnish those who like the fashions and taste of the metropolis with the newest patterns—Grecian, Card Work & Tea tables." Thomas Pomroy and Lemuel Hedge, one a native of Windsor and the other born in Northampton and coming from a newspaper background, countered Boynton's claim: they could "manufacture any kind of Cabinet Work, either in the French, Grecian, Arabian, Chinese, Italian, English, or American Style, almost as well as those who give their unqualified assurance that they will not permit their work to be equaled in Vermont." Boynton indignantly responded to their claims of global expertise that his firm was "not in the habit of bungling up their store in the 'Chinese,' 'Arabian,' or any other heathenish or savage 'style,' " and brought forth the following week this extraordinary parody lampooning the frequent invocation of metropolitan culture in so many provincial advertisements, which closed this remarkable exchange between cabinetmaking and journalistic rivals:

MINE ADVARTISMENT

T. BUNGLETON & CO

mak de pest CABINET VORK dat ever vas mak in dis country fore it vas settle. . . . Vone "Vorkman experiance" jus stop at dair Shop who travel all de vay thro de big town of Bosson, and the city New York, an bring all de fashun an de taste of de Tropolis on de back.

Later that year a disastrous fire destroyed the Tontine Building, and Pomroy and Hedge dissolved their partnership. Pomroy faded from sight, and Hedge manufactured cabinetwork and musical instruments for others. Boynton's ads appeared less frequently, and he eventually sold his shop in 1828. As the commercial histories of both Boynton and Pomroy and Hedge attest, residents witnessed the arrival of cabinetmakers and other artisans capable of providing the very latest cosmopolitan work. Artisans experienced a vast expansion of possibilities; rural locales offered new venues for aspiring cabinetmakers; and provincial grandees could commission grand sideboards to their desired specifications. Villages experienced cosmopolitan transformations.[33]

The Literati Gather Upriver

On 26 April 1797, Joseph Dennie wrote to Mary Green Dennie of Walpole:

Musing on the fate of my paradoxes . . . I sat out one evening for this place [Walpole]. . . . On the road I formed that plan which I have since realized, and which has attached some success. There was a press here conducted by a young man [Carlisle], honest, industrious, and then a partner of Thomas. I determined, by the agency of my pen, to convince him that I could be useful, and then—my humble knowledge of human agency taught me—I was sure he would encourage me when his own interest was the prompter. Without saying a word respecting a stipend, I wrote and gave him an essay on Wine and New Wine, and called it the Lay Preacher. It had been objected to my earliest compositions that they had been sprightly rather than moral. Accordingly, I thought I would attempt to be useful, by exhibiting truths in a plain dress to the common people.[34]

As Joseph Dennie made his way from Boston to Walpole, he created the persona of the "Lay Preacher," putting on the mantle of traditional ministerial authority, while also self-consciously fashioning his own path as a literary professional. But his role was as a new kind of cultural mediator, one who sold his literary products "in a plain dress to the common people" in the burgeoning marketplace for cultural commodities. Walpole, New Hampshire, across the Connecticut River from Windsor and Wilson's group of provincial cartographers, became another cosmopolitan community with a cluster of cabinet shops and avid consumers like many others in the hinterlands. But it also offered the remarkable spectacle of the Walpole Wits, a literary circle formed around the town's newspaper editor, Joseph Dennie, who made the town the central place for the Village Enlightenment—at least for a while. Dennie, often called the American Addison, led the local wits in fashioning an American literature—neoclassical in genre, caustic in its critique of democratization—from this rural outpost. These enterprising literary craftsmen, like other village entrepreneurs, decentralized production in an effort to attract the patronage of the commercializing countryside; they also placed a premium on "exhibiting truths" to promote the enlightenment of their neighbors and further their own national literary careers.[35]

Walpole's cosmopolitan community was a product of recent vintage. New England town settlement entered a new stage during the 1790s. Such communities as Walpole and Windsor coalesced at the town center, with stores and shops, merchants, artisans, and professionals. They became commercial villages, vividly described by former resident and author Jeremiah Mason: "This [Walpole] was a brisk, active village, with several traders, and many industrious mechanics, and two or three taverns. Walpole was, at that time, a place of more business than any in that vicinity, and was much resorted to by the people of the neighboring towns. There was also a considerable travel from a distance, passing on what was called the great river road. . . . The inhabitants of that part of the Connecticut river valley were then just passing from the rude and boisterous manners of first settlers to a more civilized, orderly, and settled state. There was more motion, life, and bustle than in the older parts of the country." Mason looked back nostalgically to a time when village centers served as cosmopolitan crossroads.[36]

Walpole was transformed by the commercial and cultural revolution that swept through the rural northern United States after the Revolution. Improvements in transportation promoted the passage of ideas as well as commodities to and from previously isolated communities. A post rider started visiting Walpole in 1784; by 1791, federal legislation established a weekly postal route from Concord, and a post office opened in town in 1795. Stagecoach lines proliferated in the hinterlands after 1800. A weekly stage traveled up and down the Connecticut River and to and from Boston in 1801. By 1803, the Boston stage ran through Walpole to Hanover (fifty miles away) three times a week. One English traveler to Walpole noted that residents were hungry for news: "It was entertaining to see the eagerness of the people on our arrival to get a sight of the last newspaper from Boston. They flocked to the post-office and the inn, and formed a variety of groups around those who were fortunate to possess themselves of a paper. There they stood, with open mouth, swallowing 'the lies of the day,' which would be as readily contradicted on the morrow."[37] The Third New Hampshire Turnpike was chartered in 1799 to channel the country produce of lower Vermont across the Connecticut River, through Walpole to Keene, and on to the state border, where it connected to the Massachusetts Turnpike that ended in Boston. The Cheshire Turnpike, chartered in 1804, crisscrossed the town. The boom in turnpike building, brief in its duration but momentous in its consequences, "visibly manifested the invisible economic network that was spreading across New England." Boston became the hub of a system with toll roads radiating outward toward Providence, Hartford, the Connecticut Valley, and New Hampshire and Vermont. Many of these chartered roads were linked together into longer channels for through traffic. Turnpike corporations were issued legislative charters that gave them the privilege to collect tolls in exchange for building and maintaining more direct and better constructed roads than the town-built routes.[38]

Village entrepreneurs tackled other obstacles to long-distance trade. Enoch Hale, the Cheshire County sheriff, received a charter in 1783 for a span over the Connecticut River at the site called the Great Falls—later, Bellows Falls—above Walpole. When completed two years later, the string bridge, the first across the Connecticut, spanned 365 feet and pushed the available bridge technology to the limit. The location of this bridge ensured that the Third New Hampshire Turnpike would pass through Walpole. The Bellows Falls Canal, the first navigation canal in the United States, bypassed the treacherous Great Falls that obstructed river traffic.[39]

The publishing pioneer Isaiah Thomas initiated Walpole's rise as a print center by creating a northern outpost there in 1793, opening a printing office, bookstore, and newspaper with a former apprentice, David Carlisle. His Walpole bookstore linked local production with the long-distance market and engaged in both wholesale and retail trade in books, almanacs, and pamphlets. In 1808, the shelves of the village bookstore contained 31,280 specified titles, along with several thousand other unspecified ones. Thomas promoted the circulation of information and distributed the mounting output of his presses by exchanging his stock with other printers; only one-sixth of the almost 1,500 titles that he produced, about a third of all of his books, had been printed in the region. Walpole's newspaper, the *New-Hampshire Journal*, which later became the *Farmer's Weekly Museum*, resembled other weeklies in its coarse paper and large format. The quotation from Benjamin Franklin on the masthead, "Where Liberty is, this is my country," and the motto following it, "The Liberty of the Press is Essential to the Rights of Man," suggest how the newspapers achieved a community of readers. Villagers could imagine a new nation by reading about the contentious debates in Congress or even debate these issues themselves in the pages of the paper during the volatile 1790s. Carlisle's paper produced nothing exceptional, until in October 1795, Joseph Dennie moved to town "under the pretense of practicing law" and began his "Lay Preacher" essays that brought Walpole's press to national attention.[40]

Dennie was born in Boston in 1768, attended Harvard College, and published his literary work in a leading Boston periodical, the *Massachusetts Magazine*. His family's concern for him to find a a career led him to look north for training in a Charlestown, New Hampshire, law office, but he kept his literary aspirations alive with the "Farrago" series of newspaper columns in the Windsor, Vermont, *Morning Ray*. When the town minister died, Dennie was pressed into service as the lay reader for the local Episcopal society. He briefly opened a law office in Charlestown, but his dreams of a metropolitan literary life brought him back to Boston as editor of a failing Boston magazine. He wrote to his mother on the way to Walpole to take up his labors for David Carlisle in 1797 and set up a provincial site for his cosmopolitan literary network.[41]

Dennie adopted the persona of the Lay Preacher, the title of his most famous literary work, to solve the problem of establishing cultural authority. In an early column, Dennie mixed his inherited traditions, announcing that he was neither Universalist nor New Light, but a "*moral* preacher," not whining from the pulpit or demanding a salary "but asking only for your reformation." From the secular side, he advocated such standard Enlightenment values as the efficacy of reason and the importance of hierarchy and order, while opposing superstitions, old customs, and especially "French fashions." In these periodical essays, a brief column or two of newsprint aimed at a wider audience than traditional literary magazines, Dennie offered "a performance, which should not resemble an austere monitor . . . but a pleasant friend, whose conversation at once beguiles and improves the hour."[42] He contributed political satires and summaries of "Foreign and Domestic Intelligence," all with a Federalist bent. He had been running the literary and political departments of the *Museum* for some time before he took over formal editorial control in April 1796, when Thomas dissolved his partnership with Carlisle.

Dennie's greatest genius was in collecting the local literati, the Walpole Wits. These young lawyers, who had moved to the upper Connecticut River area to advance their legal careers, were significant figures in the towns of the upper valley, and their poems and prose transformed what would otherwise have been a typical weekly newspaper into the leading periodical of its day. Dennie also cultivated a broader national network of amateur authors and cultural authorities through his correspondence and other efforts. The *Farmer's Museum and the New Hampshire and Vermont Journal* reached its heyday in 1796 with volume four. The last page was set off as a separate literary department called "The Dessert"; the first three pages were devoted to "Politicks, Biography, Economicks, Morals and Daily Details." Dennie announced on 24 July that the paper had subscribers in all the states of the republic except Georgia, Kentucky, and Tennessee, with over one thousand new readers added to the rolls in the last eighteen months. By December, he had two thousand subscribers, a larger circulation than any other village newspaper in the United States.[43]

The Walpole Wits and other Federalist literati were Janus-faced with regard to the new commercial order and its attendant cultural changes. Neoclassical satire assumed that its values would be understood by a republic of like-minded readers, enabling it to ridicule those outside its clearly drawn borders. Humor was directed at those who practiced a "false elevation" of language. The American neoclassical poets preached correctness and regularity in expression and took social and political issues as their focus; their art was to be a public art. Ironically, their satirical portrait of post-Revolutionary society was subverted for a series of aesthetic and social reasons.[44]

Dennie collaborated with Royall Tyler, poet, playwright, novelist, and fellow lawyer.[45] The Walpole Wits often resorted to satirical representations of how American culture and knowledge itself had become debased in this "leveling" age. Dennie and Tyler wrote literary "advertisements" under the title "Colon & Spondee," parodying a country store's announcement of its stock, attacking the common people's desire for their inappropriate display of higher learning. "American Learning, 1798" is a comic squib about an arriviste speculator who, having amassed a fortune, has scholarly aspirations and sends a Boston bookseller the following letter: "Sur i wants to by sum Buks—as I am prodig house fond of larnen—plese to send by the Bear here 5 hunder Dollars woth of the *hansumest* you have—Yoors &x.—." The republic of letters, with its hierarchy of talents that gave the Wits their status among the second generation of New England authors, was in danger of being toppled by a mobocracy of illiterate hoi polloi.[46]

Dennie and his contributors represented the tumultuous times with an apocalyptic tone in their public pronouncements. Tyler's "Ode Composed for the Fourth of July," ostensibly a patriotic and familiar form of verse chosen for celebrating the new nation's birthday, published on 19 July 1796, descends into drunken disorder and gloomy political prognostications:

> Squeak the fife, and beat the drum,
> Independence Day is come!!!
> Let the roasting pig be bled,
> Quickly twist off the cokerel's head,
> Quickly rub the pewter platter
> Heap the nutcakes, fried in batter

Tyler catalogues the tempting treats being prepared as the participants become boisterous and spirited.

> *Independent*, staggering Dick,
> A noggin mix of *swinging thick*;
> Sal, put on your russet skirt,
> Jotham, get your *broughten* shirt
> Today we dance to tiddle diddle.

The poem concludes with the end of the festivities and the specter of the French Revolution's guillotine linked to the homegrown Jacobin "Demos." This glorious "INDEPENDENT DAY" is less a cause for celebration than a cause for alarm. New England's religious and republican institutions seemed precarious; for Dennie and Tyler, disorder, heightened by the mobbish uprisings in the Massachusetts and Pennsylvania backcountry, always threatened to engulf the republic.[47]

The sharpest attack on the democratic errors of the age came in the Federalist mock pastorals of country customs and characters that often appeared in the *Farmer's Weekly Museum*. Thomas Green Fessenden, the son of Walpole's minister, introduced New England village characters and vernacular speech through native verse. Fessenden worked his way through Dartmouth College by teaching school and publishing poems in the *Museum*. His first published poem, "The Country Lovers, or Jonathan Jolthead's Courtship with Miss Sally Snapper," written in 1795 and published as a broadside at the Walpole press in 1796 while he was still at Dartmouth, won Nathaniel Hawthorne's praise as an "original and truly Yankee effusion." It mounted a savage critique of the claims of political and cultural democratization by lampooning the low manners and language of Jonathan Jolthead, a rustic, naive, and ultimately pitiful figure, who became the model for a standard literary type. These cosmopolitan aesthetes evoked the Yankee yeoman as their voice, heightening their reliance on the village scene to perform their cultural work. In the *Museum*, Fessenden depicted rural folk with condescension, laughing at the discrepancies between the intended meaning of the high-flown rhetoric used by the village character and the shared meaning understood by the more educated author and reader. In "Peter Periwinkle, to Tabitha Towzer," the country lover begins his description of his beloved with rustic analogies:

> My Tabitha Towzer is fair
> No Guinea pig ever was neater,
> Like a hackmatak[48] slender and spare,
> And sweet as a musk rat, or sweeter!

"Pining, poetical PETER" continues his incongruous comparisons of different parts of Tabitha's anatomy with barnyard animals. These earthy metaphors render her a grotesque object, quite the opposite of what the country lover intends as passionate romantic statements. Fessenden pokes fun at the efforts of the common folk to draw upon the conventions and vocabulary of romantic verse. Fessenden developed his satiric attacks on the democratization under way in American culture by versifying about the false pretensions of rural learning in "'Love's Labour Lost' Peter Pumpkin-head defeated by Tabitha Towzer." This piece was an expansion of his earlier satire on rural courting rituals, where the suitor—showing off an education obtained through reading Morse's *Geography* and a few novels—tells his beloved of the promising future that awaits him after spending a mere month at an academy. In the notes to the poem, Fessenden writes that the new middle classes of New England society are sending all their sons off to get advanced education, "too many for the good of the community." Their smattering of English and Latin grammar makes them unfit to return to their "former laborious occupations," so they attempt "to *crowd themselves* into the learned professions."[49]

The neoclassical authors satirized the provincial, creating a literature that, because of its vivid vernacular detail, in the long run restored provincial culture to a central place. Longing for local society infused with face-to-face social relations, post-Revolutionary authors created an imagined community for both New England and the new nation through the commercialized marketplace for print based to a large part on New England village characters and landscapes. This literary reinvention of New England used a variety of traditional genres as well as innovative institutions in the service of conservative, even reactionary, social goals. Ironically, the Village Enlightenment in New England led to the democratization of knowledge that made possible the crafting of new identities for aspiring authors and rural readers alike, moving New England further away from that idealized "golden age of homespun." Their creation of the new Yankee character achieved an indigenous transformation of "high" neoclassicism in their prose and poetry into a homegrown hybrid form, published in the upper Connecticut Valley, similar in its process of translation and mediation to the Hayes sideboard. Dennie located his effort at creating a "virtual metropolis," as historian Catherine O'Donnell Kaplan calls it, in Walpole, at a time when the United States had no literary capital.[50]

Walpole and Windsor were unique places, yet they represent the broader transformation of provincial towns into cosmopolitan commercial centers. Newly settled communities quickly developed commercial villages connected through a network of turnpikes to Boston and New York. Ideas and objects traveled in both directions. Walpole's Joseph Dennie made the *Farmer's Weekly Museum* into a central source for neoclassical literary productions. In many villages, printers and portraitists, cabinetmakers and clockmakers could supply the decorations desired by the emerging provincial gentry, such as Elijah Boardman or Elijah West.

Useful and Ornamental

James Wilson and his Windsor County neighbors formed a remarkable circle of mapmakers and engravers whose products graced the walls of schoolhouses and homes across Vermont and the entire nation. We sometimes picture a man like Wilson as a solitary genius, but he was well supplied with coworkers. From the tiny villages of Greenbush and Felchville, a cluster of more than a half-dozen rural artisans, printers, and engravers produced visual representations of Vermont, in maps, prints, and illustrated books. The men and women of this "Greenbush group" were linked by partnerships, marriages, apprenticeships, and collaborations. Through their intellectual, financial, and family connections, they helped weave Enlightenment and edification into the commercialization of the countryside.[51]

Most maps before the 1790s were compiled by British cartographers and engraved and published in London. American provincial elites had followed British customs as "maps, charts, atlases, and globes became important symbols of the enlightened gentlemen." Newspaper ads and occasional paintings testified to that high regard. Leading London map and print seller Carrington Bowles's 1790 catalogue featured plans of London as "useful and elegant furniture for screens, halls, large rooms, stair cases, &c," as the rococo design elements of many eighteenth-century maps added to their attraction as decorative household items. Many maps hung in the Williamsburg Governor's Palace. During the eighteenth century, the audience for maps, atlases, and other cartographic products expanded beyond the elite, David Bosse has found in his study of over 1,500 probate inventories. Informational and commercial purposes were also important. Arthur Dobbs celebrated his appointment as the governor of North Carolina by commissioning a portrait by William Hoare; with a globe in the background, Dobbs grasps a compass in his right hand, reminding viewers of his former station as surveyor-general of Ireland, and holds a map of North Carolina in his left. These cartographic devices suggest his office was one of authority, knowledge, and power. Sharing those assumptions and aspirations, Ralph Earl and his sitters frequently included maps and globes in his provincial portraits as well.[52]

State maps were the first American cartographic efforts after independence, and Vermont became the first state with a map, according to cartographic scholar Walter Ristow: William Blodget's *A Topographical Map of the State of Vermont*. After keeping a store, operating an iron forge, and serving as a land agent in Bennington, Blodget returned to Connecticut determined to turn his knowledge of Vermont's terrain to profit. Vermont's territory was contested by New Hampshire and New York, and Blodget's map bolstered their land claims. Armed with the manuscript town surveys of Ira Allen, the state's first surveyor-general, he turned to Yale's Ezra Stiles for help with "the scale of Lat. & Longitude." Amos Doolittle engraved the final product, and the *New Haven Gazette* informed "friends of American improvement in Arts and Manufacture" that the map was "seldom equaled" by European artists and hailed its accuracy and elegance, while making the nationalist appeal that the map "does honour to the genius and ability of our countrymen." The imposing map marked the new American landscape with towns, roads, mills, meetinghouses, forts, county boundaries, and the houses of famous Vermonters, even noting the site of the failed "Blodgets Forge."[53]

Blodget's map did little to enhance his finances, the story for many post-Revolutionary cartographic entrepreneurs as they struggled to supplant imported products, a similar pattern to print in general. Scottish surveyor James Whitelaw fared better. Whitelaw came to North America in 1773 as an agent for the Scots-American Company of Farmers, one of the many groups looking to expand settlement along the upper Connecticut River Valley after the Seven Years' War. Whitelaw secured half the township of Ryegate from its primary owner, the Reverend John Witherspoon, otherwise engaged as president of Princeton. He helped lay out a military road when General Washington was looking for the shortest route from Boston to Canada during the War for Independence. When peace came, he served as Ira Allen's deputy and succeeded Allen as Vermont's surveyor-general. From the surveys of the state's towns, he compiled *A Correct Map of the State of Vermont*, to which he added details about the state's commercial and manufacturing activities (fig. 41). The legend on Whitelaw's map displayed such familiar icons as forts and meetinghouses, but he added grist-, saw-, and fulling mills, along with grammar schools and other signs of industrial and cultural improvement. The map's large cartouche contained a delightful pastoral scene that featured the ongoing work of agricultural development taking place throughout the state: an improving farm with its cleared fields, a stump in foreground, and a two-story farmhouse in the back. Many of the early national maps and atlases featured accuracy and up-to-date content in their advertisements alongside older appeals to decorative design (see fig. 42).[54]

About 1810, Isaac Eddy established a shop in the little hamlet of Greenbush in a western corner of Weathersfield, another river town lying between Walpole and Windsor. Eddy and his son, their apprentices, and their business partners turned this remote village into a significant center of early national engraving, especially cartographic work. The Eddys produced an amazing volume of maps, illustrated books, and even globes. Isaac Eddy was born in Greenbush in 1777. The precocious nineteen-year-old entered into print with the oration *On Fatality and Predestination*, apologizing that "one in my humble condition, and of my rank" should even presume to deal with these cosmic issues. His best-known contributions were his engravings. In 1810, when Windsor publishers planned the "First Vermont Edition" of the Bible "in a style of decency and elegance . . . so every Family, in this state, will feel an ambition to be furnished with a copy of the first Bible printed in Vermont," they secured Eddy to engrave seven plates. That same year, he contributed the frontispiece, a detailed foldout engraving of the new Vermont state prison building that featured prominently in the newspaper announcement of the publication of John Russell's *An Authentic History of the Vermont State Prison*. The book celebrated this important Windsor public institution, which was awarded to the town as a consolation prize after it lost the battle to become the state capital to Montpelier at a time when towns competed to secure important institutions to improve their prospects. Russell, another enterprising nineteen-year-old, advertised the volume as an effort to secure the necessary funds "in obtaining a collegial education." The venture proved successful for all parties, and Russell entered Middlebury College the next year.

Isaac Eddy's ambitions expanded as he made a career out of the distribution of knowledge in the countryside, as well as the construction of rational systems of organizing information for sale to his neighbors. Eddy purchased a printing

Fig. 41. James Whitelaw and James Wilson, *A Correct Map of the State of Vermont: from actual survey, exhibiting the county and town lines, rivers, lakes, ponds, mountains, meetinghouses, mills, public roads, &c.*, 1810. 87 × 59 cm. James Wilson updated James Whitelaw's original 1796 state map. Dartmouth College Library, Hanover, New Hampshire.

Fig. 42. This detail of the cartouche of Wilson's 1810 map (and also the original 1796 one) celebrated agrarian improvement with its dominant pastoral scenery. Dartmouth College Library, Hanover, New Hampshire.

press and embarked on a modest program of imprints. Among his ten items, several were religious texts or written by Universalist authors; however, he did not neglect children's books or schoolbooks, such as Lewis Robinson's *Select and Original Dialogues*. His most ambitious collaboration was with James Wilson on *Chronology Delineated / To Illustrate the History of Monarchical Revolutions*. These two encyclopedists mapped out the history of the world in two 36-by-21-inch sheets to be placed together, graphically representing the growth of the mostly European nations from the time of Adam to the present. Lines soared upward from the Jews, Athens, Babylonia and other branches, with the English branch splitting at the very top to show American independence in 1776. An elaborate plan explained how the diagram worked. Eddy's prospectus for his "Chronological Chart," offered for sale by the "Hundred, Dozen, or Single," boasted of its sophisticated European pedigree. The advertisement for the new American edition was addressed to "Patrons of the Fine Arts," offering an American audience "useful, amusing and ornamental" information.[55]

Eddy and his fellow rural engravers set out on a course of improving their fortunes while making available geographical materials to individuals, families, and schools. In January 1810, fresh from chronicling world history and fabricating his first globes, James Wilson took on the engraving of a new edition of James Whitelaw's *A Correct Map of the State of Vermont*. Whitelaw had sent a printed broadside around the state asking for such alterations and additions as "the direction of Turnpikes and other public roads." When the second edition appeared that September, it reflected those concerns with a new "CENSUS of VERMONT A.D. 1810" along with a revised legend showing courthouses and other public buildings, post routes, turnpike roads, and "Turnpikes granted but not compleated." Whitelaw and Wilson's work maintained its place as the most accurate representation of Vermont of its time and sold at the popular price of $2.50. The two also looked beyond the state, engraving Whitelaw's *Map of the Northern Part of the United States and Southern Part of the Canadas* (1813).[56]

Whitelaw's Vermont map had a long life among other Windsor County engravers. Publisher Ebenezer Hutchinson bought the new editions in 1821 and 1824, as well as an 1829 edition of Whitelaw's northern U.S. map. In new editions, a vision of place transformed by enterprise and industry gradually replaced the pastoral scenes depicted in 1795 and 1810 (fig. 42, 43). Two cartouches graced the 1824 map: one depicted the thriving village of Montpelier from the mill point; the other was a fantastic scene looking west. The wilderness with its thunderous waterfall and roving wildlife was divided by an earthen urn with the map's title, the state seal, and an eagle above the whole, leading to a cultivated scene with a farmer and his livestock in the foreground, a farmer crossing the fields with a plow in the middle ground, and then a river with a puffing steamboat going by. An urban scene stood across the shore.

Ebenezer Hutchinson had set up as a copperplate printer in Quechee Village near Hartford and Woodstock. He employed Hartford native Moody Morse Peabody to engrave a *Map of Massachusetts, Connecticut and Rhode Island* for him in 1819. Hutchinson advertised that his "factory in Quechee Village" did copperplate printing and combmaking; he also sold maps, "Masonick Aprons, and Salisbury's Patent Window-springs." Peabody's earliest work was a frontispiece to Susanna Rowson's *Charlotte Temple*, an enormously popular novel, printed in 1815 in Windsor, which has led to speculation that Hutchinson also owed his training to Eddy's shop. He engraved the 1821 and 1824 Vermont maps for Hutchinson and later did portraits of Washington and Monroe, as well as book illustrations.

When Zadock Thompson, another young Windsor County native with a passion for natural history, set out to produce a *Gazetteer of the State of Vermont* in 1824, he supplied a small folding map and several smaller town maps, the only illustrations for this prodigious compendium of three hundred pages.

Fig. 43. When Ebenezer Hutchinson republished the well-known 1810 Whitelaw and Wilson map of Vermont in 1824 (*Vermont from Actual Survey*), the changed cartouches highlighted the new urban industrial sector. The 1824 map had two cartouches, with the agrarian world receding before new scenes of mill sites, steamboats, and cityscapes. Dartmouth College Library, Hanover, New Hampshire.

Thompson devoted his life to the study of Vermont, while earning a living as a schoolmaster, clergyman, and college professor. *The Gazetteer*, his first book, contained an account of every town and pond in the state and cost only a dollar. History, weather, geology, archaeology, and natural history made an appearance in his *History of Vermont, Natural, Civil, and Statistical* (1842). The reduced Vermont map owed much to its larger cousin, the original Whitelaw map, which also turned up as the frontispiece of Samuel Read Hall's *Child's Assistant to a Knowledge of the Geography and History of Vermont* (1827). Geographical instruction started early in this "little book," which supplied a concise account of a child's "own town, county, or state." Hall started with the definition of a township, ranged over Vermont's landscape and natural history, its forms of government and history, the employment of the people and the institutions of learning: two colleges and twenty-two academies, sixteen hundred common schools, and newspapers in almost all large towns so its people are well informed and "desirious of improvement."[57]

The Greenbush circle introduced new map styles and advanced production techniques. Another Eddy apprentice, George White, struck out on his own with smaller and less detailed maps of the two states straddling the Connecticut River. Born near Greenbush in 1797, the teenager entered the printing and engraving shop of Eddy as an apprentice and took over when his master left the area. He belonged to the same generation as Eddy's son Oliver. Both young men worked across the river in Walpole where O. T. Eddy engraved a map of New Hampshire in 1817 with a striking cartouche of Bellows Falls and its famous bridge. The younger Eddy later became a portrait painter, while White worked briefly for Ebenezer Hutchinson in Quechee on the large Vermont maps. When Hutchinson left publishing and the elder Eddy moved to Troy, New York, White took over his former master's small business, which included making paint and "a very superior quality of engraving ink." He served as the village postmaster to supplement his income. The part-time engraver did a variety of work; he produced two charming prints of *Kitty* (which appeared on a Metropolitan Museum of Art postcard in 1969 as the work of an unknown American artist) and *The Happy Family* (of dogs). His best-known maps traced town borders, river courses, and railroad lines. These copperplate intaglio engravings did not supply dates of settlements or icons of institutions, but they gave northern New Englanders with modest pocketbooks the opportunity to own their own maps. White moved a few miles north to Felchville, a larger community, to continue his map work; later he engraved portraits of Millard Fillmore and James Buchanan for a New York City company.[58]

Windsor County's most notorious engraver worked from the confines of a prison cell. Counterfeiting had become a real problem in antebellum America; a counter economy based on banknotes forged for the great number of financial institutions that issued paper money symbolized, according to historian Steven Mihm, the new capitalist economy and also provided opportunities for skillful artisans.[59] Christian Meadows, a British immigrant, landed in Boston and worked as a banknote engraver until he and a quantity of banknotes and dies disappeared in January 1849. Meadows claimed that he had been "led astray" by William "Bristol Bill" Warburton, a well-known bank robber and counterfeiter. The two were caught and ended up in the county jail, but they made a spectacular and nearly successful escape. Their subsequent trial, during which Warburton stabbed the state's attorney, captivated the public. Meadows was convicted and sent to the Vermont State Prison in Windsor, the very institution celebrated by Isaac Eddy. The prison's accommodating warden allowed Meadows to continue his trade; he permitted the prisoner to journey to Hanover, New Hampshire, in 1851 to sketch the campus of Dartmouth College and engrave a fine print of the college buildings. When the directors of the New Hampshire State Agricultural Society desired an engraved diploma, they inquired in Boston for the finest engraver in New England, only to find out that he resided nearby in Windsor's prison. Meadows sought only a modest compensation, but enlisted the society's notables in an effort to secure his pardon. A Meadows engraving of the New Hampshire birthplace of Daniel Webster featured an allegorical scene with Ceres, the goddess of liberty; numerous domestic animals; and an elm tree, the "Webster Elm," that grew beside the secretary of state's birthplace. A copy sent to Webster received the reply, "This is a true resemblance of the tree at my birthplace. Who is the engraver that has done this? Where does he dwell? I have been searching for such a man. We want him at the State Department to engrave some maps." Upon being told this man was a convict, he asked: "Why do you bury your best talents in your state prisons? Is Meadows an old offender?" Webster's letter, along with the support of other notables, resulted in Meadows's pardon in 1853. He settled in Windsor, but State Department patronage was not forthcoming since Webster was out of office. Meadows kept busy engraving catalogs and billheads with views of academies and other local institutions, along with occasional book illustrations.[60]

Lewis Robinson, another product of Eddy's workshop, established the first "map manufactory" in Windsor County. In the second quarter of the nineteenth century, Robinson became the leading purveyor of maps in northern New England and a major producer in the entire United States, all without leaving his hometown. Born in 1793 in Reading, Robinson was raised on his father's farm and had only a basic education before becoming an apprentice. The enterprising young man entertained several independent ventures while under Eddy's tutelage, including the publication of educational books and illustrated pamphlets. He even authored one: *Select and Original Dialogues, Orations and Single Pieces, designed for the use of Schools*, along with engraving a Masonic apron, printed on silk, all published under his pseudonym, "Roberson." Robinson found his greatest success in his cartographic ventures. He set up his own shop in South Reading that specialized in copperplate printing, map publishing, and scripture paintings. He, too, reprinted Amos Doolittle's *United States Map* (1813) in 1825, adding the new western states. Three years later he produced his own *Map of Vermont and New Hampshire*. These local productions of regional maps were "steady sellers" for the next few decades.[61]

Robinson's map factory remained in the little village of South Reading for thirty-eight years, and maps of Vermont and New Hampshire remained his chief products. They ranged in price from thirty-three cents to three dollars.

Robinson's scale of operations vastly outstripped his Windsor County counterparts. He expanded his business with individual state maps and an ambitious *Map of the United States* (1833) that spanned four sheets. He established an office in Akron, Ohio, where a series of maps of the midwestern states were produced; a Lower Canada branch followed. Robinson also handled lithographs and other engraved prints in his shop. He was an eager entrepreneur; his other enterprises included a store in South Reading, a starch mill, and a wooden-ware manufactory. Robinson marketed his products through an extensive network of peddlers and traveling salesmen. His accounts listed fifteen peddlers who sold maps, lithographs, and an occasional set of suspenders. His correspondence with John Emery of Andover, New Hampshire, ranged over the itinerant's rentals of the plates of New Hampshire and Vermont maps, an application for credit for damaged maps, and his 1850 offer to supply Robinson with local information about railroad improvements. Robinson's maps answered the call for accurate and up-to-date information. Less grand than the Whitelaw productions in size and detail, without magnificent cartouches or tables of icons, they set off the counties in varying hues, forming a colorful patchwork of northern New England in such utilitarian and readily available versions as the 1845 *Map of Vermont and New Hampshire* (fig. 44). Lewis Robinson sold nearly six thousand maps and ten thousand prints between 1840 and 1855 and made his little village "a thriving backwoods center of commercial American cartography," as Vermont cartographic historian J. Kevin Graffagnino has written.[62]

This cluster of print shops and cartographic entrepreneurs, linked by a network of kin and apprentices, began by offering local products at a variety of sizes and prices, but moved on to more specialized work. Their maps and engravings displayed images of the new cultural order: the academies and turnpikes that dotted the landscape were also the means by which these geographic products secured an audience. Cartographic commodities promoted the diffusion of knowledge and a pride in the new nation's growth—all from the workshops of provincial Vermont.

James Wilson continued to operate his shop in Bradford, but eventually success induced him to open an urban shop in Albany, New York. Wilson was not content to rest after his singular achievement in producing a globe; he kept track of cartographic advances and promoted new products. He recorded his first sales: "January 18, 1810, sold Mr. Wellman 1 globe. Jan. 25 sold Judge Niles 1 globe." Justice Nathaniel Niles of West Fairlee, sitting on the Vermont Supreme Court, must have helped Wilson by his stature and circle of acquaintances, for Wilson recorded the sale of seventeen globes on the same loose leaf of an account book, with eleven following the transaction with Niles. Those first globes had undated labels stating, "A new Terrestrial Globe on which the Tracts

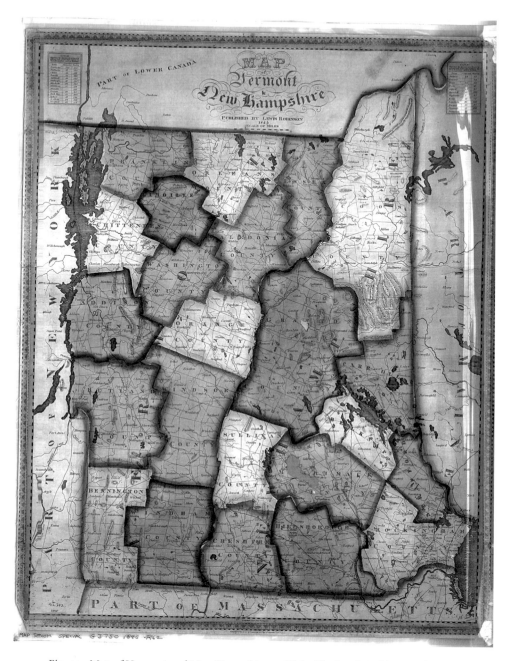

Fig. 44. *Map of Vermont and New Hampshire,* published by Lewis Robinson of South Reading, Vermont, 1845. 25-3/8 × 19-5/8 in. Evans Map Room, Dartmouth College Library, Hanover, New Hampshire.

and New Discoveries are drawn from the Accurate Observations made by Capt. Cook, Furneau, Phipps etc. By J. Wilson, Vermont," and contained a skeletal geographic depiction of North America. While the eastern coastal area was crowded with the names of the states and the major Atlantic coastal cities from St. Augustine to Halifax, Wilson left the vast interior of the continent bare from the Mississippi and Missouri river system west to the Pacific Coast.

Events deep in the Pacific and across the North American continent captured Wilson's imagination, and as he gained new information, he corrected his globes. On *A NEW AMERICAN TERRESTRIAL GLOBE on which the PRINCIPAL PLACES of the KNOWN WORLD are ACCURATELY laid down with the traced attempts of CAPTAIN COOK to discover a Southern Continent by James Wilson, 1811*, Wilson filled out the continent with place names and river systems as compared with his 1810 product. Elaborate mountain ranges ran across the southwest. To the northwest stood Nootka along with Quadra and Vancouver listed in parentheses, indicating the recent Spanish and British voyages to the Gulf of Georgia (near present-day Vancouver). He also replaced archaic eighteenth-century usages, such as the long "s," and the Western Ocean, Eastern Ocean, and Great South Sea became the Atlantic (fig. 45). These large globes sold well at fifty dollars a pair for the thirteen-inch terrestrial and celestial versions. He exhibited them in Boston along with other examples of his work, such as wall maps. Wilson secured his supplies of paper locally in Bradford as well as from Boston. His well-constructed globes, framed in ash and furnished with a brass quadrant, came packed in neatly planed and hinged pine boxes.[63]

In 1817, Wilson's sons opened a factory in Albany, New York, to meet the increased demand for their globes. The eldest son, Samuel, wrote to his father from Albany in March, as the Hudson River gradually cleared of ice: "I want to have some Globes finished by the first of June," inquiring about receiving some maps in return for sending the globes. A signed agreement between another son, John, and his father dated 1818 stated that the elder Wilson would provide "all materials required for manufacturing Globes" in Albany for one-third the profits, and "John will manage the business, employ all necessary workmen, and have two third[s] in exchange." On the new edition "with additions to 1819," the Floridas appeared as a U.S. territory and the new nation's contested northeastern and northwestern boundaries are interpreted conservatively. Soon the label reflected the latest developments in American geography and Wilson's establishment: "The American Nine Inch Terrestrial Globe exhibiting with the greatest possible accuracy Places of the Earth with New Discoveries & Political Alterations down to the present Period 1819 By J. Wilson & Co. Albany." Wilson kept abreast of the United States' territorial expansion.

Knowing there was a market for inexpensive cartographic objects, the Wil-

Fig. 45. James Wilson, detail of "A NEW AMERICAN TERRESTRIAL GLOBE on which the PRINCIPAL PLACES of the KNOWN WORLD are ACCURATELY laid down with the traced attempts of CAPTAIN COOK to discover a Southern Continent," 1811. Author's photograph. Hand-colored paper gores over papier-mâché and plaster, mounted on a wooden stand with four legs supporting a wooden circle with mounted zodiacal paper and a brass meridian ring; 34 cm in diameter. While James Wilson's 1810 globe had few places between the center of the North American continent and the Pacific coast, he had filled out the continent with place names by 1811. Library of Congress, Washington, D.C.

sons even produced three-inch terrestrial and celestial globes after their brother David, a skilled engraver, joined them in Albany. Later he went to New York City, where he became a successful miniature painter (plate 4). Citizens of the new nation eager to display their knowledge of the world could easily afford these miniature spheres.[64]

The Wilsons' first advertisements in 1820 and 1822 boasted to "the scientific community" about the "ELEGANT GLOBES" available from their "American Globe Manufactory," highlighting the "recent improvement in the elegance of the execution" as well as "the geographical and political correctness of the delineations." Superior to the best European examples, the Wilsons' globes were available at "Very low prices, particularly to schools and academies" and were

"Able to be transported anywhere in the country." The 1822 globes introduced engraved vignettes instead of text labels: an allegory of Columbia sat on the left, holding dividers over a large globe that displayed the Western hemisphere and behind which perched an eagle holding in its beak a ribbon inscribed "E Pluribus Unum."

Despite their success, Samuel reminded his father in a long 1822 letter that "the work is laborious" and "it is a life of bondage to be so strictly confined." He hoped that a few years more would yield him several thousand dollars, the opportunity to purchase a great little farm, and to go into the mercantile business, for then "you might have me for a Neighbor." But their total sales that year did not exceed $1,200. Orders were slow with their Boston agents, making them "even more dependent on the New York Market." He recounted how the previous year they had "commenced 400 Globes" in great anticipation, but they had finished and sold only 100 of them. The remaining 300 globes would be completed that winter, tying up all of their savings and leaving only a small remainder for the "necessaries of a domestic life." The son reminded the father how different life in the city was from the farm, "where every necessary of life must be bot and the cash paid for it." Still, they were finishing up some "18 inch Globes," and Samuel anticipated the completion "in stile" and success. He urged his father to visit Albany and keep on hand a ready stock of globes in Vermont for sale or trade. In fact, James's papers chronicle his building and finishing of "a brick house" with spiral stairs in the front in Bradford, with the brick suppliers and joiners taking some terrestrial globes as part of their pay.[65]

An 1828 broadside advertised the Wilsons' full range of three-inch to thirteen-inch globes on mahogany pedestal stands: "Great Pains have been taken, in the plates for these globes, to make them elegant as well as useful. . . . The correctness of the geographical divisions, &c. of *our own country*, and the western hemisphere, renders these globes more useful and interesting to the American geographer, and gives them a decided preference to imported globes, on which this continent is greatly misrepresented" (fig. 46). The celestial companion contained nearly five thousand stars, including some new constellations not found on any competitor's product. Wilson's globes were also less expensive than imported ones, the broadside boasted, "so schools and academies, even private families, could take advantage." The "popularity and usefulness of Geographical and Astronomical science" were so apparent to potential customers that no explanation was necessary.[66]

James Wilson had been withdrawing from direct business responsibilities and brought twenty-four-year-old Cyrus Lancaster, a Dartmouth graduate and schoolteacher in the Bradford Academy, into the firm around 1826. Cyrus took charge after Samuel and John died in 1833; the next year he married Samuel's

Fig. 46. Advertisement, J. Wilson & Sons, *Wilson's American Globes*, Albany, 1828. This 1828 broadside boasted of the greater accuracy and lower price of "Wilson's American Globes" as compared to their imported competition. Library of Congress, Washington, D.C.

widow. The founder remained involved. Son-in-law Cyrus wrote to James in 1834 that he was busy putting paper upon the globes, but "no papers printed for balls [globes] since you were here," and awaited James's arrival as soon as possible to help with selection of papers in local warehouses since the new papers were not taking colors well. James kept busy with his studies in geography and astronomy. A local historian described how he designed and built with his own hands a planetarium, "a machine which finely illustrated the diurnal and annual revolutions of the earth, the cause of the successive seasons, and the sun's place for every day of the year." In 1862, the eighty-three-year-old was still active; he engraved the copperplate for a print of the months of the year and signs of the zodiac, the year of his death.[67]

Neoclassical designs came from local resources and ornaments as well as from imported concepts and printed forms. Such highly symbolic household items as globes and sideboards enabled producers and consumers to participate in processes of cultural integration and hybridization. Artifacts did not just stand in for particular values, they could be understood in a variety of ways when displayed in the shop or the home and allowed their owners to negotiate claims of inclusion in certain groups and perhaps distance from others. However, these critical domestic commodities that were fabricated in provincial workshops did not just copy their coastal cousins but rather were melded from cosmopolitan and other stylistic sources into something different. Artifacts figured centrally in these dynamic and complex fields of cultural negotiation. Cultural historians must learn to draw on material artifacts and sensory experience to understand them rather than just see them as texts to be "read"; they must be "seen" and experienced as three-dimensional artifacts.[68]

Wilson's globes represented an America in which New Englanders and other consumers could see themselves. Such three-dimensional objects expressed in spatial terms and material form the aspirations of the craftsmen and consumers who constructed the Village Enlightenment. They remind us that we sometimes too readily dismiss the countryside as a source of information and innovation. The modern model of an urban monopoly on curiosity and sophistication fails to capture the intellectual world of James Wilson and his neighbors. Globes and other cartographic instruments served well as an exemplary archive of knowledge, quickly adding the "discoveries" of such explorers as Captain Cook and modeling an ideal: the creation of a natural and orderly society. Commerce and culture came together in this transformation, as men and women made a business of providing cultural commodities in the hinterlands. Entrepreneurs like Wilson took advantage of the curiosity fostered in schoolrooms and popular books and helped promote the democratization of knowledge as well as the commercialization of the countryside. In the post-Revolutionary period, this widespread movement not only made European colonials into Americans but also shifted the center of that culture from its familiar settings in Philadelphia, New York, and Boston into inland communities. Bradford, Vermont, a town perched along the upper Connecticut River where James Wilson set up his globe-making shop, seems an unlikely site for globalism. The farmer-blacksmith's remarkable saga attests to one of many rural savants navigating among the arts and sciences to produce new commercial goods and cultural identities.

CHAPTER FOUR

Itinerants and Inventors

Eli Terry and the Wooden Shelf Clock

When Eli Terry introduced the wooden-movement shelf clock in 1816, he revolutionized the American clock industry and the very concept of this household object (fig. 47). While this simple clock, an unadorned box with the numerals painted on the glass, seems an unlikely signpost in America's industrial history, Terry and his fellow Connecticut entrepreneurs transformed what had been a luxury product into a mass-consumer item through a combination of marketing and mechanical innovations. Most eighteenth-century clocks were expensive objects fashioned out of metal by skilled artisans. The possession of a tall clock signified wealth; it was the most valuable item in a house, as we have seen in the Reverend Ebenezer Devotion's household inventory. Terry's innovations extended from production through marketing, building on previous experiments and bringing clocks to a wider range of consumers. He reengineered the inner workings of the clock movement. Clockmakers, such as Benjamin Cheney, had been tinkering with ways to manufacture cheaper wooden timepieces for several decades. Terry began mass production; he reworked the system of manufacture by using water power to replace human effort, as well as by standardizing parts. Then he invented a new kind of clock. A cluster of Connecticut

Facing page: Fig. 47. Box clock made by Seth Thomas from Eli Terry's patent, ca. 1816. 20 × 14 × 4-1/2 in. National Museum of American History, Smithsonian Institution, Washington, D.C.

Fig. 48. Eli Terry, shelf clock, pillar-and-scroll style, ca. 1816. 28-7/8 × 17-3/8 × 4-1/8 in. "Eli Terry, Plymouth Ct." Printed on paper label. Yale University Art Gallery, Bequest of Olive L. Dann, New Haven.

artisans accelerated production in clock shops and manufactories. Most important, Terry developed a new system for marketing. The box clock or its successor, the pillar-and-scroll shelf clock (fig. 48), became the standard timepiece in American parlors during the second quarter of the nineteenth century; clockmakers used itinerant merchants or peddlers to bring these mass-produced goods signifying status to a vast rural market that extended as far as the rural South. That revolution in the manufacturing, marketing, and consumption of clocks, chairs, and portraits is the subject of Chapters 4, 5, and 6.[1]

Other crafts followed the clockmakers' path of innovation and itinerancy. The furniture industry was built on an extensive base of rural work sites—sawmills roughing out parts, chair shops for assembly, and farmhouses filled with cane seaters—rather than on production at a single site (Chapter 5). The division of labor facilitated the proliferation of work sites and production totals. Innovative chairmakers joined the sturdy and standardized frame of Windsor chairs and the colorful painted surface of fancy chairs, bringing these innovations together in the familiar mass-produced form of the Hitchcock chair. In portrait making, itinerant artist-artisans made a greater number of portraits (Chapter 6). Some provided inexpensive profiles, while others made more expensive portraits available to rural residents. Provincial portraitists pioneered the rapid manufacture of likenesses using stylized designs and, increasingly, mechanical methods of production, which standardized their portraits, but they distinguished their subjects by including personal items. This cycle of consumption was part of a general "cultural revolution" marked by a remarkable proliferation not only of paintings but also of items of all kinds that found their way to farmhouse doors.

These new provincial products were not merely cheaper versions of former luxury products of metropolitan origin. Artisans created such new forms as Terry's shelf clock by taking advantage of new materials and innovative manufacturing processes while rural consumers eagerly sought these new products that signified the up to date, in a new kind of gentility, superior to aristocratic excess and metropolitan fashion.[2] Those prospering in the commercial villages of New England and New York went about redecorating their homes in the new and colorful fashion (plate 5). They furnished their parlors with a growing number of factory chairs and other items of refined living, as depicted by Celestia Bull in her watercolor interior from about 1826 of "Lord Charles" and "Lady Sarah." The two, perhaps a rural couple, are seated at a drop-leaf table facing each other on two of the nine fancy chairs that are scattered about the room, the ample number indicating their relative affluence and attesting to their ability to entertain as well. The scene contains such other exuberantly decorated items as the grain-painted desk with a pair of portraits resting on it and a silhouette above, a painted sheet-iron tray for serving refreshments resting alongside the desk, painted window shades, a stenciled-frame wall mirror with a landscape, a set of stacked oval storage boxes on the right—each one brightly decorated—and a wall-to-wall striped carpet to finish the décor. The couple is engaged in refined activities; he is looking at his music books while playing the violin, and she is sewing while reading.[3]

This emerging provincial middle class espoused a new aesthetic that one recent author has labeled "American Fancy" and that contrasted with the rational restraint of the late eighteenth-century Village Enlightenment. It was a social group in the process of forming itself. The pre-Revolutionary world of Ebenezer and Martha Devotion, with its social hierarchy of relatively fixed ranks and stable indicators of power and authority, dissolved under the solvent of democratization and commercialization, giving rise to a new and shifting coalition of middle-class people with no clear and firm boundary marking them off from those below. Portraits shared the characteristics of other emblems of gentility entering provincial parlors and households as the new middle class announced their arrival by display; fashionable clothes and elaborate furnishings set the middle class off from their poorer neighbors.[4]

The Reinvention of Clockmaking

Eli Terry was born on 13 April 1772, in East Windsor, Connecticut. He received an education in the two main branches of Connecticut clockmaking—brass as well as wooden movements—from Daniel Burnap, the most significant brass-movement clockmaker in eighteenth-century Connecticut. Burnap had been exploring the fashioning of clock parts in advance of assembly, yet he averaged about four clocks a year from 1787 to 1805. By all accounts Eli Terry was the most outstanding of Burnap's numerous apprentices. He also received instruction in the craft of making wooden movements from a "Mr. Cheeney," his son Henry later reported, probably either Benjamin or his brother Timothy Cheney in East Hartford; and Terry took away a lesson in how to make clocks out of cheaper materials and distribute them to a broader market. When freed from his indentures, he stayed for only a year in East Windsor before striking out to the northwest, to the Naugatuck Valley, where a cluster of clockmakers gathered in the town of Northbury, which became Plymouth in 1795.[5]

Terry pursued both brass and wooden clockmaking in the same modest fashion as his colleagues; he used a foot-treadle lathe for turning parts and a hand-cranked clockmaker's engine to cut wood or brass teeth. Few could see the urgency of increasing production, for "so limited was the demand for clocks at this time and so inadequate his means for making them, that after finishing three or four [clock movements]," his son recounted, "he was obligated to go out with them on horseback, and put them up, where they had been previously engaged or sold. His usual way was to put one forward on the saddle on which he rode, one behind, and one on each side in his portmanteau." In this "day of small things," when his father solicited a sale at one farmhouse, the occupant replied that he could not consider "so extravagant" a purchase. Terry accepted "various kinds of farmer's produce, which made the terms of payment so easy as to conclude the bargain." His intimacy with this rural clientele must have convinced him that expensive brass clocks were not the route to prosperity. The price had to be well below the twenty-five to sixty dollars that a wooden or brass movement cost. Producing a clock cheaply enough for mass consumption meant simplifying the clock mechanisms so they could be manufactured and set up without the services of a skilled artisan; ways had to be found of distributing larger quantities more efficiently than the few clock movements hanging from Terry's saddle.[6]

By examining the works of the clocks made by Terry during these years, we can see that he was constantly experimenting. Around 1795, he made a thirty-hour wooden tall clock with crudely cut teeth that he marked "Eli Terry Watertown." He changed the design—inside and out—several times; he cut the teeth more precisely and milled them smooth for the wheels of an engraved clock. In order to make the face more economically, Terry had a dial of printed paper glued onto a wooden plate. The inexpensive material was then concealed by painted graining. Painted decoration covered many surfaces in rural homes, imitating more expensive woods and enriching household décor.[7]

As Terry substituted painted wooden dials for expensive brass ones, he gave a fashionable new look to clock faces and offered employment to local young women. He took advantage of local expertise in manufacturing and painting. Women who worked as industrial painters were important to the growth of the tin and clock industries, as a rare diary kept by a clockmaker's daughter reveals. Candace Roberts was one of the thirteen children born to Gideon and Falla Roberts in Bristol, Connecticut. She began her diary in 1802, recording days filled with spinning yarn, carding cloth, and other forms of household production. She worked outside the home by store clerking, tavern keeping, and sewing for friends and the local tailor. Roberts also found the time for school and steady reading. In June 1802, she "Flowered tin" for Nathaniel Bishop, a Bristol manufacturer. Most likely Roberts learned painting from her mother, who japanned tin and designed and painted clock dials for her husband's wooden clocks. Candace continued to decorate tin, working for Captain Elijah Montress at the largest local tin shop in December and then going to work at Asa Andrews's tin shop in Farmington. After a bout of ill health in 1804, she worked for James Harrison of Waterbury: "He wanted me to go & paint clock faces for him." She was joined there by her brother Elias and a friend from Bristol, and she found good company among the many young people employed in the tin and clock industry. Roberts enjoyed an active social life in Waterbury, attending balls and other entertainments. Her diary notes the appearance of a mysterious, romantic "elegant figure," perhaps a clock peddler since he spent his winters in the South. In February 1806, Roberts "went to live with Mr. Terry in Plymouth" and stayed for several weeks, where she "worked very diligently all day" painting dials. After returning home for a pleasant interlude of tea parties and visits with friends, she "heard the unpleasant news that Mr Terry was comeing after me on Friday." Her five periods in Terry's employ were part of his plan to boost production.

However, Roberts died of typhoid fever late that year. Her diary and the other business accounts record the pioneering role of women industrial painters, for she began painting tinware near the beginning of its local manufacture. Candace Roberts was one of the many women painters hired to decorate the dials of clocks coming out of Connecticut shops for sale across the United States.[8]

Eli Terry also took advantage of the many opportunities offered by the dense and interconnected networks of skilled artisans in Connecticut to cheapen production. He took the knowledge he had gained under Burnap's tutelage, especially of design and the crafting of precision machinery, and combined it with his experience with the Cheneys, especially in the standardization of wooden parts, to accelerate production. Other clockmakers were experimenting with new methods, but it was Terry who gathered up and integrated these various innovations into a consolidated system and put them into practice in an economically efficient manner. At the same time that Terry developed faster methods of manufacturing clock movements with wooden parts, he began to use waterpower and started cutting with saws. The advantages of substituting waterpower for footpower were well known, even in clock making. In 1802, James Harrison built the first waterwheel to drive clock-manufacturing machines in Waterbury. In 1806, Terry signed a lease with Joseph Wright to build a shop "for turning and doing mechanical business by water."[9] Those innovations could push his production from a maximum of twenty-five to several hundred clock movements a year. A year later, in the summer of 1807, Terry took another step in the move from craft to industry: he constructed a clock factory on his recently acquired property, a grist-mill site that included a dam and raceway. At about this time, Terry received a remarkable contract from two Waterbury merchants to build four thousand clock movements within three years. The merchants, the Reverend Edward Porter and his partner Levi, were already involved in various manufacturing activities, including a clock assembly shop and a button manufacturing company. The Porters would furnish the necessary supplies and capital; Terry would provide the movement, dial, hands, weights, and pendulum, but no case—all for four dollars![10]

The craft of clockmaking was on the cusp of a great change, leaving forever the world of shop production, but whether Terry's gamble would succeed rested equally on manufacturing experiments within his workshop and the marketing innovations of his partners. When Terry built his first manufactory in 1806, townspeople ridiculed his grandiose plans to produce hundreds of clock movements per year. The foolish man "would never live long enough to finish such a number," one skeptic scoffed; another retorted that even if Terry did live that long, "he never would nor could possibly sell so many." While focusing on accelerating production, Terry set others up to do distribution. He turned to the system pioneered by the Connecticut tin industry, a network of peddlers, to dispose of this increased production. Soon Terry and other Connecticut clock manufacturers were marketing their wares to new consumers across the rapidly expanding nation.[11]

Peddling Patriotism

Experience has taught me that small, i.e. quarter of dollar books, on subjects calculated to strike the Popular Curiosity, printed in very large numbers and properly distributed, wd prove an immense revenue to the prudent Undertakers. If you could get the life of Genl. Wayne, Putnam, Green & c., Men whose courage and Abilities, whose patriotism and Exploits have won the love and admiration of the American people, printed in small volumes and with very interesting frontispieces, you wd, without doubt, sell an immense number of them. People here think nothing of giving 1/6 (their quarter of a dollar) for anything that pleases their fancy. Let us give them something worth their money.

Mason Weems to Mathew Carey,
Dumfries, 11 August, 1797[12]

Mason Weems, the "peddling parson," wrote to Philadelphia publisher Mathew Carey about the potential market for inexpensive biographies of the new nation's heroes, provided they were properly packaged and widely distributed. The goal of his "campaign" was "to Enlighten, to dulcify and exalt Human Nature—by Good Books" while turning a pretty profit. Peddlers, who are often relegated to a quaint place in Yankee folklore, were significant figures in the commercial life of the early republic. Rural residents depended on itinerant merchants for their supply of books and other desired cultural commodities before the establishment of a reliable transportation and distribution network. Itinerant merchants promoted the transformative power of goods while they also advanced their own status. Although Weems's eager self-promotion made him the most famous of these colorful characters who traveled the dusty roads of the backcountry, he represents only the most visible figure among these agents of commercial expansion. Many took to the road to sell "small trifles," and a few itinerants such as Weems became significant producers of refigured cultural goods; some itinerants even added the making of likenesses to their offerings. Dissatisfied with the austere volumes in his pack, Weems sought books that were more appealing to his farmhouse customers. His best-selling item, *The Life of George Washington: With Curious Anecdotes, Equally Honourable to Himself and Exemplary To his Countrymen*, which went through twenty-nine editions, epitomized this new message.[13]

Mason Weems traveled far over the course of his career as a "Pastor and Travelling Bookseller." Born into a well-off family in Maryland in 1759, he was the youngest of nineteen children. While his neighbors were embroiled in the War for Independence, young Mason was receiving a patrician education in Scotland and England, first in medicine and then the ministry. After the end of the war, he was ordained as an Anglican priest and returned to Maryland, where he became pastor of two churches. However, Weems had already veered away from the path set for a minister in the established church. Following his marriage in 1795 to Frances Ewell, he relocated to Dumfries, a small port along the Potomac River in Prince William County, Virginia, about eighteen miles below Mount Vernon, a place that figured large in his subsequent self-fashioning. He did not remain a stationary minister for long. His preference for an evangelical Protestantism brought him closer to the revivalism that flourished in the backcountry, but distressed his fellow clergymen, who deplored Weems's "method of working up the passions that pays no respect either to reason or decency." Even worse, Weems began vending books alongside his sermons when he visited towns and villages. Initially, he sold imposing books of collected sermons; then he reprinted dramatic travel stories and sensational religious tracts. Eventually his intimate knowledge of popular tastes led him to authorship.[14]

In 1795, while visiting Philadelphia to pick up stock, he met and forged the productive partnership with Mathew Carey that brought both entrepreneurs prominence and financial success. Ever the promoter of himself and his work, Weems exclaimed to Carey in 1807 that "I am sure—very sure—*morally & positively* sure that I have it in my power (from my universal acquaintance, Industry, & Health) to make you the most Thriving Book-seller in America. I can secure to you almost *exclusively* the whole of the business in the middle & western parts of all these Southern states from Maryland to Georgia inclusive."[15] Mathew Carey had fled Ireland in 1784 after issuing an incendiary article in a radical Dublin newspaper. He began a publishing house in Philadelphia, but found the business unprofitable until the disruption of British shipping by the Napoleonic wars after 1790. A nascent desire for American cultural independence led Carey and others to start publishing lavish books by advance subscription, such as William Guthrie's *New System of Modern Geography*, which sold for twelve dollars.

Weems quickly learned firsthand the difficulties of selling such expensive tomes. He set off on foot and went from town to town selling subscriptions to these hefty volumes. Unlike previous subscription projects, these books were already published and could be delivered quickly. But the price remained a real barrier. Weems and Carey had both become aware of the need to produce inexpensive books. Weems exhorted: "I deem it glory to circulate valuable books. I would circulate millions. This cannot be effected without the character of cheapness." He admitted to Carey that "this building a high fortune on low priced books, appears to you strange"; only a mass market would ensure success. They needed to look to the south and west of Philadelphia for new customers. "This country [Virginia and Maryland] is large, and numerous are its inhabitants." Rural residents constituted a vast potential market. Weems wrote his new partner in the fall of 1796: "To cultivate among these a taste for reading, and by the reflection of proper books to throw far and wide the rays of useful arts and sciences," would spread enlightenment as well as generate profits. "For I am verily assured that under proper culture," Weems wrote from his rural base, where he cultivated culture like a crop on fertile soil, "every dollar that you shall scatter on the field of this experiment will yield you 30, 60, and 100 fold." Weems, in close contact with the real readers, regularly urged a wider range of goods upon the publisher Carey: "Let them be of the gay and sprightly kind, Novels, decent plays, elegant Histories. . . . Let the Moral and Religious be as highly dulcified as possible," as Weems advocated sweetening serious subjects and lightening public literature to meet the public taste.[16]

Weems contracted with local assistants to increase the amount of territory that he covered. He envisioned a network of two or three hundred bookstores throughout the South, small ventures where a bundle of books could be left with a well-established citizen and replenished by periodic visits from Weems or one of his assistants. Lacking a way to implement his grand plans, Weems took to the roads himself, following a set pattern of itinerancy, returning to the same places year after year and appearing at periodic events that brought rural people together: court sessions, racing days, agricultural fairs, militia musters, and market days. Weems was even an uninvited guest at private ceremonies. He made himself available to give sermons to congregations or graduations and used these opportunities to sell books to his captive audience. These strategies were successful: for example, Weems sold three hundred copies of his Washington biography during one week of racing in Charleston, South Carolina.[17]

Weems grasped the public thirst for popular biographies. No national hero stood higher in public estimation than Washington. Just weeks after the first president's death, Weems wrote Carey about the possibilities for profit: "Washington, you know is gone! Millions are gaping to read something about him. I am very nearly prim'd & cock'd for 'em. 6 months ago I set myself to collect anecdotes of him. You know I live conveniently for that work. My plan! I give his history, sufficiently minute—I accompany him from his start, thro the French & Indian &

British or Revolutionary wars, to the Presidents chair, to the throne in the hearts of 5,000,000 of People." Weems was already at work on a memorial volume, though Carey was not the publisher. He remained dissatisfied with his eighty-page effort, and by 1808 he had produced a sixth edition, three times as long, with a new title: *The Life of George Washington: With Curious Anecdotes, Equally Honourable to Himself and Exemplary To his Countrymen.*[18]

The formula that Weems developed for his popular biography was strikingly different from such weighty and tedious tomes as John Marshall's five-volume work. Instead of portraying Washington as an austere figure involved in the councils of state and the field of battle, he focused on the hero's "private life" and exemplary virtues. Through vivid anecdotes, the rising generation would find a model of character: "the dutiful son—the affectionate brother—the cheerful school-boy," and a list of other domestic virtues. By cultivating the private virtues, Weems suggested, "in these every youth may become a Washington." Familial life and stories about friendship abound in Weems's rather than previous biographers' emphasis on public performances. Weems's Washington was not "born with a silver spoon in [his] mouth"; rather an ethic of hard work accounted for his rise, while his self-control pointed toward the bourgeois ethos of the nineteenth century. Indeed, "his Washington biography, in fact, resembled nothing so much as a success manual for young Americans," according to Scott Casper. "This became not just a leveling message; it could also be used for creating new distinctions within rural society between those opting into the new commodity culture and those who did not or *could* not."[19] Washington was transformed into a secular icon, binding together a fractious new nation by creating a patriotic religiosity from the strands of emotional intimacy and social harmony. Young George was renowned for settling disputes between classmates, Weems reported. The famous myth of George's chopping down the cherry tree, in which the youth could not bring himself to lie, ended in a display of strengthened affection between George and his father, as his father cried, "Run to my arms, you dearest boy." According to historian Peter Onuf, Weems translated "Washington's self-consciously neoclassical concerns with character and reputation into a popular, democratic idiom." The peddling parson's message resonated powerfully in the new republic. He and Carey created a market for cultural commodities in the hinterlands where one had not existed before, and in the process offered new models of the self to readers.[20]

Itinerant Merchants

Itinerancy served many functions for producers, distributors, and consumers in the increasingly mobile society that emerged after the Revolution. In the mid-eighteenth century, northern rural households had varying degrees of access to consumer goods from urban importers, retail shops, and country stores. In the new republic, rural artisans began to produce a wide range of commodities in a newly decentralized system of production. Peddlers were uniquely equipped by their geographical mobility to link manufacturers who had goods to sell with consumers who had farm surpluses to exchange. Peddling could also serve as a means of social mobility for rural youth, a way out of the demographic and social constraints of the northern agrarian economy and into the possibilities offered by capitalist expansion. Peddlers and consumers could share in the self-fashioning of new identities through an exchange of goods that facilitated the democratization of gentility. In the young United States, social identity became markedly fluid.[21]

Itinerants were at the center of the process of commercialization, facilitating the shift from local exchange, fostering the expansion of production in the countryside, and expanding the role of commodities in everyday life. They distributed the growing production of rural artisans, generating a market for goods well beyond the bare "necessities." They encouraged innovations in the products themselves, so goods would be made more affordable and available to the domestic market. Most important, itinerant merchants promoted the transforming properties of goods, marketing a consumer culture throughout the hinterlands and accustoming rural people to acquiring goods. The pace of these changes varied with the product. While entrepreneurial artisans were behind most innovations in clocks, peddlers took a more active role in influencing book production. Portrait painters combined production and sales. Such dramatic changes were accompanied by conflict. Peddlers challenged country storekeepers for local trade, and in many northern states, stationary storekeepers led a licensing movement to drive out their competitors. Cultural resistance to itinerant merchants took the form of a rich folklore about peddlers. Tales about the peddler's arrival in an isolated rural community and his entry into the farm household itself served as a lightning rod for fears about changing gender relations and the morality of the market. Neither commercial nor cultural resistance had a significant effect, however. Peddlers and the system of itinerant merchandising became the vehicle for the creation of a regional marketplace and a stimulus for industrial innovation.

During the colonial period, peddlers had worked as agents for stationary storekeepers rather than acting as competitors to them; in the new republic, they had independent relationships with both producers and consumers. Itinerant merchants inserted themselves into previous systems of distribution and extended them significantly. Writing about bookselling, William Gilmore has pointed out that two distribution networks existed in the countryside, a mainstream commercial one and an informal one that "rested on the shoulders of flying stationers and peripatetic entrepreneurs, especially peddlers, but also itinerant authors selling their own and others' works." Peddlers generally traveled in regular circuits to reach their customers; and they had a variety of commercial arrangements with their principals. A wagon peddler could start out with a stock of merchandise worth anywhere from three hundred to two thousand dollars, and it has been estimated that this stock could be turned at a gross profit of 100 percent over two or three months.[22]

We are familiar with Americans' propensity to seek to rise socially by moving geographically, a tendency that is especially clearly visible by the great flux of transient individuals through northern towns and cities during the early nineteenth century. The social history of peddlers reveals enormous geographic, occupational, and class mobility. For many young villagers, peddling proved to be a stage in the life cycle, as well as a way of exploring commercial activities beyond the family farm. The itinerant life allowed dissatisfied or displaced farm youths the opportunity to construct new identities through their travels and sales of new consumer goods. By the 1820s, an increasing number of young men in their late teens or early twenties were setting out on their own.[23]

Amos Bronson Alcott, the New England Transcendentalist who was lovingly depicted by his daughter, Louisa May Alcott, as the quintessential impractical idealist, spent many of his adolescent hours hanging around clock workshops in his native Connecticut. He noted in 1816 that many young men and women "were tempted by the offer of fair wages" into working in shops or small factories, while other "young men, emulous of adventure, or of more lucrative employment during the winter months, went South as peddlers of the clocks." Soon Bronson and his brother Chatfield joined the growing ranks of these mobile merchants in 1819. The two helped their father on the farm in the summer, but persuaded him to let them journey south each winter from the age of eighteen, promising that their earnings would lighten the debts that burdened the family farm. Many youthful travelers remained tightly bound to home and family, filling their letters with expressions of homesickness and accounts of ill health.[24] Critics warned against the dangers of a wandering life and its incompatibility with family ties. Samuel Hopkins Peck cautioned his younger brother Russell: "When you find yourself getting old—you have lived such a roving life that you can never content yourself to settle down on a farm and Enjoy your (I wont say ill begotten) means." Some wavered between the charms of the hearth and the opportunities of the market. Although the clock peddler Milo Holcomb wistfully imagined his brother Nahum passing the winter evenings "in the happy farmer fashion" with wife and young child before "a cheerful fire cider and apples with other goods things to sweeten and make happy your life," he added that such a life was not for him and remained certain that clock peddling was more lucrative than farming. Despite the reports of great returns from profits or wages, peddling was a risky business. Milo was forced to sell his Hartland, Connecticut, farm to pay off his peddling debts, admitting "the undisguised truth I am too lazy for a Hartland farmer," especially "with land that has more rock than Soil."[25]

The peddling craze swept the northern countryside during the first half of the nineteenth century. Thousands set out from their New England villages to peddle clocks and combs, their ears filled with stories of riches to be made. Even Bronson's sober and studious cousin William, after reports that "some of them appeared to be getting rich," joined the ranks of the itinerant merchants; the two Alcotts took off in 1820, William's first trip and Bronson's third. From Bristol, Connecticut, Asa Upson reported to his son Rensseleaer embarking upon his peddling career in Alabama, that several young neighbors had just returned home in quite a satisfied state, "come as Clean as the Cat Come out of the Cream."[26]

In Vermont, according to licensing records, the number of peddlers working within the state rose from 15 in 1807 to between 25 and 35 each year from 1820 and 1830; the total was estimated to be at least 50 in 1833. These peddlers could not have been poor; licenses cost thirty to fifty dollars. In Worcester County, Massachusetts, 126 peddlers were listed in the 1850 census. This was a young man's trade. A majority of the Worcester County peddlers were in their twenties; 41 percent were aged twenty-one to twenty-six. Historian Joseph Rainer found that half of the identifiable peddlers in Georgia between 1826 and 1831 were between twenty-one and twenty-five years of age. They were overwhelmingly New England–born; just 5 percent were Irish. By 1860, the number of peddlers in Worcester County had doubled. In Massachusetts as a whole, there were 1,648 peddlers, 5 percent of the 35,937 people occupied in commerce. The number of peddlers was also substantial in New York State; there were 302 licensed peddlers in 1841, and the state census of 1855 listed 4,131 itinerant merchants. U.S. census takers found 10,669 peddlers in 1850 and 16,594 in 1860; two-thirds of them came from New York, Pennsylvania, Massachusetts, and Ohio.[27]

The seasonal rhythm of peddling suited the calendar for traveler and customer alike. Young men left their hometowns after the harvest, traveled south through the winter, and returned for summer farm labor, as the Alcott brothers did. In Vermont in 1809–14, most "were travelling with a horse"; a few had a cart as well. Whatever their means of transport, peddlers moved slowly. Foot peddlers carried their goods in a backpack or hand trunk. A daguerreotype, taken between 1840 and 1860, shows a trunk peddler standing stiffly; a harness and neck brace support the weight of his trunks, and the outlines of a pocketbook and account book can be glimpsed on the right side of his coat (fig. 49). A merchant with a wagon could decorate the sides with advertising to beckon customers and open the shelves and display his wares.[28] The relationship between peddlers and suppli-

Fig. 49. Daguerreotype of a trunk peddler with his two bags by his side and a harness and neck brace, ca. 1840–60. Sixth-plate daguerreotype. Library of Congress, Prints & Photographs Division, Washington, D.C.

ers ranged along a spectrum of increasing independence: the salaried employee, the commissioned agent, those who worked on credit (as clock peddlers did) or on their own account, and finally, the independent artisan who produced his or her own wares (for example, itinerant portrait makers). Initially independent entrepreneurs predominated: artisans or those merchants who worked "on their own hooks" by buying directly from wholesalers. Eighteenth-century tinsmiths often took to the road to sell their kettles, or they sent out employees. In the early nineteenth century, farmers-turned-broommakers peddled their own products. A South Hadley, Massachusetts, resident recalled: "Here was a man on horseback with a load of strange-looking articles behind him, which he was trying to sell 'only four pence for a corn broom that will out sweep and out last all the birch brooms and split brooms in creation.'" By the 1820s, tinware and clock manufacturers came to rely on a network of peddlers to sell goods. One agreement in 1817 spelled out the arrangement between Oliver Filley and Erastus Beaman, Connecticut tinsmiths, and "Nathaniel Clark, a peddler": "Said Clark agrees to go a pedling Tinware and other goods for the space of six months from the 15th day of May 1817—and to be true and faithful to his employers and to furnish himself with a good horse and wagon and to keep the same in good repair free from expense to the said Filley and Beaman and for the same to pay to the said Clark twenty-five dollars per month for the specified term of six months, he to be every way honest and faithful to his employers as above stated."[29] A peddling system emerged as the distances traveled increased, the production of village shops and factories expanded rapidly, and the financial system proved unsuited to myriad consumer transactions.

Familiar rural accounting practices lingered; the world of small exchanges of goods and services continued in this expanding economy. Clock peddlers, working in circuits, often gave twelve months' credit, returning the next year to retrieve their notes. Recalcitrant creditors posed as many difficulties as impassable roads. Lewis Robinson relied heavily upon peddlers to market his maps: on a six-month trip in 1846, Herman Gilson took in only about one-quarter of his sales in cash, but he did manage to collect raccoon skins, sheep pelts, cat pelts, and even a "green mountain gem worth 75 cents" for his employer. Others collected less exotic barter or simply came up short. Peddlers visited populous regions first and then ventured into more remote regions, Joseph Rainer found. Some floated along on the waterways as "River Hawkers," their boats outfitted with counters, shelves, and drawers.[30]

Tin peddlers were ubiquitous. Country households relied upon these cheap, lightweight utensils and containers. Tin was an easy material to work with, it could be worked cold, and only simple tools were required to shape it into such utilitarian wares as pots and pans, while bread boxes and trays could be decorated. The tinware industry expanded as the rural production system was fueled by the growing hunger for everyday goods, with producers and consumers connected by the "hawkers and walkers" of the rural world. Like many of the "small industries" of the countryside, tinware shops grew dramatically in size and dispersed across the landscape during the half century after the Revolution. Burrage Yale of South Reading, Massachusetts, began manufacturing tinware in 1805; by 1832, his capital amounted to ten thousand dollars, including thirty-five horses for his peddlers. Like the clock industry, the tin industry was centered in Connecticut, where entrepreneurs developed ingenious machines to simplify production and boost output. C. L. Fleischmann, a German visitor, remarked: "The German tinsmith may be more skilled in making objects requiring great dexterity, but when he comes to this country he must learn to work quickly and with machines, and he must also learn which kinds of objects are in demand here, which shapes and sizes are desired, in order to utilize the plate to advantage."[31] Whatever the scale of production, the peddling system was critical to distribution.

The output of Connecticut tinware manufactories quickly outstripped local demand. As early as the mid-eighteenth century, Berlin tinmaker William Pattison hired peddlers to hawk his merchandise in nearby towns. Transporting low-value tin goods long distances did not pay, so entrepreneurs set up temporary shops in southern and western villages and towns. From these depots, peddlers could be supplied: a shop with five workers could keep twenty-five peddlers on the road. They returned with a cornucopia of produce taken in exchange and waited to be restocked before venturing out again. In the late spring, the shop closed up, and the tinsmith, peddlers, and young women who painted decorative or "japanned" tinware returned to farm labor. Oliver Filley of Windsor, Connecticut, started out with a shop filled with apprentices. The numerous family members whom he trained set up shop across the new nation, from St. Louis to Baton Rouge. Filley's brother Harvey's Philadelphia tin shop sold goods in Virginia's hinterlands. A Winchester depot's goods were carried across the Allegheny Mountains. Almost 70 percent of Maine's production came from Stevens Plains. The peddler "was generally a green young man from the farm" whose outfit was "a horse. A 'tin cart' and a pair of steelyards. The tin cart was four wheels, axle trees, arms and whiffle-tree like a light truck wagon, a large box for a body with an L in front to sit on. . . . Paint the cart red, fill up with tinware and 'trinket,' hitch 'Dobbin' in his place, mount the cart, boy, and be off on trading for a few weeks!" Peddlers returned with large loads of paper rags, hog's bristles, old copper, and all sorts of peltry "generally worth double what they started off with."[32] Whatever the accuracy of that estimate of profits, the success of tinware contributed to the decline of its peddling system as local production took hold. Using small tinworking machines invented by Connecticut entrepreneurs, some peddlers set down as manufacturers or merchants in these southern or western spots. Julius Woodford wrote to Oliver Filley in 1818 from Indiana that since he had last "purchased a load of tin from you I have traveled through the state of Ohio & Kentucky and from that into the State of Indianna [sic]. Now happy to report settled in tending store in Corrydon Indiana." One set of recollections from Stevens Plains ended, "From 1800 to 1835 more young men, natives of Maine, graduated from 'tin carts' than graduated from Bowdoin College in the same time," and the author somewhat hyperbolically exclaimed, "a far less proportion of all the peddlers have been failures in life than of the college graduates."[33]

Itinerant merchants were critical figures in cultivating a market for consumer goods. Peddlers promoted the transformative power of commodities.[34] They extended the democratization of gentility that began with eighteenth-century retail shops. Storekeepers developed a new persona and invited customers to transform their social identities. One *became* gentry by buying the right things. Peddlers joined storekeepers in the role of tutor with regard to the polite world of material goods.[35] Peddlers greatly extended that invitation, economically by appearing outside the local structure of exchange, geographically through their travels, socially by providing new consumer goods that represented status, and culturally by fashioning new and enticing blandishments to present at the farmhouse door.

The pivotal role played by peddlers in the transformation of the countryside gave rise to conflict that can be traced in folk humor. The figure of the Yankee peddler in popular literature served as a rich vehicle to convey deep ambivalence about the charged encounter between itinerant merchant and consumer. Fictions about the crafty peddler, a transient passing through town, were symbolic representations to rural people of profound changes in the conduct of economic transactions. The market in the early stages of capitalism, some cultural historians have argued, became dislodged from an actual sense of place and became an amorphous, free-floating concept.[36]

John Bernard's description of the arrival of a peddler in a Virginia village shows both the promise and the perils that commodities held for isolated farm families. Bernard's itinerant Yankee arrived in the isolated community as the personification of market culture, armed with magical personal qualities to entice buyers, even if the sacred associations of a pilgrim had been lost:

A pedestrian is seen wandering down the hill, his legs, in the slanting sunbeams, sending their shadows half a mile before him. By the length of staff he might be taken for a pilgrim, but the sprawl of his walk awakens anything but sacred associations. . . . Suspicions are excited; and at length one who may have suffered more than the rest, perhaps, from the endemic [infestation] recognizes its symptoms and exclaims, "I'll be shot if it aint a Yankee!" At these words if there is not a general rout, or springing-up or banging-to of doors, it must be because their faculties are prostrated by the surprise, and they lie spell-bound, as cattle are said to do on the approach of the anaconda.

Bernard relates the mixed "wonder and contempt" that this curious species of man excited with his "prying into holes and corners to prove the extent of their needs." Such tales articulated rural residents' fears about their own susceptibility to consumerism, as well as their passivity before the magical charms of itinerant merchants.[37]

Representations of country dwellers' ambivalence toward a market society emerged in the genre of popular humor. These humorous dramatizations do contain vestiges of the reciprocal transactions that characterized the local exchange economy. Peddler and customer engaged in a contest of wiles and wills. The consumer was an active party to the deception, drawn in by the peddler and his own penchant for chicanery, an accounting immortalized by P. T. Barnum's notion of "humbug." That entrepreneur of culture learned his trade from a stint as a storekeeper in Connecticut: "The customers cheated us in their fabrics and we cheated them in their goods. Each party expected to be cheated, if it was possible." But these new mobile traders, with their up-to-date knowledge of market conditions, were better placed than their customers to judge a bargain accurately.[38]

The peddler played market analyst, entertainer, and trickster—and was always on the move. One Yankee discussed the signs that the occupants of a farmhouse would purchase a clock. "If the house had glass windows, if the man of the house did not wear [a cap] but a hat, if he had boots on—the clock was as good as sold." If the wife appeared in calico and checked apron, the traveling merchant knew she had bought from a fellow itinerant and would be "easily excited by a gaudy ribbon or a shining pair of scissors."[39] Peddlers were known to use shrewd techniques to break down rural resistance and induce demand where none had existed before. "We trust to 'soft sawder' to get them into the house," Sam Slick, the fictional Connecticut clock peddler boasted, and "to 'human natur' that they never come out of it." Slick's "soft sawder," or flattery, was a reference to the solder of the tinsmiths' trade. Villagers who had previously felt little need for Slick's wares were persuaded to buy by his appeal to their vanity and their own attachment to luxury. He pretended to leave a clock in a farmhouse temporarily, hinting that it was really intended for a neighbor, all the while chuckling that "that clock is sold for 40 dollars—it cost me just six dollars and fifty cents. Mrs. Flint will never let Mrs. Steel have the refusal—nor will the Deacon learn until I call for the clock, that having once indulged in the use of superfluity, how difficult it is to give it up." The yeoman felt flattered to be called "Squire," while his wife became concerned that another woman would secure the timepiece.[40]

Women became associated with the dangers of consumerism in popular images. In writers from Benjamin Franklin to Henry David Thoreau, Robert Gross has noted, "the complaint is invariably the same: status-conscious women first introduce the corruption of luxury into the home," the cause of excess, even frivolous expenditure on the farm. Sources as varied as James Guild's peddling journal, Asher B. Durand's *The Pedlar Displaying His Wares*, and Francis Edmonds's *The Image Pedlar* represented women as the family members most interested in the arrival of a peddler (figs. 50 and 51). The elderly peddler in Durand's 1836 painting opens his pack of trinkets for the younger women in the household, as the child shows an object to the father. Here too the peddler challenges the father's authority over his wife and daughter. Edmonds's 1844 painting has a more youthful peddler, but shows the same distinction in the

Fig. 50. Asher B. Durand, *The Pedlar* (*The Pedlar Displaying His Wares*), 1836. Oil on canvas. 24 × 34-1/2 in. Collection of The New-York Historical Society, New York City.

Fig. 51. Francis Edmonds, *The Image Pedlar*, ca. 1844. Oil on canvas. 33-1/4 × 42-1/4 in. Collection of The New-York Historical Society, New York City.

degree of interest imputed to men and women. The farmer, his father, and a son sit by the window, evidently more interested in the bust on the table than in the peddler's wares. As a contemporary critic wrote, "The grandmother drops her peeling-knife, and the mother takes her infant from the cradle, to gaze at the sights in the pedler's basket." Other paintings also highlight the role of the peddler and the shelf clock in "mediating national affiliation through the expansion of the market," as Thomas M. Allen has argued. In John Ehninger's *Yankee Peddler* of 1858, the peddler arrives to entice a family gathering of young women and children, with a clock perched on the top of his well-stocked wagon, representing the centrality of the clock to the process of national consumption.[41]

All of these themes—peddling as a stage in the life cycle, the fluidity of social identity on the road, and the message of self-transformation through goods—come together in one particularly rich text. The journal of James Guild, "Peddler, Tinkerer, Schoolmaster, Portrait Painter," begins with his first merchandising venture in 1818 when he departed from rural Vermont. By 1824, he was an artist working in a London studio. His rapid rise from peddler to profile maker, penmanship professor, and professional artist was not the common experience of those who strapped on a peddler's pack to try their luck on the back roads of the rural North, but James Guild's early adventures bear a close relation to those of many itinerants.[42]

James Guild had been born in 1797 in Halifax, Vermont, to Nathaniel and Mehitable Gaines Guild. After the early death of his father, Guild's mother "bound [him] out" at the age of nine, unable to take care of him and his three siblings. Once freed from his "confined situation" as an apprentice, Guild sank his entire fortune, a note of seventy dollars, into a "trunk of goods" and took to the road: "I began my peddling. *You* must know it was awkward for a farmer boy who had been confined to the hoe or ax to put on a pedlers face, but I believe I was as apt as any one. I got my things in rotation pedler form, so when I went into a house, do you wish to by some harecombs, needles, buttons, buttonmolds, sewing silk, beeds? If they wished to purchase, they would want to banter untill they could get it for nothing." Guild found few customers in his first few days among the "poor set of inhabitants." He endured several bouts of homesickness, fear of failure, and the dark passage through the woods on his travels. His visit to Troy, New York, brought out the "green boy," as he had never been "in so large a place before" and was daunted by the looks and manners of "the gay and polished part of that great Citty." His efforts to deceive the locals succeeded until he was confronted with a plate of parsnips, which he gobbled down faster than his partners, only to be rewarded by another plateful. But he did learn a lesson about taking on the "masks of politeness."[43] Homesickness caught up with him again; but the thought of returning to Vermont made him realize that "I cannot be a farmer boy"; like Silas Felton, he felt an aversion to farm work. Guild remained on the road and tried some tinkering. After buying some cheap scissors, he displayed the cunning of a more experienced merchant. When his reasonably priced scissors found no takers, he offered another pair of the identical scissors at a higher price. He made a quick sale when a farmer's daughter demanded that her mother purchase the more expensive ones.[44] Guild mastered the tricks of the trade and recognized the importance of women as consumers.

His sojourn in Albany proved to be a turning point in James Guild's self-fashioning. While observing a band playing in a museum, he claimed to have musical training, and the proprietor hired him to play that evening on the "tamborin." Museums offered varied forms of popular entertainment as well as cultural "improvements." During the month-long employment that followed, he received instruction in cutting profile likenesses. Soon Guild called himself "a profile cutter," exploiting the mutability of identity and the public's thirst for cultural goods and services to "make folks think I was something I was not." Traveling remained fraught with difficulties, however. A husband who returned home to find Guild painting his wife threatened him with a good horsewhipping. Evenings spent in taverns sometimes ended with wrestling bouts.[45]

Armed with a few sessions at a writing school and several manuals, Guild took on the guise of a writing master. His reliance upon printed rules of penmanship "furnished me with a bold face." He soon associated with an academy in Middlebury. Still dissatisfied with his occupational status, the "profile cutter" sought to rise in the profession. When he encountered another itinerant "who painted likenesses," he paid the painter five dollars for a day's tuition in "how to distinguish the coulers." The next day Guild was back on the road with "a picture of Mr. goodwins painting for a sample. . . . I put up at a tavern and told a young Lady if she would wash my shirt, I would draw her likeness. Now then I was to exert my skill in painting. I opperated once on her but it looked so like a rech I throwed it away and tried again. The poor Girl sat niped up so prim and look so smileing it makes me smile when i think of while I was daubing on paint on a piece of paper, it could not be caled painting, for it looked more like a strangle cat than it did like her. However I told her it looked like her and she believed it."[46] James Guild had "put on the face" of a portrait painter.

When Guild paused in his travels after two or three years, he reflected, "I find by experience if a man thinks he is something and puts him self forward he will be something." The rural North furnished a fluid environment for his social pretensions; he need not "confine himself to any class," but could rather "conform myself to the class I am in." He learned to associate with the "big caricters" and avoid the mean and "dispising those who haunt the grog shop or the gambling table." When he was in the company of "the first stile of people," Guild learned to "put on my polish as it ware." Guild had moved up, become more independent, made his own goods, and avoided commercial ties. In the cultural realm, he had learned how to posture in the social world. Guild had become a success. While he would continue to ascend, gravitating to such metropolitan centers as New York, Charleston, and Boston and achieving longer periods of residence and greater financial rewards, he had learned the critical lesson on the roads of provincial New England and New York. A visit to his Vermont hometown brought a warm welcome from his family, but Guild gradually realized that his carriage and fine frocks set him apart from his former companions' towcloth shirts and week-old beards. His family had "no ambition to shine," which made him long to return to New York where he could rejoin stylish society with its constant source of "new thing[s] to attract the eye."[47]

Ironically, he achieved his success by being a peddler, which was a problematic role in this culture. In his journal, James Guild, like P. T. Barnum, constructed a self in the role of a Yankee trickster.[48] His writings show how a rising generation of men and women greeted the possibilities of consumerism with enthusiasm and amazement rather than suspicion and criticism. But his autobiography also reveals people's ambivalent response to a peddler's arrival in their community. Guild's writings use the folklore about Yankee peddlers, a genre that projected rural residents' fears about the dangers of consumerism onto itinerant merchants.

Terry's Triumph

Eli Terry's neighbors doubted that the promised hundreds of clocks would pour out of his manufactory. They did not; rather they came out in the thousands. As he would do several times, Terry withdrew from production to rework his production line and rethink his design. For the first time he did not have to be concerned about marketing because the Porters would take care of that important sector of the business. In 1807, Terry began by fulfilling his contract with them to supply four thousand wooden tall-clock movements in three years (fig. 52). Terry converted the grist mill he bought in the south part of Plymouth into a "Wooden Clock Factory." Henry Terry observed that his father spent the first year "fitting up the machinery," the next fabricating a thousand clocks, and the final year of the contract making the remaining three thousand clocks. He hired Seth Thomas and Silas Hoadley, two young woodworkers who had no training in clockmaking, to run the operation. Terry's mentors, Harland and Burnap, had moved toward standardizing clock movements and increasing production. Terry took more dramatic steps toward mass manufacture by harnessing waterpower to drive machin-

Fig. 52. Eli Terry, tall clock, ca. 1807–9. Thirty-hour movement. Oak plates, cherry wheels, maple arbors and pinions. 84 in. One of the Porter contract clocks. Collections of Old Sturbridge Village, Sturbridge, Massachusetts. Photograph by Henry Peach.

ery and using wood for major components of clocks. Waterpower traveled through belts and pulleys to turn the various drills, saws, and other devices that fashioned the clock parts. Banks of wheels were lined up for cutting, "so a dozen or more wheels could be cut in the time it previously took to cut one."[49]

Clocks must have been coming out of the manufactory by 1 August 1808, the date on the label that stated that the clocks were made by Eli Terry for the Porter brothers of Waterbury and "warranted, if cased and well used." Detailed instructions had to be provided for setting up the clocks, since they were sold by the Porters and their peddlers over a vast expanse of territory. The label that was pasted inside the case, explained:

> Let the Clock be set in a perpendicular position. This is necessary, in order to its having an equal beat: and if it fails to beat equally, it maybe put *in beat*, by raising one or the other side of the Clock. And having found the right position, there let it be fastened. If the Clock goes too fast, lengthen the pendulum; but if too slow, shorten it, by means of the *screw*, at the bottom. If the hands want moving, do it by means of the longest, or by turning the face-wheel on the time side of the Clock: turning at any time, forwards, but never backwards, when the clock is within 15 minutes of striking; nor father [*sic*] than to carry the longest hand up to Figure XII. So, in clocks which shew the day of the month, the hand, if it varies from the truth, may be put forward with the finger. And if the Clock fails to strike the proper hour, press downward, with your finger, the small wire on the striking side of the Clock, and it will strike as often as you repeat the pressure. Keep the clock as much as possible from dust, and apply no oil, at any time, to it, unless it be a very small quantity of sweet oil, or the oil of Almonds, with a feather, to the brass or crown wheel.[50]

Terry made several important breakthroughs in order to accelerate the production of clocks. But it was the enormous scale of production and the availability of an extensive marketing network that marked the transformation of clockmaking. The successful completion of the Porter contract made Terry a wealthy man. By 1810, the Porters had transferred property worth seven thousand dollars, and the following year, Terry sold the factory to his two assistants for six thousand dollars.[51]

At the same time that Terry revolutionized the making of wooden clock movements, other clockmakers continued to experiment. Two brothers, Simon and Aaron Willard, moved from central Massachusetts to Roxbury to take advantage of its proximity to Boston's skilled artisans. Simon obtained a patent in 1802 for a wall-hung timepiece popularly known as a banjo clock for its characteristic shape (fig. 53). The banjo clock was amazingly popular, becoming a distinctive American clock form. Thousands rolled out of the Willards' workshops. In 1807, more than twenty clockmakers, cabinetmakers, and dial and ornamental painters and gilders worked for the Willards in their large workshop

Fig. 53. Patent timepiece or banjo clock, made by Simon Willard, Roxbury, Massachusetts, ca. 1805. Brass and steel. 42-1/2 × 10-1/2 × 3-7/8 in. Collections of Old Sturbridge Village, Sturbridge, Massachusetts. Photograph by Henry Peach.

or in a neighboring cluster of shops. Thousands more banjo clocks were made by authorized and unauthorized suppliers alike. But banjo clocks remained fairly expensive, costing purchasers about thirty dollars.[52]

The best prospects for large-scale clock production lay in the wooden clock movements developed in central Connecticut. James Harrison had preceded Terry by six years in setting up a waterwheel to power his small shop in Waterbury; his elder brother Lemuel, even before the Porters had disposed of their 4,000 clocks, began to make clocks in bulk by contracting with others for parts and assembly; one contractor, Ephraim Downs, recorded the assembly and finishing of 9,162 clock movements for Harrison.[53] In Plymouth, Terry's successors, Thomas and Hoadly, "Mechanics in Company," worked under contracts that specified schedules for delivery and payment, a new practice instituted with the contract between Terry and the Porters. Even Gideon Roberts, who according to Chauncey Jerome, made clocks "in the old way" in his Bristol shop and peddled them himself in New York State, soon increased his production; by 1810, he had established a Virginia agency for sales. Eli Terry represented only the most visible part of a growing network of innovative Connecticut craftsmen.[54]

Inventing the Shelf Clock: "A New Form of Clock"

Terry himself did not leave the workbench after selling his tall-case clock factory. With sufficient capital of his own, he converted a Plymouth property with a house, barn, and shop into a clock shop, where he must have worked out the design for his wooden-movement shelf clock between 1810 and 1812. The work was promising enough for him to obtain a mill site in 1812 along the Naugatuck River below Seth Thomas's shop. He intended to expand this manufacturing complex, so he purchased from a nearby farmer the privilege of "ponding and flowing water on my land so much as will be ponded by a dam fourteen feet high." Farmers and mill owners in those early years were often at loggerheads when mills flooded adjacent fields; Terry took the precaution of buying water rights in advance of raising the dam. He planned to operate on a significant scale.

Terry's new shelf clock, a revolutionary technological and aesthetic achievement, fit on a shelf or mantelpiece (see fig. 48). He reorganized the clock mechanism to make a short case possible. In 1814, Terry applied for a patent, stating "he has invented a new and useful improvement in the thirty hour brass & wooden Clocks"; it was granted in 1816.[55] The clockmaker noted many of its original features in the patent letter: he reduced the pendulum length to less than ten inches, and he reorganized critical parts, such as the pallet and pendulum, so they allowed less friction and truer operation and could be removed easily for cleaning. Looking at the clock, we can see that the winding cords come up to the top of the case and over pulleys, so the full height of the case was used for the drop of the weights. The smaller weights Terry used permit a much shorter fall. Terry's success came not by individual manufacturing prowess, but by shrewdly seizing upon several developments in the design and manufacture of clock movements taking place within the clockmaking community.[56]

For consumers, the shelf clock was cheap, good-looking, and movable. Terry's design fused the works and the case into a single unit rather than placing the movement inside a separate wooden case. His shelf clock was a simple box "about twenty inches long, fourteen wide, and three in depth or thickness." The numerals "were painted directly on the glass door which formed the dial." The back plate of the clock served as the back of the case. Compared with a tall clock, this "smaller, handsomer, less cumbersome" shelf clock was "easier moved from one room to another"; its owner was more likely to keep the weights in view and remember to wind the movement. Most important, Terry's invention was "cheaper including the case."[57]

Terry's invention of the shelf clock in 1816 transformed the clock industry. Certainly peddlers liked it; it was complete, with a handsome case for easy sales, yet small and easily transported. Before Terry's innovations, a clockmaker could produce twenty-five clock movements a year that cost twenty-five dollars each without a case; afterward, a clockmaker could produce 2,500 shelf clocks a year at ten dollars, with case included. Looking back, Eli Terry's son Henry concluded that "these things taken together *constituted a new form* of clock, a *new article* and a *new manufacture*."[58]

Terry was one of the first inventors to use the patent system, which had recently been established, to protect his mechanical and decorative inventions. Only the highly capitalized Lowell textile mills, with their integrated waterpower generation and transmission system and their machine shops where mechanical problems were addressed and resolved, held more patents on their machinery than Terry. He held six patents for his thirty-hour shelf clock alone. Many clock manufacturers realized the revolutionary nature of the shelf clock and desired to begin making shelf clocks themselves, but they feared legal action for patent infringement. However, long-established customs clashed with Terry's efforts to protect his designs. The local exchange economy paid for labor services and other work by a trade in clock movements, so his designs were bound to be spread. When cabinetmaker Chauncey Jerome left Terry's employ, he took his pay in clock movements. Eli Terry signed an agreement with Seth Thomas, licensing him to make clocks and requiring him to pay a royalty. Thomas had worked as a joiner before taking a job with Terry. After going into business for himself, he paid Terry a fifty-cent royalty for each of the five thousand clocks he produced. Soon he became one of Terry's competitors. Seth Thomas's name, not Eli Terry's, graced the largest American clockmaking firm into the twentieth century.

Terry remained fascinated with design and innovation rather than with manufacturing and marketing. He kept working on the clock movement and offered the new, improved movement to Thomas, who declined. But Thomas almost immediately began to produce the new style anyway. In 1826, Terry applied for a patent for his new design, stating, "I do not claim any one of the parts of the above designed clock separately as my invention, but I do claim the above arrangement and conformation of the whole a new and useful invention." The next year he sued Thomas and won a temporary injunction requiring Thomas to cease production. But by 1829, Terry had dropped the charges. Perhaps he realized that it was impossible to keep his Connecticut neighbors from making the shelf clock by relying on the legal system.[59] At least twenty-two other clockmakers used or adapted Terry's patent movement from 1818 through the 1820s. Other artisans ingeniously devised various ways of circumventing Terry's patent, such as Silas Hoadley, who designed an "upside down" model with an inverted train. Hoadley and Heman Clark, both former Terry apprentices, soon turned their interest to brass clocks, but the significant expense of the brass and the small scale of production meant that the brass shelf clock remained too costly for many consumers.[60]

For a public increasingly enamored of "fancy" goods, the box clock (fig. 47), though cheap, was too plain; a more attractive case would make it more desirable (see fig. 48). Chauncey Jerome, who became a major manufacturer of less expensive brass clocks in the 1830s, recounted the origin of the popular pillar-and-scroll design. "I went to work for Mr. Terry, making the Patent Shelf Clock in the winter of 1816. Mr. Thomas had been making them for about two years, doing nearly all of the labor on the case by hand. Mr. Terry in the meantime being a great mechanic had made many improvements in the way of making the cases. Under his directions I worked a long time at putting up machinery and benches. We had a circular saw, the first one in the town, and which was considered a great curiosity. In the course of the winter he drew another plan of the Pillar Scroll Top Case with great improvements over the one which Thomas was then making." Whether Thomas or Terry originated the pillar-and-scroll case remains controversial among historians; what is most interesting about Jerome's account is its narrative of collaborative work in design and manufacture. The plain box case acquired a pair of slender columns on the side, scrollwork on the top, and a set of graceful feet, along with an extra inch or two—a form inspired by the pillars and scrolled tops found on many tall-clock hoods. A separate dial was added as well. This particular example (see fig. 48) features an image of Mount Vernon, George Washington's neoclassical home and a popular subject for the colorful paintings on shelf clocks. The republican design associations are clear in the clock's scroll pediment, urn finials, and columns on the side. The pillar-and-scroll case became the basic form for the shelf clock from the 1820s on; a stenciled version soon followed. While Terry continued to tinker with the mechanism, other clockmakers created more decorative versions of the popular timepiece.[61]

Manufacturing Clocks

Clockmaking was one example of what has been called the "American System of Manufactures" during this period. American inventors including Eli Whitney and Eli Terry developed a "sequential series of operations carried out on successive special purpose machines that produce interchangeable parts," as technological historian David Hounshell defines the innovation.[62] Recent writings on the production of such small arms as rifles have dimmed Whitney's self-proclaimed genius and refocused attention on the role of the federal armories at

Springfield, Massachusetts, and Harper's Ferry, West Virginia. Inventors John Hall designed a breech-loading rifle, and Thomas Blanchard developed an automated lathe to manufacture gunstocks. The construction of metal and woodworking machinery made possible the manufacture of interchangeable rifle parts. The use of such tools as gauges facilitated precision cutting and quality control. Such "machines could make things as good and as fast as man's hands, or even better."[63]

Eli Terry and other clockmakers undertook mass production in different circumstances. They worked to develop private markets rather than relying on the federal government, and the early innovators worked not in metal but in wood, a vastly easier material to manipulate. They produced parts in roughly symmetrical shapes, such as circles and ellipses, rather than the irregular shapes required for gunstocks and the muzzles of rifles and revolvers. These technical differences made large-scale production easier for the clockmakers, which was a good thing since they had less working capital and a less reliable market than the small-arms manufacturers. But, like the innovators in the federal arsenals, Terry and his clockmaking collaborators met the goal of producing clocks in large quantities at low cost by developing tools to make interchangeable parts.[64]

The mass production of wooden-movement clocks depended on water-powered machinery to cut clock wheels and turn pinions and on such specialized tools as templates and gauges to finish the parts more easily and more precisely than a craftsman could with hand tools at his bench. The clock movements themselves, along with recently discovered wooden clockmaking machines and tools, provide mute testimony about the process of innovation. The careful analysis of artifacts sometimes can tell us stories that their makers neglected to put down and clarify matters about which participants provide conflicting testimony. For example, Terry's early shelf clocks required nine clock wheels, with 367 teeth cut out on the cherrywood blanks. Over the course of his career, he made significant progress in producing clock wheels in bulk, at high speed, and of good quality. While antiquarians paint a romantic picture of clockmakers using no machinery except a saw and jackknife to cut out their wheels, there is little truth in those accounts. Looking at the artifacts belies this simple story. An eighteenth-century Benjamin Cheney clock movement is certainly bulkier than Eli Terry's, but the teeth were laid out with a compass and rule and probably cut with a handsaw. The clocks Terry made before his contract with the Porters used less wood and had a more efficient shape. Most important, Terry borrowed key techniques and tools from brass-movement clockmakers, particularly a wheel-cutting engine that cut wheels individually and produced what were known as "milled" teeth (fig. 54). These cutters were often crudely made and left ridges on the tooth faces, which caused friction with

Fig. 54. Eli Terry, tall case clock movement, ca. 1800, with milled teeth. National Museum of American History, Smithsonian Institution, Washington, D.C.

the engaged pinions and lowered the yield per stack of wheels. But machines did make the process easier by assembling the wheel blanks on an arbor, the shaft on which the wheels and pinions are attached; a rotary cutter ran through the stack and shaped or milled the individual tooth on each wheel. The process would be repeated until all the teeth on an individual wheel were cut.[65]

Terry used such wheel-cutting machines on the first thousand clocks he made for the Porters. He adopted a circular saw for the remaining three thousand clocks. A circular saw produced teeth with smoother surfaces and more of a radial profile, resulting in less friction, and was easier to sharpen than milling cutters (fig. 55).[66] The stack of blanks, all lined up on an arbor, was turned to the proper diameter on a lathe, checked with a gauge, and then taken to the wheel-cutting machine, still on the same arbor. The stack of wheels was fed into the saws of the wheel-cutting engine, probably similar to the Hopkins and Alfred machine. Workmen slid the indexed wheel blanks into the saws on three wooden rails. The configuration of the saws changed over time. Two saws mounted on a single arbor could cut the leading edges of three teeth and the

Fig. 55. Eli Terry, tall case clock movement with circular saw–cut teeth, ca. 1808–10. American Clock and Watch Museum, Bristol, Connecticut.

trailing edges of three other teeth during each pass. In production, Terry improved upon Asa Hopkins's patented machine for cutting the cogs or teeth of the wheels, which had three mandrels, or cutting surfaces. As Eli Terry's son Henry explained, Hopkins lined up multiple fixtures so that "one row of teeth, on a number of wheels, was finished by one operation of the engine." Finding such a way to cut wheels more accurately and more quickly was the key to the mass production of clocks. Henry Terry lauded Hopkins's mechanical genius; "he had few superiors as to mechanical skill," in the clockmaking community, but "profited little from the patent" without Terry's marketing and overall entrepreneurial prowess. In contrast to Hopkins, Eli Terry made money from the application of this innovation.[67]

The cut wheels were then removed and smoothed with sandpaper. Compared with the early wheel-cutting machine that made one wheel at a time, the Hopkins and Alfred machine, which weighed four hundred pounds, stood five feet high, and required waterpower, dramatically increased the speed of the process. A most remarkable artifact is the Hopkins and Alfred clock factory itself, built about 1830 in Harwinton, Connecticut, and used for over a decade. The wooden building, with three stories and an attic, measured thirty by twenty-eight feet; the waterpower system was below. Despite its relatively small size, the factory turned out thousands of clocks.[68]

Clock manufacturers were early adopters of specialized tools for mass production. Handwork continued within these shops, but clock workers used the information contained in patterns and gauges. These devices took much of the uncertainty out of the process. In David Pye's terms, manufacturing moved from "the workmanship of risk" toward the "workmanship of certainty." Pye explains how this shift occurred: "All workmen using the workmanship of risk are constantly devising ways to limit the risk by using such things as jigs and templates. If you want to draw a straight line with your pen, you do not go at it freehand but use a ruler, that is to say a jig." The recently discovered set of Seth Thomas templates and gauges makes clear how workers performing handwork were guided by tools designed for a particular task they repeated many times. Hands measured as many as a thousand parts with marking gauges to make sure they were the same precise size or depth. Templates—pieces of sheet metal with the outline of gears or other markings cut into them—were developed to guide the hand.[69]

Terry's four-arbor, thirty-hour shelf-clock movement was manufactured with a pattern-based system. Parts were made based on models and measured against their models during the manufacturing process to ensure that the clock parts would fit together when assembled. Craftsmen used gauges for marking and verifying the dimensions of parts. In 1983, when historian of technology Donald Hoke brought together several caches of never-assembled clock parts that were made in different shops, he found the parts to be fully interchangeable; "they could certainly have been taken at random and assembled into clocks."[70] This discovery illuminates how a decentralized system of manufacturing, with shops scattered across Litchfield and Hartford counties, could produce a standardized product. The burgeoning industry still depended on a system in which various individuals fashioned parts for different clockmakers. Because major manufacturers assembled their clocks from products procured through numerous contracts, the parts had to be interchangeable when brought together at a central shop for assembly. Gauges and templates enabled parts makers to achieve the necessary precision. No longer did a clock manufacturer make all his own parts or have all the parts made in his shop. Even assembling of a mix of purchased and shop-made parts that required handwork to fit everything together was too costly.[71]

To contemporaries, production with interchangeable parts seemed magical. A visitor to Chauncey Boardman's Bristol shop in 1832 recalled this story: "One of my early recollections is going to the Boardman & Wells' clock factory on the Hartford turnpike, where I took my first lesson in clockmaking. I watched the piles of thin boards of cherry, touched by swift saws, falling as clock wheels in boxes below. Then I found that the clocks were not made by one man, but by as many sets of men and women as there were pieces; and then they were assembled." The cases, too, were mass-produced.[72]

Marketing Clocks

Merchants entered the ranks of clock manufacturers alongside the first generation of trained clockmakers. The changing case designs and expanding distribution network enticed other artisans and local storekeepers into the industry. Bronson Alcott remembered: "The public mind in a Yankee country was not content that Eli Terry should make his thousands of dollars a year, while they only got an old-fashioned living at one dollar a day or so; and one after another in the contiguous towns . . . they found their way into the same business." The enterprise established by Chauncey Jerome illuminates this development. When he decided to make "pillar and scroll cases for clock parts" in Bristol, he obtained working capital and land from George Mitchell and agreed to repay him with "Eli Terry Patent Clocks." Mitchell, one of Bristol's leading merchants, operated a large peddling network. His father had started with a tin shop and general store; he put out (by use of the outwork system) the manufacture of clothing with the stock of textiles that he bought for sale, and the tin shop led to the peddling network. Mitchell's extensive network of peddlers took a wide assortment of goods on their travels: "Bristol tin ware, clocks, leather and woolen goods, furniture, hard cider, brushes, woven goods, mirrors, wood utensils and tools." Mitchell aggressively sought out producers for those goods and, when necessary, would bring artisans to Bristol and finance them. After Jerome fulfilled his contractual obligations to Mitchell, he set up a new shop as an independent manufacturer.

Mitchell also brought Ephraim Downs to Bristol, where he assembled a water-powered mill with a turning shop. From 1826 to 1828, all of Downs's clock movements, which totaled three thousand, were delivered to Mitchell. Mitchell served as the catalyst for Bristol's clock manufacturing and was its first merchant supplier. Other merchants followed him in financing clock production, providing fixed capital and raw materials to clock manufacturers. Some also furnished credit to the clock-factory workers in their stores; the purchases were deducted from the workers' wages, so in effect these merchants loaned the manufacturers working capital with which to meet their wage bill. Equally important, merchants facilitated product distribution by using their peddling system.[73]

Erastus Hodges, a cheese merchant turned clock entrepreneur, was the central figure in Torrington's rise as a wooden clock–manufacturing center. His copious business records allow an unusual glimpse into the financial operation of clock shops. Hodges never tinkered on a workbench or trained as a cabinetmaker; he was a storekeeper above all. His father, a doctor, had turned merchant to sell the farm produce with which his patients paid for their treatment. After his father's death, Erastus's mother Rebecca expanded the store and became Torrington's major cheese merchant. Cheese was the principal source of income for Torrington farmers in the post-Revolutionary era, so a cheese merchant like Hodges played a central role in the agricultural economy. Erastus joined his mother in business when he came of age and hired a local builder to construct a fashionable mansion as a statement of his considerable ambitions. In 1816, Hodges purchased 102,000 pounds of cheese, which he shipped to Baltimore, New York, and Philadelphia; he opened up new markets in Savannah. Like other merchants, Hodges also served as a banker. He had personal relationships with prominent clockmakers as well; Riley Whiting, member of another Connecticut wooden clockmaking family, was his second cousin. The dealings between Hodges and Norris North, the clever wooden-movement maker who adapted and improved Terry's inventions, illustrate the process through which the merchant became a clock manufacturer. When North moved to Torrington, he was plagued by a perpetual lack of funds, so he kept moving his shop and rearranging his finances. In 1825, North mortgaged all his real estate to Erastus Hodges. When the loans fell due, he was unable to pay. As the principal creditor, Hodges paid North's debts, took possession of his property, and became a clock manufacturer with North as his employee. Cabinetmaker David Winship made the clock cases for Hodges and received store credits in return.[74] By 1828, North had paid off his mortgages, but the next year he fell back into debt and signed another note to Hodges. In 1831, he concluded his business relationship with Hodges by manufacturing over six thousand pillar-and-scroll clocks; Hodges was responsible for selling them, as well as providing the capital. North's fortunes did not improve after he set up a new clock shop a few miles away. He later moved to Oswego, New York, and he ended up in Iowa, where he died in 1875 at the age of eighty-five. North never attained financial success despite his inventive work in the mechanic's trade. In 1831, Erastus Hodges took over full control of what had been the Norris North clock shop.[75] Hodges became an investor and then an entrepreneur, a natural development for the wealthy merchant, given his location in the burgeoning center of American clockmaking.

Connecticut wooden-movement clock factories remained small affairs in the 1820s and 1830s. A manufacturer needed only about $2,000 worth of capital to enter the business. A handful of employees would do; the annual wage bill for ten to twenty employees ran between $3,000 and $9,000. Entrepreneurs took advantage of specialization, the division of labor, mechanization, and water-power, so that a dozen workers could make more clocks in one month than an eighteenth-century craftsman could make in a lifetime. Outside contractors provided many of the parts that went into a finished clock. Materials came predominantly from local sources; most of the rest were secured from domestic purchases, and a few were imported. Labor and raw materials were obtained on credit, in the familiar system of local exchange recorded in account books. Hodges hired five men and two boys as lathe operators, wheel cutters, metal workers, and assemblers. Family members—a father and son, or husband and wife—often worked together: Albro Cowles did "engine work" cutting wheels, while Eliza Cowles painted dials. Entries recorded the terms of the piece work being done within the shop; Harvey Moulton received $65 for "engine work for 1,000 clocks," $20.41 from making 907 verges, and lots of pendulum rods at one and a half cents each, apparently his specialty. Women and girls with school or academy training in reverse painting on glass painted the pillar-and-scroll's glass tablet. At least five casemakers provided Hodges with a variety of "small," "scroll," "looking glass (long toms)," and "short bronze" and long bronzed cases, usually working in their own shops.[76]

The major material obtained locally was wood. Clock wheels were made from cherry, the Connecticut favorite for furniture, which was easily available in the early years of wooden clockmaking but becoming scarce by the 1820s. Hodges used his peddlers to locate cherrywood and the whitewood used in cases on their peddling expeditions in western New York. The few metal pieces, such as iron clock bells and pendulum bobs, could be purchased from nearby specialty firms. Brass, the most expensive material, was needed only in small quantities; Hodges picked it up on semi-annual shopping trips to New York City.[77]

Peddling Clocks

The new mode of clock manufacture required more than the technological innovations and changes in the work process embodied in powered machinery, specialized tools, and a rational system of production using skilled mechanics, piece workers, and outside contractors. The development of mass production in clockmaking was, from its sources of capital through its system of marketing, a radical economic transformation. Terry's mechanical innovations were predicated on the concurrent development of a flexible marketing system composed of peddlers who sold standardized mass-produced objects that signified status to a vast rural market. Terry's initial contract with the Porters relieved him of the responsibility of selling his products; the merchants took over the entire matter of marketing from the manufacturer. Distributors like the Porters and merchants turned manufacturer, such as George Mitchell, used and expanded the Connecticut tinsmiths' peddling system. Clock peddlers brought this mode of marketing to full flower in the 1820s and 1830s.

The peddling distribution system ingeniously solved many of the problems that early-nineteenth-century manufacturers faced: how to extend their market from local consumers to the populace of the southern and western states; how to navigate the confusing, risky, and sometimes precarious financial system involving local banknotes and inadequate market information; and how to promote the sale and use of complex and costly new products, such as clocks or patent washing machines. Peddlers brought their persuasive sales pitch and newfangled commodities to urban areas as well as the backcountry, and they linked the developing industrial economy of the Northeast to the growing agrarian regions of the southern and western United States. Peddlers helped create a national market. The peddling system took several forms. Sometimes clock manufacturers sold small lots of clocks to individual peddlers or set up distant assembly shops to outfit peddlers. But for the most part the system relied upon middlemen organized in three levels: forwarding agents, peddling companies, and peddlers, the last link in the merchandising chain.[78]

Clock peddling grew directly out of tinware distribution, as the tin manufacturers clustered around Berlin, Connecticut. Peddlers slowly added small goods to their packs and wagons. Clock movements made by such manufacturers as Eli Terry, James Harrison, and Gideon Roberts were added to the copious assortment available on tin peddlers' wagons on longer journeys. Terry's shelf clock, with its relatively low price, small size, and integrated works and case, changed the peddling system just as profoundly as it did other aspects of the industry. Some peddlers specialized in selling shelf clocks, although they may have carried other goods. Clock manufacturers generally relied upon the wholesale trade to dispose of their ever-increasing production to peddling companies, small partnerships, and individual peddlers. The larger companies sold several thousand dollars worth of clocks a year, with a network of "stands" or warehouses that supplied peddlers over an extensive territory. Eli Terry, Jr. and Company of Terryville sold clocks to the peddling company of Gunn, Mattoon, Gilbert & Company in central Virginia. The clocks moved by wagon from Terry's factory to the port of New Haven. A forwarding agent shipped them to New York City, and a coastal schooner carried them to a Richmond, Virginia, forwarding agent who sent them inland. Simon Gunn took ownership of the clocks in Lexington, Kentucky, for distribution from the company's stand to peddlers who sold across an extensive territory. Seth Wheeler sold Ives clocks in Kentucky in the 1830s and 1840s. His clocks followed a similar southern route;

he directed his six peddlers from Paris, Kentucky, distributing 468 clocks in 1838.[79]

Clock peddlers came from the pool of young New England men who were looking for independence in a changing countryside. Their cycle of work lasted one year. In late spring, they returned to Connecticut to pay off their debts; in the summer they arranged for their next round of merchandise. In the early fall they began their journey south or west. By winter they were in full swing, selling clocks and collecting on the notes from the previous year's sales. Employment contracts required the peddler "to be diligent, faithful, sober, and industrious in the business and frugal in his expenses, and to keep good and regular accounts of notes and money and all other property." While the peddler might be required to supply himself with a "good substantial horse and harness," the employer would furnish "a good substantial wagon and other vehicles such as may be wanted to convey clocks and other goods." Peddlers were paid twenty-five to sixty dollars a month; more experienced peddlers could command higher wages.[80] Difficulties abounded: peddlers might abscond with the goods, the clocks could turn out to be faulty merchandise, and problems might occur in transit. The length and complexity of the supply chain caused stressful delays. Itinerants often wrote back to Connecticut with advice about market conditions and pleas for the timely arrival of supplies. Highly dependent on river transport, George Bartholomew wrote in late May from Alabama of the dangers of drought and the possibilities of running out of goods: "My Goods are or will be scarce before long. . . . You must be sure to send the fall goods in season for should it continue dry the country is so situated that the merchants cannot Get Goods up the becbee [Tombigbee River, tributary of the Mobile River] until next springs freshets [spring thaw]." John Bartholomew wrote to Upson, Merrimans and Company from Canton, Ohio, after having anxiously awaited his spring inventory: "Respecting the 30 Clocks Shiped last fall they arrived in Ohio late this Spring verges and wires very rusty and many of them were Swelled So that they will not run until I whittle & Smooth the wheels." Only one of the ten sold was in order without "being tinkered more or less."[81] Clock manufacturers, such as Eli Terry, Jr., were eager to hear reports from the field in this far-flung system of merchandising. He wrote to Norton & Stimson in Jacksonville, Illinois, in 1826: "We would like to know how you are pleased with our clocks— whether they run well or not etc," soliciting his information not from the peddlers themselves but from the firm with the distribution contracts.[82]

Rensseleaer Upson combed northern Alabama, western Georgia, and southern Tennessee. His partner, the merchant Philip Barnes, provided not only the financing but also the depots in which to store clocks. When Upson returned to New England in spring 1822 to settle accounts with suppliers Eli Terry and

Chauncey Jerome, he was unable to clear up all his debt; his suppliers extended his notes under the condition that the notes were endorsed by his father Asa, and they held exclusive rights to the cotton that he collected in exchange for his clocks. Upson spent the rest of his time arranging horses and wagons and ordering stocks and supplies of combs, shoes, and clocks. He bought 234 clocks and contracted for 52 more with cases and 15 without to be shipped in October at ten dollars each. In mid-September he left Bristol, Connecticut, with three fully loaded wagons and traveled to Huntsville, Alabama, a thousand-mile journey that took forty-eight days. He sold 102 of the 136 clocks, probably to merchants along the way. While in the South, Upson managed the peddling operation. In this season, he supervised three peddlers, sending Abraham Woodruff and William Hindman to Charleston to pick up clocks shipped by sea and dispatching F. W. Atkins on the first sales trip. The three men usually took about ten clocks per trip and made about seven trips during the season. They sold 184 clocks along with shoes, pumps, and combs and took in about three thousand dollars for the year, which would be enough for Upson to pay off the previous year's debt. But the success of the enterprise depended on collecting from the customers the next year.[83]

Upson's peddlers, like those of most other merchants, did not sell clocks for cash. Only about 10 percent of a survey of peddlers' accounts came from cash; another 10 percent was composed of goods taken in exchange; and 80 percent came through credit.[84] Terms varied, but averaged about one year, when a clock peddler returned to make collections. Peddling companies worked under great uncertainty, caught between their substantial debt to clock manufacturers and the need to extend credit to consumers. Farmers and other rural residents expected generous terms and flexibility from merchants, whether they were local storekeepers or Yankee peddlers. Accepting payment in such farm produce as cotton exposed peddlers to the vagaries of speculation in commodity prices, lessons that Upson and Barnes learned only too well. The plunge in cotton prices after a bumper crop in 1826 created havoc for peddling companies and clock manufacturers alike; some even went out of business. Old clocks were among the goods taken in exchange for new ones. Peddling for Seth Wheeler in central Kentucky during the late 1830s, Isaac Hotchkiss found that many of his customers already owned a nice Connecticut clock, so he swapped their old wooden clock for a new, brass-movement clock. Being paid in banknotes was often no more secure than being paid in goods. One exchange in Cow Creek left Hotchkiss with a forty-dollar note and an "old clock taken away" that he swapped the next day for a fifteen-dollar note.[85] Before the establishment of a uniform system of paper money, holding a banknote was no guarantee of receiving adequate or certain payment. Fluctuating values for notes raised the

CHAPTER FOUR

specter of depreciation, a risk faced by businessmen everywhere. As one peddler explained to Upson: "We are compelled to take *Tenn* Alabama and Mississippi paper and a Large Portion of the latter otherwise we can get nothing at all as *Miss* paper passes very current here in payment of debts and in all commercial transactions. There is more Shinplasters in circulation in this country than would cover the Kentucky purchase one inch thick."[86]

Giving too generous terms caused other problems, as Eli Terry, Jr., warned: "The best time to collect a debt of a man who buys a clock is in sixth months or at farthest one year before the clock wants repairing or the novelty is gone. You give a man two years credit & he may get sick of his clock, or he may run away or become insolvent, when if he had been required to pay in six months it might have been collected."[87] Making accurate predictions of a customer's solvency often proved impossible, and the pressure to sell clocks led peddlers to make deals even if they were uncertain they would actually be able to collect the debt later. When the clock peddlers returned, debtors had all sorts of stratagems to avoid payment. Peddlers could resort to the courts, but, as George Bartholomew learned in Mississippi, debtors could easily obtain a stay of thirty to sixty days; to meet his obligations to Upson, he explained that he had "employed a man to go into the Chock Taw [Choctaw] Nation to trade for beever [*sic*] and other skins.". To some of his correspondents, Eli Terry, Jr., suggested rewording the standard form of the promissory note; by adding the phrase "without defalcation stay of execution or offset," they might avoid some of these evasive tactics. Often debtors simply fled, leading to significant losses, even though creditors made extensive efforts to find debtors at their new locations. Alpha Hart reported to Erastus Hodges from Shelby, New York, about a situation he encountered when he tried to recover payment from J. Oldfield. The man was not at home when he called, but his wife, "pretending she would pay part, took occasion to snatch the note from me and then kept it. I took advice on the subject of a lawyer who said the debt could still be collected."[88]

Over time, clock prices tumbled because of manufacturers' expanding production and the swarms of itinerants on the road. Manufacturers cut prices in the face of cutthroat competition for the rapidly growing market, and their enterprise became less profitable than before. Clockmakers' unit costs had been reduced to about $5 by the second decade of the nineteenth century, and they might wholesale their clocks to peddling companies for $6.75 cash or $8 to $9 on credit. The peddling companies covered shipping and insurance fees along with the sizable costs of peddlers' wages and expenses. Philip Barnes & Company would debit their peddlers $20 for each clock they removed from their Huntsville, Alabama, "stand," and in turn their peddlers charged customers between $35 and $50. Other accounts reported consumer prices between $25 and $35.[89] In regions with a glut of clocks and peddling competition, such as Alpha Hall found along the Erie Canal in the early 1830s, clocks could be purchased for as low as $10 to $15. Hall found "old fashioned clocks" made by Connecticut wooden clockmaker Riley Whiting were selling for $12, and he recommended that Hodges pick up "a hundred or so of Whiting's clocks to sell in Canada, because people in a new country cannot afford high priced clocks."[90]

Another expense and burden of peddling on the road was obtaining the necessary license. Clock peddlers often had to pay higher fees than peddlers selling other sorts of goods. In Virginia, clock peddlers paid a hundred dollars annually per county, ten times the amount charged tin peddlers. Sometimes licensing laws were aimed at protecting local merchants and manufacturers who sold goods made within the state. Chauncey Jerome evaded local laws with true Yankee ingenuity:

> In 1835, the southern people were greatly opposed to the Yankee pedlars coming into their states, especially the clock pedlars, and the licences were raised so high by their Legislatures that it amounted to almost a prohibition. Their laws were that any goods made in their own States could be sold without licence. Therefore clocks to be profitable must be made in those states. Chauncey and Noble Jerome started a factory in Richmond Va., making the cases and parts at Bristol, Connecticut, and packing them with the dials, glass &c. We shipped them to Richmond and took along workmen to put them together. The people were highly pleased with the idea of having clocks all made in their State. The old planters would tell the pedlars they meant to go to Richmond and see the wonderful machinery there must be to produce such articles and would no doubt have thought the tools we had there were sufficient to make a clock. We carried on this kind of business for two or three years and did very well at it, though it was unpleasant. Every one knew it was all a humbug trying to stop the pedlars from coming to their State. We removed from Richmond to Hamburg, S.C., and manufactured in the same way.[91]

The pretense that these clocks were local products was as much humbug as the laws purporting to regulate peddlers.

The awareness of time as a means of organizing social activities and work lives waited for the ubiquity of timepieces, a level that was reached by the 1830s. Wooden clocks had brought about this great change, and peddlers had been critical to this transformation. Clock peddlers represented the face of a manufacturing and marketing revolution that drew in a broad range of consumers throughout the United States. Paul Clemens found in Fairfield County, Connecticut, that the handful of clocks owned at the end of the eighteenth century were expensive brass ones; by the close of the 1810s, over two-thirds were wooden, and the price of wooden clocks was one-quarter that of brass ones. Along the Hudson River, timepieces appeared in about a quarter of the Greene County inventories in the first decade of the nineteenth century, and their cost averaged $26.64, according to historian Martin Bruegel; two decades later, 63 percent of the population owned a clock or watch, and the cost had tumbled to a little more than $9! Shelf clocks appear frequently on mantelpieces in contemporary paintings and travelers' accounts. English scientist G. W. Featherstonhaugh found these prized possessions in the log cabins he visited in Kentucky, Indiana, Illinois, and Missouri during the 1840s; the ubiquity and zeal of "Yankee clocks peddlers" meant that "in every cabin where there was not a chair to sit on there was sure to be a Connecticut clock." Production peaked at eighty thousand clocks in 1836, before the panic of 1837 shook up the clock industry. In those Hudson Valley houses, Bruegel found the awareness of time as a means of organizing social activities and work lives waited for the ubiquity of timepieces, a level that was reached by the 1830s. Wooden clocks had brought about this great change.[92]

Eli Terry's experiments had succeeded wildly beyond his original dreams, transforming the clock industry and the very clock itself. He built his success upon a large community of mechanically minded artisans, merchandising pioneers, and a network of peddlers all across the United States—even on the far frontier. From such small beginnings as Terry's clock shop came significant industries that supplied the colorful common household objects that signified a respectable domestic interior during the 1820s and 1830s. The Connecticut mechanics who created the first mass-production consumer industry relied on itinerant merchandisers who brought the products of northeastern industry right to the farmhouse door.

Industrialization took place outside the factory system in forms that reached across northern provincial society. Rural communities with their networks of artisans were a central source of innovation, and itinerancy was an effective marketing system that transformed American material culture. The flexible and decentralized rural system of production—pioneered by clockmakers and soon to be found elsewhere—relied on the labor of countless young men and women in the countryside willing to work for wages and on the desire of middle-class families across the nation to fill up their parlors with consumer goods. Craftsmen and consumers gave a new look to some old farmhouse favorites, with paint on the surface, a reworking of the machinery within, and a reconfiguration of the product itself.

CHAPTER FIVE

A Tale of Two Chairmaking Towns

Gardner and Sterling

Two chairmaking communities located side by side in central Massachusetts complicate the story of industrial development in the northern United States. The towns of Gardner and Sterling demonstrate the distinctive paths toward capitalist manufacturing taken by the furniture industry. During the first half of the nineteenth century, consumers, distributors, and manufacturers constituted a revolution in the manufacture of light consumer goods—chairs, clocks, and textiles. Dramatic changes in middle-class interiors came about through the move from craft to industry. When we think of the industrial revolution in the United States, images of the large-scale Lowell mills with their thousands of factory girls come to mind, not Joel Pratt's modest chair shop in Sterling, Massachusetts (figs. 58 and 56). Yet, according to the 1820 manufacturing census, Pratt was manufacturing eight thousand chairs in sets of six, and Sterling chairmakers recorded an annual production of more than seventy thousand wooden-seated chairs. Numerous small workshops lined Sterling's streams. In 1837, twenty-nine towns in Worcester County listed at least one chair- or cabinet-manufacturing firm. During the middle and late nineteenth century, central

Facing page: (top) Fig. 56. Photograph of the Joel Pratt, Jr., Chair Manufactory. Sterling, Massachusetts. Late nineteenth century. Sterling Historical Society. Fig. 57. Heywood Brothers Factory, Gardner, Massachusetts, published in John Chapin, *The Historical Picture Gallery* (Boston, 1856), 186. Library of Congress, Washington, D.C.

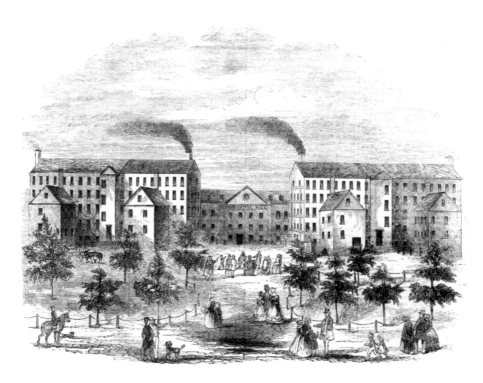

Fig. 58. Boott Cotton Mills at Lowell, *Gleason's Pictorial* (29 May 1852). Library of Congress, Washington, D.C.

Massachusetts claimed to be the center of the chair industry in the United States.[1]

Northern Worcester County—the upland region lying between the Merrimack and Connecticut River valleys—seems an unlikely location for industrial development. Here, as in other places in central New England, many young people in the generations after the Revolution turned from farming to craft pursuits. Each town developed some sort of manufacturing prowess: Leominster was known for its combs, and Gardner, dubbed "Chair City," placed a giant chair on the lawn of its town hall. During the 1820s and 1830s, the entire region was a beehive of small-scale production, so broadly had manufacturing extended in this age of wood and waterpower. Thousands of women made palm-leaf hats or chair seats in their homes, adding valuable cash to the family income. While Sterling's chair industry grew through the proliferation of small workshops, Gardner's centered on substantial factories (fig. 57). The tale of those two towns and their different paths to industrial development, from the multiplication of small shops to the consolidation of larger manufactories, reveals patterns of industrialization quite distinct from the huge textile cities created by the Boston Associates and other industrialists at Lowell, Lawrence, and Holyoke, Massachusetts, and Manchester, New Hampshire.[2]

Many years ago, I was drawn to study Worcester County by Frederick Jackson Turner's 1914 essay "The First Official Frontier of Massachusetts Bay," which featured the town of Westminster, founded during the eighteenth century by land speculators, as an example of the declension in the consensual mode of group settlement that had previously characterized New England. Turner, the frontier historian, pointed to the hordes of speculative proprietors who crowded the Boston Common looking for their share of a windfall, but soon fell into angry disputes with the homesteaders "out west" in central Massachusetts who complained about the absentee landowners' disinterest in developing their settlement into a full-fledged community. When I looked at the documents from Westminster, however, I found that a dense web of kinship ties bound eastern proprietors and western settlers. In communities founded during the eighteenth century, family farmsteads were dispersed across the landscape rather than concentrated into nuclear villages as their seventeenth-century ancestors were; the commercial market in land shaped the process of settlement to make its distribution more unequal, but farming families still sought to establish the next generation on land of its own. As towns were occupied and filled up, they hived off daughter settlements; Sterling grew out of Lancaster, for example.[3] After the Revolution, these inland towns were filled with an amazing variety of artisans seeking brighter economic prospects than agriculture afforded. Printers Isaiah Thomas and the Merriam brothers and painters Ralph Earl and Winthrop Chandler made northern Worcester County their home. The industrious agrarian household and its members provided the impetus for the small-scale and extensive development of manufacturing across the region. The varied dynamics of growth in the chair industry offer the most significant view of the nineteenth-century story of changing production and consumer products.

The conventional image of "the industrial revolution," with its connotations of a singular, drastic upheaval in the social order, is inapplicable to the long-term process of industrial development based on extensive artisanal and shop production. James Comee of Gardner began to make chairs in the back of his home, and Joel Pratt manufactured thousands of chairs in his small shop on a Sterling stream. Gardner's superior waterpower and its entrepreneurs' access to capital and transportation eventually left Sterling's chairmakers behind, while Gardner's elite became celebrated figures and its Heywood-Wakefield Company a nationally known brand name for inexpensive solid furniture. Industrialization took many forms, as small-scale rural shops as well as large-scale urban factories, and looking only at the endpoint distorts our understanding of the process. In this rapidly expanding industry, farmer-craftsmen became full-time chairmakers or furniture workers. A web of out-workers producing chair parts in workshops and chair seats in homes covered northern Worcester County and southern New Hampshire. Sawmills turning out wooden furniture parts dotted the numerous banks of streams. Making more chairs meant more sites for production. Many industries boomed with the utilization of waterpower across rural New England. The furniture industry was built across an extensive area rather than concentrated in particular sites. Handwork increased alongside machine production in furniture and other crafts. The need for increased production led chairmakers to innovations in design too: the bold, lathe-turned parts of the Windsor chair were simplified; hand-painted fancy chairs gave way to colorful stenciled designs on factory-made chairs; and these chair shops set up along the many waterways of northern Worcester County. Meanwhile, the growing ranks of northern middle-class families eagerly accumulated these cheaper but elaborately decorated items in their parlors, as seen in the 1826 watercolor of the Connecticut parlor with painted furniture (plate 5).[4]

When Solomon Sibley of Auburn made this bow-back Windsor chair around 1800, he was pursuing furniture making only about a quarter of the time, mostly during the winter months. His accounts are rounded out with farming, painting, glazing, and making wooden wares for farmers, such as rakes and grain cradles. At the turn of the nineteenth century, central Massachusetts craftsmen who made furniture were also farmers, and most practiced carpentry as well as joinery. The Worcester County deeds and inventories studied by Donna Baron and other researchers at Old Sturbridge Village identify only a few men as "shop joiners" or "chair makers" and show that most farmers owned a range of woodworking tools. Chapman Lee of Charlton, who made chairs, worked principally at farming. He worked at his trade only eighty-six days in 1804, and he spent only a tenth of his time in his shop during the peak decade of his woodworking. Lee's market was confined to a small geographic area where he supplied kitchen chairs and a few sets of Windsor chairs.[5] Farmer-woodworkers did follow changing furniture fashions. Silas Fay of Princeton, who made mostly coffins and chairs, occasionally made an up-to-date desk or dressing table.[6]

After the Revolution, the demand for furniture increased significantly, in part through population growth: Worcester County's population rose from 56,807 in 1790 to 95,313 in 1840. At the same time, the drive for rural improvement stimulated desire for consumer goods. Jack Larkin found almost eleven chairs per probated household in 1790; by the 1830s the average household

Plate 1. Miniature panorama, *Scenes from a Seminary for Young Ladies*, with a detail of two women studying a globe, ca. 1810–20. Panoramas were popular entertainments in the nineteenth century. A schoolgirl probably made this unusual watercolor and ink on silk panorama that shows the range of reading and sewing skills along with painting, music, and geography offered by female academies and seminaries. The entire panorama measures 7-1/16 × 96-5/8 in. St. Louis Art Museum, Museum Purchase and funds given by the Decorative Arts Society 89:1976.

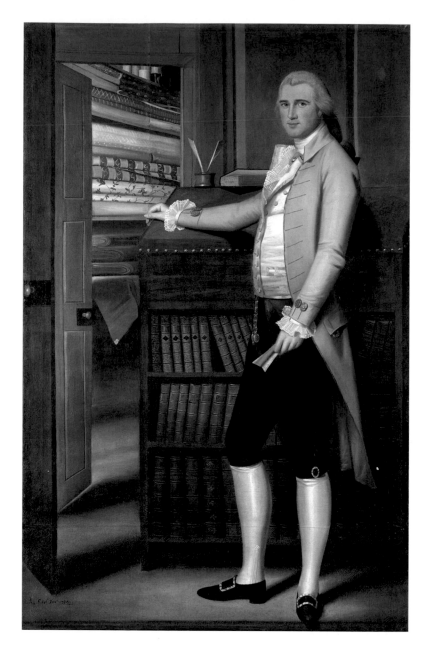

Plate 2. Ralph Earl, *Elijah Boardman*, 1789. Oil on canvas. 83 × 51 in. Bequest of Susan W. Tyler, 1979 (1979.395). Metropolitan Museum of Art, New York. Image copyright © The Metropolitan Museum of Art / Art Resource, NY.

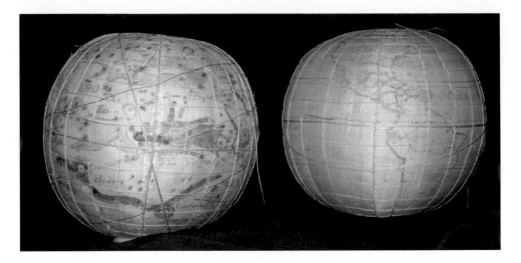

Plate 3. Terrestrial and celestial globes made by Sarah Sheppard, a student at the West-town School, Westtown, Pennsylvania, ca. 1844. Silk, paint, and ink on silk. 4-3/4 in. diameter. Monroe County Historical Association, Stroudsburg, Pennsylvania.

Plate 4. Three-inch terrestrial globe made by Wilson & Sons, ca. 1820. Albany, New York. Author's photograph. Hand-colored, paper gores over core, mounted on spindle, on a wooden pedestal with four arms supporting a wooden circle with mounted hand-colored zodiacal paper, and a brass meridian ring. Three-inch globes (this one was paired with a celestial globe) expanded the Wilson family's line of globes while still supplying customers with a great amount of detail for their small size. Library of Congress, Washington, D.C.

Plate 5 (above). Celestia Bull inscribed this exuberant watercolor and ink on paper view of a Connecticut provincial parlor: "Lord Charles Is Fiddling [and] Lady Sarah Is Sewing," along with her name and date, for Sarah Sawyer's friendship album, a popular female pastime. The nineteen-year-old artist recorded a "fancy" decorated parlor with abundant seating and colorful decorative items, along with a range of such leisure activities as music, sewing, and reading that qualify the Sawyers as provincial gentry. Watercolor and ink on paper. 8 × 6-1/2 in. Collection of Jane and Gerald Katcher. Photograph by Gavin Ashworth. Courtesy of David Schorsch and Eileen Smiles.

Plate 6 (top right). When Alden Spooner made this chest of drawers around 1810 in central Massachusetts, he inscribed it "Alden Spooner Athol" and displayed bold contrasting woods as well as a series of oval panels that alternate with the rectangular panels; the side stiles have reeding, and the top is distinguished by cross banding. Cherry with mahogany, birch, and bird's-eye maple veneers, white pine, brass. 42-1/2 × 40 × 21-1/4 in. Courtesy of Historic Deerfield, Massachusetts. Photograph by Amanda Merullo.

Plate 7 (bottom right). Ammi Phillips, *Girl in Red Dress with Cat and Dog*, 1830–35. Oil on canvas. 30 × 25 in. Collection American Folk Art Museum, New York City. Gift of the Siegman Trust, Ralph Esmerian, trustee. 2001.37.1. Photograph by John Parnell.

Plate 8. Erastus Salisbury Field, *Joseph Moore and His Family*, 1839. Oil on canvas. 82-3/8 × 93-3/8 in. Museum of Fine Arts, Boston. Gift of Maxim Karolik for the M. and M. Karolik Collection of American Paintings, 1815–65. 58.25. Photograph © 2009 Museum of Fine Arts, Boston.

Plate 9. Robert Peckham, *Rosa Heywood*, ca. 1840. Oil on canvas. 44-1/4 × 29-1/4 in. Abby Aldrich Rockefeller Folk Art Museum, The Colonial Williamsburg Foundation, Virginia.

Plate 10. Daguerreotype of a portrait of a young woman with fabric. Collection of Matthew R. Isenburg.

had twenty-one chairs, along with tables and case furniture. Some cabinet-makers and chairmakers began to work full time at furniture production. Part-time woodworkers like Sibley continued to practice their trades, but their production of furniture tapered off. While the full-time furniture makers native to the locality had been trained in shop joinery by relatives, many trained cabinetmakers migrated from eastern Massachusetts to Worcester County in search of a niche in the expanding rural economy. The earliest pieces of signed and dated furniture show the influence of eastern Massachusetts fashions, whether imported by migrating artisans or adopted by country-trained cabinetmakers.[7]

Workshops and Manufactories

The towns of Sterling and Gardner, Massachusetts, had similar beginnings in the chair industry, but veered off in different directions. The industry emerged from the rural household economy, using apprentices who lived with the chairmaker's family and relying upon farmers' woodworking skills. In about 1805, James Comee (b. 1777) set up shop at his Gardner home making wooden-seated chairs. Comee built a ladderback chair, a staple form of the eighteenth century, and a Windsor chair, a newer, post-Revolutionary style (fig. 59). Both were turned on a foot-powered lathe in the shop behind Comee's house. "In the early manufacture of chair stock," the historian of Ashburnham recalled, "the conditions required only a small room in some part of the dwelling-house, a saw, a frow and a shave, while a foot-lathe introduced the owner to the front rank among the chair makers of that period." So few tools and so little capital were required that many could add "the manufacture of chairs or chair stock" to their other employment. Meeting with success, Comee expanded his production by traditional means, training numerous apprentices and launching a new generation of Worcester County–born chairmakers. In 1820, he produced about $1,500 worth of fancy chairs and about $1,000 worth of cabinetwork. He had shifted from wooden-seated to flag-seated chairs, using dried rushes drawn from nearby marshes to make more comfortable seats. Still, he was the only chairmaker listed in Gardner. He transported his chairs to Worcester, Lowell, and Boston by teams of horses to be sold in small lots.[8]

James Comee's apprentices pushed production out of the farmhouse and began to experiment with methods of increasing output. The first of Comee's apprentices, Elijah Brick, began his apprenticeship in 1806 and then worked as a journeyman until 1814, when he built his own shop to make flag-seated chairs. Adopting a putting-out system, he had his brother make woodwork and paid local women to make chair seats in their homes. Brick marketed the goods

Fig. 59. Windsor chair made by James Comee, ca. 1800. Gardner, Massachusetts. Gardner Museum. Author's photograph.

himself with his team of horses. Another Comee apprentice, Elijah Putnam, was clever at thinking up inventions but had difficulty implementing them successfully. Starting with a foot lathe in his house, he moved to a shop where he devised a steam-powered engine of his own invention; when that failed, he tried using horsepower.[9]

Chairmaking activities were scattered all over the rural landscape. Like shoemaking and palm-leaf hatmaking, the chair industry was decentralized. Northern Worcester County witnessed the extensive spread of small-scale industrial activity, as the region's abundant woods and streams made it an ideal site first for sawmills and then for chair shops and small manufactories. Rural industries used locally available resources, such as hides, woods, and rushes, along with comparatively inexpensive but often skilled labor, to produce goods for urban markets. Worcester County's pool of skilled furniture makers, its growing commercial class, and the increasing demand for stylish furnishings all promoted a move away from "bespoke" or custom work toward production chairmaking.

That change came in many ways. In Templeton, Stephen Kilburn manufactured a shaped tablet-top Windsor chair in a style similar to the work coming out of Alden Spooner's Athol, Massachusetts, cabinetmaking shop, yet in far greater numbers. Kilburn had adopted waterpower; replacing the one-man shop with a small manufactory of several employees operating power-driven lathes. The 1820 manufacturing census noted that Kilburn annually "makes more than twelve thousand chairs." Other innovative entrepreneurs were also purchasing waterpower privileges or enlarging older facilities.[10]

A network of specialized producers—mill operators, chair "stuff" producers, assemblers, and seaters—covered northern Worcester County and southwestern New Hampshire. While the trade card for William Buttre's Fancy Chair Manufactory in New York City around 1812 (fig. 60) shows all these steps being performed in a centralized workshop, in New England these activities were spread around two counties. Increasingly, sawmills or chair mills in the northernmost tier of towns produced chair plank or squared turning billets along with lumber. "Farmers and timber dealers supplied most of the turning stock, splitting and cutting sticks to length, then trimming the corners in readiness for the lathe," according to curator Frank White. "Many manufactories specialized in turned chair stock, leaving the framing, finishing and merchandising to other establishments." Chair manufacturers could purchase seats from woodworkers who specialized in this part of the trade. Substantial manufactories stockpiled raw materials and employed local workmen to assemble chairs part time, either in their shops or more often at home as outworkers. Smaller shops might rely on the labor of the owner and one other worker. Some chair shops were located on small streams just powerful enough to drive a single lathe. Others did without a lathe by focusing on the framing and assembling of chairs. With its varied configuration, the industry transformed the region into a network of turning mills, chair mills, chair manufactories, and small shops, with the painting, seating, and finishing of chairs done in farmhouses.[11]

Sterling may have commenced chairmaking a bit later than Gardner, but it took the lead in chair manufacturing during the first decades of the nineteenth century. By 1800, a turnpike connected Sterling to Boston, and a post road ran to Worcester. Local entrepreneurs tapped into urban and more distant markets. "The sales [of Sterling chairs] are made all over the country," a local historian wrote, "but principally in the manufacturing villages, that are growing up with such rapidity." A new generation of chairmakers led this aggressive expansion. Of the town's twenty-three chairmakers listed in the 1820 census, over half were younger than thirty-four. Many must have entered the trade during the 1810s, at about the same time as James Comee of Gardner. Heman Burpee and Elijah Dresser, both about twenty-one, bought a small lot of land with buildings and

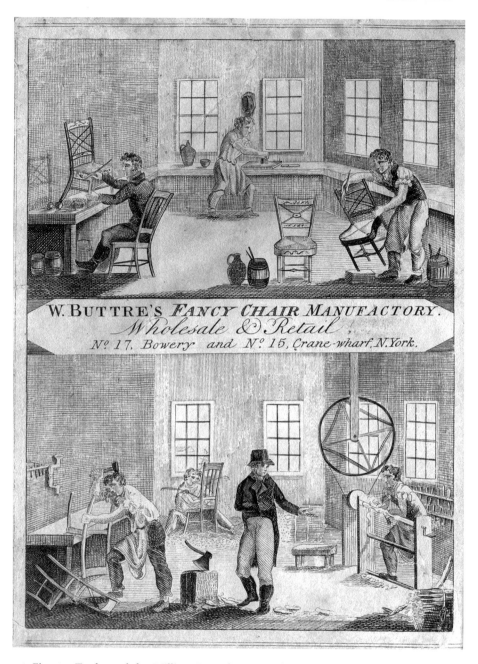

Fig. 60. Trade card for William Buttre's Fancy Chair Manufactory, ca. 1813. New York City. Buttre's manufactory illustrated the specialized nature of chair production. In the lower half, going from right to left, workmen turn a chair part on a foot-pedal lathe, weave a chair seat, and frame a finished fancy chair. An owner or perhaps a customer stands at the center. In the upper half, we see three stages of the painting process: the better-dressed ornamenter dabbing on colors; another grinding paint on a stone; and a varnisher deftly balancing the decorated chair on one leg for purposes of rotating it for faster application. Courtesy of The Winterthur Library: Joseph Downs Collection of Manuscripts and Printed Ephemera, Winterthur, Delaware.

Fig. 61. Side chair by Gilson Brown, Sterling, Massachusetts, late 1820s–1830s. Sterling Historical Society. Author's photograph.

set up a chair shop near the center of Sterling in 1814. A town map from 1830 shows chairmakers clustered in several locations around town, mostly along the waterways; ten chair mills were listed, more than the total number of sawmills and gristmills combined.[12] Newton Burpee constructed his chair mill and water-powered turning shop at a long-established mill site near Beamon Road. He obtained ready-made, rough-cut chair stock from sawmills. Henry Roper's "water lathe shop and chair shop" was located on a small stream, where he erected a rudimentary earthwork dam in order to run his lathe and a small circular saw. In Sterling as in Gardner, the scale of production was small, and many chairmaking activities were dispersed. The 1831 tax list for Sterling showed seventeen shops as "within or adjoining the house"; by 1841, the number had risen to thirty-nine. In 1820, Gilson Brown assembled three thousand chairs in his shop, which had many tools but no lathe. The rounded-end, tablet-top chair has a simple plank seat, but the profile resembles popular Boston wares; screws hold up the ornamented tablet in the manner of a fancy chair (fig. 61).[13] If an artisan could make do without waterpower, as Brown did, his shop could be located anywhere.

In chairmaking, as in the clock industry, the leaders of industrial growth were those who combined entrepreneurial energies and marketing prowess rather than relying solely on their training and experience at the workbench. The careful coordination of decentralized production was the key to making profits. Joel Pratt, Jr., became Sterling's largest chairmaker, producing eight thousand chairs in 1820. He owned a gristmill and a sawmill in 1811, and he soon added a chair mill to the site at the junction of Wiccapicca (Wickapekitt) Brook and the Leominster to Worcester Road, giving him ample waterpower and easy transportation to markets. Eventually the area became known as Pratt's Junction (see fig. 56). The available waterpower was sufficient to turn many lathes. Not only did Pratt boost production, but his accounts list charges for the "use of the lathe" or "turning" by local chair turners who rented time on his machinery for sixteen cents a day. Renting out the use of simple machinery, such as cider presses, was a common practice in rural communities. But chair manufactory owners were businessmen. Pratt opened a store and purchased parts and labor from many workers. His store accounts show transactions with more than three dozen chairmakers who supplied turned or shaved chair stuff or prefabricated chair seats, which Pratt sold either as stock or used to make framed and finished seating. Most accounts were local, but some chairmakers lived as far away as Fitzwilliam, New Hampshire. For example, Samuel Ingalls received credit for 1,766 legs and 1,788 rods or spindles in 1824. Pratt also hired his brother-in-law and other workers to turn chair parts. He even purchased completed chairs, which he marketed under his own label. Pratt and other Worcester County manufacturers made full lines of chairs, often sold in sets of six, that ranged from a cheap and simple arrowback Windsor side chair painted brown, to grained thumb-back side chairs (fig. 62), to an elaborately decorated armchair distinguished by hand-painted foliage.[14] By 1840, Pratt had a warehouse in Hartford where he sold a wide variety of chairs as advertised in his broadside:

STRANGER, LOOK HERE!
Where is the best Place to buy
CHAIRS?
J. PRATT, JR., & SON,

MANUFACTURERS, wholesale and Retail Dealers in Chairs, respect-fully inform the Inhabitants of HARTFORD and vicinity, that they have opened a Chair Warehouse . . . where they have, and intend keeping on

Fig. 62. Set of side chairs made by Joel Pratt, Jr., 1830–40. 32-1/2 × 16 × 15-7/8 in. Maple, birch, and pine with rosewood graining and stenciled metallic powder decoration. Collections of Old Sturbridge Village, Sturbridge, Massachusetts.

hand a general assortment of *Chairs*, consisting in part of a variety of patterns, of Grecian, Common Cane and Flag Seat, Common Wood Seat, Dining of all descriptions, and a great variety of Large and Small Boston Rocking chairs, Misses and Children's common do., Settees, Desk Stools, & C., &c., which they will sell in large and small lots, *at prices as low as the like quality can be bought at any other place.*[15]

Journeyman Elbridge Gerry Reed assembled chairs for local manufacturers. His daybook gives a rare view of chair workers' labor in the 1830s. He worked at home in his shop, mostly "fraiming" chairs for Benjamin Stuart. In 1833, he assembled 1,584 chairs in eight different styles, for which he was credited almost four hundred dollars. Most were high-end models, such as "large rocking chairs," but Reed also produced children's chairs and standard side chairs with screwed backs or turned tops with four- or five-rod backs. He probably could frame four to six chairs a day. Reed did more than put together chairs, however; he was a versatile craftsman. By one estimate, he turned hundreds of thousands of chair parts for shops throughout northern Worcester County. He also sawed out chair backs, bent chair stuff, transported chairs and chair stock, and made and repaired tools for other chairmakers. His accounts with several dozen chairmakers offer visible evidence of the complex and extensive network of relationships that supported the rise of the Sterling chair industry during the second quarter of the nineteenth century.[16]

The region's burgeoning furniture industry and decentralized mode of production supported an increasing number of woodworkers. Many turned parts or made seats rather than assembling chairs. North of Sterling and Gardner, sawmills made chair stock. The owners of a Hubbardston mill advertised "Chair Stuffs of all descriptions. On hand at all times Sawed and Turned Stuff . . . at a lower rate than can be found at any other Mill." In Fitzwilliam, New Hampshire, Rial Heywood sold seat blanks to Elbridge Gerry Reed and Joel Pratt, Jr.; one transaction for two loads totaled around five hundred seats.[17] Chair seaters were the largest and most significant set of woodworkers outside the chair shops.

Women Outworkers

Women in Gardner started seating chairs for Elijah Brick's shop around 1814, according to local histories. This work had previously been done by regularly employed men in manufactories. William Buttre's 1812 trade card shows a man weaving a flag seat in the back of the room with a pile of flag beside him; someone else turns stock, and another workman assembles frames that will then be ready to receive their seating (see fig. 60). This system, which prevailed in New York City, entailed high costs and limited output. The rising demand for fancy chairs that boasted flag and cane seating led rural entrepreneurs to look for a more ample and cheaper supply of labor. Women outworkers, along with inmates in prisons and juvenile facilities, became a major source of inexpensive hand toil. Sterling shops, which concentrated on plank seating, needed less seating than places that made flag-seated chairs, such as Templeton, Ashburnham, and Gardner. Flag or rush seats were made from native plants, such as cattail or sweet flag, that were harvested, dried, and wound or woven around the chair frame. All such work was done by hand as the seater worked on the floor or on a low stool, twisting and knotting the fiber to create a tight weave. "The skill lay in deciding how many rushes to twist together and how tightly to twist them so as to get a smooth, uniform surface," according to Nan Wolverton. Those broken rushes left over were stuffed in between the woven rush to provide bulk to the seat and comfort to the sitter.

Cane was different: cane weaving could be mechanized and required imported material derived from tropical rattan. Rattan was scraped and split into strips, and then woven into vertical, horizontal, and diagonal strands through holes in the chair seat frame—a relatively simple process. In Gardner in 1832, ninety-eight women and eighty-three men were employed by nine chair shops. In Ashburnham, the same number of shops employed eighty-five women and fifty-six men, suggesting that other male woodworkers labored in their homes as time permitted. Jacob Felton recorded accounts with thirteen female chair seaters who worked for him between 1836 and 1838 as outworkers. He supplied the chair frames and sometimes the flag, and when the women returned the seated chairs, they were credited with about sixteen or seventeen cents per chair. They mostly worked during the summer months when the flag was harvested. By 1837, Felton was completing a transition to cane seats, a process that was occurring throughout the region and industry.[18]

The women who seated chairs for Rial Heywood and Jacob Felton represented another face of rural industry during the first half of the nineteenth century. Outwork was one of the flexible manufacturing arrangements that facilitated the Northeast's industrialization. Farm women and underemployed rural residents produced a variety of handloom woven textiles, straw and palm-leaf hats, chair seats, and shoes for urban and southern markets. Manufacturers and merchants sent burgeoning amounts of raw materials and semi-finished goods out into the countryside. In turn, farm families used the proceeds of their outwork to purchase the new manufactured goods to decorate their households and adorn their persons. Rural women had a central position in this important process by providing outwork labor and by purchasing manufactured goods.

Handloom weaving was the first major form of outwork employment. With the advent of spinning factories that turned out thread by water-powered machinery, textile producers put out work to at least twelve thousand weavers across rural New England in 1820. But the introduction of power looms soon centralized weaving into factories, so textile outwork was short-lived. Straw and palm-leaf hatmaking more than took up the slack. Enterprising young women fashioned hats out of split and braided straw, a readily available local agricultural product, at the turn of the nineteenth century. One New Englander recalled that the income was "a great help to many families." Soon storekeepers became middlemen by supplying rye-straw braid and marketing finished hats. In Hardwick, Massachusetts, Jason Mixter's store accounts show 135 households actively braiding straw in 1818. The only tool required was a splitter for making the narrow splints for braiding. New tariff legislation and declining prices for straw braid led Mixter and others to turn to palm-leaf braid for their hatmaking trade.[19]

Worcester County became the center of the palm-leaf hat industry; residents made 1.5 million hats in 1832 and more than 2 million in 1837. Merchants fostered the growth of the industry. Dexter Whittemore of Fitzwilliam, New

Hampshire, bought imported Caribbean palm leaf from Boston wholesalers, split the leaf locally, and sold it on credit to customers who braided men's or children's hats according to the directions supplied by the manufacturer. Rural customers typically brought back the completed hats fifteen at a time, picked up additional braid, and used their credit for store purchases. Unmarried young women supplied most of this seasonal labor. This was not full-time work, but rather a way to supplement farm family income. Nonetheless, as Thomas Dublin has observed, "Hatmaking remained the only source of female wage labor in Fitzwilliam in this period." Women braiders and hatmakers toiled long hours to earn small sums of money while in sentimentalized retrospective representations, authors and artists produced images of virtuous industriousness in a comfortable country home. In 1830, Whittemore employed more than 250 individuals who made 23,000 hats a year, and by the 1850s, more than 800 workers made 80,000 hats a year in a wide swath of communities around Fitzwilliam. The outwork manufacturing system grew by extending its geographical scope rather than by intensifying its demands on its workers as the factory system did. The middlemen had little control over the productivity of the far-flung farm families they employed. This combination of flexibility and managerial challenges characterized the outwork system in hatmaking and other manufacturing systems in the rural economy. Worcester County's chairmakers took note. In chairmaking, a web of workers in shops, families, and farmhouses composed the industry's labor force; entrepreneurs supplied the capital and attempted to manage production and marketing profitably.[20]

Making Plain and Fancy Chairs

The success of Worcester County chairmakers rested upon the demand for cheaply produced but attractively designed "common" plank-seat Windsor chairs and fancy chairs. Common chairs had plank seats sawn of pine; turned pillars or back posts, legs, stretchers, and rods; sawn backs; and varying decoration. Some featured quickly turned "bamboo" lines on the legs, a crest rail painted or stenciled with a handsome flower design, or side rails striped in gold (see fig. 62). Fancy chairs had more comfortable flag or cane seats and more decoration, making them suitable for a place in the parlor. They retailed for two to two-and-a-half dollars each, twice as much as plain chairs. Both designs had cheap seats, but their mode of construction was quite different. The common chair's plank seat anchored the legs and backs, just like the Windsor, while the fancy chairs' open seat frame was secured to the continuous back posts.

Countless variations in design were fashioned within these two broad categories, as entrepreneurs cultivated changing styles in décor.[21]

Although Gardner got a slower start in chairmaking than Sterling, its entrepreneurs sped up production and incorporated far-reaching changes in machinery and industrial organization, and the two towns' paths diverged in the 1820s and 1830s. By the 1840s, Gardner chair manufacturers aggressively used the new resources of steam power, machinery, and railroad transport to consolidate the disparate elements of chairmaking into factories. Steps in the process formerly performed at several sites in town or across the region were brought under one roof. Gardner's scale of production, measured by the amount of capitalization and number of employees per enterprise, soared relative to other commercial villages where chairmaking was carried on. In 1832, Sterling had fifteen chairmakers while Gardner had nine, but the scale of production differed markedly in the two towns. All the chairmaking establishments in Sterling counted 47 employees (all men), while those in Gardner employed 181 (83 men and 98 women). That same year, 53 chairmaking establishments were scattered throughout the northern region, employing 244 men and 186 women, with production estimated at almost $190,000. By 1837, Sterling and Gardner each had about 25 chairmaking establishments, but Gardner had twice the value of production ($109,064 compared with $53,228) and almost four times as many employees (300 compared with 80). By 1845, Gardner's nearly 600 chairmaking workers made over 170,000 chairs.[22]

In other places in the Northeast, innovative entrepreneurs also took advantage of expanding national markets to build a centralized furniture industry. In Chester County, Pennsylvania, decentralized furniture making declined, and large-scale production clustered in a few central sites. West Chester, the county's major market town, stood at the crossroads. Amos Darlington, Jr., took over his father's "old stand." He made far more furniture than his father, recording almost eight hundred items in a fifteen-year period. The shop made mostly the same forms as it had before, bedsteads and tables with an occasional sideboard and bureau. Darlington employed a journeyman or two, but continued small-scale shop production. His neighbor Thomas Ogden took a different tack; he left behind his father's joinery workshop in the small village of Marshallton for a stint in Philadelphia. In 1813, Ogden returned "in possession of the neatest & newest fashions" to open a cabinetmaking business in West Chester. He advertised repeatedly for apprentices and boasted of his low prices. In 1825, he offered "Cheap Furniture . . . for instance, sideboards that were once 80 to 100 dollars, can be purchased for 40 to 50 dollars." He stocked eight-day clocks "of superior quality" made by Philadelphia makers, and he housed the clocks in his own mahogany cases "which he [could] sell very low." Ogden enlarged his business in 1819 "so as to keep ready made furniture," opening a wareroom from which he would deliver future "almost to any distance." In banner headlines, Ogden offered customers advice on achieving refinement inexpensively: sofas that "should grace every gentleman's parlor" were made in "the newest and latest Philadelphia fashions." Ogden introduced a series of marketing innovations to Chester County. Expanding his labor forces beyond the usual apprentice and journeymen, he called his business a "manufactory" where in 1829 he had "9 or 10 workmen" and six workbenches in his shop. Amos Darlington attempted to enlarge his business in 1831, but the following year he sold off his tools and materials, some to Ogden; at the age of forty-one, he left West Chester and took up farming.

Other Chester County artisan entrepreneurs followed the same path as Ogden. Joseph Jones opened a chairmaking shop in 1813, producing a ready supply of Windsor chairs in a variety of styles over his thirty-year career. In 1836, he advertised that he had on hand nearly "sixty dozen CHAIRS and SETTEES ready for the spring sale." Some were fancy chairs and others plain: "a FULL ASSORTMENT OF FANCY, RUSH SEAT SETTEES, DO.[ditto] CHAIRS, BENT AND STRAITBACK WINDSOR CHAIRS & SETTEES, COMMON BENT AND STRAIT BACK RUSH-SEAT CHAIRS, With a great variety of WRITING, ROCKING, CHAMBER, small chairs, &c . . . finished in the latest and most approved fashions . . . having purchased a large quantity of first rate materials, he will be able to furnish, at short notice, any order that he may be favored within the above line of business." He assured patrons that he had a large assortment of Windsor chairs "of the latest shapes and color finished to please the fancy of an enlightened and refined community." Jones and Ogden developed a new model of furniture production in Chester County: producers concentrated at a few central locations with optimal access to transportation, made aggressive use of advertising and pricing, built warerooms for customers to inspect ready-made goods, and transformed the labor process within their shops.[23]

In Gardner, the key to economic success was the centralization of production under one roof. Ezra Baker, who had built a dam and shop with lathes for turning posts and stretchers, purchased a circular saw and hired workers to prepare lumber for turning instead of buying stock from farmers, sawmill operators, or independent woodworkers. As the number of hands Baker employed in the shop increased, he needed more waterpower, so he transferred his machinery to a nearby gristmill. Other chairmakers followed Baker's example, locating workshops on good waterpower sites and preparing their own stock.

Gardner jumped past its competitors by adopting cane-seated furniture. The initial inspiration for this shift came through what would today be called industrial espionage. Learning that Wethersfield supplied fancy chair seats to New

York City, Elijah Putnam sent John Cowee, one of his workmen, to the Connecticut State Prison in Wethersfield to investigate the inmates' manufacture of chair seats; employing prisoners in productive, albeit unremunerated labor was a common practice at the time. Cowee watched carefully and brought one of the finished seats and some cane back with him. In Putnam's shop, Cowee and other craftsmen slowly removed the cane to determine the exact process of weaving and fashioning a cane seat, a sort of reverse engineering. Then Putnam obtained some frames and "engaged women to come to his house, where they were taught the mystery of seating, and where they [were] employed for a time in doing that part of the work, one of the rooms of this dwelling being devoted to his use." When the *Gardner News* noted the death of Phoebe Jackson in 1894, the obituary remarked that "she was the first woman in Gardner to seat a cane seat chair" and celebrated her achievement along with the community's identity as a chairmaking center. If so, she must have been one of those gathered in Putnam's household workshop. Finally, Putnam had found a route to success. Gardner chairmakers' determination to manufacture inexpensive cane seating generated a massive outwork network involving thousands of homes in the region; to open up the U.S. Census of 1850 or 1860 is to see line after line with "seater" listed in the column for occupation. Putnam and other entrepreneurs loaded up bundles of canes and batches of chair frames in wagons to drop off at farm households throughout the region.[24]

The Heywood brothers proved to be the most significant figures in assuring Gardner's eminence, first regionally and then nationally (see fig. 57). The Heywood family's six sons moved from farming into blacksmithing, storekeeping, and chairmaking in the early nineteenth century. Initially, Walter Heywood made chairs in a small shop attached to his father's house using only a foot lathe, while his older brothers Levi and Benjamin Franklin Heywood operated a store and occasionally assisted with the chair work. Walter moved to a larger shop across the street where fifteen to twenty workmen were employed, while Levi went to Boston to open a wareroom to sell chairs and opened a veneer mill in Charlestown. After fire destroyed Walter's shop in 1834, a common hazard for workshops built of wood, he rebuilt in a different location, purchasing a building with wood-turning equipment, a set of lathes, and a circular saw and securing a substantial waterpower site along the shores of Crystal Lake with potential for expansion. A partnership of the three brothers with outside partners from Boston and Providence gave the firm access to greater capital.

Levi Heywood returned to Gardner and aggressively took control of the business. His insistence on mechanization so dismayed his partners that they "withdrew from the concern," and the firm became Levi Heywood and Company. Heywood wanted to build new machinery; for example, he consulted with several experts on a continuous saw band. He also sought to adapt other woodworking machinery to the chair industry. Heywood seized upon the nascent railroad system for transportation, securing Gardner's place on the grid at the expense of its local competitors. Heywood's warehouse in Boston gave him access to the wholesale and retail trade of the metropolis, and from his position in the port city, he directed arriving Irish immigrants to central Massachusetts factories. Heywood incorporated earlier than his competitors, protecting himself from personal loss and enabling his business to expand.[25]

Factory production in Gardner grew from the extensive regional network of producers, as entrepreneurs incorporated elements of plain Windsor and fancy chair forms. Although the factory is a familiar endpoint in industrial histories, the distinct roads taken by these two inland towns—from households and workshops through vast networks of sawyers, turners, assemblers, and seaters, many of them outworkers laboring at dispersed locations—sheds new light on the industrialization of the northeastern countryside and the inexpensive manufacture of new consumer commodities.

Many possibilities existed for expanding production without centralizing work in a factory, as Sterling's raft of chair manufacturers shows. In an anonymous painting done between 1840 and 1880 (New Jersey Historical Society, Newark), David Alling stands proudly in the doorway of his chair manufactory in Newark, New Jersey, next door to his house, with an elegant chair standing alongside his front stairs, while an African American worker comes by with a loaded wheelbarrow. Over five decades, Alling's shop and shop records depict the dramatic transformation of the furniture craft into an industry. Isaac Alling, David's father and mentor, was a typical craftsman who provided a diverse set of goods and services to the local community. David moved far beyond the small-scale chairmaking practiced by his father. His shop produced chairs in unprecedented numbers, far outstripping local supply and demand; he bought thousands of chair parts from suppliers and shipped finished chairs in batches to places as far afield as the southern United States and Latin American ports. He specialized in the production of low- and medium-priced lathe-turned chairs, such as rush-bottom common chairs, Windsors, and fancy chairs. These simple designs were readily adapted to the batch production of inexpensive chairs, ornamented but made with standardized parts of local woods held together by bored socket joints rather than sawed and carved parts held together by mortise-and-tenon joints. Alling's production reached its highest point in the mid-1830s with total sales of 5,246 chairs. His shop inventory recorded sixteen large workstations, including a writing desk, but outside contracting for parts and labor played an important part in his ability to increase production without increasing his payroll or enlarging his workshop. Chair parts from out-

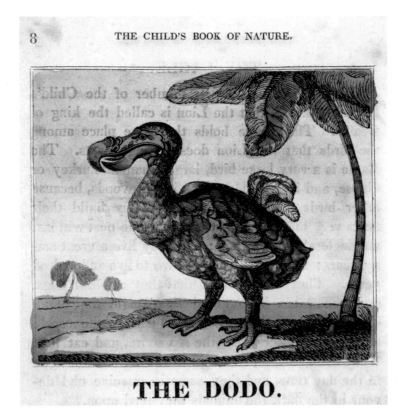

THE DODO.

Fig. 63. This color plate of "The Dodo" was handpointed by women working in the Lancaster workshop of Carter and Andrews. *The Child's book of nature; being figures and descriptions illustrative of the natural history of beasts, birds, insects, fishes, &c.* [Birds. No VII], Lancaster [Mass.]: Published by Carter, Andrews, and Co. and sold by Carter and Hendee, Boston, [1830?]. Courtesy of American Antiquarian Society, Worcester, Massachusetts.

side suppliers may account for as much as 60 percent of the total cost of a chair. Initially, Alling bought them from nearby rural New Jersey sawmill operators and woodworkers who could make chair parts economically. In the 1830s, he looked to urban contractors when chair seats became more specialized and urban labor became plentiful and cheap. Alling's network included far-flung export merchants. His was a "flexible specialization" emerging out of already existing elements. This entrepreneurially oriented producer industrialized the chairmaker's craft decades before steam-powered, factory-based mechanization.[26]

Back in Worcester County, a new generation of print entrepreneurs organized factory operations and offered a greater diversity of products, even while continuing handmade work. Carter and Andrews of Lancaster, which special-

Fig. 64. Alden Spooner made a chest of drawers in 1807 with a dramatic bow-front, French bracket feet, and fan-inlaid drawers. Cherry, ash/satinwood, with pine and brass. 35-1/2 × 39-1/2 × 17 in. Collections of Old Sturbridge Village, Sturbridge, Massachusetts. Photograph by Henry Peach.

ized in children's books and textbooks, developed a large, integrated plant to handle multiple stages of book production—printing, illustration, and binding—that had previously been done by separate shops, and they made use of such technological advances as lithography and stereotypy. The firm employed more than a hundred people at its height. In 1832, Carter and Andrews was the largest establishment in Lancaster. With almost $10,000 invested in tools and machinery, it turned out 150,000 volumes worth $50,000 and another $10,000 in copperplate engraving and printing, all of which went to Boston. That year the firm employed more than sixty workers, half women and girls, twenty-five men, and eight boys. This hand-colored illustration (fig. 63) of a dodo in the 1830 *The Child's Book of Nature* was probably painted by one of the firms' female employees working in her home. Technological advances were complemented by hand processes that embellished the mass-produced items. There were many

Fig. 65. Chest of drawers made by Joshua Moody Cumiston and David Buckminster, Saco, Maine, ca. 1809–16. White pine and holly with birch and mahogany veneers. 37-3/4 × 41 × 22 in. Buckminster was a native of Worcester County, Massachusetts, and came to Saco as a journeyman to Cumiston's shop, after a possible apprenticeship with Alden Spooner, bringing the designs for oval panel drawer fronts with him. Courtesy of Winterthur Museum, Winterthur, Delaware.

roads to increasing production of affordable commodities while also providing fancy and colorful household designs.[27]

Cosmopolitan Cabinetmaking in the Countryside

In furniture, cosmopolitan forms were becoming available in northern Worcester County and other inland areas at the same time that Sterling and Gardner became the center of plain and fancy chair manufacturing. Provincial cabinetmaking establishments operated in villages across New England, but some of these establishments produced anything but provincial-looking goods, as the work of furniture makers drew on European pattern books and seemed true to urban prototypes, made possible by a network of artisans trained in cosmopolitan workshops. The story of Alden Spooner exemplifies the paths taken by village craftsmen who sought to emulate high-style forms and continue more expensive modes of construction. Spooner was well informed of market trends, as even this sophisticated craftsman had to adopt new business practices, shifting over time from custom to ready-made work and marketing products through warehouse showrooms.

Spooner, who was born in Petersham, Massachusetts, opened a cabinetmaking business in Athol during the first decade of the nineteenth century, around the same time as James Comee. Spooner's case furniture forms betray training in Boston, Portsmouth, or elsewhere in eastern Massachusetts. The earliest known piece is an inlaid cherry bow-front bureau with "Alden Spooner/athol/july 1807" inscribed on the underside (fig. 64). The solid construction and sophisticated use of contrasting woods attest to his professional experience. The facade bears substantial similarities to designs shown in George Hepplewhite's *The Cabinet-maker and Upholsterers' Guide* (1794), which praised "drawers . . . which are elegantly ornamented with inlaid or painted work."[28] Another chest made a few years later and inscribed "Alden Spooner" is made of cherrywood with mahogany, birch, and maple veneers (plate 6). This lovely piece has cross banding along the top, side stiles with reeding, and elaborately turned legs, as well as a scrolled skirt, and is patterned after British furniture designer Thomas Sheraton's plates in *The Cabinet-Maker and Upholsterer's Drawing Book of 1793*. Most striking are the oval panels down the center, which are emphasized by rectangles of contrasting mahogany. The oval brass fittings are marked H.J., high-end products made by Thomas Hands and William Jenkins of Birmingham, England.[29] This chest closely resembles a series of chests of drawers with flashy patterns of oval panels, executed in veneers and inlays, identified by Thomas Hardiman as made by the shop of Cumiston and Buckminster in Saco, Maine, around 1809 to 1816 (fig. 65). Hardiman has hypothesized that David Buckminster, a native of Worcester County, worked with Alden Spooner in Athol and brought the design for the oval panel drawer fronts with him when he came north; in Saco, the design was combined with Cumiston's training in the Portsmouth furniture-making tradition.[30] Design traditions migrated as artisans did, generating regional styles.

By April 1808, Spooner had partnered with George Fitts. Both in their mid-twenties, the two men worked together for five years. Chests of drawers branded "Spooner & Fitts" are sophisticated pieces, displaying all the vocabulary of Boston in their contrasting woods, decorative work, drop panels, and decorative skirts. The most elaborate example, with ivory escutcheons, visually suggests a Thomas Seymour bow-front bureau of more expensive mahogany and veneered with rare Australian casuarina wood and curvy maple. Spooner also made stylish card tables derived from Thomas Sheraton's designs in his *Cabinet-Maker and Upholsterer's Drawing Book of 1793*.[31]

After Fitts sold Spooner his half of the property in 1813, Spooner worked briefly with another partner and then on his own from 1815 until 1850. He kept up with changing chair fashions, making in succession a square-back Windsor with single bows and bent backs, a slat-back Windsor, a fancy double-bow-back armchair, and a shaped tablet-top Windsor side chair between 1816 and 1822. A new Greek Revival–style sofa with scrolled arms also came from his shop. In remote Athol, Spooner put together the most fashionable forms, sometimes with spandrels and cartouches purchased from specialty inlay shops in Boston and brasses from Birmingham. Spooner's shop developed side by side with the multiplying shops of Sterling and the growing factories of Gardner. Like the manufacturers of mass-produced seating with whom he had to compete, this high-style cabinetmaker adopted the new business model of warerooms. Increasingly, he focused on purchasing specialized forms and stocking ready-made furniture. In 1827, Spooner advertised that he "has now on hand, and offers for sale . . . at his FURNITURE WARE ROOM, a large and elegant assortment of ready made Mahogany and Cherry Furniture."[32]

Still, sofas were unusual items in provincial households in the early nineteenth century—and so were family group portraits in those homes. The existence of the two household decorations announced both the arrival of Westminster's Timothy Doty, who adorned his central Massachusetts home with a sofa with Grecian scrolled arms, and the existence of artisans well aware of academic and cosmopolitan modes of production in the region. Timothy Doty commissioned a double-sized family portrait of his wife, Susan Cowee, and their son, Pearson, from a neighboring painter named Robert Peckham to celebrate Doty's status as a prosperous businessman and family head (fig. 66). At the age of forty-five, he had married Susan, a woman more than twenty years younger, and she gave birth to Pearson in 1833, ten months after their wedding. The toddler stands on the sofa between the two parents, larger than life, a visible sign of their thriving family, surrounded by other indicators of their prosperous station in life. Timothy's father, John, a blacksmith, had moved west to Hardwick and joined the suppression of Shays's Rebellion in 1787. Timothy was born the following year, and he and his father came to Westminster in 1813 when they purchased the Westminster Hotel in the town center, one of the signs of the new commercial infrastructure that connected provincial towns to each other and the urban venues.

Timothy rose in the ranks of commerce from innkeeper to merchant in Westminster. Around 1824, he built a large double house on the lot adjoining the hotel, which he turned over to Oliver Adams. He also became involved in

Fig. 66. Robert Peckham, *Timothy Doty and Family*, ca. 1834–35. Oil on canvas. 36-1/8 × 50-1/8 in. Photograph courtesy of Westminster Historical Society, Westminster, Massachusetts. Gift of Grace Klar.

the new outwork business of straw and palm-leaf hatmaking; many storekeepers organized networks of local women and children to produce bonnets and hats. Doty's store had large quantities of palm leaves, straw braid, and almost one thousand palm-leaf hats and straw bonnets valued at one thousand dollars out of a total of over six thousand dollars for the entire store inventory. When he died tragically in 1835, his probate inventory recorded also a large and varied stock of goods in his store, including ample amounts of "Irish Linen" and "English Gingham" and lots of other fabrics, ribbons, and sewing notions, along with spices, tools, teasets, and "Fancy Bowls." Westminster's residents could obtain all sorts of ready-made clothing now, such as hats and gloves as well as a wide-ranging collection of potions and medicinal products. The ambitious merchant also served the town and the state in a wide variety of public roles: early on he took on the duties of postmaster for a decade and a half; he served at the same time as selectman, tax assessor, overseer of the poor, town modera-tor, and representative to the General Court. The successful store, unencum-bered with debt, passed to his young heir, but locals called it the "Widow Doty Store," which suggests that his widow, Susan, took over the enterprise.[33]

Doty's inventory reveals that Peckham depicted the Doty family in their parlor with its upholstered sofa, valued at twenty-five dollars, and ornate draperies listed at forty dollars, the two most expensive items in the listing of "articles in the parlor" in the room-by-room inventory. Not shown are the carpet and hearth rug, Grecian center table, ladies' work table, set of six side chairs, and looking glass. The sitting room had an expensive secretary and sofa bedstead along with its ten cane-seat chairs and some Liverpool ware. The other six chambers had an assortment of tables and bedsteads, carpets and rugs, looking glasses, and bureaus, almost one of each per room; still, in most chambers, the most expensive item remained the bedstead and bedding. The kitchen had fourteen chairs. All these fashionable home furnishings, like the portrait itself, had recently entered the middle-class domestic interior.[34]

So Doty followed many other members of the new rural bourgeoisie by commissioning a portrait to commemorate his familial and material achievements. Pearson stands distracted by holding the gold chain of his father's pocket watch, the single most expensive household item appraised at forty dollars. But Doty also owned a timepiece and a brass clock too. Susan stands out with her white lace collar and lots of jewelry adorning her person: large dangle earrings, the brooch that holds together her lace collar, two rings with stones in them, and a silver belt buckle. Jewelry, with its association with wealth and vanity, was designed for show and marked the body as a site of consumption.[35]

Doty and Spooner were not isolated individuals. Upholstered sofas and stylish center tables like those in the Dotys' possessions certainly appeared in Worcester County households. Specialized and stylish forms, such as "gilt drawing chairs" and fancy bow front chests of drawers, for example, entered Sturbridge's affluent households, available locally rather than just as coastal imports. When housewright Leonard Waters died in 1825 at the age of thirty-five, he owned a wooden clock, a cherry bureau, and a card and bookcase—items making only their second appearance in town. In the 1820s, Sturbridge's less well-off families often added a clock and a chest of drawers; the acquisition of ceramic tableware and tea dishes offered signs of refinement to even poorer families.[36] Athol's cosmopolitan craftsman adopted new marketing methods to make a variety of furniture available to consumers without centralizing production. A wide range of forms came from shops like Spooner's, at different price levels, even as cheap chairs took centerstage for the manufacturers focusing on mass production in Sterling and Gardner.

Hitchcock Chairs

The most famous maker of inexpensive chairs in America, Lambert Hitchcock, lent his name to the most popular "common" chair. Hitchcock, or more significantly Hitchcock-like chairs, appeared in numerous period portraits with a gentleman seated on one or a bold gold-stripped frame of one popping up behind a family group. Born in Litchfield County, Connecticut, in 1795, Hitchcock served a traditional apprenticeship in furniture making with his brother-in-law David Pritchard, who also operated a clock shop, probably also learning clockmaking methods that made use of machines; he then served a stint as a journeyman in the Litchfield shop of Silas Cheney who ran one of the region's largest furniture operations. At the age of twenty-three, he struck out on his own in a corner of a water-powered sawmill on the Farmington River in Barkhamstead Township, an upland region with ample wood supplies. Hitchcock started out as a manufacturer of chair parts because of his limited capital, but he aspired to produce complete chairs. In 1822, drawing on funds from family and friends, he opened a "manufactory" in a two-story wooden building along the Farmington, which had easy access to the River Turnpike, a branch of the Hartford-Albany Turnpike.[37] The success of this enterprise enabled him to acquire land on both sides of the river and construct a three-story brick factory with a dam and raceway to harness more waterpower and separate rooms to house all phases of the chairmaking operation. The new factory opened in 1825. The ground floor housed the lathes, saws, and other machinery used to process the semi-prepared lumber that arrived from a nearby sawmill. The immense waterwheel turned wooden gears and shafts that ran along the ceiling, and leather belts ran off the shafts to power the rows of woodworking machines. Workers in the second floor's driving room fitted up the wooden parts made below and hammered together the chairs. Children often applied the red undercoat of paint. Women decorated and labeled Hitchcock "Fancy and Plain Chairs" in the top floor's finishing and stenciling room. Seating material came from near and far: cane from East Asia arrived through Hartford, while cattails for rush seats were available locally. Wholesale prices ran from about twenty-five cents to a dollar per chair. Retail went for about $1.50. The hamlet, with a company store and a few houses, was called by the name of its proprietor: Hitchcocksville. The chair manufacturer proudly signed his products with a stenciled name, location, and guarantee to meet the expectation that his chairs would reach a market well beyond Litchfield County: "L. Hitchcock. Hitchcocks-Ville. Conn. Warranted" on one of the back stretchers (fig. 67).[38]

Hitchcock advertised regularly. As his name turned into a brand, the proprietor of the Hartford Auction House boasted that "Hitchcock Chairs are so well known, that it is not considered necessary to give a particular description of them." Expanding production required more skilled chair workers, and Hitchcock faced a continual labor supply shortage; in 1828, for example, he advertised for "six journeymen Chair Makers." It also required more working capital, a

Fig. 67. Hitchcock, Alford and Co., roll-top side chair, cane seat, with gold stenciled decoration on back and striping on legs, "L. Hitchcock . . ." stencil, 1826–29. Courtesy of Winterthur Museum, Winterthur, Delaware.

particularly pressing problem for Hitchcock. With his low prices, profits were never large. Seating the chairs, a time-consuming and tedious task, was always a production bottleneck. Hitchcock relied on the inmates of the new Wethersfield Prison near Hartford that opened in 1827 with various workshops for inmates based on contemporary ideas about penitentiary reform; prison authorities had installed facilities for making chairs and chair seats. Hitchcock's teams of horses could bring down to the Hartford docks their loads of finished chairs and pick up seat frames and chair parts from the prison for their return journey to Hitchcocksville. In 1828, after Andrew Jackson's inauguration of fiscal policies that destabilized the credit system, his inventories of chairs mounted in the Hartford auction houses and mercantile houses, while payments to him became more uncertain. A disastrous fire in Hitchcock's uninsured general store in June 1829 pushed the entrepreneur into bankruptcy.[39]

Hitchcock could do little to solve his financial woes with his cherished factory in the hands of his creditors. An 1830 agreement gave the bankrupt manufacturer the right to operate the factory and three years to pay off his creditors, a schedule he managed to beat. Hitchcock raised chair prices and introduced a line of painted cabinet furniture with a higher profit margin. Over one hundred employees produced fifteen thousand chairs in 1831. He took his brother-in-law, Arba Alford, into partnership in 1832; they established Hitchcock, Alford, and Company and stenciled the chairs with the new firm name. With Alford supervising the manufactory, Hitchcock focused on sales and marketing to a broader national market. He opened a "New Chair Store" in Hartford and in 1835 embarked upon a western trip, following migrating New Englanders with his saddlebags full of stencils and chair designs to take orders from distributors and storekeepers. The panic of 1837 caused significant distress for most businesses, but Hitchcock's firm weathered the crisis. Neighboring firms, such as the Holmes & Roberts manufactory, were not so fortunate, and Hitchcock waited them out; by 1839, he purchased the firm's excellent waterpower site and two substantial buildings for a little cash and a series of postdated promissory notes. Hitchcock eliminated a significant competitor and added its production capacity to his own. Bedsteads and washstands from the neighboring manufactory diversified the Hitchcock product line.[40]

Hitchcock succeeded in branding his products across the nation, but he continued to seek innovations in manufacturing and chafe at the limitations of his firm's site. The prominence and profitability of the painted cabinet pieces highlighted the out-of-the-way location of the Hitchcocksville factory. Hitchcock's new position as a Connecticut state senator in Hartford gave him a better vantage point to survey economic prospects. A new Farmington Canal that stretched from New Haven as far north as Northampton seemed to offer superior facilities for an ambitious industrialist. The national economy was recovering during the early 1840s. In the summer of 1843, Hitchcock liquidated the corporation and started anew on his own. Lambert Hitchcock had produced the prototype chair of the era. Hitchcock chairs combined a simple form with brightly colored decoration: gold-striped front legs (with their inner surfaces often left bare to save time and money) and rear legs often plain; chair backs in plain, scroll-top, or roll-top shapes painted with cornucopias; and plain, rush, or cane seats. The stenciling, which applied multicolored metallic powders to varnish, required little more expense or skill than the simple construction did, but five different fruit and floral designs were available, including the "Basket of Fruit," the "Horn of Plenty," and the "Fountain with Birds." Few chairs left the factory without decoration. Hitchcock had mastered the art of offering consumers sturdy cheap seats with a variety of shapes and patterns from which to choose. While Hitchcock's name and chairs have come to represent a new mode of manufacture and design, recently decorative arts scholar Ann Smith has argued that "he was not alone in trying to find ways to adopt new manufacturing methods to furniture production." Other Litchfield County furniture makers were using machines to produce chairs and chair parts.[41]

The 1820s and 1830s were a time of significant innovation in rural craft production, and new developments in power supply, manufacturing, and marketing extended well beyond clocks and chairs. Changes flowed across crafts, from furniture to publishing, from hatmaking to portraiture. The towns of Sterling and Gardner each produced thousands of the "fancy" chairs desired by consumers all over the United States, achieving success through very different modes of industrial organization. David Alling and Joel Pratt developed a decentralized system that consisted of a variety of producers and workers spread out across a wide region. The small-scale workshop mode of clock and furniture manufacturers, such as Alden Spooner, continued, often alongside industrial methods. Decentralized and small-scale operations offered the significant advantage of flexibility and required relatively limited capital. Aggressive entrepreneurs, such as Lambert Hitchcock and Levi Heywood, concentrated resources in centralized factories, using waterpower, integrating production, and mechanizing their operations whenever possible. It remained to be seen whether their formula for success—cheap, sturdy, and decorated items for the masses produced in large quantities at low cost—would be successful, for it depended on low-cost transportation, liberal credit, and rising consumer spending. Firms like Hitchcock's struggled under the weight of debt and mounting inventories during financial panics and downturns in the business cycle.

CHAPTER SIX

Provincial Portraits

Dogs and Cats and Standardized Portraits

Folk paintings are now hot items in the marketplace, and Ammi Phillips's *Girl in Red Dress with Cat and Dog* has become *the* iconic image of American folk art. *Girl in Red Dress with Cat and Dog* was the first work of folk art to sell for over a million dollars when Ralph Esmerian purchased it privately in 1985 (fig. 68 and plate 7). A companion Phillips painting, *Girl in Red Dress*, soared past two-thirds of a million ten days later at Christie's, a record-setting price for an American folk painting sold at auction (fig. 69). Four quite similar Phillips paintings of girls in red dresses have been identified (as well as portraits of boys, figs. 70 and 71), but duplication has not diminished their value. This portrait of

Facing page, clockwise from top left: Fig. 68. Ammi Phillips, *Girl in Red Dress with Cat and Dog*, 1830–35. Oil on canvas. 30 × 25 in. American Folk Art Museum, New York City. Gift of the Siegman Trust, Ralph Esmerian, trustee. 2001.37.1. Photograph by John Parnell (also Plate 7). Fig. 69. Ammi Phillips, *Girl in Red Dress*, ca. 1835. Oil on canvas. 32-3/8 × 27-3/8 in. Daniel J. Terra Art Acquisition Endowment Fund, 1992.57. Terra Foundation for American Art, Chicago. Photograph: Terra Foundation for American Art, Chicago / Art Resource, NY. Fig. 70. Ammi Phillips, *Andrew Jackson Ten Broeck*, 1834. Clermont, New York. Oil on canvas. 39 × 34 in. Private collection. Fig. 71. Ammi Phillips, *James Mairs Salisbury*, ca. 1835. Catskill Landing, Greene County, New York. Oil on canvas. 32 × 27 in. American Folk Art Museum, New York City. Extended loan from a private collection. EX2008.1.1 Photograph by Gavin Ashworth, New York.

an anonymous child captures our view of what "folk art" is: a child embracing one pet, another at her feet, her direct gaze engaging both painter and viewer. *Girl in Red Dress with Cat and Dog* graced the covers of several catalogs of important folk-art exhibitions as well as the *Journal of the American Medical Association* and a 1998 U.S. Postal Service stamp; it has become the icon for the American Folk Art Museum in New York City. Recently, a children's author adopted Phillips's subject. The story opens: "That's me over the fireplace. When I was a little girl and living with my parents on the farm, Mr. Ammi Phillips came, and I sat for a portrait. Well, I almost sat. In those days, I couldn't sit still for long." Curator Stacy Hollander emphasizes the painting's appeal to the viewer: "I have just loved that painting since I first became aware of the whole field [of folk art]. It just spoke to me. The painting has such a quiet, timeless, classic quality. It's perfection."[1]

Ammi Phillips fits popular notions of the perfect folk painter, too. Long relegated to anonymity as the creator of unsigned "ancestor portraits," his work first surfaced at a summer fair in Kent, Connecticut, in 1924 when longtime residents exhibited their nineteenth-century family portraits. The striking collection of elegantly dressed women with long, slender necks leaning forward from gleaming dark backgrounds and men clad in dark garments holding newspapers or books drew national notice at a time when the "the folk" were just being discovered in the United States. Phillips was dubbed the "Kent limner" because his sitters clustered around Kent, Connecticut. In a 1925 *International Studio* article titled "Early American Primitives," Mrs. H. G. Nelson enthused: "These bygone souvenirs of a bygone time have a distinct artistic worth of their own. . . . It is interesting to observe how much in common this art has with certain phases of the 'modern movement' in art today." The folk-art movement gathered momentum as avant-garde artists looked beyond Europe in search of "primitive" art forms and intellectuals anxiously gazed inward to locate the roots of an indigenous American culture. Modernist artists were delighted to discover artisan-artists who shared their interest in abstract shapes, arbitrary perspectives, and bold colors, while those seeking an "authentic" American culture seized upon the European term *folk*. The nineteenth-century romanticization of *das Volk*—the people, race, or nation—and early twentieth-century nostalgia for "the world we have lost"—tightly knit communities with shared customs—led to the revaluation of traditional arts. Modernists and antimodernists shared enthusiasm for "primitive" or "folk" art.[2]

In the 1920s and 1930s, collectors cherished the preindustrial associations of the producers, who stood apart from the dramatic transformation of crafts into capitalist industries during the nineteenth century. Others delighted in folk art's democratic possibilities, seeking an art of the people, by the people, and for the people. Family portraits and tavern signs were honest and straightforward expressions of the spirit of a people, as Holger Cahill made clear in several important exhibitions and his 1932 book, *American Folk Art: The Art of the Common Man in America, 1750–1900*. The term *folk*, originally signifying "rustic" or "native," has persisted in discussions of these nineteenth-century portraits, as well as of wood carvings, weather vanes, and other utilitarian objects, even while new terms have come to the fore, including *nonacademic, untrained, amateur, naïve, popular, provincial, vernacular*, or, if from the twentieth century, *outsider*. While scholars have debated the vexed definition of the folk and even the usefulness of the term, the audience for these bold canvases has grown and the prices of the paintings have escalated.[3]

Such artists as the Kent limner or the "Border limner," another unknown painter who worked in the region along the New York and Massachusetts-Connecticut state lines, gained popularity because they stood apart from modernity. Their appeal lay not solely in their striking works but also in their quaint ways: their itinerancy along the new nation's roads and turnpikes, their untutored genius, an apparent rejection of representational strictures, and finally, the ordinariness of their subjects: these people could be one's ancestors (or at least those owning or studying the paintings in the 1920s and 1930s), in contrast to the elites whose portraits are commonly exhibited. Adopting this perspective offered a critique of contemporary society and culture, especially the separation of head and hand in the labor process and the alienation between producers and consumers, but did not draw out its political implications. Researchers have gradually pulled aside the veil of anonymity. Lawrence and Barbara Holdridge, who in 1958 purchased a portrait of *George Sunderland* signed by an unknown artist, spent over two decades uncovering the painter's identity. They relied on a few signed canvases, the lodestars, but also consulted records of births and marriages, land transactions, and estate inventories. Lo and behold: the Border and Kent limners were revealed as one and the same: Ammi Phillips (1788–1865).[4]

Phillips's life and work is representative of the numerous artisan-artists of the first decades of the nineteenth century, but also turns many cherished notions on their head. His was no brief or intermittent dabbling with a brush; he pursued a long and successful career as a commercial portraitist. Years of research in local antique shops and major museum collections have raised the total of Phillips portraits from the few shown at the Kent fair to over eight hundred at last count; one art historian estimated that he completed as many as two thousand canvases over his career. Ammi, whose biblical name means "my people," took to the road as an itinerant vendor of sought-after cultural commodities, like the many other young men coming of age after the War for

Independence who peddled notions, clocks, and sundry other goods. He painted clusters of friends, relatives, and neighbors in New York State as far north as the Adirondacks, went south to Westchester County, and then crossed to neighboring Massachusetts, Vermont, and Connecticut over his fifty-year career. As John Vanderlyn cynically told his nephew,

> I heard with pleasure that you had made some very clever attempts in portraits where you are and which had given much satisfaction. A couple of years more spent in N. York must improve you in this occupation if you pay the least attention to it and in being only a little superiour to the Philips [sic] who was here some years since, you may gain more money than you could by any Mechanical business, which you must know, is far more labourious and less genteel and considered. Were I to begin life again, I should not hesitate to follow this plan, that is, to paint portraits cheap and slight, for the mass of folks can't judge of the merits of a well finished picture, I am more and more persuaded of this. Indeed, moving about through the country as Philips does, must be an agreeable way of passing ones time. I saw four of his works at Jacobus Hardenburgh's the other day painted a year or two ago, which seemed to satisfy them—it would besides be the means of introducing a young man to the best society and if he was wise might be the means of establishing himself advantageously in the world,—property is after all, the most important thing in the country particularly, fame is little thought of, money is all and everything.[5]

Phillips's métier was painting plain likenesses devoid of shadows or modeling, and his prices were far lower than those charged by an established academic artist such as Vanderlyn. Nonetheless, his achievement was not slight.

Phillips used several painting formulas. According to art historian May Black, "repetition enabled Phillips to work efficiently, though many of the details of his poses and costumes required time-consuming and meticulous brushwork."[6] In the 1840s, he painted four portraits of Sarah Sutherland, one for each of her daughters, with the only difference being the number of circles of lace on her collar. His dogs reappeared with very slight variations. The standing children in his early portraits, such as Harriet Leavens and Harriet Campbell, had identical parasols and slippers. Most striking are the four *Children in Red*, three girls and one boy. Each child wears an identical brilliant red dress over pleated white pantaloons; all have slippers peeping out below the hem, two pairs of scarlet and two black. They sit with arms crossing their bodies diagonally and a kind-looking dog lying at their feet. One portrait includes a cat held in the girl's arms, filling the vacuum created by the waists of the other girls; it "echoes the exaggerated sweep of the full sleeves," according to folk-art scholar Stacy Hollander. Phillips lowers the child's arms to allow for the cat, but leaves the neckline uninterrupted, minimizing the disruption of his design. The girls are seated on green-upholstered benches (see plate 7). The girls all sport coral beads, a popular charm to ward off evil, but the number of coral beads and the color of their slippers distinguish the individual portraits. One painting proves the exception. Phillips painted *Andrew Jackson Ten Broeck* of Hudson, New York, in 1834 (see fig. 70), the only signed likeness, seated below a hickory-nut tree, with some husks scattered at his feet and one in his hand, a visual play on his namesake, "Old Hickory." In this series, Phillips's standardized poses and props offered consistency to his clients who knew what they were paying for while also saving him time; strong colors and bold, decorative design pushed his work well beyond the "cheap and slight."

In the years 1832–35, he was painting the patricians living along the Hudson River south of Albany: the Ten Broecks, Livingstons, and Dewitts. For these old Dutch and English patrons, Mary Black has suggested, he evolved this formula of the seated children dressed in red. Two variations on this formula have come to light. He changed the color of the dress to blue in *James Mairs Salisbury*, but the dog and other props remained (see fig. 71). For *Mrs. Mayer and Daughter*, the portraitist planted a miniature version of the child on the mother's lap, but with the same red dress and scarlet slippers (fig. 72). The *Girl in Red Dress with Cat and Dog* stands out among these dramatic paintings owing to the exaggerated sweep of the neckline and sleeves that cut across the canvas, the lace trim and double row of pleats on her gown, and the cat that visually centers the composition, demonstrating the extra care the painter devoted to this portrait.[7]

What sets Phillips apart from his numerous kin crisscrossing the Hudson River Valley and other inland areas? Was it his ability to innovate within these standardized formats? Over his long and prolific career, Phillips adopted a remarkable variety of styles to satisfy local tastes and keep abreast of changing fashions. Familiar poses, costumes, accessories, and palettes reappeared in ever-changing combinations. His earliest signed portraits from 1811, using a somber palette, resemble those of his Connecticut predecessors. A bust-length portrait of Gideon Smith, the first of many tavernkeepers, attests to the time he spent on the road and his considerable business acumen. Later in the decade, his full-length portraits of standing children (originally attributed to the Border limner) rendered in luminous colors have a dreamlike quality, visibly related to the work of J. Brown who painted in the Berkshires between 1806 and 1808 (fig. 73). The young artist has learned how to paint men and women at the same height on his canvases. By the 1820s, Phillips's work became increasingly realistic; the

Fig. 72. Ammi Phillips, *Mrs. Mayer and Daughter*, 1835–40. Oil on canvas. 37-7/8 ×
34-1/4 in. Metropolitan Museum of Art, New York City. Gift of Edgar William and
Bernice Chrysler Garbisch, 1962 (62.256.2). Image copyright © The Metropolitan
Museum of Art / Art Resource, NY.

portraits, somewhat reduced in size, feature strong, contrasting colors (see fig.
91 of Anna Doll Vanderpoel). His shift to a more realistic style may have come
through his contact with Ezra Ames, an academic artist known to be working
in the same region. In the Kent portraits of the 1830s (those originally attributed
to the Kent limner), the sitters lean in graceful but exaggerated poses in clothing
that contrasts with the dark background (see fig. 72). This body of work displays
what Stacy Hollander has called "a visual formula of almost mathematical precision in the placement, volume, and spatial relationships between the separate
elements." The sitters' minimal forms and broad areas of color required few
wasted brushstrokes. In the early 1840s, Phillips returned to more direct likenesses. What Black terms a "sculptural" style of 1848–50 shows strong modeling.
During the Civil War years, Phillips's work shows the growing influence of the
new medium of photography.[8]

Phillips's stylistic shifts were related to his changes of residence and other

Fig. 73. Ammi Phillips, *Harriet Campbell*, Greenwich, Washington County, New York, ca. 1815. Oil on canvas. 48-1/2 × 25 in. Sterling and Francine Clark Art Institute, Williamstown, Massachusetts, 1991.8 ©Sterling and Francine Clark Art Institute, Williamstown, Massachusetts.

known events of his admittedly sketchy biography. He was born in Colebrook, Connecticut, in 1788 and embarked early upon the painter's path. An 1809 advertisement in the *Berkshire Reporter* announced that "A. Phillips" was at Mr. Clarke's tavern in Pittsfield, where he offered "LIKENESSES" that were done with "correct style, perfect shadows, and elegant dresses" at prices ranging from one to five dollars, with profiles as low as twenty-five cents; simple woodcut profiles of a man and a woman illustrated the advertisement. He returned to the region six months later, and then again the next year to Great Barrington. In 1811, he painted the members of Samuel Barstow's household, as Samuel recorded in his diary: "Sunday 6th October. Mr. Ammi Phillips finished boarding at my house. He has taken Pluma & Charles likenesses at full length, Oliver half way down, Mrs. Barstow's & mine small profile view. He paid me $4.30 cents in full of my boarding bill." Dr. Barstow practiced medicine and operated a tavern where Phillips had boarded for about two weeks while working on his multiple commissions.[9]

Phillips's marriage to Laura Brockway of Schodack, New York, in 1813 marked the beginning of a pattern of patronage somewhat different from the usual itinerant's wide-ranging travels. Phillips established himself in a community and painted in that area for a period, making himself known to the local notables, which perhaps accounted for his lack of advertising and the number of significant commissions at each stage of his career. In between periods of itinerancy, he resided in one place for long intervals. Laura's death in 1830 and his remarriage to Jane Ann Caulkins led him to paint the interlocking regional elite in Dutchess and Columbia counties along both sides of the Hudson while living in Rhinebeck and Amenia, New York, Jane's hometown. Before he returned to the Berkshires in 1860, his work on a posthumous portrait, a common nineteenth-century form, revealed great emotional expression on the part of painter and patron: "23 Feb 1857, Mon. Went to see Lenny's portrait, so disappointed. Still it may be like him finally. 19 March 1857, Thurs. A letter from Mr. Phillips about [t]he portrait—so kind of him. 23 March 1857, Mon. Lenny's portrait came tonight. Mother and even Father is perfectly satisfied with it. I was so thankful—it will be a comfort and it will mean more than any thing else in the world to us, now. I am more satisfied with it than I ever thought I would be with any. I shall always be grateful to Mr. Phillips for the interest he has shown in it." The *Berkshire County Eagle* simply noted Phillips's death in 1865: "Died at Curtisville, Stockbridge, July 14th, very suddenly, Mr. A. Phillips, aged 78."[10]

Ammi Phillips and other portrait makers provide a compelling perspective on the process of commercialization, the rise of consumerism in the countryside, and the creation of a provincial middle class. Their careers followed the same path as numerous other artisans emerging from the rural economy. Obtaining their artistic training from the pages of design books or from brief encounters with other untrained painters, portraitists traversed the countryside creating images that range from stark black-and-white silhouettes to colorful, full-length oils. In the process, they innovated by developing standardized techniques of production, sometimes aided by mechanical devices, all the time distinguishing their subjects by the inclusion of distinctive details. These family portraits found a ready market among "middling" craftsmen, innkeepers, and farmers who sought symbols of middle-class identity and belonging.

This provincial middle class was a social group in the process of forming itself. As Christopher Clark remarked, "Self-making, self-shaping, and spontaneous claims to preeminence were responses to this fragmentation and multiplication of social orders." Class and culture were inextricably bound up in the new United States as respectability and refinement were the new arbiters of social place. Gentility took pride of place in defining middle-class identity. The lower middle class that populated the new provincial middle class differed from the American bourgeoisie of large merchants, industrialists, and bankers. For the provincial middle class "country style spelled virtue and simplicity," Catherine Kelly has written. Fashion was mediated by village culture, contrasting its manners from the overstated parlors of the urban bourgeois. Village culture espoused a "virtuous materialism," as Alexis de Tocqueville wrote, a simpler presentation of self, exemplified in the plain portraits from provincial painters as opposed to the aristocratic forms of urban elites.[11]

Becoming middle class meant forming new identities in a changing web of social relations. These new identities came about from a variety of overlapping practices: family customs, labor relations, and domestic consumption patterns. After his exhaustive study of the sitters of nonacademic portraits in the Old Sturbridge Village collections, the exhibition *Meet Your Neighbors,* and printed "folk art" catalogs, historian Jack Larkin concluded that the patrons were for the most part "the prosperous, upper-middling beneficiaries of New England's economic transformation in the early 19th century." These were not the isolated residents of the distant hinterlands, "but merchants, physicians, lawyers, clergymen, ship captains, manufacturers, the most successful farmers and artisan-proprietors, and their wives and children." In the Hudson Valley, paintings and pictures mostly belonged to the business class and wealthy farmers; still, the humbler sort owned the occasional family portrait. Portraits shared characteristics of other emblems of gentility entering provincial parlors and household, such as bold and colorful designs; but they were also different, representations of the self that posited and propagated a new form of identity and a new set of relations within which the self was positioned. Portraitist and patron strove together to construct a genteel indicator of their newfound middle-class status.[12]

"One of the Primitive Sort"

Rural portrait makers often entered the revered world of art without the rigorous apprenticeship of their provincial predecessors or the solemnity of their academic peers; and many "of the primitive sort" spent their lives supplying plain portraits to the growing population of provincial America. Chester Harding, who became one of America's most celebrated portrait painters, in 1806 moved with his family from New England to western New York, "then an unbroken wilderness," he recalled in his picaresque autobiography that he entitled *My Egotistigraphy*. When he reached nineteen, he thought that "there must be an easier way of getting a living" than clearing the "heavily timbered forest." First, he turned chairs with his brother. Then the War of 1812 gave Chester the chance to become "a distinguished drummer." At the close of hostilities, he found work in drum making, but the urge to make his fortune persisted; Harding searched for ways to make his fortune, even though his memoirs recount a series of seemingly limitless opportunities. When a local mechanic invented a spinning head and offered Harding the rights to sell the patent in Connecticut, he "jumped into my wagon, whipped up my horse, and was soon out of sight of what, at that moment, seemed all the world to me." During the next few years, Harding peddled clocks, established a chair manufactory, and tried tavernkeeping.[13]

None of these ventures proved rewarding or held Harding's attention for long. He did a stint as a house painter in Pittsburgh and in slow seasons painted signs, a skill allied with gilding, which he had picked up while making chairs. Next he fell in with a portrait painter named Nelson, one of "the Primitive sort." Enthusiasm rather than experience encouraged this generation of portraitists. John Neal, America's first art critic, observed in 1829 "a decided disposition for painting in this Country. . . . You can hardly open the door of a best room anywhere, without surprising or being surprised by the picture of somebody plastered to the wall, and staring at you with both eyes and a bunch of flowers." Such portraits, "wretched as they are," flourished "in every village of our country," he noted, "not as luxuries for the rich but as familiar household furniture." Neal, born in Portland, Maine, recalled that as a child he had never seen "a good picture . . . nor what I should call a decent drawing." When he discovered a pen-and-ink drawing of a head pasted on a wall over a shoemaker's bench, he was "delighted beyond measure" and thought the profile a "marvel." The shoemaker presented it to Neal, who carried it home, perched on an old leather trunk in a garret, and went to work, making copy after copy "until I had every scratch of pen daguerreotyped upon my memory."[14]

Wonder and a sense of mystery came over these "farmers' boys" when they encountered works of art. Harding's mentor Nelson used a copy of the "Infant Artists" of Sir Joshua Reynolds for his sign, incongruously inscribed: "Sign, Ornamental and Portrait Painting executed on the shortest notice, with neatness and despatch." Harding regarded "painting heads" as a marvel; after seeing the painter's work, Harding commissioned likenesses of himself and his wife "and thought the pictures perfections." Taking home what was in fact a rather crude representation, he pondered by day how it was possible for a man to produce "such wonders of art" and dreamed by night of achieving this marvel himself. Finally, "I got a board; and with such colors as I had for use in my trade, I began a portrait of my wife. I made a thing that looked like her. The moment I saw the likeness, I became frantic with delight; it was like the discovery of a new sense. I could think of nothing else. From that time, sign-painting became odious, and was much neglected." Chester Harding had found his calling. Higher commissions and growing confidence accompanied each stage of his journey. Artist and audience shared in their "discovery of a new sense." Encouraged by a receptive public, venturesome portraitists undertook more advanced training and gradually assumed the mantle of the professional artist. Other country artisans sought further instruction from academic artists in the cities and returned to the rural regions to ply their trade, retracing the journey of Ralph Earl on an abbreviated timetable as the audience for provincial portraits had expanded in the new century. A few aspiring academic painters took a turn in the provinces to build their skills and pocketbooks. While practicing his craft in northern New England in 1819, Samuel Morse found several other itinerants, whom he decried: "The Quacks have been here before me."[15]

Some amateurs, especially women with academy training who were especially adept at schoolgirl arts, made the transition to professional portrait making, following the path Mary Way pioneered.[16] Often their work used skills with textiles or familiarity with print sources, but they built upon that training, taking a different path from men who began in artisan trades. Ruth Pinney was born into a well-off family in Simsbury, Connecticut. A friend described her as a "woman of uncommonly extensive reading." She married Oliver Holcomb and two children followed, but five years later, in a newspaper advertisement, she sarcastically denounced her husband as a drunk who deserted her for the West Indies. Her earliest work dates from 1809 when she was in her thirties and recent scholarship has pointed out the references to her marital troubles in such works as "Mother and Daughter," where a seemingly domestic interior also recalls arguments between the artist and her mother-in-law, and "Couple and Casualty," copied from English fabric. She painted genre scenes, mourning pictures, and illustrations from literary sources, all common subjects in schools and academies at the time. Pinney was not strictly a copyist. Her watercolor painting was well suited to her domestic setting, "readily available, relatively inexpensive, quickly executed and easily put away." She adopted and experimented with compositional elements while exploring the themes of love, marriage, and family relationships, subjects with which she was quite familiar from her personal history and from her familiarity with eighteenth-century English prints. Pinney set off her work from her design sources and from later female amateur artists. She did vigorous watercolors with bold colors and sturdy figures; her sure draftsmanship was evident in pencil sketches. The prolific amateur found her palette in the late eighteenth century, well before the fad of theorem pictures (paintings done with stencils) and popular art-instruction books "became part of every schoolgirl's equipment" and whose work was marked by willowy figures and pale colors.[17] Pinney was an original.

Her successor, Mary Ann Wilson, drew dramatic, colorful scenes, such as *The Mermaid*, in watercolor. Her life makes an equally compelling domestic story. She and a female companion moved to western New York, joining the large-scale migration of New Englanders, according to one nineteenth-century source known as "An Admirer of Art": "The artist, Miss Willson and her friend, Miss Brundage, came from one of the eastern States, and made their home in the town of Greenville, Greene County, New York. . . . One was the farmer (Miss Brundage) . . . while the other (Mary Ann Willson) made pictures. . . . These two maids left their home in the East with a romantic attachment for each other and which continued until the death of the 'farmer maid.' The artist was inconsolable, and after a brief time, removed to parts unknown." Wilson kept to the road, inspired by such prints as the popular prodigal son, and sold her works "Way to Canada and clear to Mobile!"[18]

Ruth Henshaw Bascom never intended to become a professional portraitist, yet she made over one thousand profiles between 1828 and 1846. She had developed an early interest in art, visiting the Harvard College museum with her father in 1796; five years later, her diary notes, "I spun some and cut out profiles." As a student at Leicester Academy, she might have become acquainted with Ethan Allen Greenwood, a lawyer and artist who taught at the academy. He too became a portraitist in 1801, and he and Bascom were fast friends. As an unmarried woman, Bascom supported herself by carding and combing, spinning and weaving, sewing, and quilting with remnants. She made bonnets for local women: "Rose early & sat up late to work for others, because we have no milliner in town." At age thirty-one, Bascom married Dr. Asa Miles, who died within the year. A year later she married the Reverend Ezekiel Bascom, minister of the Congregational Church in Gerry, Massachusetts; each brought one young child to the family. While Bascom's diary records no profiles between 1806 and 1819, she sat for several portraits. Ethan Allen Greenwood did four portraits when he visited the household in 1807. In 1819, Bascom started to make profiles at home; she did twelve that year, which did not interfere with her busy life as a minister's wife, mother, and town librarian. None of these early profiles have been found, but they involved a brief sitting to take the subject's outline, no drawing, cutting the profile out of black paper, and mounting it on white paper.[19]

In 1828 she began working professionally. Her husband lost his parish as a result of illness and began to spend winters in Georgia; Ruth resided with relatives and friends throughout Massachusetts while she pursued her portrait work, especially after her husband's death in 1841. Her experience in such handicrafts as quilting and bonnet making provided expertise in color and form that are visible in her portrait technique: hard outlines, solid shapes of color, and layers of paper or fabric. These life-sized profiles depict adults in bust length and children in half or three-quarter length. She charged her customers for an accurate and pleasing likeness. She began by capturing the sitter's profile in pencil, cast on the wall by a light source, sometimes outlined by a machine or silhouette, other times sketched freehand; she recorded details of the face and clothing. Then Bascom was free to color in the picture using pastel crayons without her subject present. Finally, she filled in the background with solid colors, sometimes including stylized landscapes or swagged drapery in the corners; at other times, she made necklaces or glasses of gold-foil paper or pasted locks of hair to the paper. Her diary notes her fashion sense in her hatmaking and her work with color in her pieced quilts and carpet weaving. In her portraits, as in her quilts, the shapes of the sharply contrasting materials determine the outline. In the early nineteenth century, the prevailing aesthetic of watercolor painting also demanded that edges not be blurred. The outline of dress and bonnet were equally important to patrons. Bascom maintained relationships with many of her sitters, returning to visit and perhaps mend a tear or alter the costume to suit changing fashions.

Bascom often drew her profiles simply on a piece of paper with pencil and then used pastel to color clothing and hair. Charles Lewis Bingham of Fitchburg, son of a railroad agent, was shown as a healthy baby boy with a double chin and no neckline, oversized ears and round body, clad in an orange dress. The rattle he held entertained him during the sitting, but Bascom also used it as a decorative device, for it appears in other portraits of children. Bascom not only drew the outline of her sitters, but also brought greater definition to facial features and clothing details. Her brother Horatio Gates Henshaw's character emerges from his heavy lined brow, the strong contours of the nose, and the tightly drawn lips of a mature man (fig. 74). His ruddy complexion and the curvy locks sweeping across his brow create a dynamic portrait. Bascom occasionally experimented with other forms, such as collages. She did a silhouette of "Chin-Sung studying at Leister Academy about 1841," who boarded at her brother-in-law's. The young Chinese teacher had returned with a missionary for training. As a foreigner, he attracted considerable interest among local residents.

Fig. 74. Ruth Henshaw Bascom, *Horatio Gates Henshaw*, 1839. Pastel and pencil on wove paper. 19 × 13-7/8 in. Fenimore Art Museum, Cooperstown, New York.

Bascom drew him in a pair of profiles in fine detail and full length, capturing his "native dress," as she wrote on the reverse, along with his distinctive queue.[20]

Deborah Goldsmith took up a painter's career before her marriage, a career she would leave after her marriage. She traveled to paint a circle of kin, working outside the home as many young women were beginning to do with the expansion of manufacturing. Keeping a friendship album was a common activity for young ladies; at the age of nineteen, Goldsmith began hers with verses that she and her friends chose from popular English poets. But her album was distinguished by drawings based on pictorial prints and decorative vignettes and a few watercolor portraits of friends and relatives. Some of her friends must have had artistic training at the local Hamilton Academy. An appreciative "stranger" wrote in her album:

Painting—a secretest art that few possess
Of sketching by the eye the image true
And giving to the countenance exact

Fig. 75. Deborah Goldsmith, *The Talcott Family*, 1832. Watercolor pencil and gold paint on wove paper. 14 × 18 in. Abby Aldrich Rockefeller Folk Art Museum, The Colonial Williamsburg Foundation, Virginia.

> The mental turn & intellectual thought
> Of taste and passion & idea.
> With recognized talent in "art," she embarked upon the portrait "business"
>   as she called her artwork.[21]

Goldsmith traveled the roads of central New York towns to find work. She painted in a variety of media: oil portraits on panel, most of close relatives but one of George Washington; miniatures on ivory, including a self-portrait; and at least ten watercolor portraits, including two group portraits with interiors. *The Talcott Family*, her most ambitious work, is valuable as a document of the popular taste for "American Fancy." In her early portraits, she had difficulty rendering such anatomical features as eyes and noses correctly, but her later work displays increasing skill with anatomy and proportion and a greater use of line and shadow to create more naturalistic likenesses (fig. 75). Her basic technique for drawing a figure and placing it within a composition did not change. The group portraits, done almost ten years apart, share a passion for pattern and design in highly detailed interior settings, with billowing white curtains and decorative floor and wall treatments. Three generations of the Talcott Family appear under one roof, all seated on painted chairs. Mary Talcott, born in 1762, is dressed in black as befitting her age and sits on a rocking chair whose wooden seat is softened by a pillow; her son and daughter sit in two matching painted side chairs. Decoration is everywhere: the ornamental chair backs, a figured edge to Betsy Talcott's fichu, the bold stripes of the Venetian carpet, the grained cupboard, and the stenciled walls. The painting celebrates the fashionable fascination with pattern in decor.[22]

Her work contributed to the Goldsmith's family economy. On one of her trips, she met and painted her future husband, George Throop. He sent his "declaration" in 1832, and she replied from the road in a manner that could have come from Erastus Field or other male itinerants: "I do not know how long I shall stay in this place. I have business enough for the present, and for some reason or other, Mr. and Mrs. Lloyd seem to be overanxious for me to remain there through the summer. A lady was here a few days since from Hartford. She thought I would do better than here, and I may possibly go there, or to Cooperstown village, but I do not know yet, for I think I shall stay here as long as I can get portrait painting." She closed the letter by accepting his proposal. She continued her career as an itinerant portrait painter. In June, he wrote to her in Burlington Flats that he was happy "to learn that you are in health and successful in your business, or otherwise, would be a great satisfaction to my feelings." Upon their marriage in 1832, Deborah no longer sought portrait commissions and ended her ten-year career as an itinerant.[23]

Although women artists worked in a variety of media and painted professionally at different stages of their lives, certain patterns do emerge from this survey of women artists. Academy training and needlework could launch a professional career. Watercolors and pastels were popular pastimes compatible with domesticity. Nonetheless, many women portraitists took to the road in this era, making their way to farmhouses and villages and offering family portraits.

A different kind of craft work provided a path to painting for male artisan-artists. Jacob Eichholtz was not satisfied with his father's choice of a career for him as a coppersmith. He took advantage of itinerant instructors who wandered into Lancaster looking for commissions and consulted such printed authorities as Sir Joshua Reynolds. His account book—the often dry and careful reckoning of a businessman's debits and credits, his purchases and products, all carefully arrayed day by day in a ledger book—becomes under careful scrutiny the record of a complex figure who passed through several stages and encountered setbacks in the long trail from artisan to artist. When his account book opens in 1805, we learn about his copper and tin work along with his initial attempts in profile making. By 1809, more painting fills the pages, mostly decorative work on a wide range of surfaces—metal, wood, and canvas—as he began to offer larger family portraits on rough twill to his neighbors. When Philadelphia's esteemed portraitist Thomas Sully came to work in Lancaster, Eichholtz wrote, "I was fortunate enough to get a few half-worn brushes from Mr. Sully . . . this was a great feast to me." With a growing family to support, "relinquishing" the security of his trade remained out of the question: "Part of the day I wrought as coppersmith, the other part as painter. It was not unusual to be called out of the shop, and see a fair lady who wanted her picture painted. The coppersmith was instantly transferred to the face painter." Finally, the artist busily at work as a coppersmith found the time and resources to go as far as Boston and visit the United States' foremost portraitist, Gilbert Stuart, as well as attract an eminent patron, Nicholas Biddle, fresh from his European sojourns. Eichholtz ventured off to Philadelphia, with its cosmopolitan community of artists and cultural institutions.[24]

Building a career took time, however lofty an artist's aspirations. Enterprising artisans used the growing availability of print media along with the time-honored web of face-to-face connections to locate patrons. Often artists relied upon family members who had joined the substantial wave of migration from New England to new communities north and west to advise about conditions and line up customers. Chester Harding decided to seek his fortune in Paris, Kentucky, after receiving a letter from his chairmaker brother, who informed him that a portrait maker there was receiving "fifty dollars a head." Former sitters were a real asset, provided they liked their likenesses. Elijah Boardman nagged Ralph Earl to return to New Milford. Peddler turned portraitist James Guild told a pleased customer in Norfolk, Virginia, that he would visit his home town in North Carolina "if he would draw up a subscription paper and obtain 20 subscribers." So Guild, feeling "under a pleasing obligation," went south. Upon arrival a portraitist might set up a studio in a commercial block, a patron's home, or a tavern, the crossroads of commerce and information in most country villages. A successful sitting or two could mean all the difference between a short stay and a long sojourn. Susannah Paine, one of the few women portraitists in the hinterlands, advertised her arrival in the *Portland* [Maine] *Advertiser* in 1826 but met little response. When her landlady, instead of demanding her rent, asked her to paint her daughter with her kitten, the portrait was said to be "most excellent," and Paine found herself "inundated" with visitors the next day. "They entered my 'sanctum' with eager looks, to see whither [sic]—'a woman could paint a likeness?' When lo, they all applauded, beyond my most sanguine hopes or expectation. . . . Orders for portraits followed each other in quick succession, until I was, at length, fairly established."[25]

Aspiring artists needed to offer a range of portraits to match their sitters' pocketbooks as well as their own abilities. When the young Ammi Phillips returned to Pittsfield in 1811, he raised the top asking price to six dollars. His price schedule must have reflected the size and format; for example, Dr. Barstow's diary noted "full length," "halfway down' [half length], or "small profile views." Painting as many people as possible was the best way to gain a foothold in the countryside, as James Guild learned with his reference to a customer pleased with his portrait that resembled a "strangle cat." Harding knew this lesson well from his provincial days; looking back when he wrote a letter of advice to one young artist, he proposed sending him to "some of our country towns in New England, say Montpelier. . . . I would advise your charging so low that the cost of a picture would not stand in the way of your getting sitters, as it is not money you would want so much as practice for a year or two." The ground had been prepared by the exemplary post-Revolutionary travels and travails of Ralph Earl and his few contemporaries in Connecticut and other older regions. Phillips could look to J. Brown's portrait of Laura Hall (and a handful of other Connecticut and New York artisan-artists) for a model of how to depict a standing girl when the Barstow children posed for their full-length portraits, though Pluma rests her right hand on a draped table rather than a Windsor chair and Phillips adds a billowing dark curtain to both paintings. He showed greater sophistication four years later in his portrait of Harriet Campbell (see fig. 73).[26] More entrants crowded into the likeness trade in the 1820s and 1830s, making more paths for artists and more possibilities for consumers.

Success for a provincial painter did not mean the established comfort of an academic artist's urban studio with a steady stream of patrons. Charles Bird King did achieve that station with his impressive "Painting Room and an 'Exhibition Room'" in Washington, D.C., which sported a skylight, but only after he spent time as an itinerant along the eastern seaboard. He recalled that stage of his career in *The Itinerant Artist* (circa 1830), where the painter works on a likeness of the country matron amid a crowded and chaotic farm household (fig. 76). While the father heads out the door, gun over his shoulder, eleven others crowd around the easel, eight children in all, and a grandmother leans over the canvas to offer her opinion. King's visual recollection offers a critique of provincial consumerism as the rustic inhabitants clustered in the dark monochromatic kitchen, with its wooden floor, woodenware, and ceramics, while aspiring to a more refined station. A doorway reveals a bedroom with old-fashioned chairs. The finished portrait would be among the first consumer goods to enter the household. King's painting recalls the days when he had to make his way to farmhouses and endure the provincial comments of the residents to earn his living.[27] For every Charles Bird King or Chester Har-

Fig. 76. Charles Bird King, *The Itinerant Artist*, ca. 1830. Oil on canvas. 44-3/4 × 57 in. Fenimore Art Museum, Cooperstown, New York. Photograph by Richard Walker.

ding who ended up in a Washington, D.C., or Boston studio, many more of the "primitive sort" resembled Phillips and Joseph Whiting Stock, who remained provincial painters with long-term careers as itinerants in the countryside.

Even if Chester Harding and Charles Bird King embellished the recollections of the rustic roots of their artistic career, no doubt these itinerant artisan-artists were witness to, as well as agent of, the opening of the era of popular portraiture, part of the entry of goods signifying gentility into provincial households. The transformation of the late eighteenth-and early nineteenth-century countryside accelerated with demographic growth and the rapid entry of village residents into commercial enterprise. The trend toward more elaborate consumerism, which had taken several generations to develop during the eighteenth century, gathered momentum in the nineteenth: "As . . . the condition of the people improved, then by degrees, extended their desires beyond the mere necessaries of life; first to its conveniences, and then to its elegancies. This produced new wants, and to supply them, mechanics more numerous, and more skilful were required, til at length, the cabinet maker, the tailor, the jeweler, the milliner, and a host of others came to be regarded as indispensable." The inability of the existing commercial and cultural infrastructure to satisfy these new tastes meant that itinerants provided many of the practical and luxury items sought by village residents.[28] Painters played a key role in supplying those "elegancies."

The demand for portraits spread across social strata throughout the United States. By the 1820s and 1830s, portraitists of every description and skill level produced images at every price, similar to the profusion of chairmakers and clockmakers standardizing and diversifying their colorful commodities. Even though some earlier painters' efforts represented simple likenesses, they created a widespread desire for their offerings. Stylistic developments affected their repertoire. The villager's purse and the painter's promise combined to permit significant innovations in rural design: a more colorful look, quite different from the plain eighteenth-century mode or the newer Grecian classicism in more academic circles. However inexpert the results might be, an inexperienced audience's amazement and the enterprising artisan's enthusiasm fortified the pursuit of professional status. But the range of offerings stretched from the mechanically aided profile maker to the painter of richly embellished family portraits in oil. Craftsmen and consumers shared in "the new sense" delight in seeing a likeness and the new aspirations to display a key icon of middling status—a portrait.

Painted Stuff

In 1825, an anonymous *Encyclopedia* came off the presses in Concord, New Hampshire. Entitled *A Select Collection of Valuable and Curious Arts, and Interesting Experiments Which are Well Explained, and Warranted Genuine, and May be Prepared, Safely and at Little Expense,* this work covered various topics in the arts, manufactures, and sciences of interest to country craftsmen and to consumers eager for "improvement." The author promised instruction in a variety of skills: "To paint in figures for carpets or borders; to paint in imitation of mahogany and maple; to change wood apparently to stone; copper plate etching and engraving; mezzotint engraving; etching in aqua-tints; ornamental gilding; to make sympathetic ink for secret correspondence; luminous ink that will shine in the dark; painting on glass; best method of tracing or copying a picture; the construction and use of a copying machine; to kindle a fire under water; to produce detonating balloons; construction of a galvanic pile or battery; to freeze water in warm weather; the art of manufacturing paper hangings; to change the colours of animals." The author, Rufus Porter, painter and promoter, exemplifies in his far-reaching travels and speculations the artisan-entrepreneur's crucial role in promoting the new artisans' decorative aesthetic that was coursing through the countryside during this period. Porter's education displayed the full scope of formal and informal schooling available to mobile rural residents. Born in Boxford, Massachusetts, in 1792, Porter moved as a child with his family to the new settlement of Pleasant Mountain Gore in Maine. He left the farm for six months' schooling at Fryeburg Academy, ending his formal education at age twelve. At this point, machines caught his attention, and for the next two years he preferred dealing with waterwheels, windmills, and lathes to performing agricultural chores. His family, concerned about providing him with a secure vocation, sent Rufus back to Boxford to serve an apprenticeship in shoemaking under his eldest brother. Within a few months, he gave up this vocation and returned to Maine to play "fife for military companies and the violin for dancing parties." Then he began to paint. In 1810, working as a house and sign painter in Portland, Maine, he came up with the idea of covering the walls of ordinary rooms with inexpensive landscape paintings. The outbreak of the War of 1812 found Porter painting gunboats and playing the drum. Soon Porter was in print with his first instruction manual, *The Martial Musicians Companion containing Instructions for Drum and Fife, together with an Elegant Collection of Beats, Airs, Marches and Quick Steps* (1814).[29]

Rural residents welcomed the wide range of talents itinerant instructors and inventors brought to their villages. Over the next few years, Porter taught school, got married, and built wind-powered gristmills, all the while acquiring a reputation as a professional portrait painter and "professor of dancing." By his early twenties, he had demonstrated expertise as author, artist, and inventor. Porter began publishing *Scientific American* and a series of pamphlets and instruction manuals; he painted sleighs, houses, signs, and landscape frescoes; and he continued the profitable portrait making that sustained his other ventures. He counted a "camera obscura" among his innovations. Other inventions were more fanciful, such as a "horseless carriage" and an "airship." All throughout his career Porter continued his peripatetic ways and kept alive his early interest in mechanics. For Porter, like the readers of his *Select Collection*, "the arts," "experiments," and "little expense" were not just words incongruously collected into an eye-catching title. This artist-inventor was the rural counterpart to Robert Fulton, promoter of the steamboat, and Samuel F. B. Morse, creator of the telegraph. These individuals moved easily between art and science, finding their spatial and mechanical imaginations thoroughly compatible with their creative and entrepreneurial efforts.[30]

Innovations in standardizing production made available to rural residents a greater number of portraits, whether inexpensive profiles or more expensive portraits. This cycle of consumption was part of a general "cultural revolution" distinguished by a remarkable proliferation not only of paintings but of items of all kinds that found their way to farmhouse doors. The new look in rural design made use of itinerant artisans' training in the "Curious Arts" along with their willingness to perambulate through the villages of the northeastern United States. Some city-based artists, such as Samuel Morse, were shrewd enough to take advantage of consumerism in this vast rural terrain, but rural artisans were most successful in tapping this market. They all revealed the rural craftsmen's heavy reliance on colorful paint. Stencils and design manuals offered the tools to imitate the imported elegance of Europe, but rural residents' preference for bright colors is evident in their decorative efforts.[31]

In the early nineteenth century, every available surface was decorated in a drive to embellish the home. Some portraitists, like Chester Harding, began as artisans and brought with them their training in practical craft work rather than aesthetic speculation. Others took advantage of instruction manuals and used templates and stencils to maximize their production despite their minimal skills. The emerging provincial middle class espoused a new aesthetic, which one recent author has labeled "American Fancy," rather than the rational restraint of the late eighteenth-century Village Enlightenment. They embraced profusely decorated interiors like the parlor of New Hampshire residents Sylvannus and Mary Jane Foss, which Joseph H. Davis painted in 1836. Vivid colors and bold patterns ornament the painted walls and eye-catching carpet. Mr. Foss sports a patterned waistcoat and Mrs. Foss an embroidered scarf; they face each other across a boldly painted table with an ornamental vase and brightly bound books. The interior setting projects refined living with its dazzling array of books, music scores, cut flowers in a vase, and a landscape hanging on the wall. While Davis may have depicted the Fosses in an imaginary setting, many Americans lived among flamboyantly patterned wallpapers and brightly painted furniture, and Davis specialized in painting decorative or "fancy" interiors that featured bold designs and the necessary possessions for genteel living.[32]

Walking into a room filled with fancy things recalls a sensibility described by the eighteenth-century Scottish philosopher Thomas Reid: "Fancy may combine things that never were combined in reality. It may enlarge or diminish, multiple or divide, [or] compound" to create a more intense experience. This temperament was not entirely new; eighteenth-century artisan painters like Winthrop Chandler depicted the illusion of decoration, whimsically imitative of reality, such as his fancy overmantel, which tricked the viewer with its imitation of a bookshelf on top of a mantelpiece. Chests and other pieces of furniture were grained or painted in imitation of more expensive mahogany. But the

Fig. 77. Blanket chest, ca. 1825, Artist unidentified, Matteson type, vicinity of South Shaftsbury, Bennington County, Vermont. Painted wood. 40 × 40 × 17-3/4 in. Collection American Folk Art Museum, New York City. Gift of Howard and Jean Lipman in honor of Robert Bishop, director (1977–91), Museum of American Folk Art. 1991.10.1. Photograph by John Parnell.

more exuberant phase of fancy that burst forth between 1815 and 1840 abandoned any decorative restraint for playful conceits that exceeded imitation of genuine materials, splashing display across rooms, furniture, and paintings, filling the eye with dazzling scenes, and providing the viewer with a store of unconventional images. A Vermont blanket chest (fig. 77) goes well beyond polite imitation of wood grain and moves toward more imaginative and original designs.[33]

Porter became the leading publicist for the fancy aesthetic, both by painting ornamental landscape scenes on the walls of dozens of houses throughout Maine, New Hampshire, Vermont, Massachusetts, and Rhode Island and by publishing six editions of *Curious Arts* and other manuals. He was working as a mural painter in New Hampshire when *Curious Arts* was published. His section on "Landscape Painting on Walls of Rooms" provides precise measurements and rules for mixing colors and plotting out designs for landscapes, focusing on practical instruction rather than aesthetic speculation. While art academies and treatises focused on models of plaster casts and European masterpieces, the instruction books gave concrete directions, clear and specific as James Wilson's recipe for ink. Their aim was not to convey a "more extensive knowledge of those arts" to "professed artists," "but to communicate some of the first lines and principles" for those who "practice them [crafts] occasionally," either for "profit or amusement." Painting was considered a craft, and the goal was to produce a stylized, nonillusionistic art.

Porter's directions began not with a romantic conception of nature but with a recipe for dissolving half a pound of glue in water and preparing the colors. Planning the design begins by striking a horizon line at breast height around the room. Painting starts with "rising clouds" and sky, then rivers and mountains, each colored differently, with inch-by-inch specifications for objects at different distances.[34] Porter later wrote that the four walls of a parlor could be completely covered in watercolors in less than five hours and at a cost of ten dollars (fig. 78). In an 1822 advertisement, he offered "to paint walls of rooms, in less than the ordinary expence of papering. Those gentlemen who are desirious of spending the gloomy winter months amidst pleasant groves and verdant fields, are respectfully invited to apply . . . where a specimen of the work may be seen." Price was quite a draw, since wall paintings competed with expensive French wallpapers. Porter used sponge work, stenciling, and free brushwork to capture views of farms, villages, and seascapes. Others followed in Porter's footsteps, both literally and figuratively. For example, the "Bear and Pears" artist covered a wall in Thornton, New Hampshire, with a fantastic composite: a New England landscape, a three-story structure with palm trees, soldiers with pith helmets, and even an elephant, which one scholar has related to early-nineteenth-century French wallpapers by Joseph Dufour that depict Captain Cook's exploration of the Pacific and his untimely death.[35]

Itinerant artists kept afloat by their willingness to decorate any available surface. Even accomplished artists occasionally painted tavern signs, and the provincial artists who combed the countryside decorated many otherwise utilitarian objects. Edward Hicks, apprenticed to a coachmaker, specialized in the ornamental painting of vehicles before moving on to painting furniture, signs, houses, weather vanes, and floor cloths. Jacob Eichholtz, coppersmith turned painter, did a tavern sign for Henry Diffenbaugh, the new owner of the William Pitt, Earl of Chatham Inn, on the road to Philadelphia. No less than sixty-one tavern signs dotted the sixty-six mile turnpike between Philadelphia and Lancaster. A fetching sign with a bold expanse of color on a framed board, a form similar to profiles, could catch the traveler's eye and boost business.

Fig. 78. Rufus Porter, *Landscape Wall Mural with Farms and Grazing Cattle*, ca. 1838.
Dr. Francis Howe house, Westwood, Massachusetts. Tempera with watercolor paint
on plaster with chestnut lath support. 64 × 90-1/2 in. Courtesy of Heller Washam
Antiques and Julie Lindberg Antiques.

Eichholtz worked from the engraving of William Hoare's painting of William
Pitt, the great British wartime prime minister and champion of the American
colonists' grievances, portrayed full length, seated with his wig and lacy
sleeves. Eichholtz frequently painted and lettered objects for his customers;
during these early years, he recorded fifty-three jobs of "lettering," "painting,"
gilding, making, or repairing signs. He fashioned a sign on tin for his portrait
business that read "J. Eichholtz/Portrait Painting"; tin's shiny, smooth surface
held paint well, so boxes and coffeepots were often embellished with colorful
designs. He painted a Masonic apron in July for "Mr. Elvee," decorating fra-
ternal regalia with painted, printed, and embroidered designs. That spring of
1809, according to his account book, Jacob continued to make copper sauce-
pans and mend teakettles, while painting a backgammon table and other
pieces of furniture. He painted "a frontis piece" for John Wind, maker of
pianofortes; perhaps Eichholtz painted the curly maple board behind the key-
board of the mahogany-cased piano signed by John Wind, its "delicately
painted oval cartouche flanked by floral sprays, all executed in bright, clear

colors." Eichholtz also lettered the occasional sign or clock dial but painting faces was still his goal. That May, Eichholtz recorded his first portrait commission for "Mrs Bennett."[36] Nathan Negus, son of a sign and carriage painter in Petersham, Massachusetts, planned to tour the South to advance in the painting profession. He and his brother, Joseph, who was also a painter, were none too fussy over what they would paint. Joseph wrote to Nathan from Georgia in 1819 and proposed that they meet in New Orleans and "travel to all the most considerable places in the United States, working in each place, as we found encouragement. I think we would make money very fast in the southern states a year or two at portrait painting together with painting some rooms for wealthy men who would pay an extravagant price. We could probably obtain in many places hereabouts from $75 to $100 for an 18 foot room in style."[37]

Itinerancy was a natural condition for provincial painters. While Ammi Phillips chose a country town as a base for his travels, like many artisan-entrepreneurs working in a region, most painters kept to the road, knocking on doors to face an uncertain reception, as Guild vividly remembered, and staying as long as local custom held up. Traveling artists such as Erastus Field were keenly aware of the relationship between trade fluctuations and their own success. Joseph Whiting Stock carefully recorded in a journal his daily activities, the weather, his sitters, and his business prospects. Stock relied on the advance notice of friends and the patronage of village notables to advise him on local conditions before his arrival. Once established in "his room" or by "boarding myself," he would paint portraits as long as brisk demand continued. When business flagged, Stock moved on. One of the most prolific painters traveling in the North, Stock reported after he finished a stint in New Bedford, Massachusetts, that "I have been as liberally patronized in this town, as could be expected. Considering the great depression of business the last three months I have had as much work as I could conveniently attend to and were I disposed to stay no doubt, there would be enough to keep me untill winter. So far as I am able to judge my work has given good satisfaction and if disposed to return next Spring I am assured that I can recommence business with better prospects as money will be more plenty, and business more busy." Over his five-month stay, Stock painted thirty-seven portraits and eighteen miniatures "to order," along with several landscapes, making a substantial profit before returning home.[38]

Porter, the inveterate itinerant, found his greatest success on the road. Accompanied by a young relative named Joe, he strolled into villages with his brightly decorated camera box and distributed his handbill offering reasonably priced portraits (fig. 79). The artisan-entrepreneur sketched his subjects with

CORRECT LIKENESSES,
TAKEN WITH ELEGANCE AND DESPATCH BY
RUFUS PORTER.

Prices as follows—
Common Profile's cut double, - - $.0 20
Side views painted in full colours, - - 00
Front views, - - - - - - - 3 00
Miniatures painted on Ivory, - - - 8 00
☞ *Those who request it will be waited on, at*
their respective places of residence.

Fig. 79. Rufus Porter, handbill for "CORRECT LIKENESSES, taken with elegance and dispatch by Rufus Porter," ca. 1818–20. Sheet 8 11/16 × 5-1/8 in. Courtesy of American Antiquarian Society, Worcester, Massachusetts.

the aid of the camera obscura, a dark box fitted with a lens and mirror to throw the sitter's image onto a sheet of paper. Porter and Joe traveled from village to village, offering the public a full range of "correct likenesses," produced with Porter's mechanical aids and guaranteed to provide satisfaction. A typical Porter announcement of 1821 promised:

Fig. 80. Rufus Porter, attributed. *Young Gentlemen, possibly of the Stevens Family*, ca. 1835. Watercolor and ink on paper, in oval. 4-3/4 × 3-3/4 in. with original eglomise glass and gilt frame. Rufus Porter's two gentlemen wore similar attire. The side view with its distinctive hair, features, and coat offered ample personal details to Porter's customers. Collection of Jane and Gerald Katcher. Photograph by Gavin Ashworth. Courtesy of David Schorsch and Eileen Smiles.

Painting

The Subscriber respectfully informs the Ladies and Gentlemen of Haverhill and its vicinity~that he continues to paint correct Likenesses in full colours for two Dollars at his room at Mr. Brown's tavern, where he will remain two or three Days longer.

(No Likeness, No Pay.)

Those who request it will be waited on at their respected places of abode.

He advertised his profiles at twenty cents apiece, producing perhaps twenty silhouettes in an evening by the use of a profile machine for the features. In the popular side view, "full colours" were added to the stark profile (fig. 80). For

Fig. 81. Rufus Porter, *Full View of Man*, 1830–35. Watercolor and ink on wove paper. 4 × 3 in. Porter's more expensive full view required more time for the artist to sketch in the shirt, vest, and coat; the face's stippling added distinction to the effort. Abby Aldrich Rockefeller Folk Art Museum, The Colonial Williamsburg Foundation, Virginia.

his most detailed full view (fig. 81), the camera obscura reduced his artistic labors to a mere fifteen minutes. Some side views, such as the *Girl in Green Dress,* were loosely painted, with a rare effort to paint hands; but other side views were sparer, such as the *Profile of a Lady with Ruff* with modeling on the face, the features delicately drawn and shaded with a stippling technique, or *Young Gentlemen, Possibly of the Stevens Family* (fig. 80). Porter's later full views have more generous stippling and substantial crosshatching on the face. Since the full face was more of a challenge and quite time-consuming, he charged three times as much (fig. 81). These images still showed the subject's ears in full profile, a shortcut preserved from his side views. Copies came cheap. Porter's *Select Collection* gave instructions for "the construction and use of a copying machine," or pantograph, which reduced, enlarged, or copied images. The client could choose an affordable original along with as many copies as desired. Porter created a standardized product with the aid of his mechanical inventions and labor-saving techniques; the rural client got just as much "art" as he or she was willing to pay for.[39]

A spokesperson for ideas of rural design, Porter transmitted the rules necessary to paint everything from landscapes on walls to portraits on paper. Porter's writing and painting placed repetition and rule at the heart of the country vernacular. He made sure-footed suggestions for introducing into every American home the "embellishments" that John Neal thought would eventually improve American art. Porter emphasized color and line, both accessible to precise measurement in careful proportions. The farmhouse frescoes he envisioned had no room for romantic shadowing or sublime scenery. Instead, "improving" villagers wanted working farms and practical details on their walls (see fig. 78). Just as some rural artisans used such machines as lathes to produce ever-greater quantities of chairs and clocks, enterprising artists like Porter experimented with new machines and such techniques as stenciling to mass-produce images. Mechanical process accelerated the manufacture of consumer goods. As both producers and consumers, residents of rural America were attracted to rather than alienated by the standardized products that were becoming increasingly available in the countryside.[40]

In the final analysis, Porter's mass-produced images catered to the lower ends of the rural market while taking advantage of the popularity of the fancy aesthetic best suited to an artisan's command of color and line. In rural portraiture, decorative display predominated over geometric perspective. While Porter's artisan training in house and sign painting lingered on in his reliance on repetition and two-dimensionality, he was able to achieve enormous success within the confines of these rural rules of design. But rural communities were also familiar with artists evincing at least some urban influence and some knowledge of academic models. These portraitists offered more elaborate likenesses, more suited to their own aspirations for achieving a genteel station, a goal they shared with their patrons; there were even a few who, without forgetting their village origins or audience, pushed the possibilities of rural design to their furthest form and sought to satisfy their provincial middle-class audiences' aspirations.

Aspirations for Gentility

Over a fifty-year career covering several states, Erastus Salisbury Field passed through a number of significant stylistic stages. He moved from farm to metropolis and back again, and finally matured into the painter of a richly embellished though standardized product—the most "correct likeness" one could buy in rural America—without traveling farther than two hundred miles from his birthplace. He and Phillips represent the exemplary itinerant painters of antebellum America.[41] They offered more elaborate and expensive representations based upon some urban training and an acquaintance with studio artists. Although they stylized designs and conventions to facilitate production, these portraitists were better able to display their sitters' features and surroundings to satisfy the desires of an emerging rural middle class for the various emblems of their newly won status. Poet Fitz-Greene Halleck wrote to Thomas Hicks in Philadelphia: "I want you to paint me so that I shall look like a gentleman. Never mind the likeness. In fifty years nobody will be able to tell whether the portrait is a likeness or not; but I want to be handed down to posterity as a gentleman."[42] When a practitioner of "the noble art of painting" visited Fitchburg, Massachusetts, in 1832, there was great cause for rejoicing among its citizenry. An entire generation had grown up admiring portraits and venerating the vocation of painting likenesses. An anonymous article in the *Fitchburg Gazette* noted the uplifting effects of popular portraiture on rural residents. The mysteries of painting went beyond the mere copying of features to "transferring to canvas . . . the feelings of the heart." This "gentleman now stopping over in our village" made the appearance of gentility available to all. These paintings were created in a standardized manner. In the 1830s, the visitor to a painter's studio remarked that the "some half dozen or more" likenesses resting along the walls of the rural salon, "tho' unfinished," would clearly represent in their final form the distinguished visages of their intended patrons. Families were invited to the painter's studio to obtain "a valuable picture" as well as "a correct likeness," for there would rarely be such an opportunity "in a village like ours" to have family portraits made.[43]

Field's talents had been discovered in his childhood sketches of relatives made on the family farm in the Connecticut River hill town of Leverett, Massachusetts. His parents encouraged his artistic aspirations, first by providing him with paints to experiment with on scraps of cardboard and then, in 1824, by sending him to New York to study with Samuel Morse. There he found the artist-inventor ensconced in his studio at 96 Broadway working on his heroic portrait of Lafayette, with its grand scale and atmospheric use of color and light to establish the three-dimensional stance of its subject, a portrait in the grand manner that figured in Field's own life and works. After Morse's London training, the painter had descended into long-term despair of ever finding support in the United States for escaping the drudgery of portrait painting and ascending into history painting. But his Christmas letter to his family hit a more joyful tone: "I have everything very comfortable in my rooms. My two pupils, Mr. Agate and Mr. Field, are very tractable and very useful. I have everything 'in Pimlico' as mother would say." But the sudden death of Morse's wife that

February ended Field's brief period of formal study, and he returned to Leverett by spring. There, in his first known portrait, he completed a somber-toned likeness of his grandmother, Elizabeth Ashley, with few apparent traces of his recent master's example. Then Field left his birthplace and took to the road to further his training in provincial portraiture in central Massachusetts. In his only signed portrait commission, he captured "Biel Le Doyt/Aged 25 years" in Worcester in 1827, applying a gray ground coat that he used for some time.

He is heard from next in Hudson, New York, in 1828, writing to his father that his great aunt there was helping him "in the prospect of retaining business." He had succeeded in capturing commissions from two prominent residents suggested by his uncle, and he was using two finished works as samples to lure prospective sitters. He claimed that his artistic prowess accounted for his excellent prospects; those who had seen his portraits "think that they are good likenesses." The itinerant reported, "I like it here very much so far," and added, "I think I shall tarry here as long as I can obtain business," sounding like Vanderlyn's commentary on Phillips. His painting of his cousin Lauriette Ashley is the most ambitious of his early portraits, a six-foot-high, life-sized, full-length painting, with a landscape view included, displaying Morse's influence with its soft blurred edges around the face, arms, and hands. But Field added his own crisp painting of decorative details on chair and gown, and his inexperience shows in her somewhat awkward pose. While the young painter handled bodies awkwardly, he was making a definite effort to master human anatomy and learn modeling and composition, as fine fabrics and other emblems of status for his clientele began to fill his canvases.[44]

Rural painters were no strangers to urban studios or academic conventions. Metropolitan studios often provided provincial painters with a period of training and an alluring vision of professional status. Erastus Field and Ethan Allen Greenwood secured their studio training early on; others such as Harding made do with a long period of work in the hinterlands before encountering the upper reaches of the profession. Philadelphia and New York contained clusters of rich patrons and an emerging infrastructure of artistic institutions. An aspiring artist, such as Eichholtz, knew about urban opportunities from the arrival of Philadelphia's Thomas Sully in Lancaster in 1809, already a well-known academic artist. Eichholtz hastened to visit the city's cosmopolitan community of artists and artistic institutions, where he met valuable patrons. The busy coppersmith-artist's local supporters urged him to visit "the celebrated Stuart in Boston." To gain an audience with Stuart, an artist had to arrive with a specimen of his skill; Eichholtz took his recent portrait of Biddle. Although he met "with a handsome reception," "I had a fiery trial to undergo, my picture was placed alongside the best of [Stuart's] hand, and that lesson I considered the best I had ever received:

the comparison was, I thought, enough, and if I had vanity before I went, it left me all before my return." Eichholtz studied Stuart's half-length portraits and paid special attention to Stuart's professional advice before heading home to Lancaster.

Even brief encounters with well-known artists could have profound results. Greenwood made occasional visits to Boston as he developed his craft before becoming a full-time portraitist in 1815. An emboldened Eichholtz left the tin and copper trade behind the year after his visit to Stuart.[45] Others, like Morse and King, found themselves unhappily consigned to a stint of rural rustication seeking patronage. Ralph Earl's path to prosperity beckoned others to become long-term itinerant portraitists of the post-Revolutionary gentry. Field and many of his peers made successful careers in the hinterlands painting the likenesses of the emerging rural bourgeois, eager for cultural commodities but with their feet firmly planted in the rural idiom and rural system of production. By 1833, Field had purchased land in Three Rivers, Massachusetts, and his clientele broadened beyond a narrow band of the village elite.[46]

Provincial painters' plain styles permitted low prices. In the 1830s, Field charged $4 or $5 for large portraits and as little as $1.50 for smaller ones of children. It took him only a day to paint the Reverend and Parnell Merrill Marsh of Winchester, Connecticut, dated 16 and 17 April 1833, respectively. Other artists distinguished their styles according to the time and effort required. William Matthew Prior offers the clearest evidence of how a painter's quality of work correlated directly with the price a patron was willing to pay and the time he devoted to the task. He began his career in Maine as an ornamental painter, but he demonstrated an accomplished manner from an early age, exhibiting a portrait at the 1831 Boston Athenaeum alongside Stuart, Sully, and Washington Allston. He developed a price scale based on the time spent on the likeness and the difficulty of its composition. Early in his career his advertisements offered a "likeness at a reasonable rate" and reduced rates available for "side views and profiles of children." Later he elaborated: "Persons wishing for a flat picture can have a likeness without shade or shadow at one-quarter price." Prior was master of two styles that he offered his customers: one was a quick, flat manner with broad brushstrokes and little shade or shadow, and the other a more academic fashion with modeling and varied tones. His portrait of an unknown woman was one of his "without shade and shadow" products, a flat style that he advertised as especially suitable for side views and profiles of children (fig. 82). One such flat and broad portrait had a printed label on the back that read, "PORTRAITS/ PAINTED IN THIS STYLE!/ Done in about an hour's sitting./ Price 2.92, including Frame, Glass, &c./ Please call at Trenton Street/ East Boston/ WM. M. PRIOR." The portrait of Lucy Hartshorn, one of a pair of the newlywed

Fig. 82. William Matthew Prior, *Unknown Woman*, 1837–44. Tempera on academy board. 15-1/4 × 10-1/2 in. One of Prior's "without shade or shadow products." Collections of Old Sturbridge Village, Sturbridge, Massachusetts.

carpenter and his wife, represented his more academic style, which cost from $10 to $25 (fig. 83). The two women's portraits have certain similarities: they each wear drop earrings and have black bands securing their hair. But there are also some striking differences. Lucy turns slightly to the left to engage the viewer. The symbols of fashionable adornment, such as her elegant black décolleté garment, the drop earrings, and a paisley shawl, along with the artist's generous provision of light and shadow, confirm its status as one of Prior's top-of-the-line products.[47]

Joseph Goodhue Chandler worked in a more natural mode than Prior. His offerings did not change over time, but varied even in a single portrait: children's flatly rendered bodies are combined with carefully modeled faces with a convincing sense of volume. Parents cared more about the child's individuality coming through than about their clothing.[48] Zedekiah Belknap often resorted to nontraditional surfaces, such as wood or bedsheets, but he textured the wood panels with diagonal lines to resemble canvas.

Fig. 83. William Matthew Prior, *Lucy A. Hartshorn*, Portland Maine, 1836. Oil on cardboard. 24-11/16 × 21-7/16 in. Prior also painted in a more academic fashion with facial modeling and deeper tones. Collections of Old Sturbridge Village, Sturbridge, Massachusetts. Photograph by Thomas Neill.

Portraitists and patrons shared aspirations toward a rising social and professional status. This concern with presenting a middle-class identity is strikingly evident in artists' literary and visual self-portraits, whether they occupied a life-long station in the hinterlands or a brief period of itinerancy. Some venture-some portraitists sought further instruction. James Guild closed his journal with the words, "he Commences his Profession as an Artist," and described his entry into a circle of London artists, where he sketched nude models and learned "the human figure," a far cry from his earlier painting of a country maiden in rural New York. Chester Harding met with great success traveling downriver on a floating studio and at a stationary studio in Paris, Kentucky. But, beginning "to entertain more elevated ideas of the art," he drew upon his profits and embarked upon a two-month stint in Philadelphia, "drawing in the Academy, and studying the best pictures." He grew discouraged looking at the work of older artists: "I saw the labor it would cost me to emulate them." One effect of his visit was "to open my eyes to the merits of the works of other artists," even as it diminished his self-satisfaction. "My own pictures did not look as well to my own eye as they did before I left Paris." However, Harding determined to push on in his plan for improvement, and when he completed a successful work, "my spirits would rise."[49]

Despite their middle-class aspirations and achievements, village painters' country origins were still detectable in their likenesses. In his self-portrait, Jonathan Adams Bartlett, farmer and house carpenter in Rumford, Maine, wore his Sunday best and proudly displayed the colors of his palette, but the painting exhibits the same flat perspective he used for his rural clients. Nathan Negus, son of a sign and carriage painter in Petersham, Massachusetts, assumed a regal pose in his self-portrait. Still, he and his brother were not above painting the odd room or piece of furniture. The versatile Matthew Prior took care to make his own portrait of the artist as a young man in his "fuller" form, with modeling of the face and classic pose with brush and palette; the composition was drawn from European traditions, displaying a seriousness of ambition and stylistic sophistication with its fluid brushwork and subtle palette of colors, capped off with the signature: "Wm. Matthew Prior, Painter, Portland, Maine, Oct. 12, 1825." Ordinary Americans increasingly penned their memoirs in the decades after the American Revolution, a phenomenon that historian Joyce Appleby noted, in an effort to call attention to their personal tales of success and self-formation.[50]

Although Guild and Harding ended up with a European tour to study the old masters, Negus and Bartlett never left their decorative training far behind. Jacob Eichholtz connected to the grand tradition through a source closer at hand. In his account book, he began filling entire pages with extracts from the pronouncements of Sir Joshua Reynolds. He started with Reynolds's fifteen *Discourses on Art* on 6 August 1811. The passages jump from discourse to discourse, but Eichholtz's intent is clear, for in contrast to the opening pages of the account book on which he wrote craftsmen's recipes for mixing varnish and grinding colors, he was now pursuing something much broader—an artistic education. He began his "extracts" with a passage from the *Third Discourse*: "I will now add that Nature herself is not to be too closely copied. There are excellencies in the art of painting beyond what is commonly called the imitation of nature; and these excellencies I wish to point out. The students who having passed through the initiatory exercises, are more advanced in the art, and who, sure of their hand, have leisure to exert their understanding, must now be told, that a mere copier of nature can never produce any thing great; can never raise and enlarge the conceptions, or warm the heart of the spectator." For the talented artist who achieved the goal of apprehending nature, there must also be educated patrons. Art critic John Neal optimistically wrote that "the day is near at hand . . . when pictures that are now thought well of by good judges will not be tolerated by the multitude." Eichholtz copied from Reynolds: "When the arts were in their infancy, the power of merely drawing the likeness of any object was considered as one of its greatest efforts." The passage captured the glee of self-trained artists like Eichholtz and Harding at seeing their first image take form, the sense of wonderment about the ability to possess a likeness of oneself that they shared with their neighbors, the "common people." American art would need to move beyond the fascination with the decorative detail. Taste would be elevated when portraitist and patrons alike were no longer satisfied with the "superficial senses" and demanded the capture of the "imagination," raising the artist and overall cultural horizons to ensure success.[51]

While Reynolds devoted himself in other discourses to discussing color and composition, his was not a recipe book like Porter's *Curious Arts*, but a moral handbook and an intellectual program, as another extract Eichholtz copied made clear: "If we examine with a critical view the manner of those painters whom we consider as patterns, we shall find that their great fame does not proceed from their works being more highly finished than those of other artists, or from a more minute attention to details, but from that enlarged comprehension which sees the whole object at once and that energy of art which gives it characteristick effect by adequate expression." To be a "great artist" came not from remembering rules or viewing great works, but from the larger project— "to form a *mind*." His direct encounters with Gilbert Stuart and study of Sir Joshua Reynolds made a significant impact. In 1812, Eichholtz removed his artisan's apron. On 12 November, he recorded "mending a lamp; a few weeks later he advertised in the local newspaper: "To be Let, and possession given on the 1st of April next, a coppersmith hand tinplateworker's Shop, with Horses, Bellows, and Tools complete, together with a front store, now in possession of subscriber. The premises are so well known, that no recommendation is deemed necessary. For terms apply to Jacob Eichholtz."[52] Eichholtz had left the artisan's shop bench, never to return, determined to pursue his artistic aspirations. But neither Eichholtz nor his provincial and academic colleagues ever occupied the Olympian perch of Sir Joshua Reynolds atop the Royal Academy. They could avail themselves of the growing quantity of printed material that offered an artistic education to a man such as Eichholtz and provide the opportunity to create a new self. They remained restrained as well as buoyed by their connection to the community of local artisans and their role in creating a provincial middle-class culture. Plain painting was no mere diffusion of academic concepts but an active deployment from below. Erastus Field forged a career through the desire of his western Massachusetts clientele for affordable but elaborate and standardized but individualized portraits.

Erastus Salisbury Field

Provincial artists like Field and Phillips worked by finding a formula and set of methods to speed production, bridge the limitations of their training, and meet their customers' expectations of a pleasing likeness. Academic and provincial painters used similar poses, props, and settings: seated gentlemen and ladies in lace-topped dresses. Whereas the academic artist valued psychological insight and varieties of shadows and shading, the rural portraitist aimed at a plain style in which simplicity and linearity accompanied broad expanses of color and texture. Rural residents wanted restrained likenesses with sharply defined forms, "neatly organized compositions some with an almost mathematical precision and symmetry, and no expressive brushwork, and overall flatness and linearity." One scholar has suggested that portraitists and patrons shared in an "artisan aesthetic" where visible labor rather than invisible genius was the desired effect, produced by a neat canvas with careful outlines. Faces were fully lit and often presented frontally, rather than the dark and moody visages of the more academic sort that we see in Chester Harding's portrait of Amos Lawrence (fig. 84); flatness and verisimilitude were premium values in provincial portraiture.

Those who wanted something else could always seek out an academic artist, if they had the requisite cash and contacts. Delia Ellsworth Taintor and Henry Griswold Taintor, newly married and visiting Delia's sister in Washington after remodeling and enlarging their Hampton, Connecticut, home, sought out the gallery and studio of Charles Bird King. There they procured matching portraits with informal directness and intense shading, quite different from what was available in Hampton. Delia was the granddaughter of Oliver Ellsworth, third chief justice; a monumental Ralph Earl portrait of her grandparents hung in Ellwood, the family seat in Windsor. Such elegance did not come cheaply: the portrait cost the Taintors one hundred dollars, ten times the price of a provincial likeness.[53] Occasionally, however, prominent folk sought out rural painters. Ammi Phillips painted the entire Dorr family of Chatham, New York, around 1814. Russell Dorr, a prominent and prosperous physician, commissioned a portrait of himself, a double one of his wife and their baby, and individual portraits of his six other children, all executed as pendants, decreasing in paired sizes according to the sitters' ages. His brother's family also took advantage of Phillips's services. The patriarch sits on an upholstered chair amid his medical library, which represented a substantial investment (his inventory recorded over one hundred titles). His eldest child was painted in the pastels of Phillips's

Fig. 84. Chester Harding, once "one of the primitive sort," had mastered the techniques of the academic tradition with this portrait of *Amos Lawrence*, ca. 1845, with its deep tonality and chiaroscuro. Oil on canvas. 84-5/8 × 53-9/16 in. Given in memory of the Rt. Rev. William Lawrence by his children, Image courtesy of the Board of Trustees, National Gallery of Art, Washington, D.C.

Border period, with the familiar pose of his crisscrossing arms around a book, chair, and stand. In the portrait of Joseph Dorr, the painter started by outlining large parts of the head in pale flesh tones, then played about with the shapes, finally filling in the form with a reddish-brown line and leaving the original outline as evidence of his efforts to find the proper shape.[54]

The tall tale about how traveling artists spent their winters drawing bodies and then in summer attached each patron's head to complete the likeness was published in a 1925 article, "Early American Primitives." Not so.[55] A rare unfinished pair of canvases found rolled up in an attic over a century and a quarter ago shows an anonymous artist sketching in backgrounds and bodies to establish the overall conception, then moving on to delineate the faces, leaving the man's coat to be done later as well as the background (fig. 85). With perhaps

Fig. 85. Anonymous, *Perley Bartlett*, ca. 1831–35. Sterling, Massachusetts. Oil on canvas. 37 × 33 in. This portrait left unfinished demonstrates how the artist completed the face first with the clothing just outlined, to be completed later. Sterling Historical Society, Sterling, Massachusetts.

just one sitting, the anonymous artist worked on the couple at the same time, leaving them in the same unfinished state. Other documentation shows that artists sometimes painted a pair of portraits one at a time; Prior finished the Hartshorns on the same day. Nathan Negus "inlay'd Esq Willards portrait" one day, had a second sitting the next, and then finished two days later, starting the companion portrait two weeks later ("inlay'd" probably meant laying out the portrait). Perley Bartlett's portrait probably dates from the well-established merchant's marriage to Persis, around 1831. Perhaps the couple was not happy with the work or the artist was interrupted by an emergency. The couple remained content with provincial portraiture; later they commissioned Jones Fawson Morris, the son of a decorative painter who emigrated to Sterling and painted local families, to paint a group portrait of their three children.[56]

Like their artisanal kin, portrait painters used various means of easing their task and speeding their production. We have seen Rufus Porter's profiles and views at the lower end of the spectrum of provincial portraiture, the plainer mass-produced part; at the other upper end, Erastus Salisbury Field found a grander means of portraying the rural bourgeoisie's expectations of elegance at a low price in the 1830s while relying on stock poses to increase volume. By displaying their personal possessions, Field evolved a formula that simultaneously individualized his sitters and emphasized their status. Artists like Field offered villagers desirable commodities that evinced some exposure to academic models but were also guided by their sitters' cultural norms and desire for personal transformation. While some scholars see refinement coming from Philadelphia and Boston, ideas were also coursing across the countryside. Field developed a new kind of grand-manner portraiture toward the end of the 1830s. He provided prosperous farmers, merchants, and craftsmen with formulations of gentility that helped a new rural middle class recognize itself. Field's career found its fullest expression in the 1830s as this class of commercializing entrepreneurs coalesced; the itinerant provided them with statements of their new-found stature and familiarity with refined models.

Although Field still painted his brother stiffly seated on a hard wooden chair, his portraits of country gentlemen adopted grander poses amid more lavish surroundings. The portraits adapted some lessons learned from Morse, but more from Field's own sojourn as a rural painter of a rural bourgeoisie; he used softer modeling and surer brushwork. He always added small personal details of his sitters to their general outlines, which he quickly sketched by employing a large, dark frock coat that occupied much of the canvas. In an 1836 summer jaunt to the Berkshires, his only apparent trip there, Eleazer Bullard commissioned four portraits from Field: of himself, his second wife, and his daughter (from his first marriage) and her husband, Squire and Mrs. Brewer. Eleazer was no stranger to portraiture; his first wife, Hannah Wilson, had been painted in 1812 in a stiff but honest likeness. Eleazer apparently had that portrait reframed to match the four new portraits as they took their place in the Bullard homestead. Field depicted Eleazer Bullard (fig. 86) in measured tones. He sits sideways on a wooden chair, his right hand holding a quill and resting on the chair back, his left elbow on a table, with a cupcake-shaped inkwell beside him. His features were personalized by his ruddy complexion and unshaven cheeks, a heavily shaded upper lip, and short, curly dark hair. A table and chair are suggested by quick dabs of paint. The juxtaposition of light and dark tones lends drama to the composition. The black double-breasted, high-collar coat is open to reveal a yellowish waistcoat and a white shirt with black stock. Hands were quickly painted in a graceful position despite the blunt fingers and knuckles suggested by dots of flesh-colored pigment. This same process is revealed in his portraits of women: Field found a comfortable pose for his sitters, arranged

Fig. 86. Erastus Salisbury Field, *Eleazer Bullard*, 1835. Oil on canvas. 37-1/2 × 28 in. By the 1830s, Field had adopted a standardized portrait, individualized by Eleazer's ruddy complexion and other facial details. Abby Aldrich Rockefeller Folk Art Museum, The Colonial Williamsburg Foundation, Virginia.

their hands naturally, and added props to the foreground and details to the background, until the scene teemed with color and decorative display. The details of Emeline Sheldon Bullard's intricate ruffled cap and collar (fig. 87) add visual interest, along with the pincushion, but her sleeves remain swirls of paint. Her long nose is carefully depicted. The table on which Mrs. Bullard rests her hand is replaced in her daughter's portrait with a snail-shell chair arm, a familiar element. All four large portraits of the Bullards and Brewers exhibit Field's use of black dots to define the women's lace pattern. The four sitters wore similar clothing and assumed identical poses; the portraits were probably intended to be hung as a group. However, Field took great pains to individualize his subjects.[57]

Many Field sitters were related, suggesting a web of connections to obtain commissions. That same summer he painted the extended Bassett clan of Lee;

Fig. 87. Erastus Salisbury Field, *Emeline Bullard*, ca. 1835. Oil on canvas. 37-1/2 × 28 in. Field paid considerable attention to Emeline's lace hat and collar, but her sleeves and the background received much less detailing. Abby Aldrich Rockefeller Folk Art Museum, The Colonial Williamsburg Foundation, Virginia.

ten members of three generations sat for Field. The Bassetts' narrow, sloping shoulders contribute to the triangular design of the portraits, which focuses the viewer's attention on the faces. The family patriarchs, Anselm and Nathaniel Bassett, are represented as elderly men. The next generation is similarly posed: the two men in the woodworking trades have their right hand flung over the chair back and their left hand on the lap. Anselm's son-in-law Amos Hurlbut, a successful carriage maker, is seated sideways on a grained chair, distinguished by his ruddy complexion, a book clasped in his left hand and the books lined up in the left corner. The painting is strengthened by the dramatic juxtaposition of light and dark tones as well as the brilliantly detailed book bindings. His brother-in-law Joseph Bassett, a successful cabinetmaker, appears without books. However, both are seated on fancy chairs displaying slight differences in construction, finish, and shape that demonstrate the growing availability of mass-marketed furniture. All ten portraits share soft gray backgrounds and a shaded halo of space encircling the sitters, along with skillful modeling of the face, which was of great interest to his middling clientele.[58]

Late in the year Field returned home to Leverett. There he stretched his formula to its fullest expression that Christmas while continuing to produce portraits by the efficient shorthand technique that enabled him to complete a half-length portrait in a day, for which he charged four dollars. He arrived in March 1837 to spend a full year living with his aunt and uncle Lucretia Ashley Hubbard and Caleb Hubbard at Plumtrees, a place on the banks of the Connecticut River he had loved since childhood. He had spent many an afternoon listening to Caleb's stories of the wild animals afoot in the early days of the settlement and the exciting events of the Revolution. The Hubbard tavern, built in 1763 and famous for lodging the local Minutemen on their way to Lexington in 1775, housed all those Hubbards, the largest known Field family grouping. All eleven portraits hung together in the north parlor of the former tavern where they lived. Ashley and Betsey Dole are featured, bright red drapery to the side, and behind a white column looms the colorful landscape of Mount Sugarloaf in South Deerfield as seen from Sunderlands; Ashley holds a *Boston Statesmen* of 4 March 1837, the date of Martin Van Buren's inauguration, perhaps a reference to the political role of the Hubbard Tavern in local affairs. Field painted six of their children, the sons in bright yellow vests and the girls in green gowns. Field's command of technique and color satisfied his audience's desire to proclaim their prosperity, for the artist's craft could surround his subjects with consumer goods and sentimental domestic scenes. Field's grand-manner portraits parallel the earlier work of Ralph Earl, but in an antebellum version.[59]

The same year, he traveled east to visit Petersham to paint another extended family, the Gallond-Cooks. The identity of the patriarch and matriarch, Jeremiah and Dorcas Gallond, is clear, but scholars debate which canvases portray each of their three daughters and their husbands (including the two Cook brothers). Here Fields achieved the fullest expression of individual likenesses that made up the bourgeois American family. The two sisters Louisa and Clarissa Gallond are depicted with an extended range of personal details and tonal coloring in the grandest of Field's portrait styles. Louisa and Almira had married two brothers, William and Nathaniel Cook (fig. 88), merchants who owned a Hudson River schooner. The three portraits of the Cooks (including one of William Lauriston Cook, son of Clarissa) all share a magnificent waterfront view; the women have a fantasy of red brick and granite warehouses with intervening church steeples, ships in full sail, and a beautiful sky behind it all. Field references Renaissance European portraiture with the red drapery drawn back to

Fig. 88. Erastus Salisbury Field, *Man with a Tune Book: Possibly Mr. Cook*, ca. 1838. Oil on canvas. 35 × 29 in. Gift of Edgar William and Bernice Chrysler Garbisch, Image courtesy of the Board of Trustees, National Gallery of Art, Washington, D.C.

reveal the marble column and the landscape view (figs. 89 and 90). Clarissa wears a dress and collar similar to her sister, but the collar is clasped by a mourning pin, a possible reference to Louisa's death earlier that year. While Louisa holds a book in her right hand, Clarissa grasps a loose sheet of paper, perhaps business correspondence and a commercial reference in line with the port city in the background. A few scholars have argued that these are idealized views of Boston Harbor, with brick buildings such as Faneuil Hall and a harbor

Fig. 89. Erastus Salisbury Field, *Louisa Gallond Cook*, ca. 1835. Oil on canvas. 39-1/2 × 34-1/2 in. ©Shelburne Museum, Shelburne, Vermont.

rather than a river scene. Field starts off the portraits of William Lauriston and Nathaniel Cook with poses and a painting technique similar to his portraits from earlier in the decade such as *Eleazer Bullard* (see fig. 86), but Nathaniel's drapery folds are sharply defined, the face is more realistically modeled, and the tune book is so carefully delineated that it becomes legible. Here, as in the women's portraits, a red curtain and dramatic landscape heighten the artistic striving of both artist and sitter.[60]

In 1839, Field combined these aesthetic and economic motifs in his master-

Fig. 90. Erastus Salisbury Field, *Portrait of a Woman said to be Clarissa Gallond Cook, in Front of a Cityscape*, ca. 1838–39. Oil on canvas. 34-3/4 × 28-3/8 in. Daniel J. Terra Art Acquisition Endowment Fund, 2000.4 Terra Foundation for American Art, Chicago. Photograph: Terra Foundation for American Art, Chicago / Art Resource, NY.

piece, *Joseph Moore and His Family*, one of the great—and largest—images of a nineteenth-century American family (plate 8). In the year this portrait was made, Field had moved with his family to the home of his wife's parents in Ware, Massachusetts. Living across the street was Joseph Moore from Windham, Maine, with his wife, Almira, another of the Gallond sisters, and four children, two of which were the orphans of his wife's sister Louisa Gallond Cook. Almira had left Petersham to go to high school and live with her grandparents in Ware, where she must have met Joseph. At their wedding in 1829, Clarissa wrote: "We think that she has married well or at least we hope so." Her sister described the "very nice suit of clothes" her husband gave to her for the wedding: a gown of "white Goradanet silk" with lace in the neck and ribbons fastened with "a very nice handkerchief pin." The Gallonds noted Moore's refined manners with his attendance at a writing school, "a most beautiful copper plate" in his hand, and family prayers morning and evening. Joseph was a hatmaker in winter, itinerant dentist in summer, and professor of religion all year round.

Six nearly life-sized figures cluster in two groups in the almost seven-by-eight-foot canvas. No one figure or piece dominates; the viewer's eye jumps from the black-and-white-clad subjects to their numerous possessions. The Moores' furnishings arrest attention with their exuberant colors and prominent position. Field carefully balanced the children around the adults. Almira greatly resembles her sister Clarissa and wears the same accessories—comb, gown, pin, and belt buckle—that Clarissa wore for her portrait. The tilted perspective and bright colors of the patterned carpet with the mustard ground and Indian red design draw the eye downward from the symmetrical windows at the top of the picture. Two children stand on either side of each adult, the two Moore sons on the right and the two Cook orphans on the left. The children have the familiar pointed ears and stubby bodies of Field's work. Field suggests a natural and believable interior setting, which in the New England of 1839 would be behind closed, bright-green blinds. Field successfully juggles all these items around the stenciled furniture—chairs, stands, and mirror—that completes his study of the Moores' decor. Many of the accessories and decorative items depicted in the painting remained in the family's possession, including a Hitchcock-type chair with rush seat decorated in gold with fruit stencils, Almira's jewelry, and Joseph's dental tools and case. While Field had developed a sturdy formula for his family portraits that provided much-desired representations of genteel families and conveniently shortened his labors, he painted his sitters in their homes and individualized their features and their possessions.[61]

Aspirations for bourgeois identity came from the nascent middle class of professionals and manufacturers and successful farmers clustering in center villages, a group only gradually forging its social configuration, and remained wedded to a rustic artistic idiom that stenciled its "elegant" ornamentation and flattened its subjects' features. Rather than receding in conventional perspective, the Moores' floor is pushed upward, giving a clear view of the carpet pattern. What one scholar has called Field's "inventorial style" is well suited to display his patron's possessions: their clothes, books, musical instruments, and household furnishings. We are still in the world of Elijah Boardman's store, with its careful detailing of textiles and books. But the parlors have filled up with the new and colorful products of Sterling's chair shops, and the patrons' ranks have dramatically expanded.

The Vanderpoels Look to Ammi Phillips

When James and Ann Vanderpoel built a striking Federal-style house around 1820 in the bustling village of Kinderhook, New York, they commissioned Ammi Phillips to paint a pair of portraits to grace the walls. Phillips found great favor with the rising gentry of Columbia County, a region with a mix of Dutch colonial settlers and migrants from New England, as well as a tradition of limners pushing up the Hudson River. A thriving post-Revolutionary agricultural economy meant good times for Kinderhook and for James Vanderpoel, a well-established lawyer connected with New York's politician on the rise, Martin Van Buren. The Hudson Valley was home to many of the grand New York dynasties, such as the Livingstons and Van Rensselaers, whose estates boasted portraits of their ancestors in the grand manner and furniture from the finest New York City cabinetmakers. A new generation of men like James Vanderpoel had closer ties to the commercial activity that was transforming the region. They desired the services of Phillips and other provincial painters who combed Columbia County. Together, the Vanderpoel home, the portrait, and the domestic furnishings tell us how an upper-middle-class family furnished their new home in the metropolitan orbit of New York or Albany. They did not attempt to rival the grand style of their patrician predecessors, but adopted a myriad of cultural innovations (fig. 91).[62]

James Vanderpoel and Ann Doll had come of age after the Revolution in the rapidly growing towns of Kinderhook and Kingston in the Hudson Valley. While many adjusted to the new realities of independence, their generation experienced especially significant cultural change. Both families had deep roots in the region's Dutch culture. The Vanderpoels had lived along the Hudson for seven generations. George Doll was pastor of the Dutch Reform church of Kingston, educated in Holland and Germany and fluent in Dutch, French, and German, but not English. Their children forged their place in a new world of their own making. Although Dutch rule had been overtaken by the English capture of New Netherlands in 1664, patroons and manors in the southern part of Columbia County continued to keep tenancy alive, and conflicts over land tenancy continued into the "rent wars" of the early nineteenth century.

The Revolutionary War had brought economic distress as well as political turmoil; crops had been destroyed and communities divided. Isaac Vanderpoel,

Fig. 91. Ammi Phillips, *Anna Doll (Mrs. James) Vanderpoel*, ca. 1822. Kinderhook, New York. Oil on canvas. 31 × 24-3/4 in. Albany Institute of History and Art Purchase, Albany, New York.

James's father, was a prosperous farmer with ample lands along the region's highway, the Hudson River. He had initially supported the patriot cause, but his growing dissatisfaction with the American government led to a fateful decision to join the British. He became gravely ill while leading a company on Staten Island. He recovered his health but lost most of his assets; according to one account, he "never enjoyed a day of peace after the mistaken step he took in the Revolution." He was allowed to remove to Chatham Center and cobbled together enough to provide his three sons with professional training.[63]

When peace returned, population growth also resumed, and the pressure on the land and signs of soil exhaustion led many agriculturalists to shift toward raising fodder crops and fattening cattle for extra-local markets. Trade gave a boost to merchants and such professionals as lawyers, necessary agents of the commercialization of the countryside. A group of Quaker merchants from Nantucket transformed sleepy Claverack Landing into the new city of Hudson. Based on shipping, fishing, and shipbuilding, Hudson became an instant success and the region's legal, commercial, and print center. Aspiring industrialists exploited waterpower sites along the county's numerous streams and falls. In 1809, a group of enterprising Quakers formed the Columbiaville Manufacturing Society to embark on large-scale textile production.

Kinderhook was ideally sited to take advantage of these interlocking developments: the Post Road from Albany to New York passed through town, weekly stages stopped there, and the county's first post office was located there. Two turnpikes connected the town to urban markets. Textile entrepreneurs recognized Kinderhook Creek's excellent waterpower and proximity to the Hudson River. Four years after the Columbiaville Society, the Kinderhook Manufacturing Company was established at neighboring Valatie, with its ample waterpower. Vanderpoel hailed the hamlet: "Valatie! In 1815 a bleak uncultivated barren: in 1827 an extensive Manufacturing village, containing wealth and intelligence, industry and virtue; a practical comment on the American system." He supported the new industrial order with more than words; he signed the mortgage for the rebuilding of Valatie's second mill, the Beaver Mill. The village of Kinderhook, lacking ample waterpower, attracted numerous artisans and served as the commercial locus for a rich agricultural hinterland—just the place for an aspiring lawyer.[64]

James Vanderpoel, born in 1787, studied law with a local practitioner and had served a stint as an instructor at Kingston Academy. He intended to move west like many of his generation after he obtained his license. Instead, in 1808, the same year that he was admitted to the bar, James Vanderpoel and Ann Doll married. The newlyweds settled in Kinderhook in 1809, and George moved in with them, resigning his pastoral position because of age and the congregation's desire for services in English. Vanderpoel linked his fortunes to "the Little Magician," Martin Van Buren, who had mounted a successful challenge to the Federalist patricians and wrested control of local and state politics along with the legal business that went along with it. James was elected to the state assembly in 1810; in 1812, he succeeded Van Buren as County Surrogate, an appointed position as a judge that often went to the well connected; and he followed his mentor into the Democratic Party in 1828.

With a successful political and legal career and a growing family, James and Ann set about constructing a new house between 1815 and 1820. They chose a prominent site in the new village center at the intersection of Kinderhook's

Fig. 92. Vanderpoel House, 1815–20. Kinderhook, New York. Author's photograph.

main roads, one of the countless commercial and manufacturing byways with a few modest residences. Compact farmsteads and villagers' farms covered the town's rural hinterland. The Vanderpoels built a handsome brick dwelling on an undivided eighteenth-century lot along newly laid-out Broad Street (fig. 92). The Federal structure of brick with extensive decoration, one of the more imposing in the entire county, has been attributed to Barnabas Waterman, a Massachusetts native and "master mechanic" who relocated to Hudson. Many of the region's neoclassical dwellings were built by the New England merchants who founded the city, bringing along their interpretations of Roman designs popularized by the Adam brothers. The Vanderpoel house was identical in the front and back, set within a well-defined landscape scheme. Visitors entered a dramatic hallway with an elliptical stairway, a form introduced by Charles Bullfinch and popularized by Asher Benjamin that rises with no apparent support. The hall's exterior windows and door fanlights are adorned with patriotic embellishments, while the interior doorways are ornamented with carved wood and fine plaster detailings. Still, the Vanderpoels, like many of Phillips's and Field's patrons, were neither eighteenth-century Connecticut River Gods nor nineteenth-century manufacturing magnates, but they were not ordinary farmers or artisans either. This emerging middle class clustered in new houses in the commercial villages of the early republic.[65]

The Vanderpoels aimed at a refined style, but within the provincial fashion. The hall was furnished nicely but not grandly; in winter months, a large cast-iron stove sat in the center, and a stove pipe rose upward into the second floor hall. To the left of the hall, the elegant parlor contained the most elaborate decorations: curtains, a full-sized carpet, a full suite of painted fancy chairs, and a matching settee. While the grandest Hudson River Valley homes boasted Charles Lannuier or Duncan Phyfe furniture brought upriver from those great New York City cabinetmaking establishments, along with grand chandeliers and fine porcelain, the Vanderpoels and their peers more likely had fancy chairs resembling those owned by Dr. Russell Dorr, another Phillips sitter from Chatham, whose 1824 inventory described eight fancy chairs with turnings that simulate bamboo. The Columbia County Historical Society currently furnishes the Vanderpoel house with the Dorrs' six side chairs and one armchair with flag seats and elaborate decoration: the crest rail is ornamented with gold and black grapes, leaves, and vines, along with a center rail divided by a broad "X" and oval medallions featuring conch shells. Even the back posts and bottom rail have stylized daisies on a gold band.[66]

When Ammi Phillips painted portraits to hang in the Vanderpoels' new home, he provided fashionable three-quarter-length portraits (see fig. 91). Phillips's work in his "realistic period" offers greater sophistication by its facial modeling with light and dark. This development may have been fostered by his introduction to Albany's premier portraitist Ezra Ames; he could have ducked into Peale's Gallery of the Fine Arts on Albany's North Market Street. Anna's portrait bears a strong resemblance to Ames's 1816 painting of Louisa Crane Meads, the wife of a prominent Albany cabinetmaker. Both women are seated in chairs wearing gray Empire style dresses with drapery to the left. Louisa Meads's red paisley shawl matches the drapery. Anna Vanderpoel sits in a gold and red painted fancy chair, the gold drapery on the left accentuating the chair's gold and red colors and the whiter red and green flowered shawl on her lap. The Vanderpoels' portraits have simple stenciled frames.[67]

The region's rising gentry attracted a substantial artistic community: residents could choose from Phillips and Field, along with such local artists as James E. Johnson, a one-time resident of Kinderhook with seventeen attributed portraits of town residents, and Ira Chaffee Goodell of Hudson. Johnson and his patrons celebrated the currents of agricultural improvement transforming the rural landscape; for example, Sherman Griswold owned a substantial sheep herd, as entrepreneurs responded to the importance of wool growing and cloth

manufacture to the county economy. The portraitist paid homage to local traditions; he depicted the Spencertown custom of men giving salt to their sheep
every Sunday after church. Always alive to speculative opportunities, Griswold
sold his substantial land holdings for the chance to invest in a railway to connect
Columbia County to the Berkshires. The railroad failed, and the investors lost
everything.[68] Participation in the market did not always yield profits.

In 1835, editor William Stoddard reflected in his bimonthly journal, *The
Rural Repository*, published in Hudson, on the state of the arts in America and
the hinterland's progress toward a national culture. His "Portrait-Painting" column promoted the elevation of the nation and local society. In the traditional
hierarchy of the fine arts of portrait, landscape, and history painting, Stoddard
viewed "portrait painting" as "the pioneer of the more exalted arts," the forerunner of "an elevated taste." This process of cultural elevation was influenced
by such masters as Ammi Phillips and Erastus Field, who integrated the lessons
of the academic elite with the homespun ingenuity of village artisans. *The Rural
Repository*, a mix of craft traditions and elite aspirations representing a unique
document of American culture, closed with a ringing appeal for a new national
canon based on the most traditional form of ancestor worship: "Need I say
more for the art," exclaimed Stoddard, that "permits posterity to stand in the
presence of Washington [as painted by Gilbert Stuart] . . . and in this vast
household of liberty, makes the remotest descendants familiar with the forms
and faces of those who laid down all for their country, that it might be dear to
their children."[69]

Success in his career drew James Vanderpoel from Kinderhook to grander
quarters in Albany; they purchased a "Mansion House" overlooking Academy
Park in 1833. Many of the furnishings from his 1843 inventory come from that
residence, including a desk and bookcase produced by John Meads, a piece of
fine furniture equal to the best of New York shops. Meads, the husband of
Louisa, had left New York City after his apprenticeship and relocated in Albany.
He and his partner William Alvord supplied the upper middle class and elite
with elaborately veneered furniture, the new fashion of the 1830s. The two partners made furniture for such clients as De Witt Clinton and Solomon Van
Rensselaer. The Vanderpoel desk and bookcase uses a variety of richly patterned
mahogany and rosewood veneers, with ornate carved mutins in the glazed
doors; the piece shows off the time and money expended for its fabrication.
James Vanderpoel did not live to enjoy his grander surroundings for very long;
he suffered a series of strokes and died in 1843.[70]

James Vanderpoel and Ammi Phillips had traveled a long distance from the
Village Enlightenment of the 1790s into the era of itinerants and innovators.
The portraitist's clientele had broadened beyond a narrow band of the village

elite in this age of popular and plain portraiture. Town founders, such as Elijah Boardman, had encouraged the rise of provincial painters like Ralph Earl. Those most likely to avail themselves of services of an Erastus Field or Ammi Phillips were the prosperous beneficiaries of commercialization: the professionals, merchants, manufacturers, successful farmers and artisans, and their wives and children. While few pictures of any kind graced the colonial American household, one student of central Massachusetts probate inventories reports that from 1800 to 1840 the proportion of households with "pictures" of any kind doubled, from less than one in ten to one in five. Historian Jack Larkin suggests that the number of portraits increased severalfold during that period. But portraits remained the mainstay of American artists, material statements of family lineage and stature, much to the chagrin of such painters as Thomas Cole who yearned for a wider scope for their skills: "Those who purchase pictures are, many of them, like those who purchase merchandise: they want *quantity*, material—something to show, something palpable—*things* not *thoughts*." Things were well represented in the work of portraitists and patron in the villages of the provincial northeast.[71]

Village centers filled up with craftsmen making neoclassical sideboards and fancy chairs; country craftsmen like Eli Terry and Lambert Hitchcock experimented with old standards and ended up fashioning new ones to grace parlors throughout the United States. Artists like Rufus Porter and Erastus Salisbury Field devised modes of portrait-making for almost every size pocketbook with genteel formulas and time-saving methods. But in 1839, just when Field recorded his celebration of the itinerant artisans' achievement—his striking portrait of craftsman Joseph Moore and his family—one era of itinerancy and innovation was ending and a new one beginning.

CHAPTER SEVEN

Daguerreotypes: The Industrial Image

When I first saw the portrait of Rosa Heywood and learned about its painter, Westminster, Massachusetts' Robert Peckham, the "delineator of the 'Human Face Divine,'" it was quite a revelation (fig. 93 and plate 9). Westminster is the eighteenth-century agricultural settlement where I began my dissertation research and where I had come to know neighboring Gardner as the industrial "Chair City." Central Massachusetts was home to several well-known and lesser-known provincial portraitists, starting with Ralph Earl. Peckham's story was especially fascinating because of his lifelong residence in that small town and the recent scholarly controversy about his body of work. He signed only a few paintings, a common occurrence in those days, which makes attributions of his work difficult, a work of connoisseurship by curators who must find strong similarities between the known Peckham works and the rest; also scholars search the documentary record for bills or other items that might prove someone paid Peckham for his or her portrait. His career spanned the post-Revolutionary Village Enlightenment and the Victorian parlor culture. Like so many provincial artists, Peckham began his career with stiff New England faces, but his mature work portrays provincial notables in an academic style. I first encountered Peckham's canvases of these central Massachusetts sitters stacked

Facing page, top: Fig. 93. Robert Peckham, *Rosa Heywood*, ca. 1840. Oil on canvas. 44-1/4 × 29-1/4 in. Abby Aldrich Rockefeller Museum, The Colonial Williamsburg Foundation, Virginia. (also Plate 9). Fig. 94. Set of daguerreotypes of the employees of Wright's Lumber Mill, ca. 1859. Gardner, Massachusetts. Gardner Museum.

in the closet of the Westminster Historical Society several decades ago. Since then, curators and scholars have studied the group of post-1839 full-length portraits of children in colorful garb and in prosperous parlor interiors, the offspring of the region's industrialists.[1]

The year 1839 marked a great divide in portrait making. Louis-Jacques-Mandé Daguerre's invention of photography allowed artisan-entrepreneurs to consolidate changes in the production and reproduction of images that they had initiated as itinerants. Building upon the labor-saving techniques and marketing methods developed by traveling craftsmen, portraitists of the 1840s embarked on the full-scale industrialization of image making by constructing "the daguerreotype factory." Here, as in a host of other crafts, the new industrial order began in the countryside. A whole generation of artisan-entrepreneurs promoted this change. Rural artists who had begun their careers painting a few formal poses or making silhouettes in the early nineteenth century were by mid-century offering sentimentalized images of playful children to those still interested in, and able to afford, grand family portraits in oil. Once introduced to the wonders of personal likenesses, however, rural audiences demanded greater realism at more affordable prices. By the 1840s and 1850s, traveling portraitists had created an appetite only daguerreotypists could satisfy, and the new technique of image making began replacing painting. The democratic possibilities of the group portrait, composed of individual likenesses, greatly reduced in size and cost, are evident in the image of the lumberyard workers at Wright's Mill in Gardner around 1859 (fig. 94).

Robert Peckham's Portrait of Rosa Heywood

A few artisans' careers spanned this entire process and, indeed, promoted it. Robert Peckham (1785–1865), a longtime resident of central Massachusetts, experienced the expanding commercial opportunities and emergent industrial order of the rural North; Peckham's first efforts in the 1820s were flat portraits of his kinsmen's children. Like Erastus Field, he matured during the next decade into a painter able to record the wealth and position of the new commercial class forming in country villages. He passed through the era of popular portraiture in the 1820s and 1830s and, emerging as a mature artist, mixed stylized and realistic modes in his provincial portraits. In the 1840s, Peckham weathered the challenge of the daguerreotype and celebrated the formation of a new industrial-village aristocracy, the manufacturing magnates of central Massachusetts. The Gardner lumberyard workers' daguerreotype stands at one end and Peckham's grand group portraits at the other end of the class spectrum, making visible the cultural stratification that paralleled the dramatic economic changes transforming American society at mid-century.

Robert Peckham had strong roots in village and craft traditions of New England. His ancestors had moved in the eighteenth century from coastal Rhode Island to central Massachusetts in search of new land. His grandfather, John Peckham, a blacksmith and farmer, was accompanied by three sons who cleared farms near Petersham, Massachusetts. John Peckham left one grandson "all my tools of my trade"; he left the future painter his legacy as a village craftsman. Robert Peckham moved with his family after the Revolution to the neighboring town of Westminster but continued within the artisan fold, painting signs and carriages. In early 1809, at the age of twenty-four, he received lessons from a central Massachusetts native, Ethan Allen Greenwood. The self-taught Greenwood had started portrait making while teaching at the Leicester Academy and studied in New York with Edward Savage. Greenwood praised his pupil, noting "Peckham began to color—coming out well." They exchanged both labor and products; Peckham painted Greenwood's sleigh and clock case, while Greenwood "sold him some prints and other things in the life of our profession."[2]

In July 1809, Peckham painted his first signed portrait: his friend James Humphreys, with well-defined features though without much modeling or shading. He married Ruth Sawyer of Bolton in 1813, and two years later, he and his brother Samuel advertised "House, Sign and Ornamental Painting" to the residents of Northampton, where his first child was born. By 1815, he had moved back to central Massachusetts. By 1817, he tackled a complex group portrait of four generations of the Peckham and Sawyer families in Bolton. Drawing closer to the neoclassical style, Peckham spread out the sixteen well-dressed subjects across the interior. The light entering from the left highlights those in the center. He joined other provincial artists, such as Ralph Earl and Erastus Field, whose large group portraits offered a rich detailing of middle-class life. Peckham depicted the still life on the table and the tall case clock in the corner, marking its maker and location: "John Barton/Marlboro."[3] This complex composition includes many figures, even overlapping ones that add to its difficulty; it must have proved quite demanding for a young artist with only provincial training. Peckham had a shop in Westminster until 1829, when the new owners took over "the stand formerly occupied by Deacon Robert Peckham," where they continued "the Painting Business, such as House, Carriage, and Sign Painting." Peckham opened a portrait studio in town. In 1834, he invited those wishing "for a correct likeness" to visit, although he would travel "a distance" for those who wanted to be accommodated at home.

By the 1830s, Peckham had developed a mature style for his adult portraits that was influenced by academic conventions, even though not all his patrons appreciated them. He painted black-and-white clad figures with plain and dark backgrounds and strong modeling of the faces, a new addition to his repertoire; his careful attention to the details of the sitters' clothing and professional artifacts creates an impression of his sitters' prosperous station. In his portraits for William Cowee and his wife, her carefully delineated white collar and his white ruffled shirt draw our eyes, while he holds a flute and she opens a music book. Peckham had painted William's cousin Susan Cowee Doty and her family earlier that decade. "Peckham knew how to draw," writes curator Laura Luckey; his lively surface, realistic modeling, and prominent brushstrokes brought out the personality of his sitters.

The noted poet and fellow abolitionist John Greenleaf Whittier remembered Peckham's work less generously: "I only recall sitting to him two or three times, but how it looked I have no idea. If it was a good picture, it was a miracle, for the deacon was eminently artless." Christopher C. Baldwin (1800–1835), the first librarian of the American Antiquarian Society in Worcester, caustically commented in his diary on 24 March 1834:

> I had a visit today from Robert Peckham, a portrait painter. He now lives in Westminster where he has resided for the [last] twelve years. . . . Robert the painter, never received any instruction in his art. He is not distinguished in his profession, tho' he succeeds tolerably well in obtaining likenesses and had always gained a living by the art. His portraits are badly colored and, sometimes, are laughable caricatures. His price is ten dollars, and his business is almost wholly in the country. I have in some instances seen the name of the person intended to be painted written upon the picture, which was the surest way of identifying it. He is, notwithstanding, a very worthy and devout man.[4]

Baldwin may have exaggerated the painter's clumsiness with the brush, but he accurately described his longevity as provincial artist and village reformer.

Widely known for his passionate involvement in reform causes, Peckham remained in Westminster for fifty years. He was deacon of the First Congregational Church for fourteen years, his home headquartered the town's antislavery movement, and he led the Northern Worcester County Anti-slavery Society in 1835. His ardent beliefs precipitated a controversy over allowing such radical abolitionists as William Lloyd Garrison to speak at the local academy. The academy building also housed the church's vestry, and the dispute over rights to use the building led to heated words and his excommunication from the local church. Peckham and his family moved to Worcester for the 1850s, without the usual courtesy of a release to the church there. He returned to Westminster only after the Emancipation Proclamation when tempers had cooled, and he was asked to compose and recite a poem when the town dedicated its Civil War memorial. He took his reform activities seriously, painting two small temperance panels in the 1840s (*The Woes of Liquor* and *The Happy Abstemious Family*, each signed R. Peckham). But Peckham was best known as a portraitist, especially of children. A village resident recalled that Peckham "was a medium sized man, rather stooped, and wore his hair long with the ends curled under, a stern looking man, and his wife a very small woman, but both were kind to children."[5]

Painters found the coming of daguerreotypes, or "perfect likenesses," to be a challenge to their status as purveyors of family portraits. Some took up the camera to broaden their appeal, while others made their portraits ever grander and more colorful to contrast with the daguerreotypist's black-and-white miniatures. Peckham's portraits from the 1840s are lavish canvases that create a new image of children and consumption. The cavorting progeny of local industrialists were featured without their parents, in rooms filled with fashionable toys, colorful carpets, and upholstered seating, the very products that spilled from their fathers' factories. Curators and connoisseurs debate whether this body of paintings is really Peckham's work, for it represents a surprising departure from his earlier children's portraits, with their stiff poses and flat modeling. Attributions of the work to Peckham come from family relationships with the subjects and stylistic resemblances to his mature adult portraits. The artist used realistic and meticulous details, an arresting visual engagement with the viewer, a particular depiction of the skull, and an "almost encyclopedic depiction of furnishings" found in prosperous mid-century Victorian parlors. In *Rosa Heywood* (1840), a portrait of the only child of chair manufacturer Walter Heywood, Peckham gave little hint of the farm family or country furniture in Heywood's recent past (see fig. 93 and plate 9). Born into a comfortable middle-class home, Rosa enjoyed her parent's success in producing the cheap wooden seats and plush Victorian upholstering that were beginning to fill American homes. Rosa is depicted with clarity of detail and realistic modeling, clasping a bloom that symbolizes her first name; the colors are rich, with a royal blue dress edged with pink trim and an elaborate floral and medallion Brussels-style carpet. Rosa stands at full height; her pose is a bit stiff, and difficulties with perspective are evidenced in the planter and wainscoting. When the portrait's present owner, the Abby Aldrich Rockefeller Folk Art Center, held a contest for the most popular item in its 2001 "By Popular Demand" selection of forty paintings, *Rosa Heywood* won the honors. "Rosa looked so real I felt like I could reach out and touch her curly locks," wrote a thirteen-year-old; a visitor from Gardner said,

Fig. 95. Robert Peckham, attrib., *The Hobby Horse*, ca. 1840. Oil on canvas. 40-3/4 × 40 in. Gift of Edgar William and Bernice Chrysler Garbisch, Image courtesy of the Board of Trustees, National Gallery of Art, Washington, D.C.

"Rosa's ignoring her wealth trapping with her shy mischievous grin." Other visitors remarked about the vivid colors and her beautiful eyes, and several drew upon modern notions, especially "3D" realistic detail.[6]

Peckham did feature a new three-dimensionality in *The Hobby Horse* (ca. 1840), a work in which both painter and patron tried to conceal their rural upbringings (fig. 95). This massive canvas has two children breathlessly arriving from outdoors, the little girl in a red dress holding a straw bonnet and her brother clad in a fancy dark-blue tunic. All were dominated by the painting's centerpiece, an elegant hobbyhorse. With its showy horsehair mane and tail, highly decorated bridle, and fancy stenciling and graining on its base, this toy, which was covered with animal hide (most examples were of simple wood), was found only in well-to-do families and may have been produced by the Crandall clan. The Crandalls were a Rhode Island family of rural farmer-craftsmen whose successful toy business led them to move to Brooklyn, New York, in the 1840s. There they built one of the largest toy factories in the United States, using this facility to mass-produce elegant rocking horses, copied from a handmade German model. Other wonders of the age join the display: the astral lamp that burned sperm oil, an Empire table, and ingrained floral carpet. While the identity of this family remains unknown, similar portraits feature the central Massachusetts provincial elite who desired vivid depictions of their children and growing domestic adornments; indeed, children could be seen as among a household's prized adornments. The five children of John Thurston and Mersylvia Farwell of Fitchburg are tightly grouped and brightly garbed, each holding a prop, such as a flower or doll; an additional Peckham commission came from another prominent central Massachusetts figure, a storekeeper and political official in Royalston, a town neighboring Westminster. While many families aspired to own a fancy carpet, which was often the parlor's most conspicuous feature, for the well-to-do, Elizabeth Garrett writes, such luxuries increasingly became just one more item in a sea of opulence.[7]

As artisan-entrepreneurs, provincial portraitists played crucial roles in transforming the economic order of rural New England. They promoted a desire for personal likenesses and generated a taste for scarce commodities in the countryside. Drawing on their training as artisans and using traditional technologies to develop simple, time-saving inventions, these country craftsmen facilitated the manufacture of mass consumer goods directed toward widening circles of customers. No isolated country craftsmen or "folk" artists fleeing the encroaching market, these village artisans were often aspiring entrepreneurs, leading the charge for consumption in the countryside.

The minister and merchants of colonial America were joined by the growing middle class of the early republic. Manufacturers of various sorts came to sit for the portraitist, along with innkeepers and middle-class farmers, all enthusiastic participants in the increasing commercial activity that connected backcountry towns and regional markets. The desire for "cheap and slight" portraits, ranging from paper silhouettes to framed daguerreotypes, allowed the rest of the town to participate in this redefinition of middle-class identity, even as Peckham seems to have become the portraitist of the central Massachusetts provincial elite. More and more faces were recorded in an increasing variety of poses with softer tones. Severe expressions turned sentimental. At the same time, craftsmen and consumers created a Victorian parlor culture. The few chairs and occasional brass tall clock that stood on a bare floor had been replaced by sets of six chairs, shelf clocks with painted cornucopias, and upholstered furniture that rested on soft carpets.

"Rembrandt Perfected": The Daguerreotype Arrives in America

The daguerreotype, a mechanized means of portrait making, satisfied the growing appetite for family portraits and accelerated the transformation of images into household commodities. No longer luxury items that had dominated a room, portraits were produced at low cost as encased miniatures on shimmering silver plates. While European commentators remarked upon the artistic possibilities of the new medium, American discussions focused on more practical possibilities, especially commercial portraiture and photographic experimentation. In the midst of the post-1837 economic depression, provincial artisans and urban artists alike were caught up in the exciting possibilities of achieving "perfect likenesses." Some rural entrepreneurs went to the cities for a stint of training, similar to Erastus Salisbury Field or Ethan Allen Greenwood, before heading back out to the countryside. Others stayed and became urban suppliers and tastemakers as American commercial culture became more centralized and consolidated in the 1850s.[8]

American experimenters and entrepreneurs quickly recognized the commercial value of Daguerre's invention as an improved method of mass-producing portraits. News of "Rembrandt perfected" had crossed the Atlantic in only a few short weeks. In April 1839, N. P. Willis and Samuel Morse published accounts in the American press hailing the advent of "a revolution in art" where "all nature shall paint herself." After seeing Daguerre's work in Paris, Morse exclaimed that the "exquisite minuteness of the delineation cannot be conceived. No painting or engraving ever approached it." By September, Daguerre had penned a pamphlet that described the process in great technical detail. Morse, now back in New York, and others quickly took up a camera. Morse had experimented with trying to fix images with a camera obscura, so the new technique was allied "to his favorite art." In the midst of his telegraphy work, he translated Daguerre's tutorial—it was published in thirty editions and almost as many languages by the end of the year—and constructed a camera apparatus "made exactly after the French." Fellow professors John William Draper and Alexander Wolcott in New York attempted to produce portraits, as did other scientifically minded individuals in New York, Philadelphia, and Boston.[9]

A. S. Southworth, a twenty-eight-year-old pharmacist in Cabotville, Massachusetts, was bitten by the "perfect picture" bug and used it to make his way in the world. Joseph Pennell, a former schoolmate who had been working with

Morse on his daguerreotype experiments, wrote to Southworth inviting him to "join him as an associate in business for the purpose of making likeness." Southworth met Morse and received instruction in "the new art" when he arrived in the metropolis. The two young men made rapid progress and returned to Cabotville to begin their enterprise. Southworth anticipated great success as he wrote to his sister back on the family farm in West Fairless, Vermont:

> My mind has been in one constant scene of agitation and study. I told Brother S. in a letter written on board a steamboat, that you should know what I went to New York for.
>
> You have read of the daguerreotype, an apparatus for taking views of buildings, streets, yards, and so forth. I had an invitation to join Mr. Pennell . . . in getting one, and partly to gratify my curiosity, and partly with the hope of making it profitable, I met Mr. Pennell in New York and purchased one. I cannot in a letter describe all the wonders of the apparatus. Suffice it to say, that I can NOW make a PERFECT picture in one hours time, and that would take a painter weeks to draw. The picture is represented in LIGHT and SHADE, nicer by far than any steel engraving you ever saw. The colors of objects are NOT given, but the picture is shown in light and shade.

The two continued their technical improvements in Massachusetts; a batch of portraits they sent to New York were "pronounced superior to any made there," and samples were sent on to Europe.[10]

When Daguerre's representative, François Gourand, arrived in New York from Paris in November 1839, public interest in daguerreotypes grew. He began with private viewings to select members of the press and local notables; the painter Asher Durand received a letter of invitation to a special showing of thirty plates by Daguerre and others. Public viewings were next; then came a series of lecture-demonstrations and a "public depot" to sell photographic equipment; and the instruction of pupils completed his successful campaign. Gourand gave thirty-two lectures in New York, two a day, in French and and even in Spanish, before he moved to Boston at the end of February. He left in his wake a city enthralled with the invention. Bostonians flocked to the lectures, the *Boston Daily Transcript* reported "an audience of five hundred ladies and gentlemen, the number of whom would have been twice or thrice increased if the lecturer had not judiciously limited the issue of tickets." Prominent figures such as Edward Everett Hale and Ralph Waldo Emerson attended, and news of the event dominated conversation.[11]

The eighteen-year-old George Fuller enthusiastically wrote his father in western Massachusetts about his visit with his brother Augustus to view Gourand's specimen daguerreotypes. Fuller anticipated how the French mechanical invention could translate into a great consumer product in the potentially enormous American likeness market: "This [invention] can be applied to taking miniatures or portraits on the same principles that it takes landscapes." With only a sixty-one-dollar investment, ten dollars for instruction and the rest for the apparatus, "we could clear ourselves of all expenses in two weeks." Fuller bought a camera, purchased lessons from Gourand, and took to the country roads with his brother.[12] "This is a new invention, and consequently a great novelty, of which everyone has heard, and has a curiosity to see. It is just what the people of this country like, namely something new. I think any one would give $7 for their perfect likeness."[13]

Josiah Johnson Hawes had already given up farm life for a carpenter's bench before the portrait-painting bug hit him: "Happening one day to come across an ordinary oil painting which I was admiring, a friend of mine asked me to close one eye and look at the picture through my hand with the other eye. The surprising change which took place, from its being an ordinary flat canvas to a realistic copy of nature with all its aerial perspective and beauty, so affected me, that from that time, I was ambitious to become an artist. I purchased books, colors, and brushes, and commenced the study of art. . . . I practiced miniature painting on ivory, likewise portraits in oil, landscapes, etc. with no teacher but my books." Seeing Gourand's plates in Boston converted Hawes from painter to daguerreotypist: "The excitement of the discovery of the daguerreotype . . . and some specimens of it which I saw in Boston changed my course entirely. I gave up painting and commenced daguerreotyping in 1841." He conducted the business in the familiar ways of an itinerant portraitist.[14]

The first daguerreotypes were not well suited for commercial portraiture; they required lengthy poses outdoors in bright sunshine. But mechanically minded Americans quickly reduced the exposure times sufficiently to open the world's first daguerreotype portrait studios. Wolcott and Johnson opened a commercial studio in New York in March 1840; others followed in Philadelphia and Boston. Jeremiah Gurney, one of the earliest studio operators in New York, recounted the enthusiastic response of numerous customers willing to part with five dollars: "My sign at the doorway was a frame of four small daguerreotypes and the first, I believe, ever exposed for this purpose on Broadway. It was perfectly astonishing to see the multitudes who stopped to look at these pictures, and one perhaps in a thousand would rush upstairs to know something more about this new art. But it usually resulted in the knowledge, simply, that they went away with five dollars less in their pockets, in exchange for a shadow *so thin* that it often required the most favorable light to detect that it was anything more than a metallic looking-glass." Despite the poor quality of the miniature images, many purchased one of these 'great novelties.'"[15]

Residents of rural areas received news of the remarkable invention almost immediately. In western Massachusetts, the local newspaper announced in March 1840, "THE DAGUERREOTYPE . . . Each particular shade of the face is given with astonishing exactness." Entrepreneurs set out to improve the new technology, concentrating their energies on producing commercially viable portraits and taking advantage of the commercial and mechanical expertise that abounded in the New England countryside. Back in Cabotville, Southworth and Pennell had experimented with a mirror camera that allowed shorter exposure times. They reported with pride on their progress in September 1840:

> I have just succeeded in managing the Daguerreotype so as to make perfect likenesses, and if I should leave it now, those who have assisted me, would not be pleased. Besides, I have not now funds to bear expenses. . . . You would like to know my prospects for making money, and so forth. It must be to somebody a profitable business. Mr. Pennell is with me and we have very far surpassed any body in this country, and probably in the world, in making miniatures. We have exchanged with some of the New Yorkers, and have sent some to Boston. They are as far beyond the one I sent home as that is beyond one you could make with a pen. . . . We make them not larger than a five-cent piece or as large as the one you have. Since we commenced, the opinions of people with regard to our success have changed about as many times as the weather. . . . In a fair day it requires three minutes sitting and we know positively that we can have an apparatus that will not require more than thirty seconds.[16]

Experiments in sensitizing the plate with various chemical compounds proved the surest route to lowering exposure times while expanding the tonal scale and image quality.

Southworth and Pennell decided their future lay at the upper end of the business, best pursued in cosmopolitan Boston. Southworth painted a bright future to his sister: "Our daguerreotypes are by far the best in America, probably the world." He urged her to join them, as they needed someone to "wait upon the ladies when they call upon us." He promised light work that would be "a pleasant employment for ladies": "the hardest part of it is to clean the silver plates" and frame the miniatures. Southworth wrote from their new rooms in the Scollay Building, a few doors down from the site of Gourand's exhibition in a building that once housed John Singleton Copley. By 1843, Hawes replaced Pennell as a partner in what became Southworth & Hawes, one of the illustrious names in the trade.[17]

Many more young men and an occasional woman with little training and even less capital catered to the provincial market. The lure of easy profits and an independent life enticed rural youth into the trade. Nathaniel Hawthorne's fictional daguerreotypist Holgrave in *The House of the Seven Gables* exemplifies the varied experiences and restless movement of young men who sought opportunities in the expanding commercial sector of the countryside and who landed in the portrait business. "Though now but twenty-two years old . . . he had already been, first, a country schoolmaster, next, a salesman in a country store, and either at the same time or afterwards, the political editor of a country newspaper. He had subsequently traveled New England and the Middle States, as a peddler, in the employment of a Connecticut manufactory of cologne water and other essences. In an episodical way, he had studied and practiced dentistry, and with very flattering success, especially in many of the factory towns along our inland streams."[18] The geographic and social mobility of the post-Revolutionary limners like Rufus Porter increased in its speed and range. Equipment could be bought cheaply and training was easy to come by during those early days. In western New York, W. H. Sherman found it natural to "enlist under the (photographic) black flag" with his "early taste for drawing and mechanical contrivance." He began as a printer, but acquired his knowledge of daguerreotyping from a "Professor Avery." Sherman later recalled: "The first daguerreotypists, outside the cities, were generally those who had no previous training suited to fit them for the calling. One had been brought up on a farm, and fancied he would find in it easier work and better pay than following a plow or swinging a scythe. Another had learned a trade which he thought less promising than the new art, which he could learn in a few weeks. A doctor or schoolmaster, who had leisure time at his disposal, saw, or believed he saw, a profitable way of employing it."[19] Many an itinerant "professor" was but a recent student of the craft himself.

The ranks of such rural artisans as Hawes and Sherman provided the major source of daguerreotypists. The West Stockbridge craftsman and inventor Anson Clark's cache of daguerreotypes, mechanical devices, and papers offers a rare glimpse into the business of a rural daguerreotypist. Clark, born in 1788, started out as a marble cutter in the local quarries. He soon displayed a penchant for devising mechanical devices, including several for marble cutting and polishing. He built a cooperage and made melodeons and other wooden musical instruments; his papers also mention a "Domestic Scrubbing Machine." Anson and his son Edwin opened a gallery in his home as early as 1841, where he

Fig. 96. Daguerreotype self-portrait of Anson Clark. Sixth-plate daguerreotype, ca. 1842–45. West Stockbridge, Massachusetts. Stockbridge Public Library.

supplemented his woodworking and stone-cutting business (fig. 96). They opened a branch in Great Barrington and took to the road; one of their broadsides for "Daguerreotype PORTRAITS" has a blank space to fill in the venue of their traveling studio, in the familiar mode of Rufus Porter. A longer broadside begins its advertising pitch by praising "this invention of a celebrated French Chemist": "The value of a portrait depends upon its accuracy, and when taken by this process it must be accurate—from necessity, for it is produced by the unerring operation of physical laws of human judgment and skill. . . . The precise expression of the face at the time of setting in its minutest features will be at once and forever fixed, engraving as it were by the sunbeams, and as the operation seldom exceeds a minute, and is often finished in a few seconds." The Clark broadside goes on to proclaim that the daguerreotype captures "flashes of the soul," "which are too fleeting to be caught by the painter. By such flashes of the soul we remember our friends, and these cannot appear in the canvass." Dissatisfied with the crude equipment available, Clark ground his own lenses and built his own cameras.

Fig. 97. Engraving of one-dollar bank note, Housatonic Bank, made by Anson Clark, West Stockbridge, Massachusetts, 1850s. Daguerreotype. 3-1/2 × 7-1/2 in. Metropolitan Museum of Art, New York City.

Clark's papers include a scrapbook filled with advertising puffs placed in local newspapers, along with news of technical advances. Numerous letters from prospective students eager to set up in the trade request instruction and equipment. Clark, a recent student himself of the craft, told one inquirer that for a hundred dollars he would receive "our best Apparatus with every article necessary to commence taking Portraits (excepting Plates & Cases) together with the necessary instructions." Clark assured him that "the time required to learn to take Portraits & Landscapes is short, say from one to two or three days and some persons are enabled to take perfect likenesses with half a days practice." One of his students, George Reed, had made a profit of over sixty dollars in one month. Clark's penchant for inventing and experimenting with "engraving with the sunbeams" extended into the practical use of the new medium to make copies of banknotes; he daguerreotyped one- and two-dollar banknotes and then engraved the daguerreotyped plate to print new bills (fig. 97).[20] An entrepreneurial artisan's ingenuity sometimes extended into the illegal.

Instruction and supplies came from a variety of sources in the new and relatively disorganized industry. Urban studios often supplemented their portrait-making business by supplying country operators with equipment and training. The Boston firm of Southworth and Hawes was flooded with inquiries about their terms for instruction. "Can you instruct a young man in Daguerreian science?" a student of medicine asked in 1841. Dolly Burr wrote from central Massachusetts in 1843 about her desire for a camera and "all the apparatus to do with that I shall need . . . at your lowest price." Former students sent technical questions along with their orders. John Lawton wrote from Chester, Vermont, that he had not been successful in "making good likenesses." He wondered whether the problem lay in the weather or his chemicals. Worrying that perhaps "I have lost some of my skill," he implored his teachers to "please suggest some suggestions" concerning his botched pictures. Others were eager to be kept abreast of the latest improvements or to receive quick tips to bring their efforts closer to their teacher's mastery. A former student in Chicopee, Massachusetts, wrote that "the likeness does not appear on the plate as distinct" as it did when "I was in Boston . . . perhaps you can inform me what the trouble is." Correspondence had slowed down by the middle of the decade, but Sarah Holland asked, "Will you tell me how I can avoid a shade upon one side of the face?"[21]

By mid-century, itinerant daguerreotypists had reached further into the hinterlands. In 1843, L. C. Champney, one of Southworth's first students, advertised in Franklin County, Massachusetts, offering "Daguerreotype miniatures with all the latest improvements in coloring." Two months later, a Dr. Gates was charging two to five dollars for likenesses "warranted to be recognisable at first sight" and taken in less than three minutes. By 1847, Greenfield, the county seat, had a permanent daguerreotype establishment. Such rural daguerreotypists as Anson Clark quickly established studios in center villages with populous and prosperous hinterlands to draw on for customers. Every city and town had at least one gallery, and "itinerant daguerreotypists traveled to remote backwoods and frontier areas in their horse-drawn 'saloons,' or floated down the rivers in houseboats."[22] Itinerants encroached on the trade of miniaturists who were ranked among craftsmen. Ambrose Andrews wrote in 1846: "It is seldom that I have any miniatures to paint now-a-days, since that the Daguerretype [sic] invention has spread throughout the length & breadth of the land. People everywhere go in now for 'cheap things' & a truly moderate price for a well-painted miniature on ivory 'seems enormous.'" Soon he decided to take up daguerreotypes himself.[23] Many provincial painters acquired cameras. Some, such as Joseph Whiting Stock and Noah North, offered daguerreotypes in addition to oil likenesses. Others altered their way of work, using the daguerreotype as an aid in taking likenesses to facilitate paintings. Erastus Salisbury Field used daguerreotypes to collect images of individual family members as studies for a group portrait. Another itinerant, Isaac Augustus Wetherby, painted posthumous portraits from daguerreotypes; Wetherby had been so excited by the new technology that in the spring of 1841 he bought a daguerreotype apparatus for twenty-five dollars, but he "did not succeed with it [apparatus] and waited another twelve years before he tried again."[24]

The intense competition and the flood of eager operators made daguerreotypes available for as little as twenty-five cents. One "floating gallery" owner

Fig. 98. Daguerreian saloons varied greatly. For those looking for daguerreotypes to send home from the California gold fields, Perez Mann Batchelder's traveling studio wagon advertised "Walk in and examine specimens." Isaac Wallace Baker (1810–ca. 1862), *Baker in Front of Batchelder's Daguerreian Saloon.* Quarter-plate daguerreotype, 1851. Courtesy of the Oakland Museum of California, Gift of anonymous donor.

boasted to the readers of the *Photographic and Fine Art Journal* that he "took near one thousand likenesses, travelled (by water) near fourteen hundred miles," on his most recent three-month trip down the Mississippi. J. R. Gorgas claimed to have spent three years on a "floating gallery," the happiest years of his life, accompanied by a good cook, a flute, violin, and guitar; he "did not need any advertising, and never did any Sunday work." As country and city drew closer through business relationships and the circulation of print, rural residents demanded some version of fashionable urban products. The latest in urban elegance—the commercial daguerreotype parlors and salons that instructed the new urban middle class in gentility—appeared in the countryside in the significantly different form of itinerant operators' "Daguerreotype Saloons" (figs. 98 and 99).[25]

GURNEY'S DAGUERREAN SALOON—BROADWAY, NEW YORK.

Fig. 99. On New York City's fashionable Broadway, Jeremiah Gurney's Daguerreian Gallery was a celebrated site, with its "reception saloon" of celebrity portraits and well-dressed patrons. From "Gurney's Daguerreian Rooms, Broadway, New York," *Illustrated News* (New York) 2 (12 November 1853): 277. Courtesy of American Antiquarian Society, Worcester, Massachusetts.

Itinerants were greeted by an enthusiastic clientele. At Lockport, New York, well sited on the Erie Canal, a traveling daguerreotypist, a recent entrant to the trade, wrote to his brother in 1845: "There is a regular excitement here, my room being crowded full most of the time. The high ones are going a rush for it. I have taken some of the best families in Lockport and am going to have lots this week . . . we took 42 from monday to friday night . . . my half of the profits amounted to $19.39."[26] Darker shadows accompanied the arrival of the daguerreotype in the countryside. Danger and duplicity lurked in early accounts of the taking of a likeness, an association often fostered by rural daguerreotypists who enveloped their business with the aura of magic. Daguerreotypist Abraham Bogardus remembered "the public estimate of the 'dark room,'" where customers believed "the operator conducted some hocus-pocus affair." Rural operators, often ill-informed themselves, intensified the sense of mystery as they retreated into their dark closets to ply their craft. "They imposed themselves as magicians on the credulous villagers," an early historian of photography writes, and "like magicians, they readily acquired the title of professor." The magical, perhaps demonic machinations of the daguerreotypist, T. S. Arthur told the readers of *Godey's Lady's Book*, so frightened one farmer, fearful of having his soul captured, that he "dashed down stairs as if a legion of evil spirits were after him." Other sitters swore that a magnetic attraction drew their eyes toward the lens during the process of taking a likeness. Phoebe Pyncheon complained in *The House of the Seven Gables* that, conversely, the portrait image was always "dodging away from the eye, and trying to escape altogether." The mirrored surface of the daguerreotype, with its image moving in and out of view according to the angle of observation, increased the transience of the experience. With the meaning of daguerreotype likenesses not yet fixed and the stability of the self placed at risk by the daguerreotype process, country patrons expressed their fears of the new mechanical technology.[27]

Rural customers maintained their notions of what constituted a proper family portrait; continuities remained strong with the older mode of portraiture in the rapidly changing countryside. L. C. Champney wrote in 1843 from Bennington, Vermont, to his teacher, A. S. Southworth, about the distinctly different expectations in the rural marketplace. "I think I shall stay up this way for the present. They all say that my pictures are the best that they ever saw. I have tride [*sic*] the light as you proposed, but they do not like the dark on one side of the face, and I cant sell a picture that where one side of the face is darker than the other, altho it seems to stand out better and look richer." When a rural daguerreotypist in Kingston, New York, imparted his "System of Daguerreotyping" to a student, he passed along the precept: "One object in getting a good picture is getting an even light over the countenance and body and not have one side dark and the other light—to accomplish this you sometimes have to work considerable." Other daguerreotypists remembered that a public familiar with plain portraits "wanted their pictures made white and flat, with no expressional lines or detail," to the chagrin of the photographer who sought a more "artistic" image (figs. 100 and 101).[28]

Customers' expectations along with continuities in personnel resulted in the persistence of a rural aesthetic marked by the forthright qualities of composition, lighting, and pose common to both painting and daguerreotyping. Portraitists continued to rely on clothes, jewelry, or the tools of a trade to produce a good likeness in the 1840s, but unlike the painted portrait, they relied heavily on the participation of the sitter for a successful likeness. The motives and methods of portraiture remained familiar, representing the achievement of gentility. In the early years, Abraham Bogardus remembered, "To have a daguerreotype taken was the ambition of every aspiring man. It was a great event to most sitters. A black suit, a white vest and thumb in the armhole of the vest, the other hand holding an open book—an attitude of spirit and importance—was considered just the thing." The portrait's portability and low cost made it an

Fig. 100. Anonymous, *American Gothic*. Quarter-plate daguerreotype, n.d. Collection of Matthew R. Isenburg.

ideal present to send to loved ones who were far away. Elijah Carpenter, a resident of western Massachusetts, had his likeness taken, perhaps by the itinerant L. C. Champney, to send as a memento to his son working on the Rochester and Erie Canal Railway.[29]

Many themes in early daguerreotyping—easy access to the trade, the aura of gentility and science that surrounded operators, the eagerness of rural customers for likenesses, and the eventual consolidation of commercial and cultural meanings—come together in James Ryder's autobiography, *Voightlander and I*.[30] The young farm boy was introduced to "the new wonder from New York" when Ryder's next-door neighbor burst into their house, "excited as a child," with a likeness of her sister. An accompanying letter explained that the remarkable new discovery was called the daguerreotype. In short order, the "so-called Daguerrian artist" made an appearance in Ryder's small village. Ryder, a young printer's apprentice with a vague idea of "following the Ben Franklin route," pinned his hopes on the unlikely figure of Professor Brightly, who attempted to strike a genteel pose with his silk hat—except, Ryder remembered, the professor

Fig. 101. Southworth and Hawes, *Young Girl, Hand on Shoulder*. Whole-plate with hand-tinted colors. Collection of Matthew R. Isenburg.

always wore rubbers. Brightly had been a country schoolteacher and itinerant lecturer in phrenology and biology when, Ryder learned, the "new art of daguerreotypy attracted his attention and had been gathered in as another force with which to do battle in the struggle for fame and dollars," a not uncommon occurrence. Ryder succumbed to the professor's flattering phrenological predictions of his success as a daguerreotypist. "The new business of likeness-taking was admitted to be a genteel calling, enveloped in a haze of mystery and a smattering of science."[31] When Brightly devoted his energies to his phrenological career, he "discarded his rubbers for day ware" and offered Ryder a position in the Ithaca Daguerreian Gallery around 1847.

Country operators learned by trial and error; no professional literature was available, and "professors" were more plentiful than informed instructors. Ryder covered his ignorance by blaming botched likenesses on his sitters: "*You moved!!* headed the list." Rival daguerreotypists struck terror into the heart of the young lad. Professor Bartholomew, Ryder remembered, "looked like a real professor," with a double-breasted overcoat. The eager youth purchased lessons from whoever crossed his path, many armed with urban studio experience or new technical improvements. A Mr. Johnson passing through the region greatly impressed him with technically sophisticated specimens. Soon Ryder was ready to set out on his own.[32]

The young daguerreotypist chose a prosperous farming area near Ithaca where he was sponsored by an acquaintance, Deacon Lyon, a rich fruit grower, who proudly announced his arrival to his neighbors, "it being something of a novelty to have a daguerreotype man at one's house." He lent his porch for Ryder to use as a studio and gallery. The surrounding countryside had many "well to do farmers" who could "easily afford to spend a few dollars for family likenesses." As his pocket filled with dollars, his confidence rose, and he resolved to plunge into the nearby metropolis, a village with two streets, two mills, and a store and post office. The postmaster's wife offered her parlor for sittings and hung his specimen likenesses on the gate. Since Ryder's camera was the first ever in the village, he became a sensation and commercial success: "I was busy with customers all the days and dollars rolled in mightily." The once timid apprentice now found himself regarded by all the locals with respect and courtesy, except the village blacksmith who denounced him as a humbug who was "too lazy to get an honest living." After a profitable stay, the daguerreotypist was soon on the move again.[33]

As he moved west from rural New York, Ryder was often "the first likeness man" to visit a community; exploiting the novelty of obtaining a daguerreotype proved profitable. As he looked back on those early days, he recalled, "People attached a more grave importance to having likenesses taken then. It was more the parents having likenesses taken for the children, a matter more seriously considered; something more in the way of duty, possibly a last duty—certainly a sacred one—from parents to children, a legacy of love."

In Ohio, he took a young man who wanted to learn the trade as an assistant. Ryder sent the trainee to smaller towns when his skills developed sufficiently. In 1853, Ryder went to Cleveland to keep informed about the latest urban developments and look up the "Mr. Johnson" who had made such a strong impression in central New York. C. E. Johnson offered him a position as manager of his Cleveland operation while he opened a branch in New Orleans. Ryder put his itinerant's trunk away to "step into an established studio . . . a city gallery, with fine accessories and surroundings."[34] As this devotee of the Franklin model marked his arrival as an urban professional, he mentioned the contemporaneous founding of professional journals and the solidifying of an artistic hierarchy that rendered his self-made tale more difficult for those who might follow him to duplicate. Ryder and his rural customers supported a robust daguerreotype trade where many characteristics of popular portraiture of the 1820s and 1830s, such as easy entry into the trade and flat likenesses, had also extended into the 1840s. In the 1850s, the fluidity of the nascent daguerreotype business yielded to the processes of industrial consolidation and professionalization.

Consolidation and Professionalization

Professionalization and standardization in the 1850s involved strategies to curtail the cultural drift of the 1840s whereby all could participate in the daguerreian wonder. Journal editors and leading daguerreotypists attempted to restrict entry into the practice of portraiture by proclaiming daguerreotypy as an artistic profession, not a mechanical trade; they also defining the meaning of what constituted a good likeness. At the end of the 1840s, entrepreneurs with a keen sense of business management consolidated the daguerreotype trade into an integrated business system, seeking to limit grassroots authority by daguerreotypist and customer alike and install a more hierarchical structure in its place. Well-placed studio owners, photographic suppliers, and journal editors took over the craft from the mechanics, the "professors," and the public. These new arbiters sought to end the haphazard state of mechanical knowledge and the grassroots nature of cultural authority that characterized the first decade of daguerreotyping. In its place, they would position cultural authority in the hands of professionals; daguerreotypists aspired to be artistic guardians of photographic truth. The commodities produced by this consolidation were distinctive and expensive emblems of middle-class family status, purchased from "proper" artists in elaborate commercial parlors and displayed amid other "household treasures" in the well-defined vocabulary of the Victorian parlor.

Industrial consolidation began in the late 1840s as enterprising studio owners expanded their operations by setting up branch studios throughout the United States. John Plumbe opened a chain of sixteen galleries scattered throughout the United States, Cuba, and Europe, supervised by individual managers but run in a standardized fashion and supplied and overseen by a central office. Rising technical standards required more expensive equipment, while the intense competition for customers led to increasingly elaborate studios. The era of artisan experimentation and itinerant instruction waned when a professional literature emerged in 1849 with the publication by Henry Hunt Snelling of *The History and Practice of the Art of Photography*. A few months later, Samuel Humphrey, an upstate New York daguerreotypist, started the *Daguerreian Journal*. The following year a rival publication, the *Photographic and Fine Art Journal*, began, laying claim to the mantle of the fine arts. Both journals published foreign and domestic treatises on photographic techniques, as well as news from a far-flung network of correspondents. Editors urged readers to trust in their articles as well as to rely on other publications by experts, exhorting operators and customers to stop relying for their knowledge on chance encounters with itinerant "professors" or personal experimentation. Finally, national supply houses were established with a complete stock of equipment and materials. The small dealers, many of them studio owners, were pushed out of the trade as they could not muster the immense amount of capital needed for such large operations.[35]

This new industrial structure promoted the professionalization of daguerreotyping whereby "genteel artists" would drive out the "mere mechanics." Professional journals implored daguerreotypists to shed identification with their artisanal origins and assume an elevated stature, a genteel and artistic pose that would distinguish the "true artists" from "the cheap johns" who offered discounted wares. S. D. Humphrey, the editor of the *Daguerreian Journal*, claimed that "were it not for the enterprising few engaged, our art would sink into deep insignificance. Thanks to the noble and generous who are striving to promote the interest of the Daguerreian Art, by keeping pictures up to such prices as will demand respect. We may almost look in vain to see our art elevated to its deservedly high eminence, until the public shall be enabled to discriminate between a fifty cent and a three dollar daguerreotype. We look upon a person visiting a Daguerreian Artist's Room for the purpose of obtaining a cheap picture, as one who thinks little of the art, and less of his friends." The intense competition among operators and the threat that the mechanical camera would devalue the portraitist's skill spurred the enterprising daguerreotypist to assume the stature of artistic steward and gatekeeper of romantic truth working with nature (see fig. 99). A professional hierarchy developed, with the operators of elegant New York studios at the top. Such industry leaders as Mathew Brady set out to raise the daguerreotype, one journal editor announced proudly, to "the dignity and beauty of an art of taste."[36]

The strategy to elevate the artist and ward off the mechanical "operator" had several parts: practitioners were urged to assume an artistic stance and also achieve high technical qualities; a proper (and lavish) studio setting was essential for attracting the desired middle-class patron; finally, public patronage should be guided by genteel guidelines and a general elevation of taste by the American public—all supervised by the "daguerreian artist." The training and stance of the "true artist" could be traced back to Jacob Eichholtz's transcriptions of Reynolds's guide to young artists, in contrast to the practical advice of Ryder's Professor Brightly. Marcus Root, in his 1853 treatise "Qualifications of a First-Class Daguerreotypist," discussed the proper sphere of operation for "the Loftiest and most expansive of artistic geniuses" and listed "Michael Angelo" and Rembrandt; "the artist is a creator" who breathes life into his work. Root coined a term for such an individual, the *heliographer;* genius and culture would be required and "mere mechanical operators . . . be excluded from the profession." Such a gifted individual needed a genteel culture to "secure the admiration of his patrons" by his grace and conversation and to call forth the proper countenance of his subject, as Gilbert Stuart was reputed to have done.[37] Technical training was not to be neglected. "Substance and shadow" became the code words. The "just disposition of lights and shadows" could be achieved by pose and lighting. Root studied the Old Masters "to learn much about the magic effects of light and shadow" and achieve the desired effect of a well-rounded, distinctively "relieved face, so rarely found," instead of the "flat, meaningless maps of the face, with little or no shadow, but with half of the face white, and the other in a shadow," that were too often found. Fitzgibbon concluded "never for one moment think of letting a picture leave your gallery that has no *shadow or out-line to the features*," which bring no credit to "art or the artist." Southworth even referred to "chiaroscuro," the classic Renaissance technique of dramatic juxtaposition of light and dark later associated with Rembrandt (see fig. 101).

Pose had its place. Inexperienced operators insisted that "the truth of the picture exists principally in the eyes staring the beholder full in the face," when a "three-quarter or two-thirds view was best," said a "True Artist" who prescribed a studious "hour passed in the gallery of fine arts" would provide "opportunities for observing the due effect of lights and shadow" in addition to "accustomed study of every day life, as presented in the *Daguerreian Attiller* [*sic*]." Tastemakers did not neglect the setting, advocating the "proper setting up of the daguerreian rooms, a waiting room with books . . . [the] finest engravings" lying on the table, all appealing to elevation of taste and the profession. Care was given to all aspects of the setting, down to the details of the paint on the walls and the furniture in the rooms, contributing to the creation of "a temple of beauty and grandeur." Finally, consumers needed to be "improved" too; these tastemakers looked forward to "the artistic education of the masses."[38]

The elevation of the daguerreotypist and the establishment of aesthetic standards were strategies aimed at characterizing customers and discount operators alike as unsuitable judges of the daguerreotypist's art. John Fitzgibbon wrote that the botched cheap goods that represented likenesses to an ignorant public were just as much the consumers' fault as the professors'. Efforts were directed at wresting cultural control of the process of portraiture from patrons who, editor Humphrey noted, had clearly set notions of how they wanted to be "delineated." Unfortunately, customers demanded "a clear white but flat impression," continuing a preference for the rural aesthetic; they remained ignorant of the higher artistic standard of the romantic shadowing of the face and features, while demanding cheap likenesses. Popular and professional periodicals contained numerous comic accounts of country bumpkins and obstinate customers sitting for the put-upon artist. Some called for the formation of a professional association, the National Photographic Society, to "elevate the character of those engaged in the business" and "establish a fixed scale of prices for the finest productions of the art." During the 1850s, editors advocated standardization of prices and operating practice as journals moved from publishing general aesthetic treatises to detailed formulaic accounts of correct pose, background, and facial expression.[39]

As social and professional fluidity became restricted, the division of labor within the portrait-making industry increased. A gallery owner such as Brady did not take portraits; he hired the best operators and darkroom technicians. He acted as "the controlling aesthetic intellect in the creation of the portrait," posing the sitter and supervising the process. Within the daguerreotype establishment, the increasing scale and size of operations curtailed the independence of the operator and sitter. In large galleries, numerous technicians were responsible for small parts of the process. The English visitor John Werge dropped into one "'portrait factory' on Broadway, where likenesses were turned out as fast as coining, for the small charge of twenty-five cents a head. . . . The arrangements for such rapid work were very complete." The visitor purchased "a dollar's worth of these 'factory' portraits" at the desk and took his or her place in a crowded waiting room. Customers slid their way toward the entrance to the operating room, "answering the cry of 'the next' in much the same manner that people do at our public baths." When it was Werge's turn, he found the operator "stationed at the camera, which he never left all day long, barking out a chorus of 'Sit down' and 'Look thar'" before putting his hand into a hole in the wall—the "coating room"—to receive a sensitized plate. After the exposure, the plate went out through "another hole in the wall" to the "developing room."

> The operator had nothing to do with the preparation of the plates, developing, fixing, or finishing of the picture. He was responsible only for the "pose" and "time," the "developer," checking and correcting the latter occasionally by crying out "Short" or "Long" as the case might be. Having had my number of "sittings," I was requested to leave the operating room by another door which opened into a passage that led me to the "delivery desk," where, in a few minutes, I got all my four portraits fitted up in "matt, glass, and preserver,"—the pictures having been passed from the developing room to the "gilding" room, thence to the "fitting room" and the "delivery desk," where I received them. Thus they were

all finished and carried away without the camera operator ever having seen them.

A surprised Werge pronounced the images excellent: "Three of the four portraits were as fine Daguerreotypes as could be produced anywhere." Still, the controlling hand of the daguerreotypist receded in the upscale studio and "portrait factory" alike. The division of labor promoted the industrialization of image making while also increasing the scale of production and the employment of less-skilled operatives behind the scenes, as Werge observed, following a similar process to what we have seen in other household manufactures.[40]

Such industrial developments spelled trouble for the portrait painter John Toole, who entered into a business relationship with a local St. Petersburg, Virginia, entrepreneur. Mr. Minis supplied daguerreotypes from which Toole could paint oil portraits. At first, the "Face maker" was eager to take advantage of the possibilities of these new "Daguerreotype factories." But he soon found that the "face factory" challenged his independent way of working:

> Minis wants me to work by the year, but such an arrangement would not suit me. Were I to bind myself for a year he might be grumbling whenever I would go home, or take any recreation. I prefer working by the piece, and if he should not have the constant employment, I could work on my own engagements. I am willing to paint all he wants done so long as it suits me to stay, but not to bind myself whether it suits me or not. He knows he cannot do better than employ me on my own terms. He is to furnish a room for me to work in and give me twenty-five dollars for each large size portrait I paint for him and fifteen for head size, besides paying me extra for hands.[41]

Toole repeated "bind myself" twice, loathe to give up his independence like many other artisans caught up in the new manufactories; he was content to engage in piece work under the supervisory scrutiny of an entrepreneur who supplied him with customers and rooms.

The allure of scientific discovery enticed some young men into picking up a daguerreotype apparatus; those eager to leave the family farm in a manner similar to Silas Felton two generations earlier were now caught up in a rapidly changing trade. George Pyle grew up in Chester County, Pennsylvania. Although the death of his father when George was eight ended his formal education, he left the family farm in West Marlborough and began teaching school. His interest in chemistry led him to seek out Philadelphia's John Jabez Mayall in the spring of 1846 for lessons in daguerreotypy for fifty dollars. Mayall and others in this center of photographic innovation had developed sensitizing solutions and other methods to shorten exposure times to a few seconds. Pyle was an apt pupil; he recorded detailed notes of the various procedures necessary to make a daguerreotype in his "Formula and Lesson Book." "Lesson 1st" included a comparison of French, German, and American plates before moving on to buffing; the operation of the camera was the subject of later lessons. Mayall sold Pyle an apparatus and chemicals at a cost of $129.79 and encouraged him to pose subjects leaning on chairs or holding their chins in a natural manner, as in his portrait of Mayall circa 1846. He bade farewell to his young student with the news that he had sold out his concern to the "writing master" Marcus Root and was returning to England; Pyle set up on his own back home.[42]

Word quickly spread among family and friends in Unionville that the young schoolteacher owned a camera. By the end of the year, he began compiling a register of all his sitters and their residences, a wonderful resource for learning about business history in the early days of photography. Pyle photographed fellow teachers Jonathan and Eliza Gause on 29 March 1847, probably posing the couple outdoors since a homemade fabric backdrop has been suspended behind them. They sit comfortably, Jonathan with spectacles on his head and his hand in a book in three-quarters view, Eliza gazing at the camera with her hands clasped in her lap (fig. 102). His register notes other family members that same day. That month he recorded twenty-six customers, which probably undercounts the actual number. During the summer, Pyle went on the road to nearby towns, still relying on urban suppliers. He moved in wider circles of the provinces as he looked for markets where no daguerreotypist had recently been. From Gettysburg, Pennsylvania, he learned from his friend Levi Scarlet, whose following of the court circuit left him well informed about business conditions in the central and western parts of the state, "There is no one taking likenesses in this place—the last taken here was done a year ago." That itinerant obtained two to five dollars for his likenesses; a local bookstore owner was willing to board Pyle and conjectured, "You could do a good business if you can afford to take likenesses at $1.50." Scarlet added a postscript from Carlisle that the well-known politician/photographer and former blacksmith "Mr. Bear 'The Buck Eye black smith'" had removed there; his likenesses were somewhat improved, but remained "middling."[43]

Pyle kept moving west in 1848: to Pittsburgh by train and packet boat, spending six months in Ohio and arriving in Indiana by the summer of 1849. He scribbled in a journal in the back of his daguerreotype register, "Notes of incidents of travels in the west" to see the "Wonders of the mighty west"; he recorded his thoughts of the dangers—"steam boats blow up, cars running off the track"—and almost a year after he left home, he marked that he was "now

Fig. 102. Daguerreotype portrait of Jonathan and Eliza Gause made by George Pyle, 1847. Quarter-plate daguerreotype in case. Inscribed "Jonathan and Eliza Gause taken by George Pyle, Unionville, Chester Co., Penna. March 29, 1847." Chester County Historical Society, West Chester, Pennsylvania.

in Greenfield Hancock Co,. Ia." He advertised in the *Vincennes Gazette* that he had obtained rooms; for shorter stays, he must have posted broadsides for "Likenesses in a Superior Style," with a blank space for his traveling studio. He kept in touch with his family, reporting in the fall that "the cholera has together with the failure of the wheat crop in this section of country . . . made business very dull, daguerreotypes as well as everything else nearly." The epidemic and the lack of business sent him back to the farm. Meanwhile, new establishments with elaborate studios appeared at home. Philip Pierce and Levi Crowl opened the first daguerreotype studio in Chester County in 1850, across the street from the county courthouse in West Chester.[44] Urban studios raised the status and cost of the craft.

These centralizing developments squeezed out marginal operators like Southworth's pupil L. C. Champney, who had been lured into the trade in the early boom years. Other painter-daguerreotypists could not escape the increasing market for photographic portraits. Ambrose Andrews, a painter who "went into the daugerreian business," did "tolerable well" for a while but soon found that photography in New York was "entirely overdone. It is so easy for one to learn the process that thousands upon thousands have jumped in it and the number is still increasing everyday." By 1853 he was advertising his daguerreotype equipment for sale, but he still took on the coloring of photographs for "one of the principle [sic] photographic establishments in Broadway."[45] Out in the countryside, W. H. Sherman found that the limited training required and lofty prospects drew many aspirants, but "before long hardly a country village could be found" along his travels that had not "its resident daguerreotypist already on the retired list, but not, I grieve to say, on half pay. Rather because he had not been able to make it half pay." The 1850 census recorded George Pyle's occupation as a farmer, and his papers recorded no more likenesses. When he fell on hard times in 1871, an inventory of his property included a "trunk of daguerreotype fixtures" valued at only five dollars.[46]

Rules were promulgated for the acquisition and display of daguerreotypes by consumers. As Shirley Wajda reminds us, "Rather than considering merely the proliferation of portraits, we need more carefully to attend to the details of acquisition: who was denied, by cost or by social strictures, this testimony to bourgeois membership." T. S. Arthur concluded that every individual could own a likeness of an ancestor and every home could be a Daguerreian gallery: "A few years ago it was not every man who could afford a likeness of himself, his wife or his children; these were luxuries known only to those who had money to spare; now it is hard to find the man who has not gone through the 'operator's' hands from once to half-a-dozen times, or who has not the shadowy faces of his wife and children done up in purple morocco and velvet, together or singly, among his household treasures." Enterprising daguerreotypists and elite consumers in the 1850s sought stratagems for securing their membership in a new middle-class social order while also shoring up barriers against pretenders or cheap johns and professors. The "household treasures" that Arthur described were produced by commercial parlors to be encased as miniaturized, privatized mementoes of family ancestry, procured in a marketplace where increasingly exclusionary rules of production, distribution, and consumption were being set in place.[47] More daguerreotypes were being produced, but their terms of production and consumption were now bound up in an increasingly restricted set of rules of middle-class culture; consolidation did not mean progress as the democratic potentials of popular portraiture were restricted.

For clockmakers, chairmakers, portraitists, and many other artisan-entrepreneurs, the 1840s proved to be the beginning of a period of centralization and consolidation, similar to the experience of daguerreotypists. Entrepreneurs sought to stave off ruinous competition while also meeting the ever-increasing demand for inexpensive timepieces and stylish chairs. But in the fall of 1837, clock manufacturer Chauncey Jerome sat in his room in Richmond, Virginia, pondering the perilous state of the wooden-clock industry that he and many other Connecticut artisans had turned into a national marvel. Eli Terry's neighbors had once scoffed at the idea of making a few thousand wooden-movement clocks, but dozens of producers had followed Terry's successful manufacture of the cheap and attractive household objects until the ruinous competition had forced down wholesale prices from nine dollars in 1830 to four dollars by 1837. Most firms like Jerome's were in serious financial trouble, and a few had gone bankrupt. The final blow was the severe financial recession sweeping the entire nation, precipitated by President Andrew Jackson's withdrawal of federal deposits during the Bank War when, Jerome remembered, "Clock makers and almost every one else stopped business."[48]

Jerome was in Richmond to try and collect some debts and pick up "some scattered clocks" in an effort to stay afloat financially. Clock-peddling operator Philip Barnes reported from Great Barrington, Massachusetts, to his partner Rensselaer Upson: "Some of the heaviest of banks in this state have failed, and many others are expected daily to follow. . . . Money is ten time as scarce as last year." Prospects seemed bleak for the Connecticut wooden-movement clock industry, ending an era of small shops and itinerant innovators that had metamorphosed into a major industry.[49]

"Feeling very much depressed," Jerome could not bear to give up. As he looked at the wooden clock on his table, "it came into my mind instantly that there could be cheap one day brass clock that would take the place of the wood clock." Brass movements—expensive, relatively rare, and formed from imported metal—had been abandoned by the clock industry. Connecticut artisans, most notably Joseph Ives, had continued to experiment and produce these eight-day movements because of their superior timekeeping, but they had been unable to compete with the inexpensive one-day wooden ones. An inspired Jerome feverishly figured out how it could be done: "The case would cost no more, the dials, glass, and widths and other fixtures would be the same, and the size could be reduced." Jerome lay in his bed mulling over "this new thing" all night and rose in the morning convinced "there was a fortune in it." As he continued his southern journey, he could think of nothing else, drawing plans

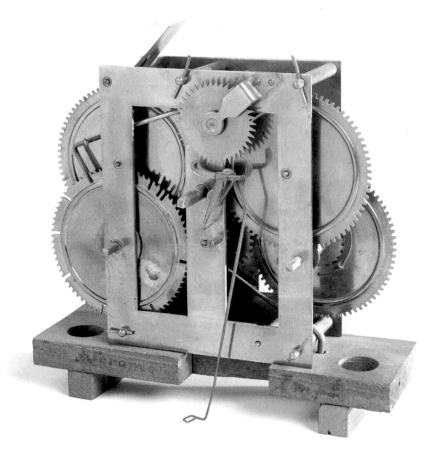

Fig. 103. Brass clock movement made by Chauncey Jerome, the first cheap thirty-hour brass clock, 1839. 26 × 15-1/2 × 4-3/8 in. National Museum of American History, Smithsonian Institution, Washington, D.C.

and making calculations. However, when he met his head man in Georgia with the news that he "could get up something when I got home that would run out all the wood clocks in the country," his hopes met with a hearty laugh.[50]

By the next summer, when his Georgia foreman came north to Connecticut, Jerome had a "Shelf full of them running." His brother Noble, the mechanic in the family, perfected and patented a thirty-hour brass movement based on a local example. Early models had their solid brass wheels visible for all to see (fig. 103). The cheap brass clock was an immediate success. Housed in simple ogee cases, well designed, rugged, and efficient, they were sold by several firms and produced in tremendous quantities, with little improvement during their seventy-five years of production. Hiram Camp, Jerome's nephew, recorded that there was such a "great demand for these clocks people would come and leave money in advance for them." Jerome said he made $35,000 on the clocks. He moved on to secure greater capital, and other clock manufacturers such as Seth Thomas abandoned their older designs and set off to Jerome's manufactory to learn how to make the new movements. Jerome's new brass clock restored the health of the clock industry while it also fostered an upheaval in its structure.[51]

Central Massachusetts chair manufacturers also strengthened their position in the 1840s. Gardner's Levi Heywood aggressively used the new resources of steam power, machinery, and railroad transport to consolidate the far-flung elements of chair making within their growing factories. Gardner's large-scale production superseded the region's several commercial villages where the artisans of the 1820s and 1830s had built their enterprises. In 1820, Gardner had less than one-third as many chairmakers as Sterling. In 1832, the chairmaking establishments in Gardner counted over three times the number of employees as those in Sterling. By 1837, each town had about twenty-five chairmaking firms, but Gardner had twice the value of production ($109,064 compared with $53,228) and over four times the number of employees (300 compared with 80). By 1845, Gardner had 20 establishments, and its almost 600 chairmaking workers made over 170,000 chairs worth over $100,000. By 1855, that total had dropped to 14 firms, but their capitalization had jumped tenfold, and employment had increased to 2,112, about one-quarter men and three-quarters women.[52]

The Heywood family set up the substantial group of factory buildings depicted in the company's advertisement (see fig. 57). Wagons carried large quantities of chairs as far as Albany and Boston. Heywood seized upon the railroad system for transportation and secured Gardner's place on the grid. His warehouse in Boston gave him access to the wholesale and retail trade of the metropolis, and he directed Irish immigrants arriving at the port of Boston to his central Massachusetts factories. Heywood incorporated his business earlier than his competitors, protecting himself from personal loss and securing capital for expansion. Factory production grew from the extensive network of producers as new designs incorporated elements of Windsor and fancy chair forms.[53] Skilled painters like Thomas and Edward Hill dabbed on the gold scrolls and flowers that decorated the miniature chairs used for samples. The Victorian side chair (fig. 104) was a standardized product with simple turned legs and rails, distinguished by its elaborate freehand painting. By mid-century, Heywood Brothers and other Gardner chair companies sold a diversified line of factory-made chairs though a widespread network of factories and showrooms.[54]

Elements of the work process, formerly performed at decentralized sites, were drawn together under one roof. Levi Heywood kept expanding his chair "shop" located on Crystal Lake so that by 1850 it bore little resemblance to the small buildings that still dotted the countryside. His continual introduction of

Fig. 104. Victorian side chair made by Heywood Brothers, ca. 1860. 31 × 17 ×
14-1/2 in. Gardner, Massachusetts. Gardner Museum.

new sources of power and production methods transformed the industry. Levi's
insistence on mechanization drove his brothers out of the firm as he installed
water-powered turning lathes and circular saws. He perfected machines for
making wooden seats and bending wood with high temperatures. After Francis
Thonet, the famous Austrian designer and chair manufacturer, visited the factory, he wrote Levi: "I must tell you that you have the best machinery for
bending wood that I ever saw." The product line was diversified with such
specialized forms as baby carriages and cribs. Gardner manufacturer Philander
Derby's Boston rockers and stenciled chairs gained popularity.[55]

Connecticut clockmakers consolidated too. The thicket of clock shops
thinned out and mechanization advanced. The clock industry's successful
transition to inexpensive brass mechanisms relied on a series of mechanical
innovations that raised productivity and lowered costs. Eighteenth-century
clockmakers had depended upon cast brass, which was bulky and difficult to
work. The rise of an American brass industry in nearby Waterbury in the 1830s
made high-quality sheet brass available locally. Clock plates were made from

single stamped sheets, but more efficient machines were required for gear teeth and wheels. Soon a single die could stamp out an entire gear using thin brass strengthened by a raised bead around the circumference of the wheel. By the early 1840s, stamping presses had replaced saws, dies were used instead of wooden gauge markers, and machines rather than hands did the polishing. A visitor to Jerome's factory in 1845 saw a fantastic vision: "The movements are all cut in proper forms and sizes by dies, with great precision and rapidity, even to the pivot holes in the plates, which have before been drilled. The cogs in the wheels, the second, minute, and hour stops, are grooved out by the same rapid and skilful process. The posts, pins, and smaller pieces of the inside work are turned from the more rough material, polished and finished at the same time, while the plates and wheels are cleansed and polished by rinsing first in a strong solution of aquafortis, and then in pure water." Some fifty different hands worked on various processes before the movement was completed. Jerome boasted that with his equipment, three men could "take the brass in the sheet, press cut and level under the drop, then cut the teeth, and make all the wheels to five hundred clocks in one day."[56]

The manufacture of cases was also changed by the substitution of machine for hand labor: "On entering, our ears were greeted with the mingled hum of buzz saws, the thunder of two powerful steam engines, and the clatter of machinery." The sawing works drew the most attention, where "the cases are cut out and fitted as if by magic." Then the finer saws took over "and cut in perfect order for being matched and put together; no other smoothing or levelling process is used except what these saws accomplish." Finally, the veneering and varnishing finished the job; the clock case was the product of a few hands and many machines, the visitor noted in wonderment, and "will compare in elegance with the finest articles of furniture in the cabinet warerooms of our city." The former cabinetmaker's ogee cutter split the twelve different pieces of the rectangular case for its veneer and then fit it all together with no extra handwork. Jerome boasted that "labor costs less than twenty cents for each case, and with stock, less than fifty cents: a cabinet maker could not make one for less than five dollars."[57]

Steam had once only powered Jerome's New Haven factory, but soon all the other manufactures followed suit. These innovations progressively enlarged production in Jerome's establishment: the largest one went from under ten thousand wooden clocks in the mid-1830s, to fifty thousand brass ones in the mid-1840s, and almost a quarter of a million brass clocks by the mid-1850s at a price of about $1.50 to $2. Capitalization climbed from a mere $2,000 in the wooden era to a more robust $25,000 by 1850 and doubled over that decade. Entrepreneurs started with internal sources of capital but quickly encountered difficulties with keeping a working capital balance; with no commercial banks in the vicinity, they sought out Hartford bankers and wealthy individuals in the region. Financiers gradually replaced the original entrepreneurs. The roving agents for R. G. Dun, the credit agency, came around and recorded capsule biographies of each entrepreneur in town, down to the small farmer. In Gardner, Levi Heywood stood on top each year, receiving a terse but steady approval of his credit worthiness, except for the fact that he took advantage of the Massachusetts General Incorporation Law, which the Dun correspondent remained skeptical about in 1858: "We have not much confidence in such Corporations." The Heywood Chair Manufacturing Company, as it was called then, maintained good credit through the 1857 panic, with the Dun reporter's discussion of the financial pressure that made it hard for them; but they were "'a rich concern' and Heywood is a wealthy man abundantly able to meet all his liabilities."[58]

While Jerome relocated his manufacturing operation to New Haven, Gardner industrialists sought to break out of the constraints imposed by their inland location and its burdensome costs for transporting raw materials and finished furniture. The Vermont and Worcester Railroad would bring Vermont's forest products to Gardner and take her chairs to Boston markets. In 1842, Alvah Crocker, president of the proposed railroad and Fitchburg's leading industrialist, planned to extend the line northwest from Fitchburg; he raised local interest and sold stock to Gardner and Templeton residents. When the proposed route reached the legislature in 1844, Gardner found that its place on the rail line had been taken by Winchendon in an effort to ensure Fitchburg's regional supremacy, a common feature of railway battles that determined the primacy of urban centers. Two years of conflict exhausted the county commissioners and state legislature before Levi Heywood resolved the issue in Gardner's favor. Furniture manufacturers secured an improved way to obtain their stock and market their products. A north-south route to Worcester was not built for another two decades.[59]

Chairmaking and clockmaking artisans were also on the move as their industries centralized. Expanding production and the growth of a regional and national market favored industrial consolidation. Connecticut clock manufacturers turned to urban factories and wholesalers. Some furniture makers retired to the sidelines to pursue custom or repair work; others turned to retailing. Sterling's Joel Pratt had set up a "Chair Warehouse" in Hartford with a full range of furniture.[60]

Only a few took the riskier path of expanding factory production. Production costs were lower in rural areas with ample supplies of wood, labor, and waterpower. Some Worcester County chairmakers moved north; Peter Wilder established a chair factory in southern New Hampshire to produce Windsor and other wooden-seated chairs that were indistinguishable from the products of Sterling shops. Peter's grandson Josiah Prescott Wilder recorded making more than twenty-five thousand chairs between 1837 and 1839 in over forty styles; many went to the growing factory town of Lowell, where at least six stores sold Wilder's products.[61]

The furniture industry reorganized geographically as manufacturers relied upon water and steam power and improved transportation. By the 1830s, such entrepreneurs as Anthony Van Doorn established water-powered cabinet manufactories and warerooms in the southern Vermont town of Brattleboro. Van Doorn migrated from Rhode Island around 1815, and his shop was "newly fitted up and the Machinery enlarged and much improved." By 1840, eight men worked under his roof, and his advertisements circulated widely in the state; the 1850 industrial census recorded his capitalization at $5,500, with eighteen employees and an annual output of chairs, bureaus, sofas, tables, and other forms worth $12,000. His cabinet manufactory and wareroom produced and sold increasingly standardized items, such as a secretary (Historic Deerfield) that used stock turned legs and drawer pulls on a standard carcass frame. Little besides his printed label distinguished it from items produced in any of the dozens of other factories in the northeastern United States. Orange County, Vermont's Simeon Willard Edson and Ara Howe mass-produced worktables and chairs from templates and interchangeable parts. Tens of thousands of chairs spilled out of Brookfield's well-capitalized factories along the White River's tributaries. Ara Howe had come from Sterling and learned the craft of making chairs in bulk with simple cutout shapes for their tablet back, scooped seat, and turned legs.[62]

These dramatic changes within furniture workshops not only displaced mature artisans but also affected young men looking for a place in a consolidating industrial society. Fourteen-year-old Edward Carpenter, after a stint in a factory village, began his apprenticeship with the cabinetmakers Miles and Lyon in Greenfield, Massachusetts, in 1842. In his journal, he recorded a steady regimen of bureaus and secretaries, finishing one every two or three weeks. The firm had a clear hierarchy of skill and cost; the two bosses still produced better "bespoke furniture," according to historian Christopher Clark, "while cheaper goods were made by the apprentices or journeymen for sale to peddlers or the firm's 'ware room.'" On 17 February, Carpenter noted: "I finished a Bureau today & began a Mahogany Secretary, they have sold the one in the wareroom." While working on a card table in April, Miles sold a bureau, so "I had to quite it again & make another Bureau to take the place of the one that he sold." In the changing work environment, the youth was caught somewhere between being an apprentice learning a skilled craft and a wage worker manufacturing standardized products. Carpenter and many other young men sought instruction in "the mysteries of a craft," but for the employers, these young men served increasingly as a "source of inexpensive labor in an increasingly competitive market." By 1845, Miles and Lyons reorganized their manufactory. They had the apprentices eat breakfast one-half hour earlier, set work "stints" for Carpenter to speed up production, established a water-powered mill site, and added three more journeymen.[63]

Provincial marketing extended into urban centers and beyond the borders of the United States. Chairmakers retailed their merchandise in the countryside and nearby towns and cities. From the mid-1830s, Jacob Felton of Fitzwilliam, New Hampshire, hired teamsters to cart as many as 425 chairs in a single load to Boston for as little as six cents per chair. Northern Worcester County manufacturers transported their chairs in "huge wagons, drawn sometimes by six horses" to the Boston market, a two-day journey; special large barns were built along the route to accommodate these "chair racks." After the Blackstone Canal from Worcester to Providence opened in 1822, one author recalled, "Chairs, chairs everlasting in number, brought into town in large loads from the northern parts of the country seemed to me to be the principal loading of the boats down the canal." Wagons "piled high with chair-seat frames and bundles of cane" called at local farmhouses where women and children seated chairs by hand. Worcester County chairs ended up in the southern United States, the West Indies, and even South America.[64]

The new brass clock movements facilitated far-reaching changes in marketing. Clockmakers dependent on peddling networks rooted in the Connecticut countryside now turned to a new urban-based distribution system in a change of direction. New York City jobbers became the center of trade and the chief suppliers for country merchants. Urban wholesalers who had regarded wooden clocks as suitable only for country consumers witnessed the new brass clocks in great demand in urban households and retail shops. Changes in design, such as the more sophisticated ogee case, also attracted urban consumers.[65]

Wooden clocks had proved difficult to transport long distances, especially by water, as their works would swell and their accuracy diminish. Jerome realized that "metal clocks can be sent anywhere without injury." The venturesome entrepreneur looked across the Atlantic to extend the market for clocks beyond the land of "wooden nutmegs." When Jerome's representatives convinced an English merchant to carry some items, they rapidly sold them out and he ordered more; English merchants soon got over their prejudice against "Yankee clocks." Britain's revenue laws allowed customs officers to seize shipments they believed were undervalued and being "dumped" by paying the shipper 10 percent over their stated price. So the clocks were confiscated and Jerome thwarted, "thinking we would put the prices of the next cargo at higher rates." When a third shipment arrived, exasperated officials "came to the conclusion that we could make clocks much better and cheaper than their own people."[66]

Chester County's furniture makers, once housed in farm-based workshops sprinkled throughout the region, moved to larger shops. They increased their production and sold to larger markets via newspaper advertising and wareroom displays. When John Hartman came of age after finishing an apprenticeship in his father's workshop, he relocated, acquired machinery, and featured specialized products. His wareroom with three bureaus and seven chests was more modest than Pratt's, but his sixty beds offered the public a wide range of stock to inspect. The constant need to borrow money kept him in a precarious situation, but Hartman doubled his labor force over the decade as he built a more highly capitalized manufactory. Others turned away: chairmaker Jesse Esbin of East Goshen made less and less new furniture and repaired and bottomed old chairs; he soon focused on house painting. Many cabinetmakers who once made coffins as a sideline turned into specialized producers.

In the 1840s, furniture workshops and warerooms concentrated in West Chester, while they disappeared in the rest of the county. Chairmaking had always been the most receptive branch of the furniture industry to centralization; chairmakers had more opportunities to exploit economies of scale by selling sets, and chair parts could easily be standardized and stockpiled, a development grasped early by Lambert Hitchcock. Joseph Jones, who began his chairmaking business in West Chester in 1819, enlarged his sales and added a line of iron stoves in 1824. His 1836 ad boasted of an assortment of chairs "of the latest shapes and color finished to please the fancy of an enlightened and refined community." Still, by 1841, Jones decided to focus his entrepreneurial skills on the iron business rather than compete with the factory-produced chair arriving in town.

Customers drove these developments. Shoppers traveled to West Chester and Philadelphia to compare goods in various warerooms. Shopping became a pastime. City and countryside grew closer. West Chester furniture manufacturers adopted several successful business strategies in the 1840s. Thomas Ogden aggressively combated the lure of Philadelphia, boasting that his work matched the quality available there and was as "Cheap as the city prices." By the 1850s, however, the number of furniture firms in West Chester had dwindled to three. William Hoffman emphasized his "superior workmanship," while Daniel Nields promoted a cheaper line. Soon all three retailed factory-made goods from Philadelphia and New York.[67]

The clockmaking industry was deeply affected by the panic of 1837. At first, the earlier pattern of falling prices and rising production seemed familiar; but the days of an industry composed of many firms of comparable size were gone. Small producers could not compete with the economies of scale and capital requirements in one-day brass-clock manufacture, as output soared from fewer than 50,000 clocks in 1840 to over 550,000 in 1850. By 1850, ten firms accounted for over 90 percent of all clocks made in Connecticut; Jerome's company alone made over half the total. Entrepreneurs lowered costs by centralizing production of clock parts at one site, similar to chair production. The system of independent subcontractors did not end until the turn of the century, but they clustered under one roof, using the machinery and materials of the clock manufacturers. Jerome stood out by the scale of his entrepreneurial efforts. He leased a former Satinet factory with "so much of the Gearing and Water power . . . as may be necessary to manufacture twelve thousand Brass Clock Movements." He modernized the factory, supplied tools, stock, and power—everything but the labor—and leased it to a partnership that agreed to supply 40,000 brass movements at $1.40 each. It turned out to be a better deal for the working partners than for the capitalist; Hiram Camp recalled that these movements "did not cost half as much" as Jerome was paying the partners, including his brother, and disparagingly added the "movements were not so good, either."[68]

Jerome's consolidation of his operations proved more successful. Wood for casemaking came by ship through New Haven before moving on to Bristol; the finished clocks went back through New Haven. So Jerome thought: why not set up a casemaking plant in New Haven? He packed up the movements in Bristol, "one hundred in a box," and sent them to New Haven where they were cased and shipped. This expansion worked well until a disastrous fire in 1845 was set off by some boys playing with matches under the factory where the shavings fell. The devastating loss was barely covered by inadequate insurance, but Jerome recovered. He uprooted his Bristol "movement makers" and concentrated all his operations in New Haven. The ruinous competition convinced Jerome and seven of the other firms to try forming an association to control output and prices. The venture did not succeed, and several firms went under because of the association's weak financing and lack of unity. Jerome increasingly turned his attention to various civic endeavors, and his firm failed stunningly after a disastrous partnership with the century's most famous producer of entertainment spectacles, P. T. Barnum.[69]

Jerome's failure was part of a general collapse of major firms in the 1850s, which were plagued by the mounting difficulty of maintaining enough working capital, the burden of opening jobbing houses, and vicious cost competition. New entrepreneurs from Connecticut's brass industry rescued the clock manufacturers. Of the six major firms at the onset of the Civil War, only two were directed by men with ties to the clock industry and only one, William Gilbert,

Fig. 105. Emerson Bixby House, originally Barre Four Corners, Massachusetts, built 1807–44. Now at Old Sturbridge Village, Sturbridge, Massachusetts. Photograph by Thomas Neill.

was an important entrepreneur in clockmaking. After Seth Thomas died in 1859, his firm passed to a new generation. The leading firm in 1860, the New Haven Clock Company, had roots in Jerome's subcontracting back in Bristol and was run by his former foreman Hiram Camp, but Camp too relinquished control to New Haven entrepreneurs.[70] Centralized and well-capitalized industrial concerns were in the ascendancy in clockmaking and chairmaking.

Fashioning Parlor People

Emerson Bixby participated in the transformation of provincial culture that swept across New England in the early nineteenth century. In the 1840s, he embarked upon the project of refining his domestic environment, both inside and around the house (figs. 105 and 106). Adding a bedroom to one corner with a garret above provided private sleeping space for the parents and their three daughters. The Bixbys reconfigured the older downstairs rooms to provide a new entrance through the ell and, most important, to create a parlor.

In 1822 the young blacksmith Bixby moved to Barre Four Corners with his wife and baby daughter. Two years later, he purchased a small, single-story

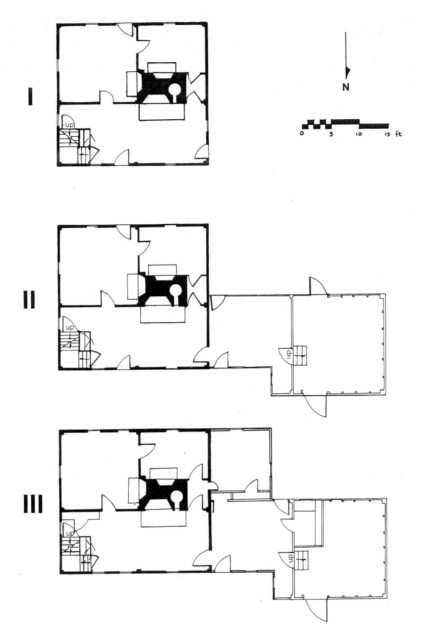

Fig. 106. Three views of the Emerson Bixby House as it developed over its history; I, the original structure, ca. 1807, with a kitchen in the front and a bedroom (top left) and sitting room (top right) in the back; II, the addition of an ell and woodshed, ca. 1815–20; III, a new bedroom added on the southwestern corner (top right) along with one in the garret, and the original bedroom (top left) turned into a parlor and its door to the outside removed for greater privacy, ca. 1845. Collections of Old Sturbridge Village, Sturbridge, Massachusetts.

house across the road from his blacksmith shop and adjacent to the shop of the wheelwright with whom he often worked. The asymmetrical structure had unpainted clapboards, and the long kitchen opened directly onto the road. Ascending the stone steps around back, visitors immediately entered the best room, with plastered walls and ceiling and graced by Federal-style detailing on the mantelpiece and painted imitation molding around the room, where the family displayed its prized possessions. The space doubled as the parents' bedroom and the family dining room. The cluttered sitting room, like the kitchen, was primarily a work space. The Bixby's three growing daughters slept in the unfinished garret. Around 1830, Bixby bought a small lot up the road where he housed and pastured the animals. After he bought the adjacent half-acre lot and carriagemaker's shop in 1841, Bixby converted it into a barn and cultivated a garden. Having improved the surroundings, the family ceased to sweep their refuse out the best-room door and also began to plan improvements to the house. Still, people passing along the road would have seen a small brown house set in a yard strewn with household refuse, without a proper entryway and with dark interior colors.[71]

The Bixbys became parlor people in the early 1840s. The door to the best room was removed and replaced by a window. An entryway prevented visitors from entering the house directly. The family also closed off doorways. By adding a finished bedroom on the ground floor for the parents and a finished chamber in the garret for their three daughters, the family separated these intimate activities from spaces where they entertained. The family presented its best face to the public in the parlor. The dark woodwork took on a pale gray and green tint, while the floors were painted yellow-orange to resemble pine. Light-colored wallpaper with a fashionable monochrome treatment covered the walls of the best room, the sitting room, and the passage. The sheathed kitchen walls were painted in a light color. The entire house, inside and out, was brightened. The exterior was reclapboarded and painted white. Neighbors noticed.[72]

The Bixbys, like many other provincial families throughout the Northeast, fashioned a parlor for performing the rituals of social life. Limiting entryways gave greater control of the access to their living spaces and suggested greater formality. Still, there were limits to this transformation. The Bixby house remained asymmetrical, and the entryway was unfinished. They could not enclose the staircase (see fig. 106). A carpet never covered the parlor floor; no cookstove graced the kitchen. Since they could not afford a fashionable Empire-style sofa, they cut down a bedstead to serve that function and upholstered one of their chairs. Most important, the house remained a workplace. The Bixby daughters had come of age, and their waged outwork—braiding straw, making palm-leaf hats, and sewing shoe uppers—played an increasingly important role in the family economy as their father's blacksmithing business declined. The enclosed ell housed the young women's supplies, benches, and tools, as well as serving as the entryway. Almost every house in Barre Four Corners underwent such changes, although houses in mill villages were improved later than those in more commercial villages.

Prospering merchants and farmers, such as David Goodale of Marlborough, Massachusetts, promoted improvement in many aspects of rural life. He took an interest in scientific farming and market-oriented agriculture, attending cattle shows and reading agricultural periodicals. He expanded his dairy, selling butter and cheese in urban markets. In 1841, the Goodales remodeled the farmhouse at a cost of $654, with a new roof, stenciled designs on the plaster walls with a different pattern in each room, and wallpapers on the first floor. They acquired new furnishings, such as a chaise for reading. Millicent Warren Goodale read *Mother's Magazine* and such advice books as Catharine Beecher's *Youth's Companion for Children*. Still, the Goodales placed clear boundaries on their consumption. Although they were among the wealthiest 10 percent of the town's farmers, their clothing purchases were frugal; Millicent purchased moderately priced fabrics and remade old gowns.[73]

A similar reconfiguration of space took place inside many provincial households. Rural families adopted an ideology of domesticity that took the parlor as its centerpiece. The transformation of the domestic interior was made possible by innovative artisans like Eli Terry who manufactured furnishings more cheaply. An array of center tables and Argand lamps, pianos and parlor carpets, family portraits and parlor suites of furniture was available by the 1850s. When Sylvia Wright was married to Frank Gale in 1858 in Colchester, Vermont, Frank gave Sylvia the money to paper all the rooms of their house, "except the parlor bedroom" that already had good paper. Her father provided the newlyweds with quite a bounty of furniture: "2 good tables, a fall leaf stand & a washsink, not a stand a nice bureau $11.00 and 14 chairs, 8 canebottomed, 2 cane rocking chairs & 6 wooden ones, 2 lookinglasses & 2 bedsteads, 1 red & the other a dark colored one with little posts up & down in the foot board." The new manufactories of the Northeast produced an abundance of inexpensive furniture.[74]

Portraits were among aspiring families' grander gestures. Newton Hubbard and Sarah Puffer, both teachers, marked their wedding in 1842 by commissioning Robert Peckham to paint companion portraits. When Newton and Sarah took over his parent's house in Brimfield, Massachusetts, they reconfigured the space. While the "main features of the house" remained the same as in his parents' day, the "main arrangement inside has greatly changed." During his childhood, he recalled, "there were no carpets on the floors, no blinds on the house, and no stoves within." The family remained mostly in the back part of the house. "But all this is changed." The spinning wheel was removed to the attic, and bare surfaces became covered and comfortable. "Blinds protect the windows and ornament the house, carpets cover the floors, and stoves are through the house."[75]

When Ebenezer Strong Snell, a member of the first graduating class of Amherst College who later taught mathematics there, married Sabra Cobb Clark in 1828, Ebenezer paid $77.66 to a Brookfield, Massachusetts, cabinetmaker for substantial furniture: seventeen chairs, including two rocking chairs and two armchairs; a bird's-eye maple bureau; a French bedstead; and tables. Over the next two decades, they added to their furnishings. They put together a dining room with wallpaper, furniture, and a looking glass. They spent twenty dollars for a portrait, perhaps a daguerreotype. Ebenezer and Sabra were fond of photographs of themselves and their five daughters.[76]

Portraits hung on once-bare walls and scores of chairs graced the edges of wallpapered rooms. The probate inventories of central Massachusetts families record a steady rise in the number of chairs per household, from less than eleven in the 1790s to almost twenty-one in the 1830s. Instead of a rare armchair reserved for the family patriarch and a few others scattered around the house, with barely enough for all to sit on for meals, provincial families filled their parlor and sitting room with fashionably painted sets of six chairs, vastly expanding the possibilities for genteel sociability. Lambert Hitchcock, Levi Heywood, and a host of small furniture manufactories had devised ways of making thousands of cheap chairs and less costly cabinet furniture that was distributed throughout the United States. In the 1770s, few in Delaware's Kent County could display furniture fashioned from such costly woods as walnut and mahogany; only a third of the wealthiest households owned such items. By the 1840s, a third of the poorest families possessed some item made of walnut or mahogany, while they were ubiquitous in better-off households. Still, the commercial classes and prosperous farmers owned more paintings and more furniture along the Hudson River Valley in that decade. Furniture forms diversified, with sideboards and secretaries going beyond the eighteenth-century standards of chairs, tables, and chests.

Central Massachusetts homes featured sofas and other upholstered furniture in noticeable numbers by the 1820s. Sturbridge "households at all economic levels owned carpets, cushioned seating furniture, rocking chairs, wash stands, and other amenities of comfortable habitation," historian Holly Izard has determined from probate inventories. Wealthy Benjamin Bullock, Jr., whose father had purchased his cosmopolitan furnishings from Salem, owned a Grecian table and a pianoforte along with carpeting in several rooms, but he also held on to a gilt-frame looking glass and a secretary from his father's inventory. At the upper middle-class level, farmer and blacksmith Zenas Dunton owned ten parlor chairs, a wooden clock, and lots of other chairs in his unpainted house. Jonas Rice stood in the middle of local society with a two-story hall and parlor dwelling. His family parlor had a stove, a dozen dining chairs, a pair of circular tables, a bureau, a lightstand, a clock, and a pair of glass lamps. A map of the United States and four framed pictures decorated the walls. But even financially distressed machinist David Atherton, with many of his household goods mortgaged, displayed his family's refined taste with two carpets, two tables, a clock, a bureau, and a dressing table, along with silver teaspoons and sugar tongs. Improved transportation and local manufactories provided Sturbridge residents with mass-produced furnishings and ceramics.[77] Diverse offerings became available to suit different budgets. When Vermont's Simeon Willard Edson made a lady's worktable in his water-powered manufactory, the table had the same shape and function as its handmade counterpart, but the two were dramatically different in their construction methods and cost. The Thomas Ackely Straw worktable had robustly turned cherry legs and drawer fronts of bird's-eye maple; it would have taken an artisan some time to turn the elegant shapes and match up the wooden surfaces. Edson's worktable had simply turned legs that supported a solid wooden carcass and a minimal design in its skirt; the turning of the legs required less time and skill. The bold grain of the maple added a decorative note.[78]

Candlesticks and looking glasses proliferated in central Massachusetts and Delaware households. Looking glasses were important additions to the parlor or sitting room, ornamenting the walls, allowing personal grooming, and throwing back reflected light. While they had once been a singular item in wealthier homes, looking glasses—often two or three—were found on the walls of almost half of the less affluent and nearly all of the wealthier households in Kent County. Lamps enhanced the "circle of light" around the family. A majority of nonfarming families in central Massachusetts owned one or two pairs of lamps by the 1830s, which brightened domestic interiors even though they puffed smoke and required daily cleaning and refilling with whale oil.

Carpets represented a new sensibility of "covering floors," Richard Bushman reminds us, to lighten the tread and heighten the contrast with the muddy environment outside the house. Carpets remained the prerogative of wealth in the eighteenth century, with none found in Kent County at any wealth level; but by the 1840s, a third of those in the bottom quarter of the population owned one while all those at the top level did. Carpets varied from simple, homemade rag rugs to a brightly colored Brussels or Axminsters woven on power looms. These large and soft carpets "strewn with gargantuan roses" decorated parlors such as that shown in Peckham's *Hobby Horse* (see fig. 95), contrasting with dark woods and simply colored walls. Distinctions by profession and income remained; in Catskill, New York, shipper David Porter, owned two bedroom carpets and two parlor carpets, with a value totaling ninety dollars. Following the Bixbys, middle-class families embellished their homes, but often mixed store-bought with homemade. A few miles from the Porter's household, the Dubois family produced their own "window curtains with fringe on" rather than making a store purchase; the women of the family wove more than thirty-three ells of fabric into "rag carpet[s] for kitchen and bedroom." Window treatments softened the light inside, giving the family privacy within while signaling gentility to those outside. A shelf clock made possible by Connecticut's innovative itinerant entrepreneurs graced the mantel in almost all central Massachusetts households headed by merchants and professionals, two-thirds of artisans' homes, and half of the farmhouses.[79]

The parlor became a key site for the construction and display of middle-class identity. The means of creating a proper parlor along with establishing a family ancestry through portraiture became available to all those willing and able to purchase the necessary mass consumer goods. In the parlor, which John Kasson describes as "a miniature museum," meaning was made material by goods. Within the Victorian parlor, "the meaning of a good is best (and sometimes only) communicated when this good is surrounded by a complement of goods that carry the same significance." The parlor and its objects were ritual adjuncts in an effort to stabilize social meanings and social relations. Objects were culture in tangible form, historian Katherine Grier writes, and the parlor, with its formulaic vocabulary of furniture, carpets, decorative lighting objects, center tables, pianos, and portraits, was a "theater of culture" in the Victorian age.[80]

Looking at a sample of Worcester County chairmakers' inventories in the 1840s gives us a chance to see how those working in the Heywood and other factories had benefited from the increase in manufactured commodities. Almost all these chairmakers held over one thousand dollars in probated wealth; however, Levi Heywood's real estate was valued at over $28,000 in 1850; by 1860, his total rose to $40,000 in real estate and $48,000 in personal estate. Chairmakers owned lots of chairs. The price of such factory-made household furnishings as chairs had dropped, often the result of the work of industrial workers in manufacturing; other furniture forms remained rare or a worker might just have one. Caleb Young died in 1849 at the age of thirty-two with an estate of about $1,000. He owned six cane-seat chairs and a dozen wooden-seat chairs along with a clock, a looking glass, and a chest of drawers. Smyrna Glazier had died of consumption at the age of twenty-eight with only two hundred dollars

Fig. 107. Henry F. Darby, *The Reverend John Atwood and His Family,* Concord, New Hampshire, 1845. Oil on canvas. 72-1/8 × 96-1/4 in. A provincial parlor with up-to-date furnishings. Inscriptions: Lower right: H. F. DARBY, Painter./1845. Museum of Fine Arts, Boston. Gift of Maxim Karolik for the M. and M. Karolik Collection of American Paintings, 1815–65. 62.269. Photograph © 2009 Museum of Fine Arts, Boston.

of inventoried wealth; he owned almost a dozen chairs, including two rocking chairs, and eight lamps, but not much more beyond kitchenware and bedding.[81]

Piety and prosperity were on display on a monumental scale similar to Erastus Field's *Joseph Moore and His Family* when the young Henry Darby painted *Reverend John Atwood and His Family* in their parlor (fig. 107). The artistic prodigy and the provincial pastor collaborated in a celebration of the new middle-class parlor culture in painstaking detail. Atwood had served several churches in Maine and New Hampshire before advancing in 1843 to the prestigious positions of state treasurer and chaplain of the state prison in the state capital, Concord. Lydia Dodge had married John when he was the pastor of her hometown Baptist church; she is depicted amid her six children. Henry Darby, the painter, was born in 1829 in North Adams, Massachusetts, a son of a small cotton manufacturer. He recalled receiving his first box of watercolors at age five, but saw few pictures besides prints during his childhood, except for "two poor pastels at my Grandmother's." When an Irish portrait painter who also served as a writing master arrived in town when Darby was thirteen, he sought instruction from the itinerant on "how to begin a head." He practiced by painting acquaintances on any surface that could be found, such as cardboard, polished wood, and ivory. When he was only fourteen, a nearby family invited him to paint them, his first commission. As his "rude likenesses" improved, he fit up a room in his father's house and worked on "family pieces," often modeled on "some magazine print."

During the summer of 1845, Darby boarded with the Atwoods and painted the family for fifty dollars. He marked his name and date in large letters in the lower right of the canvas and identified himself as "painter"—a bold assertion for a youth of sixteen. The stern Atwoods are shown engrossed in their daily Bible study; at least five Bibles lie open in the life-sized painting, attesting to their piety. Two devotional pictures hang high on the wall: a hand-colored print of Samson and a mourning picture dedicated to their dead son. The Atwoods' prosperity is not neglected, however, with their up-to-date furnishings. The parlor is decorated with ornamented wallpapers, and the floor has a painted stenciled pattern. A piano, a staple of middle-class parlor life, graces the back wall, as a richly painted brown drapery flutters in the breeze. As in *The Moore Family*, children cluster around each of the two parents in a symmetrical arrangement around the table; a new type of oil-burning Argand lamp with a cut-glass prism sits on a crocheted mat. The center table with its circle of light heightens the sense of domesticity and devotion. Family members seem absorbed in introspective thought, perhaps an inadvertent result of the fact that Darby painted each at a separate time. Several of the pieces of furniture depicted, including the footstool, remained in the family's possession. Unlike Erastus Field who emphasized decorative color, Darby focused on forms—solid faces, clearly detailed objects—in a monochromatic scene. All the faces and all the features are chiseled in a hyper-realism that Darby and other painters adopted after the invention of the daguerreotype. Darby went on to partner with Mathew Brady on a series of portraits of famous Americans in New York City and Washington, D.C. In 1855, he recorded Brady's New York studio as his place of business. Often Darby would work from Brady's photograph, producing an "enhancement" of the image by adding his oils, but sharing the monochrome palette and precise detail. Darby was content to remain in the shadows as Brady received the lion's share of the credit.[82]

In the 1850s, with Brady leading the way, daguerreotypists constructed increasingly elaborate establishments for their customers that accompanied their own newly elevated personal status. The visitor entered the commercial parlor amidst "marble-cut columns . . . richly embroidered drapery, valuable pictures in elegant frames; rich carpets," and other carefully chosen furnishings, to be instructed in the proper domestic decor and behavior. The production of portraits was hidden from view. The entranceways, reception rooms, and other chambers were a spatial and object-coded method of exclusion, casting out of the heterogeneous "masses" and stabilizing the meaning of the portrait as a cultural commodity, not so much through the object itself, but by the context in which it was consumed (see fig. 99). Commercial daguerreotype parlors extended that tutorial in gentility by creating portrait galleries where not just sitters but all viewers encountered the images of respectable men and women and learned to identify correct representations of middle-class identity. In these ways, the middle-class aspirant became familiar with the vocabulary of parlor design and saw how the daguerreotype was essential to the creation of that comprehensive system of goods.[83]

The commodity produced by those entrepreneurs, the daguerreotype minia-ture, offered a special promise of controlling and patrolling cultural meaning. Ancestral family portraits had been imposing objects displayed by the elite at a time when almost everyone else's house was devoid of reproduced images. Instead of a life-sized painting, the image was only one-sixth of a plate, typically measuring two and three-quarters by three and a quarter inches and encased in a small covered box (plate 10). A viewer opening the case would find a swatch of turkey red calico from the young woman's dress alongside the hand-tinted colors of the sixth-plate daguerreotype.[84] While seeming to promise to bring the past back to life, the daguerreotype miniature, with its erasure of reproduction and its jewellike precision, offers the consumer a fantasy of control, a triumph over the natural forces of time and space. Portrait viewing became a private rather than a public experience.[85]

Daguerreotypist and consumer in the 1850s sought stratagems to secure membership in a new middle-class social order. What Arthur described as a "household treasure" was produced by commercial parlors and encased as a miniaturized and privatized memento of family ancestry, procured in a market-place where increasingly exclusionary rules of production, distribution, and consumption were set in place.[86]

Middle-class consumers followed the lead of commercial parlor makers and created the whole—the parlor, or "Daguerreian Gallery," as T. S. Arthur called it—out of the parts, the affordable and miniaturized mass-produced goods: daguerreotypes, shelf clocks, Hitchcock chairs, and popular books. Each com-modity took its meaning from the ensemble, the overall system of goods, rather than from any individual object. The system of objects, as developed by Jean Baudrillard, offers insights about the transformation of the social meaning of objects. Family portraits, tall clocks, and other objects lost their individual value as they became repositioned in a new design totality. The parlor's universal code constructed social standing, but at a cost, the impoverishment of independence and value.[87]

The meanings of daguerreotypes and other parlor furnishings reinforced domesticity, abundance, artifice, and ultimately, cultural cohesion. Standardized, mass-marketed chairs, clocks, books, and pictures filled domestic interiors. This new abundance required some ordering principle, some visual schema to fix meaning. The middle-class aesthetic, beginning around 1840, Miles Orvell writes, became "a densely decorative style, an interior stuffed with things," whose significance came not from any individual object but from "the volume of things." Mark Twain satirically described one such country parlor:

> There was a clock on the mantelpiece, with a picture of a town painted on the bottom half of the glass front, and a round place in the middle of it for the sun, and you could see the pendulum swinging behind it. . . . Well, there was a big outlandish parrot on each side of the clock, made out of something like chalk and painted up gaudy. . . . On a table in the middle of the room was a kind of lovely crockery basket that had apples and oranges and peaches and grapes piled up in it which was much redder and yellower and prettier than real ones is, but they warn't real because you could see where pieces had got chipped off and showed the white chalk or whatever it was, underneath. . . . There were a Hymn Book, and a lot of other books. And there was nice split-bottom chairs. . . . They had pictures hung on the walls.[88]

Family portraits took their places in vividly decorated spaces. The aesthetic of artifice complemented that of abundance. Imitative graining or stenciling had existed before, as seen in *The Joseph Moore Family*, but it had been occasional. At mid-century, the practice became systemic, as imitation became the foundation of middle-class culture.

These developments in domestic decor took place as part of a long process of the commercialization of rural crafts and the growth of rural consumerism. The connections between technological innovation, patterns of itinerancy, and rural consumerism facilitated the emergence of a new industrial order in the rural North during the first half of the nineteenth century. In the early decades, the rural design aesthetic, with its exuberant and colorful motifs, had been fashioned out of local materials and manufactured by country craftsmen for rural customers. Miniaturization and artifice constituted a new cultural order that sharply set off its middle-class claimants.

Ironically, the Victorian parlor with its urban manufactured goods and its codified cultural rules excluded many of the enterprising artisans and eager farmers who had participated in that rural revolution. The flow and direction of cultural change shifted direction by mid-century. For every James Ryder who successfully transformed himself from village daguerreotypist to city business-man, there were many L. C. Champneys or John Tooles who did not make it. Rural families like the Dotys and Beals became dependent on advertisers, urban tastemakers, and other outside authorities for their design decisions. Once sin-gular objects lost their unique stature and became mere elements of a standard-ized and commodified design vocabulary.

Epilogue

The path of our artisan-entrepreneurs and consumers through provincial America was a rocky and risky road. For every Chester Harding or Silas Felton who fled the farm for the more enticing prospect of selling cultural commodities or consumer goods, others stayed in the hinterlands for their entire lives; some trained their sights on an urban studio. At the community level, our "tale of two cities"—Sterling and Gardner—shows how early nineteenth-century towns became commercial centers or even manufacturing sites for a generation, with a village newspaper and a cluster of shops, including a slew of furniture ware-rooms displaying a wealth of newly fashionable and "fancy" goods. The number of "refined" rural residents skyrocketed, as families purchased cheaper clocks and parlor furniture to fill their "best room," even as consumers like the Bixbys left a bed in their new parlors and kept alive some of their older customs in the new era of abundance.

Coming of age after the War for Independence, this generation of Americans had experienced a unique passage. They had grown up in a world of scarce goods and had witnessed, indeed made possible, a new world of abundant commodities and colorful household interiors. The innovative ways of provincial manufacture often had come about from a chance encounter on the road with "one of the primitive sort" or a particular invention made by an artisan in a small village shop. However, all told, the collective work of these provincial manufacturers and consumers did bring about a new configuration of industry and consumption in the middle of the nineteenth century.

The widespread decentralization of the village "Franklins" like Felton or the ranks of the numerous Sterling and Walpole entrepreneurs gave way to an increasing consolidation of cultural production and prestige, clustered around urban stations. A codified parlor vocabulary took shape from the dictates of urban tastemakers, such as *Godey's Lady's Book* periodical or Henkel's Furniture Wareroom in Philadelphia. Inveterate itinerants found the countryside to be a less hospitable terrain for their enterprise and moved to the city. The direction of cultural innovation changed. Many of the enterprising artisans and provincial families whose grassroots activity had brought vitality to the village center and promoted rural innovation now found themselves excluded from fully participating in the new abundance of the Victorian parlor. The imposing scale of provincial design also shifted; once such singular household commodities as tall clocks or family portraits were reduced in size and significance by industrial techniques and codified cultural rules, household goods, such as daguerreotypes and parlor suites, filled the domestic interior.

The social and cultural fluidity of the early nineteenth century had dissolved the hierarchical pre-Revolutionary social world of the Devotion family, with its vertical integration and reciprocal obligations. Now a new hierarchy developed, one marked by an emerging structure of social classes and characterized by a cultural separation between groups. This suggests a model of change whereby stability undergoes change and then fluidity is followed by rigidity, developments that can be traced in the paths of some artisan-entrepreneurs featured in previous chapters.

Chauncey Jerome was among the founding generation of clockmakers—those who had made the critical manufacturing and marketing innovations to bring about the mass production of clocks for the domestic interior. His successful production of a cheap, mass-marketed brass-movement clock set the course for the clock industry for the rest of the century; but he did not enjoy the fruits of that vision. The financial position of his Jerome Manufacturing Company, the largest in the clock industry, was insecure; the firm was overextended and undercapitalized. Jerome had served a year as mayor of New Haven and was less involved in company management. When the famous showman P. T. Barnum, who had become involved in the clockmaking industry by forming the Terry & Barnum Manufacturing Company, approached S. B. Jerome, Chauncey's son, to merge the two firms, the promise of the prosperous Barnum to endorse notes for the Jerome firm seemed just the solution to their liquidity problems. The reverse turned out to be true. The Barnum Company had substantial liabilities that had been vastly understated. When these creditors appeared and the Jerome Company had to cover the debts, its position became more exposed. The firm failed in November 1855.[1]

Chauncey Jerome never recovered from this financial catastrophe. One of the founding generation of entrepreneurs whose expertise had carried clockmaking from the wooden-shop era to the new brass-clock factory was forced to operate within an industry ruled by capitalist financiers. Chauncey moved to Waterbury to supervise a casemaking department for the Benedict and Burnham partnership. A hurricane and snowstorm in 1857 sent the steeple of the Second Congregational Church tumbling into the Jeromes' apartment next door, but he and his wife were unharmed. That spring he moved to make clock cases for William Gilbert in Ansonia, Connecticut, based on a new style he had patented. The share in the business he had been promised never materialized, while Gilbert pasted Jerome's labels on his clocks to boost their sales. Only with difficulty did Jerome extract a bonus of $1,900 on English sales from "this miser." His precarious situation only got worse. Jerome invested all the money he had in the factory of Joseph Remer in Derby, Connecticut, where he carried on his work within the factory as a subcontractor. When Remer found out the aging manufacturer was out of cash, he refused to pay any of Jerome's bill and denied that any financial arrangement between the two existed. Jerome was penniless. Only a last-minute helping hand from a friend allowed him to move back to New Haven. He worked on his *History of the American Clock Business for the Past Sixty Years; and the Life of Chauncey Jerome*, published in 1860, an effort to settle scores and reconstitute his fortune. His activities for the next five years are shadowy, but in 1866, he became a superintendent of the United States Clock and Brass Manufacturing Company in Austin, Illinois. Several clocks have Jerome's labels pasted over the company's labels, showing that his name still sold clocks. There the biographer James Parton found him: "Chauncey Jerome . . . is now at the age of seventy-three, far from his home, without property, and working for wages. I saw him the other day, near Chicago, with his honorable gray hairs, and his still more honorable white apron, earning his living by faithful labor for others, after having had hundreds of men in factories of his own." This firm only lasted a year. Chauncey Jerome returned to New Haven where he died on 20 April 1868 at the age of seventy-four.[2]

Ebenezer Merriam and his two brothers, Dan and George, had set up a print shop in central Massachusetts in 1798. They faced some rough early days; their newspaper lasted only a short time, and several book-publishing ventures proved difficult. They kept afloat by printing psalm books, primers, and sermons—the staples of rural print shops. Eventually they found success by printing books for large urban publisher-booksellers and exchanging their own publications with them. Little cash changed hands, as in many transactions within rural communities. But credit relations and cashless exchanges were dying out as cash became the medium in publishing, like many other industries. The number of country printers, which had grown as print shops proliferated in country towns after the War for Independence, started to contract as urban publishers extended their control over an emerging national marketplace. Ebenezer held out until 1848, the last of the founding generation of Merriams to stay in the countryside, spending fifty years in Brookfield. His shop eventually folded as the economics of the book trade were transformed.[3]

The younger generation of Merriams and other printers did not abandon the trade but chose urban venues as the key to a successful career. George and Charles Merriam, two of Ebenezer's brother George's eight sons, left Brookfield in 1831 for the rising town of Springfield, Massachusetts, its population of almost seven thousand three times that of Brookfield. George had apprenticed with his uncle Ebenezer in Brookfield. After his apprenticeship, Charles worked in Philadelphia and Boston print offices. In 1831, he received an offer from Springfield's orthodox ministers to establish a newspaper to combat the Unitarian menace—similar to Ebenezer's invitation to set up shop in Brookfield over forty years earlier. The brothers visited Springfield and were convinced of its commercial promise. The new firm took the name G. C. Merriam and continued the familiar pattern of a provincial print shop, producing moderate runs of law books, Bibles, and schoolbooks. The younger brothers William and Homer went off to Greenfield, Massachusetts, the shire town of Franklin County, and then moved on to Troy, New York, a burgeoning industrial center, the nineteenth largest city in the United States in 1830.[4]

George and Charles Merriam did not continue in the old ways for long. They acquired the rights to Noah Webster's *American Dictionary of the English Language*, the monumental unabridged dictionary Webster had spent almost three decades compiling. Issued in two volumes, it sold for twenty dollars, well beyond the reach of a popular audience. He had not used stereotyping, a metal plate cast from a mold of the type, because of his penchant for constant revisions. His heirs sold the unbound sheets of the 1841 edition to an Amherst firm that resold them to G. and C. Merriam at a profit. The brothers also engaged from the Webster heirs what proved to be far more valuable—the rights to publish revisions. The Merriams quickly published a cheaper enlarged edition in one volume. Chauncey Goodrich of Yale did the revisions, the Merriams stereotyped it, and the volume sold for six dollars. Webster's heirs thought such a low price foolish. But the Merriams were proven right, and the heirs received more than $250,000 in royalties over the next twenty-five years. *An American Dictionary of the English Language (New Revised Edition)* was an instant success, selling well enough to become a common household possession. Mason Weems's vision of a popular market for cheap editions and Alexis de Tocqueville's idea of manufacturers producing larger volume at lower prices added up to stupendous profits in this emerging national market. The Merriams based their prosperity on extensive advertising and agents in the field; they had a knack for publicity and specialized in only one or two fields of print. In the "War of the Dictionaries," they bested Webster's former assistant, Samuel

Worcester, with their illustrated version and a long list of endorsements. They set to work on a completely new edition by Noah Porter that was published in 1864. The fortunes of the Springfield firm were linked to the popular and numerous editions and versions of the Webster and then the Merriam-Webster dictionary. The Merriams maintained their Springfield location, even as New York became the cultural capital of print by mid-century.[5]

New York City also captured Rufus Porter, that most inveterate of itinerant provincial artisan-entrepreneurs. He made his mark in the metropolis by founding the periodical *Scientific American* in 1845. Porter had continued to hawk his provincial profiles and portraits, with wall murals taking on greater importance in the 1820s and 1830s. Inventing increasingly alternated with his painting career. His obituary in *Scientific American* in 1884 only cataloged a few of those inventions: "a flying ship, an air blower, punching press, trip hammer, pocket lamp, pocket chair, fog whistle, wire cutter, engine lathe, clothes drier, grain weigher, camera obscura, spring pistol, engine cut off, balance valve, revolvidal boat, rotary plow, reaction wind wheel, portable house, paint mill, water lifter, odometer, thermo engine, rotary engine, and scores of other inventions." Portables preoccupied Porter, from his folding chair-cane to the "portable dwelling house, elegant, warm, and comfortable, and which can be constructed, painted and finished for less than $200." Time-saving conveniences and labor-saving devices also appealed to him, such as his 1838 corn sheller. Often when Porter had a new idea, he would dash off a drawing and then sell the whole or a share "for a small sum," only to move on to something else. In 1844, he devised a revolving rifle that he sold to Samuel Colt for one hundred dollars. Porter continued his promotional bent, seeing the future of the republic in mechanical devices and patents. For that purpose, he took on a new role as an editor and founder of artisans' periodicals, which required an urban station.[6]

Porter promoted his inventions through print and celebrated the contributions of the "American Mechanic." He came to New York to work as an electroplater, one of the new techniques that facilitated larger runs and cheaper prices for the publishing industry. In 1841, he took an interest in the *New York Mechanic*, the first scientific newspaper in the United States. Porter's most famous and long-lived venture was *Scientific American*, founded in 1845 with an initial investment of one hundred dollars. Both journals sought to inform the "American Mechanic," featuring lists of patents and enthusiastic discussions of Porter's and other inventions, all with illustrations and diagrams. He celebrated the mechanic as "nature's nobleman" and "guardian of the institutions of his country." While his 1825 *Curious Arts* had emphasized rural recipes, easily copied, now Porter expanded his repertoire and added a tribute to the self-taught with a series titled "The Art of Painting." The series offered prescriptions for the use of stencils for outlining "houses, arbors, villages &c" and a penchant for drawing farms in his nine essays on "Landscape Painting on Walls," offering images of the agricultural prosperity of the northeastern United States to rural residents. He provided art instruction for the amateur that avoided an academic approach but introduced an appreciation of the American scene. Porter offered his instructions to enable readers "in the occasional employment" for their "own amusement or convenience," to benefit "ordinary practitioners in the art to attain higher improvements." After six months of his editorship, a "desire for a change" came over Porter, and he returned to New England and his inventions.[7]

Porter's airship became his idée fixe over his long career. He said the idea of flying came to him on the road in the 1820s, and he set out to work on the details. In 1834, he published his first plans for his "Travelling Balloon, or Flying Machine," a long, thin vessel kept aloft by hydrogen gas with a steam-driven propeller. Porter reprinted the plans in the 1840s, accompanied by articles about the practicality of traveling by air. When the discovery of gold in California gave an urgency to transcontinental travel, Porter authored *Aerial Navigation*, a sixteen-page booklet detailing the "practicability of traveling pleasantly and safely from New-York to California in three days" when clipper ships took three months. He constructed his first model in 1833, and larger working models followed in the 1840s, drawing favorable newspaper notices in Boston and New York. In 1853, he displayed a twenty-two-foot model in Washington, D.C., as he was petitioning the Senate for funds. Meanwhile, he launched an "Aerial Navigation Company" to sell shares of public stock and a newspaper called the *Aerial Reporter*. Funds proved difficult to attract, but the seventy-seven-year-old Porter was hopeful in 1869 when he announced plans in *Scientific American* for an aeroport for travel to Europe.

Porter spent his later years in factory towns and cities, until his death in West Haven in 1884. He made his mark in New York City, where many transplanted New Englanders flocked at mid-century, but from that urban venue, he published his tribute to the "flourishing villages" of New England that had given birth to an "air of independence" and innovation:

They are not like many towns in other parts of the country, in which a herd of people from various nations huddle together, without any other apparent occasion but to live on the breath of society; neither are they constituted by the proud mansions of retired aristocrats; but they are supported by cheerful and liberal industry, being constituted by the union of agricultural and manufacturing interest, concentrated by facilities of transportation, and cemented by education and temperance. The houses are comparatively new, in moderately elegant style, well painted and arranged in tasteful order. The surrounding well cultivated fields, and the hum of machinery in the mills, equally proclaim independence and plenty, all are independent and cheerful . . . even the operatives of the factories and work-shops, when proceeding to their houses for their stated meals exhibit an air of independence.[8]

Porter had learned his itinerant and innovative ways along the roads and villages of New England.

Erastus Salisbury Field undertook the greatest artistic journey of his long career after he returned to his hometown in rural New England. He left portrait painting behind and assumed the mantle of visionary by using the new image-making technology of photography while relying on historical and personal themes for his inspiration. After the completion of his provincial masterpiece *Joseph Moore and His Family*, Field spent a seven-year stint in New York City. There, "Erastus Salisbury, portrait painter" occupied a studio in Greenwich Village, perhaps drawn by the desire to acquire an expertise in daguerreotypy, the new technology that his mentor Samuel Morse had brought back from Paris, and perhaps also motivated by a decline in provincial portrait commissions. He exhibited some of his portraits and new landscapes at the annual American Exhibition at Niblo's Garden and changed his directory listing to "artist," foreshadowing his turn from portraying the faces of his provincial neighbors to painting imagined historical and biblical scenes.[9]

Field returned to western Massachusetts in 1847, according to family reminiscences, to help with his father's farm. He brought along his photographic apparatus that served as the basis for his remaining portrait work, along with his aspirations to express a more personal artistic vision. He occupied a single-story yellow cottage in the Plumtrees section of the town of Sunderland, living there by the generosity of the Hubbard family whose portraits he had painted as children. He used the camera as the source for all his portrait work, posing his subjects and then enlarging the images in color on canvases. Victorian settings now dominated his sitters' faces. An ambrotype of Field, probably colored by him, shows the artist circa 1853. He still ventured afield occasionally. In the winter of 1855, he boarded with the North Amherst family of William Henry Smith, a very similar situation to his 1839 Moore commission (fig. 108). The artist was a longtime friend of the family; he had painted the parents fifteen years before. But the result was quite different from the *Joseph Moore Family*:

Fig. 108. Erastus Salisbury Field, *The Smith Family*, probably North Amherst, Massachusetts, ca. 1865. Oil on canvas. 36 × 47 in. Abby Aldrich Rockefeller Folk Art Museum, The Colonial Williamsburg Foundation, Virginia. Gift of Mrs. Carl C. Mullen.

the assembled figures, captured individually by Field's photographs, are brought together in an awkward composition, figures lost in space, overwhelmed by their surroundings, in a decor dominated by its upholstered Victorian sofa and pink draperies, the height of middle-class elegance. The family members do not engage but rather look outward, a sign of Field's novel method and a new middle-class individualism.[10]

With the death of his wife in 1859, Field increasingly retreated to a hut dug out of a hillside, working every day in his two-room studio lined with scrap lumber. There Field concentrated on his historical and religious painting, withdrawing from depictions of the contemporary world that no longer needed his portraiture services. The Garden of Eden was a familiar theme, used in popular prints, along with the plagues of Egypt, or exotic places far away from Plumtrees, such as the Taj Mahal, which he painted three times in oil and drew twice, a tomb popularized by President Ulysses Grant's visit to India (which also drew his attention).[11]

What absorbed Field most during the decades after the Civil War was his retrospective *The Historical Monument of the American Republic*, a project that he began in 1867. On a huge canvas, Field set out his "grand historical an[d] allegorical picture twelve feet long and nine wide, representing the country's history and the landing of the Pilgrims to the death of Lincoln," with an announcement in the *Hampshire Gazette* of his intention to exhibit it throughout the nation along with an "explanatory lecture," following the example of panoramas and other educational traveling exhibits. Field took on some academic models, such as his mentor Samuel Morse's *House of Representatives*, the images of John Trumbull's *The Death of General Warren at the Battle of Bunker Hill*, and Benjamin West's *William Penn's Treaty with the Indians in 1683*, that appeared as bas-reliefs on Field's towers. The artist fashioned eight towers, with two more in 1888, and added an exhibition hall with hopes of exhibiting at the Philadelphia Centennial Exposition in 1876. Lincoln appeared several times, once on the central tower with his assassination and transport to heaven. The artist celebrated the survival of the republic and the union, not in the era's usual self-congratulatory form, art historian Paul Staiti has written, but with a visual sermon rooted in the historical understanding and regional ideology of the early nineteenth century. Field pulled these anachronistic pieces into a coherent social vision. The canvas, forgotten like many of his fellow artisans' works, was found rolled up in a pigsty in the 1940s.[12]

When Erastus Salisbury Field died in the opening year of the twentieth century, a local journal celebrated his achievement in an article titled "Old Folks of the Country": "Although Mr. Field was an all-around painter of the old school, his work which had been most highly appreciated is that of portrait-painting—his likenesses of people of past generation are as nearly correct as can well be made in oil, and give to posterity faithful ideas of the personal appearance of their ancestors."[13] Field and "the Primitive Sort" of artisan-painter had constructed a new industrial order and sanctioned a new cultural code of consumption that changed the face of rural America. Artisans and consumers had worked long and hard plying their trade in the provincial regions of nineteenth-century America.

Notes

PREFACE

1. Sumpter Priddy, *American Fancy: Exuberance in the Arts, 1790–1840* (Milwaukee, 2004).

2. Richard Bushman, *The Refinement of America: Persons, Houses, Cities* (New York, 1992); Cary Carson, "The Consumer Revolution in Colonial British America: Why Demand?" in *Of Consuming Interests: The Style of Life in the Eighteenth Century,* ed. Cary Carson, Ronald Hoffman, and Peter J. Albert (Charlottesville, 1994); Gordon Wood, *The Radicalism of the American Revolution* (New York, 1992).

3. See Joyce Oldham Appleby, *Inheriting the Revolution: The First Generation of Americans* (Cambridge, Mass., 2000) for such a cohort-based discussion.

4. Jack Larkin, "The Faces of Change: Images of Self and Society in New England, 1790–1850," in *Meet Your Neighbors: New England Portraits, Painters, and Society, 1790–1850,* ed. Caroline Sloat (Sturbridge, Mass., 1992), 11.

5. Laurel Thatcher Ulrich, *The Age of Homespun: Objects and Stories in the Creation of an American Myth* (New York, 2001); Bernard L. Herman, *Town House: Architecture and Material Life in the Early American City, 1780–1830* (Chapel Hill, 2005); also see the recent study by Ann Smart Martin, *Buying into the World of Goods: Early Consumers in Backcountry Virginia* (Baltimore, 2008).

6. John Styles, *The Dress of the People: Everyday Fashion in Eighteenth-Century England* (New Haven, 2007), 16; John Styles and Amanda Vickery, "Introduction," in *Gender, Taste, and Material Culture in Britain and North America, 1700–1830* (New Haven, 2006), 22

7. Michael Baxandall, *Painting and Experience in Fifteenth Century Italy: A Primer in the Social History of Pictorial Style* (Oxford, U.K., 1972), 152; Michael Baxandall, *The Limewood Sculptors of Renaissance Germany* (New Haven, 1980).

8. Michael Ettema, "History, Nostalgia, and American Furniture," *Winterthur Portfolio* 17 (1982): 135–44.

9. Styles and Vickery, *Gender, Taste, and Material Culture,* 20; also see Philip Zea, "A Revolution in Taste: Furniture Design in the American Backcountry," *Antiques* 159 (January 2001): 186–95.

CHAPTER 1. PAINTERS AND PATRONS

1. Ebenezer Devotion, Sr.'s Probate Inventory (Windham Probate District 1107, Connecticut State Library, Hartford) has been transcribed and published by Robert F. Trent and Nancy L. Wilson, in "New London County Joined Chairs, 1720–1790," *Connecticut Historical*

Society Bulletin 50 (Fall 1985): 191–95. The New London Historical Society in Connecticut owns an account book in which Judge Ebenezer Devotion recorded his furniture purchases. See also the essays in *The Devotion Family: The Lives and Possessions of Three Generations in Eighteenth-Century Connecticut,* ed. Lance Mayer and Gay Myers (New London, Conn., 1991).

2. See Richard Bushman, *Refinement of America: Persons, Houses, Cities* (New York: Knopf, 1992), xii; Christopher Clark, *The Roots of Rural Capitalism: Western Massachusetts, 1780–1850* (Ithaca, N.Y, 1990), 91–100; Carole Shammas, *The Pre-Industrial Consumer in England and America* (New York, 1990); and John Brewer and Roy Porter, eds., *Consumption and the World of Goods* (New York, 1993).

3. Neil McKendrick, "Introduction" and "Josiah Wedgwood and the Commercialization of the Potteries," in *The Birth of a Consumer Society: The Commercialization of Eighteenth-Century England,* ed. Neil McKendrick, J. H. Plumb, and John Brewer (London, 1982), 1–8, 100–145; and T. H. Breen, "An Empire of Goods: The Anglicanization of Colonial America, 1690–1776," *Journal of British Studies* 25 (October 1986): 267–99. Also see Jean-Christophe Agnew, "Coming Up for Air: Consumer Culture in Historical Perspective," in *Consumption and the World of Goods,* ed. Brewer and Porter, 19–39.

4. Shammas, *Pre-Industrial Consumer*; Lois Green Carr and Lorena S. Walsh, "Changing Lifestyles and Consumer Behavior in the Colonial Chesapeake," in *Of Consuming Interests: The Style of Life in the Eighteenth Century,* ed. Gary Carson, Ronald Hoffman, and Peter J. Albert (Charlottesville, 1994), 59–166; Gloria L. Main and Jackson T. Main, "Economic Growth and the Standard of Living in Southern New England, 1740–1774," *Journal of Economic History* 48 (March 1988): 27–46.

5. Maxine Berg, *Luxury and Pleasure in Eighteenth-Century Britain* (New York: Oxford University Press, 2005), ix; John Styles, "What Was New?" in Michael Snodin and John Styles, *Design and the Decorative Arts: Britain 1500–1900* (London, 2001), 281–307. See Gary Carson, "The Consumer Revolution in Colonial British America: Why Demand?" in *Of Consuming Interests,* 483–697; and Bushman, *Refinement of America.*

6. Regarding the use of artisan-artist, Winthrop represented the important group of early American portraitists who painted on a variety of surfaces, coming out of the artisanal ranks. Bushman, *Refinement of America,* xii; Elizabeth Donaghy Garrett, *At Home: The American Family, 1750–1870* (New York, 1980), 47; Clark, *Roots of Rural Capitalism,* 91–100; Shammas, *Pre-Industrial Consumer*; Brewer and Porter, *Consumption and the World of Goods.*

7. Franklin Bowditch Dexter, *Biographical Sketches of the Graduates of Yale College,* 6 vols. (New York, 1907), 1: 451–53. See also Mark A. Noll, "Ebenezer Devotion: Religion and Society in Revolutionary Connecticut," *Church History* 45 (September 1976): 293–307.

8. Christopher Grasso, *A Speaking Aristocracy: Transforming Public Discourse in Eighteenth-Century Connecticut* (Chapel Hill, 1999), 9; David Daggett, *An Oration, Pronounced in the Brick Meeting-House, in the City of New Haven* (New Haven, 1787), 6; Richard D. Brown, *Knowledge Is Power: The Diffusion of Information in Early America, 1700–1865* (New York, 1989).

9. Ellen D. Larned, *The History of Windham County, Connecticut,* 2 vols. (Worcester: By the Author, 1880), 1: 278; and "Declaration against itinerant preachers, November, 1744," Connecticut Historical Society, Hartford, quoted by James Oliver Robertson and Janet C. Robertson, in "The Devotion Family in Eastern Connecticut," *Devotion Family,* 28; Noll, "Ebenezer Devotion," 301.

10. Carl Bridenbaugh, ed., *Gentleman's Progress: The Itinerarium of Dr. Alexander Hamilton, 1744* (Chapel Hill, 1948), 161.

11. Scotland, Connecticut, Brunswick Separate Records, 1746–1846, quoted in Noll, "Ebenezer Devotion," 296.

12. Ebenezer Devotion, *The Mutual Obligation upon Ministers, and People to Hear, and Speak the Word of GOD* (New London, 1750), 1, 10–11; Devotion Probate Inventory; Larned, *History of Windham County*, 54–55. See Devotion Probate Inventory for "1 Negro boy named Dick."

13. Grasso, *A Speaking Aristocracy*, 99.

14. Ebenezer Devotion, *The Examiner Examined; a Letter from a Gentlemen in Connecticut, to His Friend in London* (New London, 1766); William F. Willingham, "Windham, Connecticut: Profile of a Revolutionary Community, 1755–1818" (Ph.D. diss., University of Pennsylvania, 1972); Noll, "Ebenezer Devotion," 301, 305; Robertson and Robertson, "The Devotion Family," 30–31.

15. Books and Periodicals: Devotion Family Collection, Brookline Public Library, and Private Collection; Kevin J. Hayes, "Portraits of the Mind: Ebenezer Devotion and Ezra Stiles," *New England Quarterly* 70 (December 1997): 621–22; Devotion Probate Inventory; Brown, *Knowledge Is Power*, 73. See also Hugh Amory and David D. Hall, eds., *The Colonial Book in the Atlantic World*, vol. 1 of *A History of the Book in America* (New York, 2000).

16. Brown, *Knowledge Is Power,* 73; Robertson and Robertson, "The Devotion Family," 29.

17. For information on the Devotions' possessions, see Devotion Family Collection, Brookline Public Library; Mayer and Myers, "Bringing Together a Family's Past," in *Devotion Family*, 11–24; and Beverly J. Johnson, "The Material World of the Devotion Family," in *Devotion Family*, 45–59; Devotion Probate Inventory; Trent, "New London County Joined Chairs See also Beverly Jean Johnson, "Winthrop Chandler and the Rural Gentry of Northeastern Connecticut" (master's thesis, University of Delaware, Newark, 1990).

18. Trent, "New London County Joined Chairs," 27–29; Johnson, "Material World," 51.

19. Rodris Roth, "Tea-Drinking in Eighteenth-Century America: Its Etiquette and Equipage," in *Material Life in America, 1600–1860*, ed. Robert Blair St. George (Boston, 1988), 439–62; Johnson, "Material World," 47–49; Kevin Sweeney, "High-Style Vernacular: Life Styles of the Colonial Elite," in *Of Consuming Interests*, ed. Carson, Hoffman, and Albert, 8–10; Ann Smart Martin, "Tea Tables Overturned: Rituals of Power and Place in Colonial America," in *Furnishing the Eighteenth Century*, ed. Dena Goodman and Kathryn Norberg (New York, 2007), 169.

20. The best source for biographical and artistic information about Chandler is Nina [Fletcher] Little, "Winthrop Chandler, Limner of Windham County, Connecticut," *Art in America* 35 (April 1947): entire issue.

21. Little, "Chandler," 93–94; Richard H. Saunders and Ellen G. Miles, *American Colonial Portraits: 1700–1776* (Washington, D.C., 1987), 304.

22. *Diary and Autobiography of John Adams*, 16 January 1766, ed. Lyman H. Butterfield, 4 vols. (Cambridge, 1961), 1: 294, quoted by T. H. Breen, "The American and Consumer Revolutions of the Eighteenth Century," in *Of Consuming Interests*, 451–52.

23. Copley to Benjamin West or Captain R. G. Grace, 1767?, in Guernsey Jones, ed., *Letters and Papers of John Singleton Copley and Henry Pelham, 1739–1776* (Boston, 1914), 65–66; Paul Staiti, "Class and Character," *John Singleton Copley in America* (New York, 1995), 54; Susan Rather, "Carpenter, Tailor, Shoemaker, Artist: Copley and Portrait Painting around 1770," *Art Bulletin* 79 (June 1997): 275–85.

24. Carson, "Consumer Revolution in Colonial British America," in *Of Consuming Interests*, 523, 608–17.

25. Bushman, *Refinement of America*, 5–7.

26. W. T. Baxter, *The House of Hancock: Business in Boston, 1724–1775* (Cambridge, Mass., 1945), 188; Breen, "Empire of Goods"; Neal W. Allen, Jr., ed., *Province and Court Records of*

Maine, 6 vols. (Portland, Maine, 1975), 6: 72–76; Sweeney, "High-Style Vernacular," in *Of Consuming Interests*, 8–10.

27. Allen, *Records of Maine*, 6: 72–76; "An Act Against Hawkers, Pedlars, and Petty Chapman," *Acts and Laws, of Her Majesties Province of the Massachusetts-Bay in New England* (Boston, 1714), Chapter 7; Breen, "Empire of Goods," 467.

28. Bushman, *Refinement of America*, 17.

29. Bridenbaugh, ed., *Gentlemen's Progress*, 15–16.

30. Bushman, *Refinement of America*, 3–8.

31. Shammas, *Pre-Industrial Consumer*, 184; Carr and Walsh, "Changing Lifestyles and Consumer Behavior," 130–32; Bushman, *Refinement of America*, 75–77.

32. Charles Willson Peale to Rembrandt Peale, 28 October 1812, Peale Family Papers, microfiche IIA/51G2, quoted in Ellen Miles, "The Portrait in America, 1750–1776," in *American Colonial Portraits*, 38.

33. Philip Zea, "Rural Craftsmen and Design," in *New England Furniture: The Colonial Era*, ed. Brock Jobe and Myrna Kaye (Boston, 1984), 47–72; Brock Jobe, "Urban Craftsmen and Design," in *New England Furniture*, 9; Miles, "Portrait in America," 28–76.

34. Stephen Botein, "'Meer Mechanics' and an Open Press: The Business and Political Strategies of Colonial American Printers," *Perspectives in American History* 9 (1976): 152; Chris H. Bailey, *Two Hundred Years of American Clocks and Watches* (Englewood Cliffs, N.J., 1975), 46–47; Miles, "Portrait in America," 30–31.

35. Robert Blair St. George, *Conversing by Signs: Poetics of Implication in Colonial New England Culture* (Chapel Hill, 1998), 321.

36. Bruce Daniels, *The Connecticut Town* (Middletown, Conn., 1979), 148; Susan Geib, "'Changing Works': Agriculture and Society in Brookfield, Massachusetts, 1785–1820" (Ph.D. diss., Boston University, 1981), 137; James T. Lemon, *The Best Poor Man's Country* (Baltimore, 1972), 147; Clark, *Roots of Rural Capitalism*, 95–97; Zea, "Rural Craftsmen and Design."

37. Zea, "Rural Craftsmen and Design," 63–65; Ann W. Dibble, "Major John Dunlap: The Craftsman and His Community," *Old Time New England* 3–4 (Winter–Spring, 1978): 54–55; John Gaines II and Thomas Gaines I, Account Book, 1707–1761, Winterthur Museum Library, Winterthur, Del.; Robert E. T. Hendrick, "John Gaines II and Thomas Gaines I, 'Turners' of Ipswich, Massachusetts" (master's thesis, University of Delaware, 1964).

38. Jack Larkin, "The Merriams of Brookfield: Printing in the Economy and Culture of Rural Massachusetts in the Early Nineteenth Century," *Proceedings of the American Antiquarian Society*, 96 (April 1986): 42; see also Ann Smart Martin, *Buying into the World of Goods: Early Consumers in Backcountry Virginia* (Baltimore, 2008).

39. Bettye Hobbs Pruitt, "Self-Sufficiency and the Agricultural Economy of Eighteenth-Century Massachusetts," *WMQ* 41 (July 1984): 33–64; James A. Henretta, "Families and Farms: *Mentalité* in Pre-Industrial America," *WMQ* 35 (January 1978): 3–22; Daniel Vickers, "Competency and Competition: Economic Culture in Early America," *WMQ* 47 (January 1990): 3–29; Michael Merrill, "Putting 'Capitalism' in Its Place: A Review of Recent Literature," *WMQ* 52 (April 1995): 315–26; Clark, *Roots of Rural Capitalism*; Richard L. Bushman, "Family Security in the Transition from Farm to City, 1750–1850," *Journal of Family History* 6 (Fall 1981):238–56; Robert A. Gross, *The Minutemen and Their World* (New York, 1976); Allan Kulikoff, *Agrarian Origins of American Capitalism* (Charlottesville, 1992), and *From British Peasants to Colonial American Farmers* (Chapel Hill, 2000).

40. Charles F. Hummel, *With Hammer in Hand* (Charlottesville, 1968), 221.

41. Zea, "Rural Craftsmen and Design"; Edward S. Cooke, Jr., *Making Furniture in Preindustrial America: The Social Economy of Newtown and Woodbury, Connecticut* (Baltimore, 1996).

42. Botein, "'Meer Mechanics' and an Open Press," 152–54; Amory and Hall, *Colonial Book*, 163–67; see also Richard Sennett, *The Craftsmen* (New Haven, 2008).

43. William Hosley, Jr., "Timothy Loomis and the Economy of Joinery in Windsor, Connecticut, 1740–1786," in *Perspectives in American Furniture*, ed. Gerald Ward (New York, 1988), 127–51.

44. The woodworking shop has been reconstructed at the Winterthur Museum, and the placement of the tools determined by Historical American Buildings Survey conducted in 1940, with a molding plane rack, the tool racks, and a long ash pole with its support that powered the pole lathe; see Hummel, *With Hammer in Hand*, 7–13, with illustrations.

45. Hosley, Jr., "Timothy Loomis," 128–29.

46. Zea, "Rural Craftsmen and Design," 63–65; Philip Zea, *The Dunlaps and Their Furniture* (Manchester, N.H., 1970); Zea, *The Dunlap Cabinetmakers: A Tradition in Craftsmanship*, 1st ed. (Mechanicsburg, Pa., 1994).

47. Philip Zea and Robert Cheney, *Clock Making in New England, 1725–1825: An Interpretation of the Old Sturbridge Village Collection* (Sturbridge, Mass., 1992), 15–17.

48. David Pye, *The Nature and Art of Workmanship* (New York: Cambridge University Press, 1968), 4–5; Forman conversations referenced in Philip Zimmerman, "Workmanship as Evidence: A Model for Object Study," *Winterthur Portfolio* 16 (Winter 1981): 287; Cooke, *Making Furniture*, 35.

49. Zimmerman, "Workmanship as Evidence" 288; Cooke, *Making Furniture*, 13–32; Dibble, "Major John Dunlap," 54–55; Henretta, "Families and Farms," 3–22; and David Jaffee, "Artisan Entrepreneurs in Worcester County, Massachusetts," in *Rural New England Furniture : People, Place, and Production,* ed. Peter Benes (Boston, 2000), 100–119.

50. Bailey, *Two Hundred Years of American Clocks and Watches*, 63; Gerald W. R. Ward and William N. Hosley, Jr., eds., *The Great River: Art and Society of the Connecticut Valley, 1635–1820* (Hartford, Conn.:, 1985), 341, 345–46 (Youngs).

51. Zea and Cheney, *Clock Making in New England,* 23–24; Ward and Hosley, *Great River*, 349–50; Philip Zea, "Diversity and Regionalism in Rural New England Furniture," in *American Furniture 1995,* ed. Luke Beckerdite and William N. Hosley (Milwaukee, Wisc., 1995), 79–80; Bailey, *American Clocks and Watches*, 46–47.

52. Cooke, *Making Furniture*, 13–32; Zea, "Rural Craftsmen and Design," 47–72; Sweeney, "High-Style Vernacular"; Aileen Ribeiro, "'The Whole Art of Dress': Costume in the Work of John Singleton Copley," *John Singleton Copley in America*, 107–8.

53. John Chester to Joshua Huntington, 4 July 1769, "Huntington Papers: Correspondence of the Brothers Joshua and Jedediah Huntington During the Period of the American Revolution, 1771–1783," *Connecticut Historical Society Collections* 20 (1923): 159–60. Joshua was a distant relative of Felix Huntington; see Huntington Family Association, *The Huntington Family in America: A Genealogical Memoir of the Known Descendants of Simon Huntington from 1633 to 1915* (Hartford, Conn., 1915), 504, 627.

54. Livingston Letter Files, American Wing, Metropolitan Museum of Art, quoted by Morrison Heckscher and Leslie Bowman in *American Rococo, 1750–1775: Elegance in Ornament* (New York, 1995), 25; George O. Rogers, Jr., "Changes in Taste in the Eighteenth Century: A Shift from the Useful to the Ornamental," *Journal of Early Southern Decorative Arts* 8 (May 1982): 20; Sweeney, "High-Style Vernacular," 46–50.

55. Hugh Amory, "Reinventing the Colonial Book," in *Colonial Book*, 45; Isaiah Thomas, *The History of Printing in America*, 2 vols. (Worcester, 1810), 2:31.

56. James Raven, "The Importation of Books in the Eighteenth Century," in *Colonial Book*, 164; Botein, "'Meer Mechanics' and an Open Press."

57. Amory, "Reinventing the Colonial Book," 52; Isaiah Thomas quoted in Amory, *Colonial Book*, 51; David D. Hall, "The Atlantic Economy in the Eighteenth Century," in *Colonial Book*, 154; James Parker to Benjamin Franklin, 22 March 1765, *Franklin Papers*, 8: 86–91, quoted in Botein, "'Meer Mechanics' and an Open Press," 147.

58. Franklin to Hall, 18 April 1759, *Franklin Papers*, 8: 319, quoted in James N. Green, "Part One: English Books and Printing in the Age of Franklin, in *Colonial Book*, 272.

59. Elizabeth Carroll Reilly, "The Wages of Piety: The Boston Book Trade of Jeremy Condy," in *Printing and Society in Early America*, ed. William L. Joyce et al. (Worcester, Mass., 1983), 83–125, 112, 108; Bushman, *Refinement of America*, 36, 41–44; David D. Hall, "Learned Culture in the Eighteenth Century," in *Colonial Book*, 411–33.

60. Thomas, *History of Printing*, 1;369; Hugh Amory, "The New England Book Trade, 1713–1790," in *Colonial Book*, 335; Clifford K. Shipton, *Isaiah Thomas: Printer, Patriot, and Philanthropist, 1749–1831* (Rochester, N.Y., 1948), 3–43; Marcus McCorison, "Foreword," *The Press and the American Revolution*, ed. Bernard Bailyn and John B. Hench (Boston, 1981), 2–9.

61. Ezra Stiles, *The Literary Diary of Ezra Stiles*, 3 vols., ed. Franklin Bowditch Dexter (New York, 1901), 1: 33; Ebenezer Devotion, Jr., Account Book, cited by Robertson and Robertson, "The Devotion Family," 31–33; Willingham, "Windham, Connecticut," 91–92.

62. Judge Devotion to Dr. Waldo, quoted by Larned, in *History of Windham County*, 2: 186, 115–17; Dexter, *Biographical Sketches of Yale Graduates*, 2: 578–79; Willingham, "Windham, Connecticut," 179; correspondence between Ebenezer Devotion and Joshua Huntington, Huntington Papers, *Connecticut Historical Society Collections* 20 (1923): 52, 78, 215; Robertson and Robertson, "The Devotion Family," 32–34; Richard Buel, *Dear Liberty: Connecticut's Mobilization for the Revolutionary War* (New York, 1980).

63. Larned, *History of Windham County*, 2:230–31, 416; Devotion Family Collection, Brookline Public Library, and Private Collection; Dexter, *Biographical Sketches of Yale Graduates*, 2: 578–79; Robertson and Robertson, "The Devotion Family," 36–38; *Huntington Family in America*, 124, 627.

64. Little, "Chandler," 99–100; Robertson and Robertson, "The Devotion Family," 34.

65. Mayer and Myers, "A Family's Past," in *Devotion Family*, 20.

66. Mayer and Myers, "A Family's Past," 19–20, 27; Trent, "New London County Joined Chairs"; Devotion Probate Inventory.

67. Johnson, "Material World," 52–56; Nancy Coyne Evans, *American Windsor Chairs* (New York, 1996), 285–92, 302–4; Nancy E. Richards and Nancy Goyne Evans, *New England Furniture at Winterthur: Queen Anne and Chippendale Period* (Winterthur, Del., 1997), 84–86.

68. Zea and Cheney, *Clock Making in New England*, 106; Chris Bailey, "Thomas Harland of Norwich: Forerunner of the Clock Manufacturing Industry," *Connecticut Historical Society Bulletin* 51 (Fall 1986): 230–31.

69. Susan P. Schoelwer and Dawn Hutchins Bobryk, "A Craftsmen's Life: New Evidences on Eliphalet Chapin," in Thomas P. and Alice K. Kugelman, *Connecticut Valley Furniture: Eliphalet Chapin and His Contemporaries, 1750–1800*, ed. Susan P. Schoelwer (Hartford, Conn., 2005), 460–67; Heckscher and Bowman, *American Rococo*, 185, 214–16.

70. Hosley and Ward, *Great River*, 228–32; Joseph Lionetti and Robert F. Trent, "New Information About Chapin Chairs," *Antiques* 192 (May 1986): 1082–95; Richards and Evans, *New England Furniture at Winterthur*, 84–86; see also Susan P. Schoelwer, "Writings on Eliphalet Chapin: A Case Study in American Furniture History," in *Connecticut Valley Furniture*, 443–59.

71. Hosley and Ward, *Great River*, 229; Lionetti and Trent, "New Information About Chapin Chairs," 1084; Richards and Evans, *New England Furniture at Winterthur*, 84–86; Kugelman and Kugelman, *Connecticut Valley Furniture*, 133–36.

72. Deborah Chotner, *American Naive Paintings* (Washington, D.C, 1992), 63–65; Little, "Chandler," 113–14.

73. *Massachusetts Spy*, 19 August 1790; Little, "Chandler," 87–89.

74. Kevin Sweeney, "Mansion People: Kinship, Class, and Architecture in Western Massachusetts in the Mid–Eighteenth Century," *Winterthur Portfolio* 19 (Winter 1984): 221; Johnson, "Chandler and the Rural Gentry."

CHAPTER 2. THE VILLAGE ENLIGHTENMENT

1. For recent writing on reading and literary societies, see Mary Kelley, *Learning to Stand and Speak: Women, Education, and Public Life in America's Republic* (Chapel Hill, 2006).

2. *Silas Felton Biography, 1790–1801*, unbound journals-F, Manuscripts and Rare Books Collection, New York Public Library; reprinted in Silas Felton, "The Life or Biography of Silas Felton Written by Himself," ed. Rena L. Vassar, *Proceedings of the American Antiquarian Society* 69 (1959): 119–54; Charles Hudson, *History of the Town of Marlborough* (Boston, 1862), 266. Besides Felton's 1802 autobiography, the Felton Family Papers at the American Antiquarian Society contain Silas Felton's copybook with his speeches, letters, and other writings.

3. See J. M. Opal, *Beyond the Farm: National Ambitions in Rural New England* (Philadelphia, 2008).

4. Philip Zea, "Diversity and Regionalism in New England Furniture," in *American Furniture 1995*, ed. Luke Beckerdite and William N. Hosley (Milwaukee, 1995), 61–112.

5. Felton, "Life," 126.

6. Cyrus Felton, *A Genealogical History of the Felton Family* (Marlborough, Mass., 1886); Hudson, *History of Marlborough*; Jacob Felton Inventory, Felton Family Papers, 1750–1883; Opal, *Beyond the Farm*, 84.

7. Felton, "Life," 126–28; Jay Fliegelman, *Prodigals and Pilgrims: The American Revolution Against Patriarchal Authority, 1750–1800* (New York, 1982).

8. Felton, "Life," 128–29.

9. Felton, "Life," 130; Opal, *Beyond the Farm*, 85–86.

10. Cathy N. Davidson, *Revolution and the Word: The Rise of the Novel in America* (New York, 1986), 42; David Hall, "The Uses of Literacy in New England, 1600–1850," in *Printing and Society in Early America*, ed. William L. Joyce et al. (Worcester, Mass. 1983), 1–47; Opal, *Beyond the Farm*, 86.

11. Davidson, *Revolution*, 44.

12. Felton, "Life," 130–31.

13. Mary Kelley, ed., *The Power of Her Sympathy: The Autobiography and Journal of Catharine Maria Sedgwick* (Boston, 1993), 74; Mary Kelley, *Private Woman, Public Stage: Literary Domesticity in Nineteenth-Century America* (Chapel Hill, 1984).

14. Caroline Chester quoted in Lynne Templeton Brickley, "The Litchfield Female Academy," in *To Ornament Their Minds: Sarah Pierce's Litchfield Female Academy, 1792–1833*, ed. Catherine Keene Fields and Lisa C. Kightlinger (Litchfield, Conn., 1993), 45; Emily Noyes Vanderpoel, ed., *Chronicles of a Pioneer School from 1792–1833, Being the History of Miss Sarah Pierce and Her Litchfield School* (Cambridge, Mass., 1903), 150–60; Kelley, *Learning to Speak and Stand*, 156; Kelley, "Reading Women/Women Reading: The Making of Learned Women in Antebellum America," in *Reading Acts: U.S. Readers' Interactions with Literature, 1800–1950*, ed. Barbara Ryan and Amy Thomas (Knoxville, Tenn., 2002), 59.

15. Margaret Bayard Smith, "My Books," *Ladies Magazine* 4 (Sept. 1831): 404–5; Charlotte Sheldon Journal, 9 June 1796, in *American Women Writers to 1800*, ed. Sharon M. Harris (New York, 1996), 78; Catharine Maria Sedgwick, *Means and Ends, or Self-Training* (Boston, 1839), 247–49; Lucinda L. Damon-Bach, "To 'Act' and 'Transact': Redwood's Revisionary

Heroines," in *Catharine Maria Sedgwick: Critical Perspectives,* ed. Lucinda L. Damon-Basch and Victoria Clements (Boston, 2003), 58–59. Margaret Bayard Smith was a novelist as well as a diarist and letter writer; her husband, Samuel Harrison Smith of New Brunswick, New Jersey, was a longtime congressman, and her letters describing Washington life are in the Library of Congress.

16. E. Latimer, *Life and Thought, or, Cherished Memorials of the late Julia A. Parker* (Philadelphia, 1856), 62. See also Laura Hadley Mosley, *The Diaries of Julia Cowles: A Connecticut Record, 1797–1803* (New Haven, 1931); Caroline Cowles Richards, *Village Life in America* (New York, 1913); Eliza Southgate Bowne, *A Girl's Life Eighty Years Ago* (New York, 1887); Benjamin Wisner, ed., *Memoirs of the Late Mrs. Susan Huntington, of Boston, Mass.* (New York, 1829).

17. [Mrs. Rebecca Hammond Lord], *Miscellaneous Poems on Moral and Religious Subjects by a Lady* (Woodstock, Vt., 1820), 19–20; Catherine E. Kelly, "Between Town and Country: New England Women and the Creation of a Provincial Middle Class, 1820–1860" (Ph.D. diss., University of Rochester, 1992), 359–61; Catherine Kelly, *In the New England Fashion: Reshaping Women's Lives in the Nineteenth Century* (Ithaca, N.Y., 2002).

18. Steven Watts, *The Republic Reborn: War and the Making of Liberal America, 1790–1820* (Baltimore, 1987); Fliegelman, *Prodigals and Pilgrims.*

19. Gordon Wood, *The Radicalism of the American Revolution* (New York, 1992), 271–76.

20. Solomon Sibley, Account Book, 1793–1840, Ms., Old Sturbridge Village Research Library (hereafter referred to as OSV Library); Zea, "Rural Craftsmen and Design" 57–58; Christopher Clark, *The Roots of Rural Capitalism: Western Massachusetts, 1780–1860* (Ithaca, N.Y., 1990), 99; Daniel Vickers, *Farmers and Fishermen: Two Centuries of Work in Essex County, Massachusetts, 1630–1850* (Chapel Hill, 1994), 314.

21. Charles Grier Sellers, *The Market Revolution: Jacksonian America, 1815–1846* (New York, 1991).

22. Clark, *Roots of Rural Capitalism,* 61–62; Robert A. Gross, "Culture and Cultivation: Agriculture and Society in Thoreau's Concord," *Journal of American History* 69 (June 1982): 56.

23. Joseph Hasmer, "Concord in Ye Olden Time," 1889, Adams Tolman Newspaper Scrapbook Collection, Concord Free Public Library, quoted in Gross, "Culture and Cultivation," 49–50.

24. Zadock Thompson, *History of Vermont, Natural, Civil, and Statistical: In Three Parts* (Burlington, Vt., 1853), 213–14; Wood, *Radicalism of the American Revolution,* 300; Bushman, *Refinement of America*; David Jaffee, "Peddlers of Progress and the Transformation of the Rural North, 1760–1860," *Journal of American History* 78 (September 1991): 517–35.

25. Priscilla Robertson, *Lewis Farm: A New England Saga* (Norwood, Mass., 1952), 34; Louise Hall Tharp, "Bonnet Girls," *New England Galaxy* (Spring 1960): 5, cited by Caroline Sloat, "'A Great Help to Many Families': Straw Braiding in Massachusetts Before 1825," in *House and Home,* ed. Peter Benes (Dublin, N.H, 1988), 90; Sarah Anna Emery, *Reminiscences of a Nonagenarian* (Newburyport, Mass., 1879), 61–62, 89–100; Gregory Nobles, "Rural Manufacture and Urban Markets: A Case Study of Broom-making in Nineteenth-Century Massachusetts," *Journal of the Early Republic* 4 (Autumn 1984): 287–308.

26. Leigh Keno, "The Windsor-chair Makers of Northampton, Massachusetts, 1790–1820," *Antiques* 117 (May 1980): 1,100–101, 107; Evans, *American Windsor Chairs,* 387–92.

27. Duane E. Ball, "Dynamics of Population and Wealth in Eighteenth-Century Chester County, Pennsylvania," *Journal of Interdisciplinary History* 6 (Spring 1976): 629; Paul Clemens and Lucy Simler, "Rural Labor and the Farm Household in Chester County, Pennsylvania, 1750–1820," in *Work and Labor in Early America,* ed. Stephen Innes (Princeton, 1988), 111; James T. Lemon, *The Best Poor Man's Country: A Geographical Study of Early Southeastern Pennsylvania* (Baltimore, Md., 1972), 227; Barry Alan Kessler, "Of Workshops and Ware-

rooms: The Economic and Geographical Transformation of Furniture Making in Chester County, Pennsylvania, 1780–1850" (master's thesis, University of Delaware, 1987).

28. Margaret Berwind Schiffer, *Furniture and Its Makers of Chester County, Pennsylvania* (Exton, Pa., 1978), 62–65.

29. Penrose Hoopes, *The Shop Records of Daniel Burnap, Clockmaker* (Hartford, Conn., 1958), 6; Chris H. Bailey, "Thomas Harland of Norwich: Forerunner of the Clock Manufacturing Industry," *Connecticut Historical Society Bulletin* 51 (Fall 1986): 227–47.

30. John Fitch, *The Autobiography of John Fitch*, ed. Frank D. Prager (Philadelphia, 1976), 34–43; William Rorabaugh, *The Craft Apprentice: From Franklin to the Machine Age in America* (New York, 1986), 10–11.

31. Norwich (Conn.) *Packet*, 9 December 1773, reprinted in Willard I. Willard, "Thomas Harland, Clockmaker, Watchmaker and Entrepreneur," *National Association of Watch and Clock Collectors Bulletin* (April 1995): 187; Silvio A. Bedini, "Thomas Harland of Norwich, Connecticut," *Professional Surveyor* (July–August 1991): 60; Bailey, "Thomas Harland of Norwich"; Penrose Hoopes, *Connecticut Clockmakers of the Eighteenth Century* (New York, 1930), 86; Francis Manwaring Caulkins, *History of Norwich, Connecticut* (Hartford, Conn., 1874), 608.

32. Hoopes, *Shop Records of Daniel Burnap*, 96; also, see Daniel Burnap, Account Books, 1786–1839, Connecticut Historical Society, Hartford, Conn.

33. Hoopes, *Shop Records of Daniel Burnap*, 9; Donald Fennimore, *Metalwork in Early America* (Winterthur, Del., 1996), 20.

34. George Eckhardt, *Pennsylvania Clocks and Clockmakers: An Epic of Early American Science, Industry, and Craftsmanship* (New York, 1955), 30–31; Hoopes, *Shop Records of Daniel Burnap*, 6.

35. Hoopes, *Shop Records of Daniel Burnap*, 44–52; Bailey, "Clocks and Watches," in Ward and Hosley, *Great River*, 342 Fennimore, *Metalwork in Early America*, 302; Thomson clock, illustrated in Ward and Hosley, *Great River*, 356–59.

36. Kenneth Zogry, *The Best the Country Affords: Vermont Furniture, 1765–1850* (Bennington, Vt., 1995), 107; Ward and Hosley, *Great River*, 361; Bailey, *American Clocks and Watches*, 68; Heckscher and Bowman, *American Rococo*, 68; Hoopes, *Shop Records of Daniel Burnap*, 24–28, 68.

37. Rorabaugh, *Craft Apprentice*, 35.

38. Carl F. Kaestle, *Pillars of the Republic: Common Schools and American Society, 1780–1860* (New York, 1983), 25; Carl F. Kaestle and Maris A. Vinovskis, *Education and Social Change in Nineteenth-Century Massachusetts* (New York, 1980).

39. Emory Washburn, *Brief Sketch of the History of the Leicester Academy* (Boston, 1855); 6–13. 54–56 *The Centenary of Leicester Academy held September 4, 1884* (Worcester, Mass., 1884). Claudius Herrick to Thomas Lewis, June 26, 1799, Deerfield Library, quoted in Suzanne Flynt, *Ornamental and Useful Accomplishments: Schoolgirl Education and Deerfield Academy, 1800–1830* (Deerfield, Mass., 1988), 12; Margaret A. Nash, *Women's Education in the United States, 1780–1840* (New York, 2005), 41; Jason Opal, "Exciting Emulation: Academies and the Transformation of the Rural North, 1780s–1820s," *Journal of American History* 91 (September 2004): 445–70; Penny L. Richards, "'Could I but Mark Out My Own Map of Life': Educated Women Embracing Cartography in the Nineteenth-Century American South," *Cartographica* 39 (Fall 2004): 1–17.

40. Kelley, "Reading Women/Women Reading," 59.

41. Litchfield and Tapping Reeve: Alain C. White, *The History of the Town of Litchfield, Connecticut 1720–1920* (Litchfield, Conn., 1920), 98–106.

42. Catherine Kelly, "Object Lessons: Miniature Worlds," *Common-Place* 3(2) (January

2003): available at http://www.historycooperative.org/journals/cp/vol-03/no-02/lessons/ (accessed 25 June 2009); Kelley, *Learning to Stand and Speak*, 28.

43. Lynne Templeton Brickley, "The Litchfield Female Academy," in *To Ornament Their Minds*, 22. Pierce to Sarah Pierce quoted in Richard Bushman, "Portraiture and Society in Late Eighteenth-Century Connecticut," in *Ralph Earl: The Face of the Young Republic*, ed. Elizabeth Kornhauser (New Haven, 1991), 69–84, quote on p. 77.

44. Lucy Sheldon journal quoted in Brickley, "The Litchfield Female Academy," 46, 54; Emily Noyes Vanderpoel, *Chronicles of a Pioneer School from 1792 to 1833: Being a Chronicle of Miss Sarah Pierce and Her Litchfield School*, ed. Elizabeth C. Barney Buel (Cambridge, Mass., 1903).

45. Edward Hitchcock, *Reminiscences of Amherst College, Historical, Scientific, Biographical, and Autobiographical* (Northampton, Mass., 1863), 282; George Sheldon, *A History of Deerfield, Massachusetts* (Deerfield, Mass., 1895–96)2: 827–28; Opal, "Exciting Emulation"; Records of Young Ladies Literary Society, 1813, Memorial Hall Digital Collections, available at http://memorialhall.mass.edu/collection/itempage.jsp?itemid + 876 1 (accessed 25 June 2009).

46. Felton, "Life," 130–34; David F. Allmendinger, Jr., *Paupers and Scholars: The Transformation of Student Life in Nineteenth-Century New England* (New York, 1975), 3.

47. Flynt, *Ornamental and Useful Accomplishments*, 28

48. Felton, "Life," 140–41.

49. Isaiah, Thomas, *The History of Printing in America*, 2 vols. (Worcester, 1810), 1:9; Richard Brown, "The Emergence of Urban Society in Rural Massachusetts, 1760–1820," *Journal of American History* 61 (June 1974): 43–44.

50. On Thomas, see George Lyman Kittredge, *The Old Farmer and His Almanack* (Cambridge, Mass., 1920), and Robb Sagendorph, ed., *The Old Farmer's Almanac Sampler* (New York, 1957). I use *The Farmer's Almanack* since that was Thomas's title after the first issue in 1792. Thomas presented his autobiography in several installments in *The Farmer's Almanack* from 1833 through 1839.

51. Thomas, "A Concise Memoir of the Author," *The Farmer's Almanack for 1835* (Boston, 1834), n.p.; *The Farmer's Almanack for 1833* (Boston, 1832), n.p.; Robert B. Thomas, "Preface," *The Farmer's Almanack . . . for . . . 1794* (Boston, [1793]), n.p.; Robert B. Thomas, "Farmer's Calendar" for December, *The Farmer's Almanac . . . for . . . 1793* (Boston, [1792]), n.p.; "Farmer's Calendar" for February, *The Farmer's Almanack . . . for . . . 1812* (Boston, [1811]), n.p.

52. Robert Thomas, *Robert B. Thomas, Has for Sale at his Book & Stationary Store, in Sterling . . .* (Leominster, Mass., 1796).

53. John Prentiss, "Autobiographical and Historical Recollections of Eighty-Eight Years," "Recollections," 18–19, John Prentiss Papers, 1795–1871, American Antiquarian Society, Worcester, Mass.; also, see David R. Proper, Keene, New Hampshire , Press, 1787–1876 (master's thesis, Simmons College, 1967); Cornelius Railey Lyle II, "New-Hampshire's 'Sentinel': The Editorial Life of John Prentiss, 1799–1846" (Ph.D. diss., Northwestern University, 1972).

54. Prentiss, "Recollections," 11–12, 18–19.

55. Jack Larkin, "The Merriams of Brookfield: Printing in the Economy and Culture of Rural Massachusetts in the Early Nineteenth Century," *Proceeding of the American Antiquarian Society* 96 (1986): 39–73; Homer Merriam, "My Father's History and Family," Merriam-Webster Papers, Beinecke Library, Yale University, typescript, OSV Library.

56. Prentiss, "Recollections," 11–12, 18–19.

57. Milton W. Hamilton, *The Country Printer: New York State, 1785–1830* (New York, 1936), 85–88; Phinney to William Cooper, 4 January 1796, quoted in James Fenimore Cooper, *The Legends and Traditions of a Northern County* (New York, 1921), 163; *Otsego Herald*, 1 May 1795; Levi Beardsley, *Reminiscences; Personal and Other Incidents* (New York, 1852), 63–66.

58. William J. Gilmore, *Reading Becomes a Necessity of Life: Material and Cultural Life in Rural New England, 1780–1835* (Knoxville, Tenn., 1989), 57.

59. Homer Merriam, "My Father's History and Family," Merriam-Webster Papers, Beinecke Library, Yale University, typescript, OSV Library; Larkin, "Merriams of Brookfield," 61.

60. Larkin, "Merriams of Brookfield," 61.

61. Kornhauser, *Ralph Earl*, 154–56; Robert St. George, *Conversing by Signs: Poetics of Implication in Colonial New England Culture* (Chapel Hill, 1998), 298–364.

62. Elizabeth Kornhauser, "'By Your Inimmitable Hand': Elijah Boardman's Patronage of Ralph Earl," *American Art Journal* 23 (1991): 8; Kornhauser, *Ralph Earl*, 156. See also William Sawitzky, *Connecticut Portraits by Ralph Earl 1751–1801* (New Haven, 1935); Margaretta M. Lovell, *Art in a Season of Revolution: Painters, Artisans, and Patrons in Early America* (Philadelphia, 2005), 2–6.

63. On merchants as "the central agents of social transformation in their communities," see Gregory Nobles, "The Rise of Merchants in Rural Market Towns: A Case Study of Eighteenth-Century Northampton, Massachusetts," *Journal of Social History* 24 (Fall 1990): 5–23, 6. See also Christopher Clark, "Taking Stock of the Nineteenth-Century Country Store," paper presented to the annual meeting of the Organization of American Historians, Minneapolis, Minn., April 1985 (in Jaffee's possession); Thomas Dublin, "Women and Outwork in a Nineteenth-Century New England Town: Fitzwilliam, New Hampshire, 1830–1850," in *The Countryside in the Age of Capitalist Transformation: Essays in the Social History of Rural America*, ed. Steven Hahn and Jonathan Prude (Chapel Hill, 1985), 51–70.

64. Kornhauser, "By Your Inimmitable Hand," 14.

65. Kornhauser, *Ralph Earl*, 23.

66. Ibid., 156.

67. St. George, *Conversing by Signs*, 300–302; Bushman, "Portraiture and Society."

68. William Lamson Warren, "Mary Way's Dressed Miniatures," *Antiques* (October 1992): 540–49; Catherine Kelly, "Object Lessons"; Ramsay MacMullen, *Sisters of the Brush: Their Family, Art, Lives and Letters, 1797–1833* (New Haven, 1997), 17–21.

69. Warren, "Mary Way's Dressed Miniatures," 544; On Holt's newspaper career, see Jeffrey L. Pasley, *"The Tyranny of Printers": Newspaper Politics in the Early American Republic* (Charlottesville, 2003), 134–47.

70. Chandler portrait of Jonathan Devotion, see Mayer and Myers, *Devotion Family*, 16; Anne Sue Hirshorn, "Anna Claypoole, Margaretta, and Sarah Miriam Peale: Modes of Accomplishment and Fortune," in *The Peale Family*, ed. Lillian B. Miller (New York, 1996), 228–29; Catherine Kelly, "Object Lessons."

71. Columbian, December 1811, quoted in Warren, "Mary Way's Dressed Miniatures," 544; MacMullen, *Sisters of the Brush*, 22–24; Robin Jaffee Frank, *Love and Loss: American Portrait and Mourning Miniatures* (New Haven, 2004), 199–204.

72. Eliza Champlain to George Champlain, 25 November 1820, in MacMullen, *Sisters of the Brush*, 161–62; Catherine Kelly, "Object Lessons"; Warren, "Mary Way's Dressed Miniatures," 544.

73. Bushman, "Portraiture and Society," 76–77, and Kornhauser, *Ralph Earl*, 44–45; Catherine Keene Fields and Lisa C. Kightlinger, *"Though Inanimate They Speak": Ralph Earl Portraits in the Collection of the Litchfield Historical Society* (Litchfield, Conn., 1990), 10–11.

74. Dan Huntington, *Memories, Counsels, and Reflections: by an Octogenary* (Cambridge, Mass., 1867), 55.

75. Thomas Collier, *Litchfield Monitor* (Litchfield, Conn.), 1784–1807, American Antiquarian Society, Worcester, Mass.; Silas Cheney, Ledger and Daybooks, 1799–1846, Litchfield

Historical Society, Litchfield, Conn; Ann Y. Smith, Town Histories," 14, and Deerin Bray, "Litchfield County Joiners," 18–22, in *To Please Any Taste: Litchfield County Furniture and Furniture Makers, 1780–1830,* ed. Edward S. Cooke, Jr., Ann Y. Smith, Derin Bray (Litchfield, Conn., 2008).

76. Bushman, "Portraiture and Society," 76; White, *The History of the Town of Litchfield,* 144; Brickley, "The Litchfield Female Academy," 22–23.

77. Kornhauser, *Ralph Earl;* 156; Samuel Orcutt, *History of the Towns of New Milford and Bridgewater, Connecticut, 1703–1882* (Hartford, Conn., 1882); Charlotte Goldthwaite, *Boardman Family Genealogy, 1525–1895* (Hartford, Conn., 1895), 331–32; John F. Schroeder, ed., *Memoir of the Life and Character of Mrs. Mary Anne Boardman* (New Haven, 1849), 397–99; Elijah Boardman Files, American Wing, Metropolitan Museum of Art, New York.

78. *Litchfield Weekly Monitor;* Kornhauser, *Ralph Earl,* 172; St. George, *Conversing by Signs.*

79. Elijah Boardman to Ralph Earl, 3 April 1795, Boardman Files, Metropolitan Museum of Art; reprinted in Kornhauser, "By Your Inimmitable Hand," 7; Advertisement, *Litchfield Weekly Monitor,* 18 May 1796, 3.

80. Kornhauser, *Ralph Earl,* 217; William I. Warren, "William Sprats, Master Joiner: Connecticut's Federalist Architect," *Connecticut Antiquarian* 9 (December 1957): 14–20; Boardman Files, Metropolitan Museum of Art; Smith, "Town Histories," *To Please Any Taste,* 14.

81. Kornhauser, *Ralph Earl,* 202–3; Stephen Kornhauser, "Ralph Earl's Working Methods and Materials," in *Ralph Earl,* 88–91; Orcutt, *History of New Milford and Bridgewater,* 300–302.

82. Franklin Bowditch Dexter, *Biographical Sketches of the Graduates of Yale College* (New York, 1907), 4: 52–54, 219–20. See Ralph Earl, *Mrs. Noah Smith and Family,* 1798 (Metropolitan Museum of Art), and the following: St. George, *Conversing by Signs,* 338; Smith, "Town Histories," *To Please Any Taste,* 12; Martin Bruckner, *The Geographic Revolution in Early America: Maps, Literacy & National Identity* (Chapel Hill, 2006), 122–23; Mrs. Noah Smith Portrait Files, American Wing, Metropolitan Museum of Art, New York.

83. Silas Felton, "Copy of the Constitution of the Social Enquirers" and "An Oration on the Happy Effects of *Social Enquiries,* delivered before the Society of Social Enquiries By Silas Felton," Silas Felton Notebook, Felton Family Papers, 1750–1883, American Antiquarian Society, Worcester, Mass.

84. Records of the Deerfield, Massachusetts, Young Ladies Literary Society, Pocumtuck Valley Memorial Society, Deerfield; digital records available at http://memorialhall.mass.edu/collection/itempage.jsp?itemid=8761 (accessed 25 June 2009); Kelley, *Learning to Stand and Speak,* 113.

85. Flynt, *Ornamental and Useful Accomplishments,* 28; Kelley, "Reading Women/Women Reading," 421; Rev. William Styles, *A Biographical Sketch of Mrs. Orra White Hitchcock* (Springfield, Mass., 1863), 4; Eugene Worman, "The Watercolors and Prints of Orra White Hitchcock," *A. B. Bookman's Weekly* 83 (13 February 1989): 646–68; Theresa A. Marchè, "Orra White Hitchcock: A Virtuous Woman," *Working Papers in Art Education* 10 (1991): 40–52; Suzanne Flynt, Christina Meade Cohen, Eugene C Worman, Daria D'Arienzo, and Robert Moorhead, *Orra White Hitchcock, 1796–1863* (Deerfield, Mass., 1992); Robert L. Herbert, ed., *A Woman of Amherst: The Travel Diaries of Orra White Hitchcock, 1847 and 1850* (New York, 2008); see Jordan D. Marché II and Theresa A. Marché, "A 'Distinct Contribution': Gender, Art, and Scientific Illustration in Antebellum America," *Knowledge and Society* 12 (2000): 77–106, for a discussion of Orra White Hitchcock and several other women illustrators.

86. Felton, "Constitution of the Social Enquirers" and "Oration on the Happy Effects of

Social Enquiries," Silas Felton Notebook; Hudson, *History of Marlborough*, 266–67; J. S. Wood, "Elaboration of a Settlement System: The New England Village in the Federal Period," *Journal of Historical Geography* 10 (October 1984): 331–56.

87. Felton, "Oration on the Happy Effects of *Social Enquiries*," 80–81; Felton Notebook, 127; Opal, *Beyond the Farm*, 161–64.

88. Jesse H. Shera, *Foundations of the Public Library: The Origins of the Public Library Movement in New England, 1629–1855* (Chicago, 1949), 61–62; Robert Gross, *Books and Libraries in Thoreau's Concord: Two Essays* (Worcester, Mass., 1988), 166; Brown, "Emergence of Urban Society." See Konstantin Dierks, "Middle-Class Formation in Eighteenth-Century North America," in *Class Matters: Early North America and the Atlantic World*, ed. Simon Middleton and Billy G. Smith (Philadelphia, 2008), 103.

89. Robert Darnton, "The High Enlightenment and the Low-Life of Literature," in Darnton, *Literary Underground of the Old Regime* (Cambridge, 1985), 1–40. I am indebted to Robert Gross for pointing out the implications of the French comparison.

CHAPTER 3. COSMOPOLITAN COMMUNITIES

1. Harold W. Haskins, "James Wilson—Globe Maker," *Vermont History* 27 (October 1959): 319–30; Leroy E. Kimball, "James Wilson of Vermont, America's First Globe Maker," *Proceedings of the American Antiquarian Society*, n.s. 48 (April 1938): 29–48; Kenneth Zogry, *The Best the Country Affords: Vermont Furniture, 1765–1850* (Bennington, Vt., 1995), 139; James Wilson: Collections Records, Bennington Museum, Bennington, Vermont; Wilson Family Papers, University of Vermont, Burlington, Vermont.

2. Silvio Bedini, *Thinkers and Tinkers* (New York, 1975), 379–80; Jerald E. Brown, *The Years of the Life of Samuel Lane, 1718–1806: A New Hampshire Man and His World* (Hanover, N.H., 2000), xxxviii.

3. David Jaffee, "The Village Enlightenment in New England," *WMQ* 47 (July 1990): 327–46.

4. *The Papers of Benjamin Franklin*, ed. Leonard W. Labarree, vol. 4 (New Haven: Yale University Press, 1961), 323, quoted in Margaret Beck Pritchard, "Maps as Objects of Material Culture," *Antiques* 159 (January 2001): 215.

5. Ann Leane, "The Construction and Conservation of Globes," and Gloria Clifton, "Globe Making in the British Isles," in *Globes at Greenwich*, ed. Elly Dekker (Oxford, U.K., 1999), 21–32, and 45–58; Elly Dekker and Peter van der Krogt, *Globes from the Western World* (London, 1993); also see T. K. McClintock Ltd., Conservation Report, Terrestrial Globe, James Wilson, 1810, 1 August 2001, Harvard Map Collection, Harvard College Library, Cambridge, Mass.

6. Denis Cosgrove, *Apollo's Eye: A Cartographic Genealogy of the Earth in the Western Imagination* (Baltimore, 2001), 188; Matthew Edney, "Reconsidering Enlightenment Geography and Map Making: Reconnaissance, Mapping, Archive," in *Geography and Enlightenment*, ed. David N. Livingstone and Charles W. J. Withers (Chicago, 1999), 165–98.

7. Haskins, "James Wilson—Globe Maker," 320–22; Kimball, "James Wilson of Vermont," 31–32; Zogry, *The Best the Country Affords*, 139; *Encyclopaedia Britannica, or a Dictionary of Arts, Sciences, Miscellaneous Literature, Constructed on a Plan, by which the Different Sciences and Arts are Digested into the form of Distinct Treatises or Systems*, 3rd ed. (Edinburgh, Scotland, 1788–1797), in Collection of the Bennington Museum; Richard Saunders and Virginia Westbrook, *Celebrating Vermont: Myths and Realities* (Middlebury, Vt., 1991), 126; James Wilson: Collections Records, Bennington Museum; Wilson Family Papers.

8. Wilson Family Papers; Kimball, "James Wilson of Vermont," 32–35.

9. See Martin Bruckner, *The Geographic Revolution in Early America: Maps, Literacy and National Identity* (Chapel Hill, 2006).

10. For such a map sampler see the Mary Franklin sampler: Betty Ring, *Girlhood Embroidery: American Samplers and Pictorial Needlework, 1650–1850* (New York, 1993), 2: 317. The Ruth Wright globe is discussed and illustrated by Martin Bruckner, "The Material Map: Lewis Evans and Cartographic Culture, 1750–1775," *Common-Place* 8 (April 2008); available at http://www.historycooperative.org/journals/cp/vol-08/no-03/lesson s/ (accessed 24 May 2009).

11. Judith Tyner, "The World in Silk: Embroidered Globes of Westtown School," *Map Collector* 74 (Spring 1996): 11–14; Helen G. Hole, *Westtown Through the Years, 1799–1842* (Westtown, Pa., 1942); Mary Jane Edmonds, *Samplers and Samplermakers: An American Schoolgirl Art, 1700–1850* (Los Angeles, 1991), 113; Ring, *Girlhood Embroidery*, 2: 388–95; Collections Records, Winterthur Museum, Winterthur, Del.; Samuel R. Gummere, *Definitions and Elementary Observations in Astronomy; also, Problems on the Globes* (Philadelphia, 1822).

12. Watson W. Dewees and Sarah B. Dewees, *History of Westtown Boarding School 1799–1942* (Westtown, Pa., 1942), 56, quoted in Margaret B. Schiffer, *Historical Needlework of Pennsylvania* (New York, 1968), 51.

13. Martin Bruckner, "Lessons in Geography: Maps, Spellers, and Other Grammars of Nationalism in the Early Republic," *American Quarterly* 51 (June 1999): 313; John Rennie Short, *Representing the Republic: Mapping the United States, 1600–1900* (New York, 2001), 9–79.

14. Deanne Levison and Harold Sack, "Identifying Regionalism in Sideboards: A Study of Documented Tapered-Leg Examples," *Antiques* 141 (May 1992): 820–33; Philip Zea, "The Emergence of Neoclassical Furniture Making in Rural Western Massachusetts," *Antiques* 142 (December 1992): 842–51; Zogry, *The Best the Country Affords*, 111; James Wilson: Collection Records, Bennington Museum; Edward S. Cooke, *Making Furniture in Preindustrial America: The Social Economy of Newtown and Woodbury, Connecticut* (Baltimore, 1996). For Vermont, see Janet Houghton, "Household Furnishings in Southern Vermont, 1780–1800" (master's thesis, University of Delaware, 1975).

15. William N. Hosley, "Architecture and Society of the Urban Frontier: Windsor, Vermont, in 1800," in *The Bay and the River: 1600–1900; The Dublin Seminar for New England Folklife*, ed. Peter Benes (Boston, 1982), 73–86; Hosley, "Architecture and Society of the Urban Frontier: Windsor, Vermont, 1798–1820" (master's thesis, University of Delaware, 1981), 10; Zogry, *The Best the Country Affords*, 98–99; Herbert Wheaton Congdon, *Old Vermont Houses, 1763–1850* (New York, 1940); also Congdon collection, Photographs, Special Collections, University of Vermont, Burlington; Henry Steele Wardner, *The Birthplace of Vermont: A History of Windsor to 1781* (New York, 1927); Timothy Dwight, *Travels in New England and New York*, ed. Barbara Solomon (Cambridge, Mass., 1969), 2: 69–70.

16. Kevin Sweeney, "High-Style Vernacular," 51; Wendy A. Cooper, *Classical Taste in America, 1800–1840* (New York, 1993).

17. Robert and James Adam, *The Works in Architecture of Robert and James Adam, Esquire*, vol. 1 (London, 1773), 3, quoted in Charles F. Montgomery, *American Furniture: The Federal Period, in the Henry Francis DuPont Winterthur Museum* (New York, 1966), 373.

18. Philip Zea, *Pursuing Refinement in Rural New England, 1750–1850* (Deerfield, Mass., 2000), 36–57; Levison and Sack, "Identifying Regionalism in Sideboards," 824–33; J. Michael Flanigan, *American Furniture from the Kaufman Collection* (Washington, D.C., 1986), 208.

19. Sweeney, "High-Style Vernacular," 46–50; Heckscher and Bowman, *American Rococo*.

20. Jonathan L. Fairbanks, *American Furniture, 1620 to the Present* (New York, 1981), 236–37.

21. John F. Page, *Litchfield County Furniture, 1730–1850* (Litchfield, Conn., 1969), 84–89; Silas E. Cheney, Ledgers and Daybooks, 1799–1846, microfilm, Joseph Downs Collection of Manuscripts and Printed Ephemera, Winterthur Museum and Library, Del.; Ann Y. Smith, "Furniture Characteristics," *To Please Any Taste*, 52, also see Sarah Pierce's Fancy chair illustrated on p. 53; Zea, *Pursuing Refinement*, 56.

22. Julius Barnard to Mills Olcott from 28 February 1801, Letter, Mills Olcott Paper, Dartmouth College Library, Hanover, N.H.; James D. Wing, "Mills Olcott and His Papers in the Dartmouth Archives," and Margaret Moody Stier, "Note," *Bulletin of the Dartmouth College Library* 22 (April 1982): 76–86; Windsor *Post-Boy*, 24 September 1805; Zogry, *The Best the Country Affords*, 99; William N. Hosley, Jr., "Vermont Furniture, 1790–1830," in *New England Furniture: Essays in Memory of Benno Forman*, ed. Brock Jobe (Boston, 1987), 245–86.

23. Ethan Allen Greenwood, Diaries, 1809, Ethan Allen Papers, 1801–1839, Manuscript Collection, American Antiquarian Society, Worcester, Mass.; Georgia B. Bumgardner, "The Early Career of Ethan Allen Greenwood," in *Itinerancy in New England and New York: Dublin Seminar for New England Folklife 1984*, ed. Peter Benes (Boston, 1986), 212–25.

24. Greenwood, Diaries, 1809; Bumgardner, "The Early Career of Ethan Allen Greenwood."

25. *Vermont Journal*, 17 March 1794; Zogry, *The Best the Country Affords*, 107; Hale Account Book, Windsor Public Library, Windsor, Vt.

26. Zea, *Pursuing Refinement*, 78; Zogry, *The Best the Country Affords*, 107–08; Lilian Carlisle, *Vermont Clock and Watchmakers, Silversmiths, and Jewelers, 1778–1878* (Burlington, Vt., 1985); Ward and Hosley, *Great River*, 349–51.

27. Philip Zea, "Clockmaking and Society at the River and the Bay: Jedidiah and Jabez Baldwin, 1790–1820," in Benes, *The Bay and the River*, 45–53; Charles S. Parsons, *New Hampshire Clocks and Clockmaking* (Exeter, N.H., 1976), 55, 100–101, 318–19; Jedediah Baldwin, Account Books and Daybooks, 1799–1809, Papers, Baker Library, Dartmouth College Library, Hanover, N.H.; Zea and Cheney, *Clock Making in New England*, 108–12. See also Charles Parsons, "Jedidiah Baldwin, Clockmaker & Silversmith when at Hanover, New Hampshire; and his nine volumes of Account Books, 1794–1810," 1987, typescript, Winterthur Library, Winterthur, Del.

28. Zea and Cheney, *Clock Making in New England*, 197; Nichols Goddard, Diary, 1795, Downs Collection, Winterthur Museum and Library, Winterthur, Del.; Dawn Hance, "Rutland's Early Clockmakers: Lord and Goddard," Rutland Historical Society Quarterly 26 (1996): 103–14; Zogry, *The Best the Country Affords*, 37; Zea and Cheney, *Clock Making in New England*, 107.

29. New Hampshire Historical Society (NHHS), *Plain and Elegant, Rich and Common: Documented New Hampshire Furniture, 1780–1880* (Concord, N.H., 1979): 124–27, 146; Margaret Moody, *American Decorative Arts at Dartmouth* (Hanover, N.H., 1981), 23; Zea, "Rural Craftsmen and Design," 77, 142–46 (George Bright).

30. Nancy E. Richards, et al., *New England Furniture at Winterthur: Queen Anne and Chippendale Periods* (Winterthur, Del., 1997), 379–81; Ward and Hosley, *Great River*, 256–67. The Amos Denison Allen chest is illustrated in John T. Kirk, *Connecticut Furniture: Seventeenth and Eighteenth Centuries* (Hartford, Conn., 1967), 40–41.

31. Easy Chair, in NHHS, *Plain and Elegant, Rich and Common*, 146; Collection Records, New Hampshire Historical Society, Concord, N.H.; Decorative Arts Photographic Collection, Winterthur Museum (DAPC), Winterthur, Del.; *Farmer's Weekly Museum*, 2 January 1798, 3 April 1798. Sturbridge Inventories, see Holly V. Izard, "Another Place in Time: The Material and Social Worlds of Sturbridge, Massachusetts, from Settlement to 1850" (Ph.D diss., Boston University, 1996), 147–52, 195.

32. Windsor, Vt., *Washingtonian*, 13 July 1812; Thomas Boynton, Account Books, 1811–1847, Baker Library, Dartmouth College, Hanover, N.H.; Zogry, *The Best the Country Can Afford*, 99–100.

33. *Vermont Republican and Statesman*, 23 and 30 March, 6 April 1818; Thomas Boynton, Account Books, 1811–1847, Baker Library, Dartmouth College, Hanover, N.H.; Hosley, "Vermont Furniture," 249–50; Charles A. Robinson, *Vermont Cabinetmakers and Chairmakers Before 1855: A Checklist* (Shelburne, Vt., 1994).

34. Joseph Dennie to Mary Green Dennie, Walpole, 26 April 1797, in *The Letters of Joseph Dennie*, ed. Laura G. Pedder (Orono, Maine, 1936), 158.

35. George Aldrich, *Walpole as It Was and as It Is* (Claremont, N.H., 1880), 79–83; Harold Milton Ellis, *Joseph Dennie and His Circle* (Austin, Tex., 1915); *Farmer's Weekly Museum*, 5 April 1796, 14 March 1797; Catherine O'Donnell Kaplan, *Men of Letters in the Early Republic: Cultivating Forms of Citizenship* (Chapel Hill, 2008), chapter 4; Michael T. Gilmore, "The Literature of the Revolutionary and Early National Periods," in *The Cambridge History of American Literature*, ed. Sacvan Bercovitch (New York, 1994), 1: 567–69; Joseph Dennie, "Advertisement," in *The Lay Preacher*, ed. Milton Ellis (New York, 1943), 3; Christopher Grasso, "Print, Poetry, and Politics: John Trumbull and the Transformation of Public Discourse in Revolutionary America," *Early American Literature* 30 (1995): 5–31.

36. Jeremiah Mason, *Memoirs and Correspondence of Jeremiah Mason*, ed. George Stillman Hillard (Cambridge, Mass., 1873), 29; Jaffee, "Village Enlightenment in New England"; Clark, *Roots of Rural Capitalism*, 59–117; Larkin, "Merriams of Brookfield; Wood, *Radicalism of the American Revolution*; Joseph Wood, "Elaboration of a Settlement System: The New England Village in the Federal Period," *Journal of Historical Geography* 10 (October 1984): 331–56; Brown, *Knowledge Is Power*.

37. John Lambert, *Travels Through Canada and the United States of North America* (London, 1813), 2: 497–98; Aldrich, *Walpole as It Was*, 97; Donna-Belle Garvin and James L. Garvin, *On the Road North of Boston: New Hampshire Taverns and Turnpikes, 1700–1900* (Concord, N.H., 1988), 84–92; Jeremy Belknap, *History of New-Hampshire* (Boston, 1792), 3: 61, 106; Dwight, *Travels in New England*, 4: 117.

38. Wood, "Elaboration of a Settlement System"; Fisher Ames quoted in Roger N. Parks, *Roads and Travel in New England, 1790–1840* (Sturbridge, Mass., 1966), 17; Frederic Wood, *The Turnpikes of New England and the Evolution of the Same through England, Virginia, and Maryland* (Boston, 1919), 215–48; Garvin and Garvin, *Road North of Boston*, 48–52; Martha McDanolds Frizzell, *A History of Walpole, New Hampshire* (Walpole, N.H., 1963), 1: 25, 34–35.

39. Aldrich, *Walpole as It Was*, 73; Garvin and Garvin, *Road North of Boston*, 55–56; Dwight, *Travels in New England*, 2: 62–64; Robert Fletcher and Jonathan P. Snow, "A History of the Development of Wooden Bridges," in *American Wooden Bridges* (New York, 1976); P. H. Gobie, *Bellows Falls and Vicinity of It* (Bellows Falls, Vt., 1912).

40. David Carlisle and Isaiah Thomas, Memorandum of Agreement, Feb. 12, 1798, Isaiah Thomas Papers, Account of Stock, 1798–1818, Walpole, Thomas Papes, American Antiquarian Society, Worcester, Mass.; Isaiah Thomas, *Catalogue of Books for Sale by Thomas and Thomas at Their Bookstore in Walpole* (Walpole, N.H., 1803); William J. Gilmore, *Reading Becomes a Necessity of Life: Material and Cultural Life in Rural New England, 1780–1835* (Knoxville, Tenn., 1989), 24, 59; Isaiah Thomas, *History of Printing*, 182.

41. Frizzell, *History of Walpole*, 19–21; Pedder, *Letters of Joseph Dennie*, 141–55.

42. Aldrich, *Walpole as It Was*, 81; Ellis, *Joseph Dennie and His Circle*, 9–83; Lawrence Buell, *New England Literary Culture from the Revolution Through the Renaissance* (New York, 1986), 26–27; Joseph Dennie, *The Farrago*, ed. Bruce Granger (Delmar, N.Y., 1985); Joseph Tinker Buckingham, *Specimens of Newspaper Literature, with Personal Memoirs, Anecdotes,*

and Reminiscences (Boston, 1852), 2: 99; Joseph Dennie, Papers 1783–1815, Houghton Library, Harvard University, Cambridge, Mass.

43. *Farmer's Weekly Museum*, 4 April, 24 July 1797; Kaplan, *Men of Letters,* 118–22; Ellis, *Joseph Dennie and His Circle*, 90–93.

44. *Farmer's Weekly Museum*, 16 September 1796, 27 July 1798; Linda K. Kerber, *Federalists in Dissent: Imagery and Ideology in Jeffersonian America* (Ithaca, N.Y, 1970), 78; Gilmore, "Revolutionary and Early National Periods," 558–72; Buell, *New England Literary Culture*; Lewis P. Simpson, "The Satiric Mode: The Early National Wits," in *The Comic Imagination in America*, ed. Louis D. Rubin (New Brunswick, N.J., 1973), 49–61; George L. Roth, "American Theory of Satire, 1790–1820," *American Literature* 29 (1958): 399–407; Roger B. Stein, "Royall Tyler and the Question of Our Speech," *New England Quarterly* 38 (December 1965): 454–74.

45. Mason, *Memoirs*, 28–32; *Farmer's Weekly Museum*, 24 April 1798; Joseph Dennie, *The Spirit of the Farmer's Museum, and Lay Preacher's Gazette* (Walpole, N.H., 1801); Marius Peladeau, ed., *The Verse of Royall Tyler* (Charlottesville, 1968); Marius Peladeau, ed. *The Prose of Royall Tyler* (Charlottesville, 1972); G. Thomas Tanselle, *Royall Tyler* (Cambridge, Mass., 1967); Ada Lou Carson and Harry Carson, *Royall Tyler* (Boston, Mass., 1979); Royall Tyler, *The Algerine Captive*, ed. Donald L. Cook (New Haven, 1970); Robert A. Gross, "The Confidence Man and the Preacher: The Cultural Politics of Shay's Rebellion," in *In Debt to Shay's: The Bicentennial of an Agrarian Rebellion*, ed. Robert Gross (Charlottesville, 1993), 316; Joseph Dennie, "Miscellany," *Port Folio*, n.s., 3 (25 April 1807): 259, and "Legal Character," *Port Folio*, n.s., 5 (20 April 1805): 112–13; Kerber, *Federalists in Dissent*, 13–17, 174–77.

46. *Farmer's Weekly Museum*, 16 August 1796, and 18 February, 11 April, 27 May 1799; Peladeau, *Verse of Royall Tyler*, 249; Gilmore, "Revolutionary and Early National Periods"; Kerber, *Federalists in Dissent*, 17.

47. *Farmer's Weekly Museum*, 19 July 1796; Kerber, *Federalists in Dissent*, 174–77; Buell, *New England Literary Culture*, 307–12; Cameron Nickels, *New England Humor: From the Revolutionary War to the Civil War* (Knoxville, Tenn., 1993), 48–50.

48. Hackmatack is a poplar tree.

49. *Farmer's Weekly Museum*, 20 August 1798; Nickels, *New England Humor*, 46–47; *Farmer's Weekly Museum*, 18 February 1797; Thomas Green Fessenden, *Original Poems* (Philadelphia, 1806), 130–39.

50. "A Town," *Farmer's Weekly Museum*, 15 March 1795 and 21 July 1797; Buell, *New England Literary Culture*, 312; Kaplan, *Men of Letters*, 129.

51. J. Kevin Graffagnino, *The Shaping of Vermont: From the Wilderness to the Centennial, 1749–1877* (Rutland, Vt., 1983), 103–4; *Windsor County Engravers, 1809–1860* (Montpelier, Vt., 1982); George R. Dalphin and Marcus A. McCorison, "Lewis Robinson—Entrepreneur," *Vermont History* 30 (October 1962): 297–313; Carl Taylor, Jr., "George White—Vermont's 'Unknown Artist,'" *Vermont History* 42 (Winter 1974): 3–11; Harold Goddard Rugg, "Isaac Eddy Printer–Engraver," *Bibliographical Essays: A Tribute to Wilberforce Eames* (Cambridge, Mass., 1924), 313–29.

52. Carrington Bowles, *New and Enlarged Catalogue of Accurate and Useful Maps, Plans, and Prints, of Various Sorts* (London, 1790), 32, quoted in Margaret Beck Pritchard, "Maps as Objects of Material Culture," *Antiques* 159 (January 2001): 212; Lester Jesse Cappon, "Geographers and Map-Makers, British and American, from about 1750–1789," *Proceedings of the American Antiquarian Society* 81 (October 1971): 243–71; David Bosse, "Maps in the Marketplace: Cartographic Vendors and Their Customers in Eighteenth-Century America," *Cartographica* 42 (Spring 2007): 17–23.

53. Graffagnino, *Shaping of Vermont*, 59–62; Walter W. Ristow, *American Maps and Mapmakers: Commercial Cartography in the Nineteenth Century* (Detroit, Mich., 1985), 85–88;

Phyllis Kihn, "William Blodget, Map Maker 1754–1809," *Connecticut Historical Society Bulletin* 27 (April 1962): 33–37; Bosse, "Maps in the Marketplace," 24–25.

54. Graffagnino, *Shaping of Vermont*, 79–82.

55. Isaac Eddy, *Chronology Delineated to Illustrate the History of Monarchical Revolutions* (Weathersfield, Vt., 1813); John Russell, *An Authentic History of the Vermont State Prison* (Windsor, Vt., 1812); *Windsor County Engravers*; Rugg, "Isaac Eddy Printer-Engraver," 324–25; Dalphin and McCorison, "Lewis Robinson—Entrepreneur"; Graffagnino, *Shaping of Vermont*, 103–6; Edith Bishop, *Oliver Tarbell Eddy 1799–1868* (Newark, N.J., 1950).

56. James Whitelaw, "Sir, I Am About Publishing a New Edition . . ." (Ryegate, Vt., 1810); Graffagnino, *Shaping of Vermont*, 79–81; Haskins, "James Wilson—Globe Maker"; Kimball, "James Wilson of Vermont."

57. Hutchinson: The Society, *The Society of Colonial Wars in the State of Vermont* (Burlington, Vt., 1925), 109–10; Zadock Thompson, *A Gazetteer of the State of Vermont; containing a brief general view of the state, a historical and topographical description of all the counties, towns, rivers, &c . . .* (Montpelier, Vt., 1824); S. R. Hall, *The Child's Assistant to a Knowledge of the Geography and History of Vermont* (Montpelier, Vt., 1827).

58. Graffagnino, *Shaping of Vermont*, 26–30, 103–6; Taylor, "George White," 410.

59. Stephen Mihm, *A Nation of Counterfeiters: Capitalists, Con Men, and the Making of the United States* (Cambridge, Mass., 2007).

60. Thomas Hamilton Ormsbee, "Christian Meadows, Engraver and Counterfeiter," *American Collector* 13 (January 1945): 6–9; *Windsor County Engravers*, 14.

61. Eighteenth-century Masonic aprons, a badge of membership and status in the lodge, were elaborately decorated with watercolors. In the new century, aprons became engraved and printed on leather or silk by such engravers as Amos Doolittle and Abner Reed. Robinson offered a source closer to home; according to Dalphin and McCorison, he "supplied most of the lodges in Vermont and New Hampshire, with aprons, which were signed with his name" (Dalphin and McCorison, "Lewis Robinson," 307). Lewis Roberson, *Select and Original Dialogues, Orations and Single Pieces Designed for the Use of Schools* (Weathersfield, Vt., 1816); Graffagnino, *Shaping of Vermont*, 114–17.

62. Gilbert H. Davis, *Centennial Celebration, Together with an Historical Sketch of Reading, Windsor County, Vermont* (Bellows Falls, Vt., 1874), 145; Hosley and Ward, *Great River*, 482; Graffagnino, *Shaping of Vermont*, 114–15; Dalphin and McCorison, "Lewis Robinson," 297–313 .

63. Discussion from the examination of the 1810 and 1811 globes in the collections of the Vermont Historical Society, University of Vermont, and the Library of Congress. Kimball, "James Wilson of Vermont"; Graffagnino, *Shaping of Vermont*, 79–81; Kimball, "James Wilson of Vermont," 34; Wilson Family Papers.

64. Agreement between James Wilson and John Wilson, 10 March 1818, James Wilson Papers, Division of Maps and Geography, Library of Congress.

65. Samuel Wilson to James Wilson, 30 March 1817, James Wilson Papers; Samuel Wilson to James Wilson, 12 October 1822, Wilson Family Papers; Kimball, "James Wilson of Vermont," 39. Also, see announcement of "WILSON'S AMERICAN GLOBES [3, 9 AND 13 inches in diameter] being sold in Samuel Wood's New York bookstore in Thomas Keith, *A New Treatise on the Use of the Globes* (New York, 1832).

66. *Wilson's American Globes* (Broadside, Albany, N.Y., 1828), Library of Congress.

67. James Wilson to James Wilson, and Cyrus Lancaster to James Wilson, 11 August 1834, Wilson Family Papers; Kimball, "James Wilson of Vermont," 41–44; Bruckner, "Lessons in Geography."

68. For extended arguments along these lines, see Barbara Maria Stafford, *Good Looking: Essays on the Virtue of Images* (Cambridge, Mass., 1996); W. J. T. Mitchell, "Interdisciplinarity

and Visual Culture," *Art Bulletin* 77 (December 1995): 540–41; Laurel Thatcher Ulrich, *The Age of Homespun: Objects and Stories in the Creation of an American Myth* (New York, 2001).

CHAPTER 4. INVENTORS AND ITINERANTS

1. On Eli Terry and clock making, see Henry Terry, *American Clock Making, Its Early History and Present Extent of the Business* (Waterbury, Conn., 1870), 4–6; Kenneth D. Roberts and Snowden Taylor, *Eli Terry and the Connecticut Shelf Clock*, 2nd ed. (Fitzwilliam, N.H., 1994); John Joseph Murphy, "Entrepreneurship in the Establishment of the American Clock Industry," *Journal of Economic History* 26 (June 1966): 168–86; and Chris H. Bailey, *Two Hundred Years of American Clocks and Watches* (Englewood Cliffs, N.J., 1975), 102–5, 116.

2. Maxine Berg, *Luxury and Pleasure in Eighteenth-Century Britain* (Oxford, 2005), 234; Donna K. Baron, "Definition and Diaspora of Regional Style: The Worcester County Model," *American Furniture 1995* (Milwaukee, Wisc., 1995), 167–90; Evans, *American Windsor Chairs*, 387. For its pioneering discussion of uneven developments in industrialization, see Raphael Samuel, "The Workshop of the World: Steam Power and Hand Technology in Mid-Victorian Britain," *History Workshop Journal* 3 (Spring 1977): 6–72.

3. Richard Miller, "Records of Life," in *Expressions of Innocence and Eloquence: Selections from the Jane Katcher Collection of Americana*, Jane Katcher, David A. Schorsch, and Ruth Wolfe eds. (Seattle, Wash., 2006), 79–80, 328–29.

4. Sumpter T. Priddy, *American Fancy: Exuberance in the Arts, 1790–1840* (Milwaukee, 2004), xxv; Jack Larkin, "The Faces of Change: Images of Self and Society in New England, 1790–1850," in *Meet Your Neighbors: New England Portraits, Painters, and Society, 1790–1850*, ed. Caroline Sloat (Sturbridge, Mass., 1992), 11.

5. Chris Bailey, "Clocks and Instruments," in Ward and Hosley, *Great River*, 342–43, and Terry's first wooden-movement tall clock, 362–64; Henry Terry, "A Review of Dr. Alcott's History of Clock–Making," *Waterbury American*, 10 June 1853, reprinted in Roberts and Taylor, *Eli Terry*, 46–49; Henry Terry, *American Clock Making*, 5–6; Penrose Hoopes, *Connecticut Clockmakers of the 18th Century* (New York, 1930); and Hoopes, *Shop Records of Daniel Burnap, Clockmaker* (Hartford, Conn., 1958).

6. Terry, "Review of Alcott's History of Clock-Making," in Roberts and Taylor, *Eli Terry*, 47; Henry Terry, *American Clock Making*, 4; Zea and Cheney, *Clock Making in New England*, 121; Chauncey Jerome, *History of the American Clock Business for the Past Sixty Years* (New Haven, 1860); Roberts and Taylor, *Eli Terry*, 9, 24.

7. Roberts and Taylor, *Eli Terry*, 14–29; for an example of a Terry Grained Clock, in the collections of the American Clock and Watch Museum, Bristol, Conn., see illus. on page 29 of *Eli Terry*; Bailey, *Two Hundred Years of American Clocks*, 29; Frances Manwaring Caulkins, *History of Norwich, Connecticut* (Hartford, Conn., 1864), 221–23; Michael O'Malley, *Keeping Watch: A History of American Time* (New York, 1990), 1–8.

8. Candace Roberts, Diary, 1801–1806, Bristol Public Library, typescript, OSV Research Library, edited by Gail Leach, Bristol, Conn., 2001, 15, 25, 39, 49; Zea and Cheney, *Clock Making in New England*, 121; Donna Lathrop, "Candace Roberts, Dial Painter," *NAWCC Bulletin* (Dec. 2001); Mimi Handler, "Brush Strokes in the Face of Time," *Early American Life* 23 (1992): 59–62.

9. Alcott, "History of Clock-Making," quoted in Roberts and Taylor, *Eli Terry*, 32; Roberts and Taylor, *Eli Terry*, 24, 32–36; Wright Deed, Plymouth Land Records, 23 January 1806, reprinted in Roberts and Taylor, *Eli Terry*, 34; Hoopes, *Daniel Burnap*.

10. Roberts and Taylor, *Eli Terry*, 36–37; Porter clock, in Ward and Hosley, *Great River*, 364–65; Henry Terry, *American Clock Making*, 5; David S. Hounshell, *From the American*

System to Mass Production, 1800–1932 (Baltimore, 1984), 52–53; Zea and Cheney, *Clock Making in New England*, 121–22.

11. Jerome, *American Clock Business*, 17.

12. Emily Ellsworth Ford Skeel, *Mason Locke Weems: His Works and Ways*, 3 vols. (New York, 1929), 2: 72.

13. Weems to Carey, Lexington, 15 March 1811, in Skeel, *Mason Locke Weems*, 3:42–43. The best work on Weems remains Marcus Cunliffe's introduction to Mason L. Weems, *The Life of Washington* (Cambridge, Mass., 1962). Also see James Gilreath, "Mason Locke Weems, Mathew Carey, and the Southern Book Trade, 1794–1810," *Publishing History* 10 (1981): 27–49; Lewis Leary, *The Book-Peddling Parson: An Account of the Life and Works of Mason Locke Weems* (Chapel Hill, 1984); R. Laurence Moore, "Religion, Secularization, and the Shaping of the Culture Industry in Antebellum America," *American Quarterly* 41 (June 1989): 216–42.

14. Skeel, *Mason Locke Weems*, 1: 257–58; Cunliffe's introduction to Weems, *Life of Washington*, ix–xii; Lawrence C. Wroth, *Parson Weems: A Biographical and Critical Study* (Baltimore, 1911), 3.

15. Weems to Carey, Savannah, 24 May 1807, in Skeel, *Mason Locke Weems*, 2:362; Wroth, *Parson Weems*, 36.

16. Weems to Carey, February 1801, in Skeel, *Mason Locke Weems*, 2:167; Weems to Carey, 12 October 1796, in Skeel, *Mason Locke Weems*, 2:44: Weems to Carey, in Skeel, *Mason Locke Weems*, 1:257–58; James N. Green, *Matthew Carey, Publisher and Patriot* (Philadelphia, 1985); Green, "From Printer to Publisher: Mathew Carey and the Origins of Nineteenth-Century Book Publishing," in *Getting the Books Out: Papers of Chicago Conference on Books in Nineteenth-Century America*, ed. Michael Hackenberg (Washington, D.C., 1987), 26–44; Rosalind Remer, *Printers and Men of Capital: Philadelphia Book Publishers in the New Republic* (Philadelphia, 1996), 128–32.

17. Gilreath, "Mason Locke Weems, Mathew Carey," 37–39; Ronald J. Zboray, *A Fictive People: Antebellum Economic Development and the American Reading Public* (New York, 1993), 42–52.

18. Weems to Carey, 12 or 13 January 1800, in Skeel, *Mason Locke Weems*, 2:126.

19. Steven Watts, *The Republic Reborn: War and the Making of Liberal America, 1790–1820* (Baltimore, 1987), 142–44; Weems, *Life of Washington* 1–3; Scott Casper, *Constructing Lives: Biography and Culture in Nineteenth-Century America* (Chapel Hill, 1999), 71–75. See also Christopher Harris, "Mason Locke Weems's Life of Washington: The Making of a Bestseller," *Southern Literary Journal* 19 (Spring 1987): 92–101.

20. Peter S. Onuf, ed., *The Life of Washington* (Armonk, N.Y., 1996), xvii; Moore, "Religion, Secularization," 216–42.

21. See David Jaffee, "Peddlers of Progress and the Transformation of the Rural North, 1760–1860," *Journal of American History* 78 (September 1991): 511–35; Richardson Wright, *Hawkers and Walkers in Early America: Strolling Peddlers, Preachers, Lawyers, Doctors, Players, and Others, from the Beginning to the Civil War* (Philadelphia, 1927); Peter Benes and Jane Montague Benes, ed., *Itinerancy in New England and New York* (Boston, Mass., 1986). Some of the collections of peddlers' papers that I have consulted include Vestus Haley Parks, Diary, 1827–1829 (OSV Library, Sturbridge, Mass.); James K. Storey, Daybook, 1836 (OSV Library); Morillo Noyes, Memorandum Books and Papers, 1859–1877 (Mss. 778, Manuscript Collection, Baker Library, Harvard Business School, Cambridge, Mass.); William C. Holbrook, Diary for 1854 (Manuscript Collection, New York State Library, Albany); David Daly, Account Book, 1836–1841 (Manuscript Collection, Vermont Historical Society (VHS), Montpelier, Vt.); and James Guild, Diary, 1818–1824, VHS, available as "From Tunbridge, Vermont, to London, England—The Journal of James Guild, Peddler, Tinker, Schoolmaster, Portrait Painter, from 1818–1824," *Proceedings of the Vermont Historical Society* 5 (September 1937):

249–313. Also see the letters of Rensseleaer Upson (clock peddler) in Priscilla Carrington Kline, "New Light on the Yankee Peddler," *New England Quarterly* 12 (March 1939): 80–98; the Abraham Kohn diary available in Abram Vossen Goodman, "A Jewish Peddler's Diary, 1842–1843," *American Jewish Archives* 3 (June 1951): 81–111; "Journal of a Peddling Trip, Kept by Ebenezer Graves of Ashfield, Massachusetts: Memorandum for the Year 1853, Commencing March 21st," *Old-Time New England* 56 (January–March 1966): 81–90, and (Spring 1966): 108–16.

22. William J. Gilmore, "Peddlers and the Dissemination of Printed Material in Northern New England, 1780–1840," in *Itinerancy in New England and New York*, ed. Benes and Benes, 84–88; Invoice of Peddlers Goods, 31 October 1842, MSC 174, Manuscript Collection, VHS. On changes in the cultural infrastructure of the countryside, see Brown, "Emergence of Urban Society," 29–51; William J. Gilmore, *Reading Becomes a Necessity of Life: Material and Cultural Life in Rural New England, 1780–1835* (Knoxville, Tenn., 1989); Jaffee, "Village Enlightenment in New England."

23. Joseph Kett, "Growing Up in Rural New England, 1800–1840," in Tamara K. Hareven, ed., *Anonymous Americans: Explorations in Nineteenth-Century Social History* (Englewood Cliffs, N.J., 1971), 1–16; Joseph T. Rainer, "The 'Sharper' Image: Yankee Peddlers, Southern Consumers, and Market Revolution," *Business and Economic History* 26 (Fall 1997): 31–33; also see, Rainer, "The Honorable Fraternity of Moving Merchants: Yankee Peddlers in the Old South, 1800–1860" (Ph.D. diss., College of William and Mary, 2000).

24. Amos Bronson Alcott, *New Connecticut* (1881; reprint Boston, 1970), 210–11; Amos Bronson Alcott to Mr. and Mrs. Joseph Alcott, 24 1820, Norfolk, Va., in Richard L. Herrnstadt, ed., *The Letters of A. Bronson Alcott* (Ames, Iowa, 1969), 1–2; Amos Bronson Alcott to Mr. and Mrs. Joseph Alcott, 30 November 1818, Norfolk, Va., in Frank Wagner, "Eighty Six Letters (1814–1880) of A. Bronson Alcott," *Studies in the American Renaissance* (1979): 245–48; Chatfield Alcott, "Journal to the South, 1821," Alcott Family, Additional Papers, 1707–1904, Autobiographical Collections, Volumes 1 and 2, Amos Bronson Alcott Papers, Houghton Library, Cambridge, Mass.; Odell Shepard, *Pedlar's Progress: The Life of Bronson Alcott* (Boston, 1937), 44–48.

25. Samuel Hopkins Peck (Augusta, Ga.) to Russell Upson Peck (Berlin, Conn.), 6 August 1826, Russell Upson Peck Correspondence, Connecticut Historical Society, Hartford, Conn.; Milo Holcomb (Uniontown, unknown) to Nahum Holcomb and Nahum Holcomb, Jr. (West Granby, Conn.), 29 January 1831, Milo Holcomb (Warren Court House, Ill.) to Nahum Holcomb (West Granby, Conn.), 27 July 1835, Holcomb Family Papers, Connecticut State Library, Hartford; Also, see Power of Attorney made by Milo Holcomb of Hartland, Conn, appointing his brother Nahum Holcomb, Jr. of Granby, Conn., to pay his debts and satisfy creditors, Lexington, Rockbridge County, Va., Dec 16, 1834, Holcomb Papers; Rainer, "Fraternity of Moving Merchants," 40–43.

26. Shepard, *Pedlar's Progress*, 56–57; William A. Alcott, Recollections of Rambles in the South (New York, 1854), 14–15; Asa Upson (Bristol, Conn.) to Rensselaer Upson (Huntsville, Madison County, Alabama), 6 April 1823, Personal and Business Correspondence, 1821–1854, Upson Papers, Connecticut State Library; Rainer, "The 'Sharper' Image of Yankee Peddlers," 31–32.

27. Vermont material in Gilmore, "Peddlers and the Dissemination of Printed Material," 82–86; and Georgia in Rainer, "The 'Sharper' Image of Yankee Peddlers," 32–33. I am indebted to Ron Daigle, Old Sturbridge Village, for sharing his tabulations on peddlers in the 1850 Worcester County Census. In New York, the annual average of 192 peddlers in the 1840s dropped to 113 in the 1850s: "New York Peddlers Licenses Pursuant to Act of March 23, 1840," vol. 1, Manuscript Collection, New York State Library, Albany; T. Headley, *Census of the State of New York, 1855* (n.p., n.d.). I am grateful to Christopher Clark for the last refer-

ence. U.S. census figures quoted in Fred Mitchell Jones, *Middlemen in the Domestic Trade of the United States, 1800–1860* (Urbana, Ill., 1937), 63.

28. On Vermont, see Gilmore, "Peddlers and the Dissemination of Printed Material," 86; and Gerald Carson, *The Old Country Store* (New York, 1954), 48. On clock peddlers, see John Joseph Murphy, "The Establishment of the American Clock Industry: A Study in Entrepreneurial History" (Ph.D. diss., Yale University, 1961), 114–73; and Lee Soltow, "Watches and Clocks in Connecticut, 1800: A Symbol of Socioeconomic Status," *Connecticut Historical Society Bulletin* 45 (October 1980): 116.

29. Sophie E. Eastman, *In Old South Hadley* (Chicago, 1912), 214, quoted in Michele P. Barker, "Peddlers in New England, 1790–1860," research paper, OSV Library, Sturbridge, Mass.; Oliver Filley and Erastus Beaman, Connecticut tinsmiths, and Nathaniel Clark, "a peddler" in 1817, Agreement, May 1817, quoted in Barker, "Peddlers in New England."

30. Rainer, "Fraternity of Moving Merchants," 117; Robert Sutcliff, *Travels in Some Parts of North America, in the Years 1804, 1805, and 1806* (York, England, 1816), 90–91; George R. Dalphin and Marcus A. McCorison, "Lewis Robinson—Entrepreneur," *Vermont History* 30 (October 1962): 297–313; Morillo Noyes Papers, Burlington, Vt., 1859–1877, Archives, Harvard Business School, Cambridge, Mass.

31. Carl Ludwig Flischmann, *Trade, Manufacture, and Commerce in the United States*, (1852; Jerusalem, 1970), 88. On tinware, see Shirley Spaulding DeVoe, *The Tinsmiths of Connecticut* (Middletown, Conn., 1968), 146–53; and Margaret Coffin, *The History and Folklore of American Country Tinware, 1700–1900* (Camden, N.J., 1968), 46–48, 68–76.

32. *Portland Argus*, 1888, quoted in Esther Stevens Brazier, "The Tinsmiths of Stevens Plain," in *Antique Metalware*, ed. James R. Mitchell (New York, 1976), 204–5; Jeannette Lasansky, *To Cut, Piece, and Solder* (College Station, Pa., 1982), 12–13; Marilyn Arbor, *Tools and Trades of America's Past: The Mercer Collection* (Doylestown, Pa., 1981); Malcolm Keir, "The Tin Peddler," *Journal of Political Economy* 21 (March 1913): 256.

33. Brazier, "Tinsmiths of Stevens Plain," 205; Shirley DeVoe, "The Perry Tin Shop of Saxtons River," in *Decorative Arts: 18th and 19th Century Research and Writings of Shirley Spaulding DeVoe*, comp. and ed. Shirley S. Baer and M. Jeanne Gearin (New York, 1999), 118–20; G. & P. E. Perry Tin Shop, Papers, 1828–1845, Saxtons River Historical Society, microfilm in Downs Collection, Winterthur Museum, Winterthur, Del..

34. *The Marlboro' Medley* (Marlboro, 1787), Broadside Collection, Manuscript Collection, American Antiquarian Society, Worcester, Mass.

35. Richard Bushman, "Shopping and Advertising in Colonial America," in *Of Consuming Interests, 233–51*; Jaffee, "Peddlers of Progress."

36. Mary-Lou Hinman, "The Yankee Peddler: His Role in American Folklore and Fiction" (Ph.D. diss., University of Connecticut, 1975); Gary Lindberg, *The Confidence Man in American Literature* (New York, 1982); Jean-Christophe Agnew, *Worlds Apart: The Market and the Theater in Anglo-American Thought, 1550–1750* (New York, 1986); Jackson Lears, *Fables of Abundance: A Cultural History of Advertising in America* (New York, 1995).

37. John Bernard, *Retrospections of America, 1797–1811*, ed. Bayle Bernard (1887; reprint New York, 1969), 43–44; Jackson Lears, "The Stabilization of Sorcery: Antebellum Origins of Consumer Culture," Paper presented at the Annual Meeting of Organization of American Historians, Philadelphia, 1897, 10–15.

38. P. T. Barnum, *Barnum's Own Story: The Autobiography of P. T. Barnum—Condensed from the Various Editions Published During His Lifetime by Waldo R. Browne* (New York, 1961), 26; Neil Harris, *Humbug: The Art of P. T. Barnum* (Chicago, 1973); James W. Cook, *The Arts of Deception: Playing with Fraud in the Age of Barnum* (Cambridge, Mass., 2001). On popular humor, see Christopher Clark, "Popular Humor and Economic Change in New England, 1780–1860 University of York, August 1983, 25–28. On the magical associations of peddlers,

see Jackson Lears, "Beyond Veblen: Rethinking Consumer Culture in America," in *Consuming Visions: Accumulation and Display of Goods in America, 1880–1920*, ed. Simon J. Bronner (New York, 1989), 78–79.

39. Carson, *Old Country Store,* 46.

40. Thomas Chandler Haliburton, *The Clockmaker: or The Sayings and Doings of Sam Slick, of Slickville* (Philadelphia, 1837), 10, 12–17, esp. 10, 13.

41. Thomas M. Allen, *A Republic in Time: Temporality & Social Imagination in Nineteenth-Century America* (Chapel Hill, 2008), 97–98; Robert A. Gross, "America's Agricultural Revolution, 1750–1850," quoted in Stephen Innes, ed., *Work and Labor in Early America* (Chapel Hill, 1988), 34; H. Nichols, B. Clark, *Francis W. Edmonds: American Master in the Dutch Tradition* (Washington, D.C., 1988), 75–78; "Editor's Table," *Knickerbocker* 23 (June 1844): 597.

42. Guild, "From Tunbridge, Vermont, to London, England," 249–313; James Guild, "Diary ," 1818–1824, Manuscript Collection, Vermont Historical Society, Montpelier; Nina Little, *Little by Little: Six Decades of Collecting American Decorative Arts* (Boston, 1998), 267–75; Arthur and Sybil Kern, "James Guild: Quintessential Itinerant Portrait Painter," *Clarion* 17 (Summer 1992): 48–57; John Vlach, *Plain Painters: Making Sense of American Folk Art* (Washington, D.C., 1988), 65–68.

43. Guild, "Journal," 251, 256–57; Charles Burleigh, *The Genealogy and Hisory of the Guild, Guile, and Gile Family* (Portland, Maine, 1887), 75.

44. Guild, "Journal," 257–59.

45. Ibid., 261.

46. Ibid., 264, 267–68, 279.

47. Ibid., 308.

48. Ibid., 279. On the formation of the urban middle class, see Mary P. Ryan, *Cradle of the Middle Class: The Family in Oneida County, New York, 1790–1865* (New York, 1981); and Karen Halttunen, *Confidence Men and Painted Women: A Study of Middle-Class Culture in America, 1830–1870* (New Haven, 1982).

49. Henry Terry, *American Clock Making,* 5; Donald Hoke, *Ingenious Yankees: The Rise of the American System of Manufactures in the Private Sector* (New York, 1990), 56; Francis Atwater, *History of Plymouth, Connecticut* (Meriden, Conn., 1895), 237; Bailey, *Two Hundred Years of American Clocks,* 105; Roberts and Taylor, *Eli Terry,* 34–37.

50. "Clocks Made by Eli Terry for Levi G. and E. Porter," reprinted in Roberts and Taylor, *Eli Terry,* fig. 12a, 38, 41.

51. Bailey, *Two Hundred Years of American Clocks,* 205.

52. Zea and Cheney, *Clock Making in New England,* 46–49; Carlene E. Stephens, *On Time: How America Has Learned to Live by the Clock* (Washington, D.C., 2002), 49, David F. Wood, "Concord, Massachusetts Clockmakers, 1789–1817," *Antiques* 157 (May 2000): 760–68; Paul J. Foley, *Willard's Patent Time Pieces* (Roxbury, Mass., 2002).

53. Bailey, *Two Hundred Years of American Clocks,* 105–8.

54. Bailey, *Two Hundred Years of American Clocks,* 110–14, 118; Zea and Cheney, *Clock Making in New England,* 119–20, 123–28; Snowden Taylor, *The Clocks of Mark Leavenworth* (Fitzwilliam, N.H., 1987).

55. Brooke Hindle and Steven Lubar, *Engines of Change: The American Industrial Revolution, 1790–1860* (Washington, D.C., 1986), 223; Roberts and Taylor, *Eli Terry,* 60–66.

56. Zea and Cheney, *Clock Making in New England,* 127; Henry Terry, "Review of Dr. William Alcott," in Roberts, *Eli Terry,* 47; Henry Terry, *American Clock Making,* 5–6; Murphy, "Establishment of the American Clock Industry," 63–64.

57. Specifications of Eli Terry's Letters Patent, 12 June 1816, reprinted in Roberts, *Eli Terry,* 62; Zea and Cheney, *Clock Making in New England,* 127.

58. Henry Terry, *American Clock Making*, 7.

59. Bailey, *Two Hundred Years of American Clocks*, 119–20; Zea and Cheney, *Clock Making in New England*, 127–30; Chris H. Bailey, "160 Years of Seth Thomas Clocks," *Connecticut Historical Society Collections* 38 (July 1973): 77.

60. Roberts and Taylor, *Eli Terry*, 151–68; Bailey, *Two Hundred Years of American Clocks*, 121–24; Jerome, *American Clock Business*, 48; Zea and Cheney, *Clock Making in New England*, 120.

61. Jerome, *American Clock Business*, 33, 41; Chris Bailey, *From Rags to Riches to Rags: The Story of Chauncey Jerome*, NAWCC Bulletin Supplement 15, Spring 1986, 5–7; Bailey, *Two Hundred Years of American Clocks*, 119; Roberts and Taylor, *Eli Terry*, 79; Allen, *Republic in Time*, 91.

62. Definition of "American System" from Eugene Ferguson, *Bibliography of the History of Technology* (Cambridge, Mass., 1968), 298, quoted in David A. Hounshell, *From The American System to Mass Production, 1800–1932: The Development of Manufacturing Technology in the United States* (Baltimore, 1984), 15; Hoke, *Ingenious Yankees*, 44; Merritt Roe Smith, *Harpers Ferry Armory and the New Technology: The Challenge of Change* (Ithaca, N.Y., 1977); Roberts, *Eli Terry*.

63. Hounshell, *From the American System to Mass Production*, 43; Hoke, *Ingenious Yankees*, 65.

64. Murphy, "Establishment of the American Clock Industry," 59–61.

65. Hoke, *Ingenious Yankees*, 48. 55; Roberts and Taylor, *Eli Terry*, 52–57; Hounshell, *From the American System to Mass Production*, 55–57.

66. Roberts and Taylor, *Eli Terry*, 52–54; Hoke, *Ingenious Yankees*, 56; Brook Hindle, ed. *Material Culture of the Wooden Age* (Tarrytown, N.Y., 1981).

67. Roberts and Taylor, *Eli Terry*; Terry, *American Clock Making*, 5–6.

68. Hopkins and Alfred Day Book, 1834–41, American Clock and Watch Museum; Shirley DeVoe, "Hopkins and Alfred: Clockmakers of Harwinton," *Connecticut Historical Society Bulletin* 35 (October 1970): 122; Hoke, *Ingenious Yankees*, 56, 87; Murphy, "Establishment of the American Clock Industry"; Hindle and Lubar, *Engines of Change*, 178.

69. David Pye, *The Nature and Art of Workmanship* (New York, 1971), 4–8; Murphy, "Establishment of the American Clock Industry," 89–90; Seth Thomas parts in Connecticut Historical Society: illustrations in Hounshell, *From the American System to Mass Production*, 55–57.

70. Hoke, *Ingenious Yankees*, 65, 86–91.

71. Hindle and Lubar, *Engines of Change*, 225; Hoke, *Ingenious Yankees*, 64–65, 85–91; Hounshell, *From the American System to Mass Production*, 54.

72. Joseph Hawley, "Address," in *Centennial Celebration of the Incorporation of the Town of Bristol, June 17 1885*, comp. John J. Jennings (Hartford, Conn., 1885), quoted in Roberts, *Eli Terry*, 235.

73. Alcott quoted in Zea and Cheney, *Clock Making in New England*, 130. On "George Murphy, Merchant Supplier," see Murphy, "Establishment of the American Clock Industry," 139–47. On Jerome, see Bailey, *From Rags to Riches to Rags*, 7–9; Bailey, *Two Hundred Years of American Clocks*, 135–36, 140.

74. Theodore B. Hodges, *Erastus Hodges, 1781–1847: Connecticut Manufacturer, Merchant, and Entrepreneur* (West Kennebunk, Maine, 1994), 110; contract between Erastus Hodges and David Winship, January 1825, reprinted in Hodges, 109–10.

75. Hodges, *Erastus Hodges*, 33, 80–81, 107, 117, 138.

76. Ibid., 123–26, 146–49. Moulton wages are recorded in Hodges Store Daybook, 1830–1932, Hodges papers (in Theodore Hodges's collection, quoted in ibid., 148; Shirley DeVoe,

"Women Industrial Painters of Connecticut, 1779–1830," *Spinning Wheel* 29 (1973): 112–15, republished in *Decorative Arts,* 132–35.

77. William A. Alcott, "The History of Yankee Clocks and Clock-Making," *Boston Dailey Evening Traveller,* 13 April 1853, reprinted in Murphy, "Establishment of the American Clock Industry," 296; Joseph Hawley, "Address," in *Centennial Celebration of the Incorporation of the Town of Bristol, June 17, 1885,* comp. John J. Jennings (Hartford, Conn., 1885), quoted in Hoke, *Ingenious Yankees,* 94; Hodges, *Erastus Hodges,* 151.

78. See also Bailey, *Two Hundred Years of American Clocks,* 116–17; Murphy, "Establishment of the American Clock Industry," 114–73; Kline, "New Light on the Yankee Peddler."

79. Rainer, "The 'Sharper' Image of Yankee Peddlers," 29–30; Eli Terry, Jr., and Co. (Terryville, Conn.) to Simon W. Gunn (Lexington, Kent.), 14 February 1838, Letter Books of Eli Terry, Jr., American Clock and Watch Museum.

80. Abel S. Wetmore contract with Erastus Hodges, 14 Feb, 1831, reprinted in Hodges, *Erastus Hodges,* 202–3; also, see numerous contracts in Upson Papers and Seth Wheeler Papers, Connecticut State Library; Rainer, "The 'Sharper' Image of Yankee Peddlers," 31.

81. George Bartholomew (Athens, Alabama) to R. Upson, Bristol, Conn., 28 May 1826; John Bartholomew (Canton, Ohio) to R. Upson, Merrimans & Co., 10 August 1837, George Rensseleaer Upson, Upson Papers, Connecticut State Library.

82. Letter to Messrs. Norton & Stimson, Jacksonville, Ill., 4 July 1826, Terry, Jr., American Clock and Watch Museum.

83. George Rensseleaer Upson, Account Book, 1822–1835, in Upson Papers, Connecticut State Library; also see letters of George Rensseleaer Upson, reprinted in Kline, "New Light on the Yankee Peddler"; and "Rensselaer Upson, Clock Peddler," in Murphy, "Establishment of the American Clock Industry," 122–135. See also Hodges, *Erastus Hodges,* chap. 6, "The Lonely Life of a Peddler"; Lee Soltow, "Watches and Clocks in Connecticut, 1800: A Symbol of Socioeconomic Status," *Connecticut Historical Society Bulletin* 45 (October 1980): 116.

84. Analysis of account books by Rainer, "Fraternity of Moving Merchants,"145–46; see also George Rensseleaer Upson, Account Book, 1822–35, and Isaac Hotchkiss, Account Book, 1837–38, Box 2, Seth Wheeler Papers, Connecticut State Papers

85. John Elledge and Thomas Smithers, Estill County, Kent., December 22–23, 1837, Isaac Hotchkiss, Account Book, Seth Wheeler Papers, Connecticut State Papers; also see George Bartholomew (Athens, Georgia) to Rensseleaer Upson, Bristol, Conn., Dec. 27, 1825, Upson Papers; Murphy, "Establishment of the American Clock Industry," 100; Kline, "New Light on the Yankee Peddler," 82–84; Hodges, *Erastus Hodges,* 209–10.

86. H. Atwood to Rensseleaer Upson, Bolivar, Tenn., 10 Dec. 1837, Upson Papers, Connecticut State Library; Rainer, "Fraternity of Moving Merchants," 148; Kline, "New Light on the Yankee Peddler," 81–82; Hodges, *Erastus Hodges,* 249–50.

87. Eli Terry, Jr., & Co (Terryville, Conn.) to G. Brawley & Co (Athens, Ohio), 2 Dec. 1837, 27 March 1838, Letter Books of Eli Terry, Jr., American Clock and Watch Museum.

88. George W. Bartholomew (Monroe County, Miss.) to Rensseleaer Upson (Bristol, Conn.), 29 Jan. 1826, Upson Papers, Connecticut State Library; Eli Terry, Jr., (Terryville, Conn.) to J. C. Lewis (Baltimore, MD), 10 June 1837, Letter Books of Eli Terry, Jr., American Clock and Watch Museum; Alpha Hart, Shelby, N.Y., to Erastus Hodges, 21 Oct. 1827, Letter, quoted in Hodges, *Erastus Hodges,* 221; Kline, "New Light on the Yankee Peddler," 81–84, Rainer, "Fraternity of Moving Merchants,"153.

89. Hodges, *Erastus Hodges,* 210–13; Murphy, "Establishment of the American Clock Industry," 165–67, 132;; Rainer, "Fraternity of Moving Merchants," 144–45.

90. Letter from Alpha Hart, Galen, N.Y., to Erastus Hodges, 15 June 15, 1828, quoted in Hodges, *Erastus Hodges,* 207.

91. Murphy, "Establishment of the American Clock Industry," 152; Jerome, *American Clock Business*, 54–55; Jaffee, "Peddlers of Progress"; Kline, "New Light on the Yankee Peddler," 91–93.

92. Martin Bruegel, *Farm, Shop, Landing: The Rise of Market Society in the Hudson Valley, 1780–1860* (Durham, N.C., 2002), 85; G. W. Featherstonhaugh, *Excursion Through the Slave States, from Washington on the Potomac to the Frontier of Mexico; with Sketches of Population, Manners and Geological Notes,* 2 vols. (London, 1844), 2:27; Paul G. E. Clemens, "The Consumer Culture of the Middle Atlantic, 1760–1820," *WMQ* 62 (October 2005): 590.

CHAPTER 5. A TALE OF TWO CHAIRMAKING TOWNS

1. Donna K. Baron, "Definition and Diaspora of Regional Style: The Worcester County Model," *American Funiture 1995* (Milwaukee, 1995), 172–73; David Jaffee, "Artisan Entrepreneurs in Worcester County, Massachusetts, 1790–1850," in *Rural New England Furniture: People, Place, and Production,* ed. Peter Benes (Boston, 2000), 100–119; John P. Bigelow, *Statistical Tables Exhibiting the Condition of Certain Branches of Industry in Massachusetts* (Boston, 1838).

2. Thomas Dublin, *Women at Work: The Transformation of Work and Community in Lowell, Massachusetts, 1826–1860* (New York, 1981); Anthony F. C. Wallace, *Rockdale: The Growth of an American Village in the Early Industrial Revolution* (New York, 1980); Thomas Dublin, *Transforming Women's Work: New England Lives in the Industrial Revolution* (Ithaca, N.Y., 1995); David Jaffee, *People of the Wachusett: Greater New England in History and Memory, 1630–1860* (Ithaca, N.Y., 1999).

3. Frederick Jackson Turner, "The First Official Frontier of Massachusetts Bay," in *The Frontier in American History* (New York, 1920), 54; Jaffee, *People of the Wachusett.*

4. John Brooke, *The Heart of the Commonwealth: Society and Political Culture in Worcester County, Massachusetts 1713–1861* (New York, 1989); Daniel Vickers, *Farmers and Fishermen: Two Centuries of Work in Essex County, Massachusetts, 1630–1850* (Chapel Hill, 1994); Baron, "Definition and Diaspora of Regional Style," 167–90; Nancy Evans, *American Windsor Chairs* (New York, 1997), 387; Beverly Jean Johnson, "Winthrop Chandler and the Rural Gentry of Northeastern Connecticut" (master's thesis, University of Delaware, 1990); Mayer and Myers, *Devotion Family.* For its pioneering discussion of uneven developments in industrialization, see Raphael Samuel, "The Workshop of the World: Steam Power and Hand Technology in Mid-Victorian Britain," *History Workshop Journal* 3 (January 1977): 6–72.

5. Solomon Sibley Account Book, OSV Library; Philip Zea, "Preindustrial Rural Cabinetmaking in New England," research paper, 1975, OSV Library; Zea, "Rural Craftsmen and Design," 57–58; Evans, *American Windsor Chairs,* 489; Frank O. Spinney, "Chapman Lee, Country Cabinetmaker," *New-England Galaxy* 1 (Winter 1960): 34–38; Chapman Lee, Ledger, 1790–1850, OSV Library; Donna K. Baron, "Furniture Makers and Retailers in Worcester County," *Antiques* 143 (May 1993): 785.

6. Silas Fay, Account Book, 1790–1835, Princeton Historical Society, Princeton, Mass.; Donna K. Baron, "Cabinetmaking: A Craft in the Process of Change, Worcester County, 1750–1850," research paper, February 1993, OSV Library.

7. Baron, "Definition and Diaspora of Regional Style," 173; Population Tables—Worcester County, in *The Gazetteer of Massachusetts* (Boston, Mass., 1846), 322–30; Jack Larkin, "The Faces of Change: Images of Self and Society in New England, 1790–1850," in *Meet Your Neighbors: New England Portraits, Painters and Society, 1790–1850,* ed. Caroline Sloat (Sturbridge, Mass., 1992), 10; Jack Larkin, "Massachusetts Enters the Marketplace, 1790–1860," in *A Guide to the History of Massachusetts,* ed. Martin Kaufman, John W. Kaufman, and Joseph Carvalho III (New York, 1988), 69–82; Jack Larkin, Probate Inventory Sample of

Worcester County Farmers, Mechanics and Merchants 1790–1850, and other Probate Inventory Samples, Department of Research, OSV Library (kindly shared by Jack Larkin).

8. Ezra S. Stearns, *History of Ashburnham . . . 1734–1886* (Ashburnham, Mass., 1887), 408; 1820 Census of Manufactures, Worcester County, State of Massachusetts; William D. Herrick, *History of the town of Gardner, Worcester County, Mass.: from the incorporation, June 27, 1785, to the present time* (Gardner, Mass., 1878), 166; Herrick, "Gardner," in *History of Worcester County, Massachusetts* ed. D. Hamilton Hurd (Philadelphia, 1889), vol. 1, 828–30; Esther G. Moore, *History of Gardner Massachusetts, 1785–1967* (Gardner, Mass., 1967), 53, 195; Evans, *American Windsor Chairs*, 490.

9. Herrick, "History of Gardner," in *History of Worcester County*, 1: 828–29; Moore, *History of Gardner*, 195; Storch Associates, "Historic Documentation Report for Gardner Heritage State Park," Gardner, Massachusetts, 19 February 1981 (in author's possession).

10. Evans, *American Windsor Chairs*, 492; 1820 Census of Manufactures, State of Massachusetts; Stephen Kilburn Chair (Historic Deerfield), illustrated in Jaffee, "Artisan Entrepreneurs in Worcester County," 9; also see Dean A. Fales, *The Furniture of Historic Deerfield* (New York, 1976), 109.

11. 1820 Census of Manufactures; Samuel Osgood, "Sterling," *History of Worcester County*, 1: 486–90, 502–3; Evans, *American Windsor Chairs;* and Nancy Evans, *Windsor-Chair Making in America* (Lebanon, N.H., 2006), 160–61, 490; Frank White, "Chairmaking in Northern Worcester County," 1993, OSV Library; Frank G. White, "Sterling, Massachusetts: An Early-Nineteenth-Century Seat of Chairmaking," in Benes, *Rural New England Furniture*, 120–21.

12. "History of the County of Worcester—Sterling," *Worcester Magazine and Historical Journal* 1 (October 1825–April 1826): 378; White, "Sterling, Massachusetts," 121–23; Map of Sterling, Massachusetts, Sterling Historical Society, Sterling, Massachusetts; Chairmakers Probate Inventories, Old Sturbridge Village, Sturbridge, Mass. (kindly provided by Jane Nylander).

13. Archaeological Report, 1992, Old Sturbridge Village, 125–27, and Brown: Worcester County Probate, 76: 256, in White, "Sterling, Massachusetts," 129–30; Evans, *American Windsor Chairs;* Osgood, "Sterling," 1: 489–95. Also roll-top side chair with scroll seat DAPC c 1825—see J. D. Pratt: Evans, *American Windsor Chairs*, 496; Joel Pratt, Jr., Account Book, 1822–30, and Elbridge Gerry Reed, Account Book, 1829–51, OSV Library.

14. White, "Sterling, Massachusetts"; Evans, *American Windsor Chairs*, 493 (armchair); Baron, "Definition and Diaspora of Regional Style," 175–79; Henry W. Miller, Chair Factory Account Book, 1829–31, Henry W. Millers Papers, Worcester Historical Museum, Worcester, Mass.; Joel Pratt Account Book.

15. Joel Pratt, Jr., "STRANGER LOOK HERE," Broadside Advertisement, 1 July 1840, Acc. 68.108.1, Henry Ford Museum, Dearborn, Mich; illustrated in Evans, *Windsor-Chair Making in America* (Milwaukee, Wisc., 2006), 108.

16. Eldridge Gerry Reed, Account Book; White, "Sterling, Massachusetts," 130–31; Evans, *American Windsor Chairs*, 497; B. Stuart and Sons, Account Book, 1854–62, American Antiquarian Society, Worcester, Massachusetts.

17. *Massachusetts Spy* (Worcester), 16 March 1836; Joel Pratt Account Book; White, "Sterling, Massachusetts," 132.

18. Jacob Felton, Daybook, Fitzwilliam, N.H., 1836–1838, OSV Library; "Gardner," 829; McLane, *Documents Relative to the Manufactures in the United States* (Washington, D.C., 1833), 293, 493, 553; Nan Wolverton, "Bottomed Out: Female Chair Seaters in Nineteenth-Century Rural New England," in Benes, *Rural New England Furniture*, 182; Trade Card of William Buttre's Fancy Chair Manufactory in New York, ca. 1813, Joseph Downs Collection,

Manuscripts and Printed Books, Winterthur Museum, Winterthur, Del.; Evans, *American Windsor Chairs*, 214–19.

19. Caroline Sloat, "A Great Help to Many Families: Straw Braiding in Massachusetts Before 1825," in *House and Home*, ed. Peter Benes (Dublin, N.H., 1988), 89–100; Gregory Nobles, "Rural Manufacture and Urban Markets: A Case Study of Broom-making in Nineteenth Century Massachusetts," *Journal of the Early Republic* 4 (Fall 1984): 287–308; Thomas Dublin, "Women and Outwork in a Nineteenth-Century New England Town: Fitzwilliam, New Hampshire, 1830–1850," in Hahn and Prude, *The Countryside in the Age of Capitalist Transformation*, 51–69; Thomas Dublin, "Rural Putting-out Work in Early Nineteenth-Century New England: Women and the Transition to Capitalism in the Countryside," *New England Quarterly* 64 (Dec. 1991): 531–73.

20. Thomas Dublin, *Transforming Women's Lives: New England Lives in the Industrial Revolution* (Ithaca, N.Y., 1994), 59; see "Idyll of the Palm Leaf Hat," *Frank Leslie's Illustrated Newspaper*, 15 July 1871, reprinted in Dublin (60) for an example of one of these sentimental scenes.

21. White, "Sterling, Massachusetts," 123; Baron, "Definition and Diaspora of Regional Style," 176–77, Evans, *American Windsor Chairs*, 492–95.

22. Bigelow, *Statistical Tables of Industry in Massachusetts*, 50; John Gorham Palfrey, *Statistics of the Condition and Products of Certain Branches of Industry in Massachusetts* (Boston, 1846), 103; Frances DeWitt, *Statistical Information Relating to Certain Branches of Industry in Massachusetts* (Boston, 1856), 491–92; Baron, "Furniture Makers and Retailers in Worcester County," 785; Storch, "Historic Documentation Report for Gardner Heritage State Park," 21.

23. Margaret Berwind Schiffler, *Furniture and Its Makers of Chester County, Pennsylvania* (Philadelphia, 1966), 131–25, 172–87, 64–68; Barry Allen Kessler, "Of Workshops and Warerooms: The Economic and Geographic Transformation of Furniture Making in Chester County, Pennsylvania, 1780–1850 (master's thesis, University of Delaware, 1987), 34–48.

24. Peter Whitney, *The History of the County of Worcester in the Commonwealth of Massachusetts* (Worcester, Mass., 1793), 308; Wolverton, "Bottomed Out," 184–85; Herrick, "History of Gardner," 831, 836; Herrick, *History of Gardner*, 208–10.

25. Heywood-Wakefield Company, *A Completed Century, 1826–1926: The Story of the Heywood-Wakefield Company* (Boston, Mass., 1926), 1–3; Richard Greenwood, *The Five Heywood Brothers, 1826–1951, A History of the Heywood-Wakefield Company* (New York, 1951); Baron, "Furniture Makers and Retailers in Worcester County"; Moore, *History of Gardner*, 222–23; Herrick, *History of Gardner*, 300–306; Heywood, "History of Gardner," 835–36, 872–74.

26. Don C. Skemer, "David Alling's Chair Manufactory: Craft Industrialization in Newark, New Jersey, 1801–54," *Winterthur Portfolio* 22 (Spring 1987): 10, 16; Evans, *Windsor Chairmaking*, 107.

27. *The Child's Book of Nature* (Lancaster, Mass., 1830); *Lancaster Gazette*, 4 March 1828; McLane, *Documents Relative to Manufactures*, 1: 500–501.

28. George Hepplewhite, *The Cabinet-maker & Upholsterer's Guide* (1794, repr. New York, 1969), 13; Baron, "Definition and Diaspora of Regional Style"; Frank White, "Sterling, Massachusetts: An Early Nineteenth Century Seat of Chairmaking," in *Rural New England Furniture*, ed. Benes, 119–38; Brock Jobe, *Portsmouth Furniture: Masterworks from the New Hampshire Seacoast* (Boston, 1993), 112–13.

29. Hepplewhite, *Cabinet-maker & Upholsterer's Guide*, 13; Thomas Sheraton, *Cabinet-Maker and Upholsterer's Drawing Book of 1793* (rpt. 1972); Baron, "Definition and Diaspora of Regional Style," 167–90, 172–13; Jaffee, "Artisan Entrepreneurs of Worcester County."

30. Jobe, *Portsmouth Furniture*, 116–17; Thomas Hardiman, Jr., "Veneered Furniture of

Cumiston and Buckminster, Saco, Maine," *Magazine Antiques* 159 (May 2001): 754–58; Benjamin Hewitt, Patricia Kane, and Gerald Ward, *The Work of Many Hands: Card Tables in Federal America, 1790–1820* (New Haven, 1982), 179–81; Zea, "Rural Craftsmen and Design," 57–58; see Cumiston and Buckminster chest of drawers, acc. 57.564 and curatorial files for related objects, Winterthur Museum, Winterthur, Del.

31. Accession Files, OSV Library; Spooner Files, Decorative Arts Photographic Collection (DAPC), Winterthur Library; Baron, "Definition and Diaspora of Regional Style," 173; Jobe, *Portsmouth Furniture*, 112–13; Donald Fennimore, "Brass Hardware on American Furniture, Part Two: Stamped Hardware, 1750–1850," *Antiques* 140 (July 1991): 89–91; Robert Mussey, *Furniture Masterworks of John and Thomas Seymour* (Salem, Mass., 2003),242–43; Hardiman, "Veneered Furniture of Cumiston and Buckminster," 754–58; Benjamin Hewitt, *Work of Many Hands*, 179–81; Gerald Ward, *American Case Furniture in the Mabel Brady Garvan and Other Collections at Yale University* (New Haven, 1988), 179–82; Sheraton, *Cabinet-Maker and Upholsterer's Drawing Book*.

32. *Athol Freedom's Sentinel*, 18 December 1827; Walter G. Lord, comp., *History of Athol, Massachusetts* (Athol, Mass., 1953), 281; Lilley Caswell Brewer, *Athol, Massachusetts, Past and Present* (Athol, Mass., 1899); Donna Baron, Frank White, and Karen Blanchfield, "Cabinet Furniture and Chairs, Cheap: Making and Selling Furniture in Central New England, 1790–1850," Research Paper, 1993, OSV Library; Evans, *American Windsor Chairs*, 490–94; Accession Files, OSV Library. For a fascinating case study of a sophisticated cosmopolitan furniture maker in southern Worcester Country at the turn of the nineteenth century, see Brock Jobe and Clark Pearce, "Sophistication in Rural Massachusetts: The Inlaid Cherry Furniture of Nathan Lombard," in *American Furniture 1998* ed. Luke Beckerdite (Milwaukee, 1998), 165–96.

33. *Vital Records of Westminster, Massachusetts, to the end of the Year 1849* (Worcester, Mass., 1908); William Sweetser Heywood, *History of Westminster, Massachusetts* (Lowell, Mass., 1893), 323, 326, 365, 427, 445, 499–504.

34. · Worcester County, Probate Records, Inventory of the Estate of Timothy Doty, 28 March 1835, Case No. 17298, 76: 307–13; Sloat, *Meet Your Neighbors*, 88–89.

35. Marcia Pointon, "Jewelry in Eighteenth Century England," in *Consumers and Luxury: Consumer Culture in Europe, 1650–1850* (Manchester, England, 1999), 123.

36. Izard, "Another Place in Time" 204–9.

37. John Tarrant Kenney, *The Hitchcock Chair: The Story of a Connecticut Yankee— L. Hitchcock of Hitchcocks-ville—and an Account of the Restoration of His 19th-Century Manufactory* (New York, 1971), 17–18, 44–57; Evans, *American Windsor Chairs*, 456–57, 459; Smith, "Town Histories," *To Please Any Taste*, 16; Silas Cheney Account Book, Microfilm, Downs Collection, Winterthur Museum, Winterthur, Del.

38. Kenney, *Hitchcock Chair*, 57–95; Evans, *American Windsor Chairs*, 459; John Warner Barber, *Connecticut Historical Collections* (New Haven, 1836), 460–61; Page, *Litchfield County Furniture*, 118–21; Smith, "Town Histories," 25, and "Furniture Characteristics," 57 in *To Please Any Taste*.

39. Barzillia Hudson ad: *Connecticut Courant*, 13 April 1829, quoted in Evans, *American Windsor Chairs*, 459; Kenney, *Hitchcock Chair*, 98–99.

40. Kenney, *Hitchcock Chair*, 97 (Ad), 98–136, 142–43; Evans, *American Windsor Chairs*, 460; McLane, *Documents Relative to Manufactures*, I: 1019; C. H. Nickerson, "Robertsville and Its Chair Makers: I. The Story of Holmes & Roberts," *Antiques* 8 (August 1925): 147–49; Nancy Goyne Evans, "American Painted Seating Furniture: Marketing the Product, 1750–1840, in *Perspectives on American Furniture*, ed. Gerald W. R. Ward (New York, 1988), 156.

41. Smith, "Town Histories," *To Please Any Taste*, 16; Kenney, *Hitchcock Chair*, 136,

148–56; Evans, *American Windsor Chairs*, 460; Cynthia V. A. Schaffner and Susan Klein, *American Painted Furniture* (New York, 1997), 128–29.

CHAPTER 6. PROVINCIAL PORTRAITS

1. Rita Reif, "'$682,000 Is Bid for a Portrait by Folk Artist," *New York Times*, 27 January 1985; Nicholas B. A. Nicholason, *Little Girl in a Red Dress with Cat and Dog* (New York, 1998), v; Stacy C. Hollander, *American Anthem: Masterworks from the American Folk Art Museum* (New York, 2002), 314; Stacy C. Hollander, *American Radiance: The Ralph Esmerian Gift to the American Folk Art Museum* (New York, 2001), 400.

2. Mrs. H. C. Nelson, "Early American Primitives," *International Studio* (March 1925): 456; Peter Burke, *Popular Culture in Early Modern Europe* (New York, 1978).

3. Holger Cahill, *American Folk Art: The Art of the Common Man in America, 1750–1900* (New York, 1932); John Vlach, *Plain Painters: Making Sense of American Folk Art* (Washington, D.C., 1988); Virginia Tuttle Clayton, Elizabeth Stillinger, and Erika Lee Doss, *Drawing on America's Past: Folk Art, Modernism, and the Index of American Design* (Washington, D.C., 2002).

4. Barbara C. Holdridge and Lawrence B. Holdridge, *Ammi Phillips, Portrait Painter, 1788–1865* (New York, 1969); Stacy C. Hollander, *Revisiting Ammi Phillips: Fifty Years of American Portraiture* (New York, 1994); Colleen Cowles Heslip, *Between the Rivers: Itinerant Painters from the Connecticut to the Hudson* (Williamstown, Mass., 1990).

5. John Vanderlyn, Sr., to John Vanderlyn, Jr., 9 September 1825, Senate House State Historic Site, Kingston, N.Y., quoted in Holdridge and Holdridge, *Ammi Phillips*, 14.

6. Mary Black, "Ammi Phillips: The Country Painter's Method," *Clarion* 11 (Winter 1986): 34; Hollander, *American Radiance*, 400.

7. Hollander, *Revisiting Ammi Phillips*, 54; Black, "Ammi Phillips," 35–37.

8. Hollander, "Introduction," 14, and Black, "Ammi Phillips," 24, in *Revisiting Ammi Phillips*.

9. Lila S. Parrish, "Dr. Samuel Barstow's Great Barrington Diary, Part III," *Great Barrington Historical Society Newsletter* (Summer 1983): 3.

10. Diary of Anna Olcott Dakin, Diaries, 1855, 1857, Cherry Valley, New York, Samuel Dakin papers, 1792–1860, New York State Historical Association, and the *Berkshire County Eagle*, quoted in Hollander, "Introduction," *Revisiting Ammi Phillips*, 15.

11. Christopher Clark, "Comment on the Symposium on Class in the Early Republic," *Journal of the Early Republic* 25 (Winter 2005): 559; Catherine Kelly, *In the New England Fashion: Reshaping Women's Lives in the Nineteenth Century* (Ithaca, N.Y., 1999), 239; Sven Beckert, "Propertied of a Different Kind: Bourgeoisie and Lower Middle Class in the Nineteenth-Century United States," in *The Middling Sorts: Explorations in the History of the American Middle Class*, ed. Burton J. Bledstein and Robert D. Johnston (New York, 2001), 287–88; also see Dror Wahrman, *The Making of the Modern Self: Identity and Culture in Eighteenth-Century England* (New Haven, 2004).

12. Jack Larkin, "The Faces of Change: Images of Self and Society in New England, 1790–1850," in *Meet Your Neighbors: New England Portraits, Painters, and Society, 1790–1850*, ed. Caroline Sloat (Sturbridge, Mass., 1992), 11; Bruegel, *Farm, Shop, Landing*, 177. See Kathleen Foster's discussion of Thomas Chambers's folk-art contemporaries in *Thomas Chambers: American Marine and Landscape Painter, 1808–1869* (Philadelphia, 2008).

13. Chester Harding, *My Egotistigraphy* (Cambridge, Mass., 1866), 12; Leah Lipton, *A Truthful Likeness: Chester Harding and His Portraits* (Washington, D.C., 1985).

14. John Neal, "American Painters and Painting," *The Yankee: and Boston Literary*

Gazette 1 (1829): 45; Neal, *Wandering Recollections of a Somewhat Busy Life* (Boston, 1868), 108; also, see John Neal Collection, 1793–1876, Maine Historical Society, Portland.

15. Harding, *My Egotistigraphy*, 26–27; Leah Lipton, "William Dunlap, Samuel F. B. Morse, John Wesley Jarvis, and Chester Harding: Their Careers as Itinerant Portrait Painters," *American Art Journal* 12 (Summer 1981): 34–50; Joyce Hill, "New England Itinerant Portraitists," in *Itinerancy in New England and New York*, ed. Peter Benes (Boston, 1986), 160.

16. Ramsay MacMullen, *Sisters of the Brush: Their Family, Art, Lives and Letters, 1797–1833* (New Haven, 1997); Catherine Kelly, "Object Lessons: Miniature Worlds," *Common-Place* 3, no. 2 (January 2003), available at http://www.common-place.org/vol-03/no-02/lessons/ (accessed 26 June 2009).

17. Susan Foster, "Couple and Casualty: The Art of Eunice Pinney Unveiled," *Folk Art* 21 (Summer 1996): 34; Jean Lipman, "Eunice Pinney," in *American Folk Painters of Three Centuries*, ed. Jean Lipman and Tom Armstrong (New York, 1987): 145–49; Gerald Ward, et. al., *American Folk* (Boston, 2001), 96.

18. "An Admirer of Art," ca. 1850, in the M. and M. Karolik Collection of the Museum of Fine Arts, Boston, quoted in Stacy Hollander, "Mary Ann Willson: Artist Maid," *Folk Art* 23 (Summer 1998): 20; N. F. Karlins, "Mary Ann Willson," *Antiques* 110 (November 1976): 1040–45; Ward, *American Folk*, 28–29.

19. Lois Avigad, "Ruth Henshaw Bascom: A Youthful Viewpoint," *Clarion* 12 (Fall 1987): 35–41; Mary Eileen Egan, "Ruth Henshaw Bascom, New England Portraitist" (Honors thesis, College of the Holy Cross, Worcester, Mass., 1980); "American Folk Art: Two Groups of Family Portraits by Ruth Henshaw Bascom and Erastus Salisbury Field," *Worcester Art Museum Bulletin* 5 (May 1976): 1–12; Allison Johnson, "The Journal of Ruth Henshaw Bascom, 1789–1796: Issues of Community and Change in the Lives of Young Women in the Early Republic" (master's thesis, University of New Hampshire, 1993); Ruth Henshaw Bascom, Journals, 1789–1846, American Antiquarian Society, Worcester, Mass.

20. For Chin-Sung, see Sloat, *Meet Your Neighbors*, 81–82; also on Bascom, see Paul D'Ambrosio, *Folk Art's Many Faces: Portraits in the New York State Historical Association* (Cooperstown, N.Y., 1987), 30–37.

21. Friendship Album, Deborah Goldsmith, II, 70, quoted in Sandra C. Shaffer, "Deborah Goldsmith, 1808–1836: A Native Artist in Upstate New York" (master's thesis, SUNY Oneonta, New York, 1968), 13.

22. Jean Lipman, "Deborah Goldsmith, Itinerant Portrait Painter," *Antiques* 44 (November 1943): 227–29; Beatrix T. Rumford, *American Folk Portraits: Paintings and Drawings from the Abby Aldrich Rockefeller Folk Art Center* (New York, 1981), 109–10; AARFAC Goldsmith Files; Priddy, *American Fancy*, 162; D'Ambrosio, *Folk Art's Many Faces*, 86–89.

23. George Throop to Deborah Goldsmith, May 20, 1832, Deborah Goldsmith to George Throop, May 29, 1832, George Throop to Deborah Goldsmith, Jun 7, 1832, reprinted in Olive Cole Smith, *Ancestral Charts of George Addison Throop, Deborah Goldsmith* (East St. Louis, Mo., 1934), 70–71; Rumford, *American Folk Portraits*, 108; also, Friendship Albums, 1826–30, Throop Family Papers, 1836–60, Manuscript Collections, New York State Historical Association, Cooperstown, N.Y.; Deborah Goldsmith, Common Place Books, 1826–32, microfilm, Archives of American Art, Washington, D.C.

24. Sully cited in William Dunlap, *A History of the Rise and Progress of the Arts of Design in the United States* (1969, rpt., New York, 183: pt. 1, p. 230; John Calvin Milley, "Jacob Eichholtz, 1776–1842, Pennsylvania Portraitist" (master's thesis, University of Delaware, 1960), 69; Monroe Fabian, *Mr. Sully, Portrait Painter: The Works of Thomas Sully (1783–1872)* (Washington, D.C., 1983), 10–14.

25. Harding, *My Egotistigraphy*; James Guild, Diary, 1818–1824, Vermont Historical Soci-

ety, available as "From Tunbridge, Vermont, to London, England—The Journal of James Guild, Peddler, Tinker, Schoolmaster, Portrait Painter, from 1818–1824," *Proceedings of the Vermont Historical Society* 5 (September 1937): 249–313; Gordon Wood, *The Radicalism of the American Revolution* (New York, 1993), 361–64; Nina F. Little, *Little by Little: Six Decades of Collecting American Decorative Arts* (Boston, 1998), 267–75; Arthur and Sybil Kern, "James Guild: Quintessential Itinerant Portrait Painter," *Clarion* 17 (Summer 1992): 48–57; Susanna Paine, *Rose and Thorns* (Providence, 1854), 61.

26. Heslip, *Between the Rivers*, 50; D'Ambrosio, *Folk Art's Many Faces*, 49–51; also, see Chapter 4 for discussion of Guild's journal.

27. Sloat, *Meet Your Neighbors*.

28. Zadock Thompson, *History of Vermont, Natural, Civil, and Statistical: in Three Parts* (Burlington, Vt., 1853), 213–14.

29. Rufus Porter, *A Select Collection of Valuable and Curious Arts* (Concord, N.H., 1825), iii–iv. For Porter's varied career, see Jean Lipman, *Rufus Porter, Yankee Pioneer* (New York, 1969, rev. ed. 1980), and "Rufus Porter, Founder of the Scientific American," *Scientific American*, 6 (6 September 1884): 144.

30. See *Scientific American*, 6 September 1884, for Porter's biography. Artisan-inventors are discussed by Brooke Hindle, *Emulation and Invention* (New York, 1981); Eugene S. Ferguson, "The Mind's Eye: Nonverbal Thought in Technology," *Science* 197 (August 1977): 827–36; Anthony F. C. Wallace, *Rockdale* (New York, 1980); Brooke Hindle and Steven Lubar, *Engines of Change: The American Industrial Revolution, 1790–1860* (Washington, D.C., 1986).

31. Neil Larson, "The Politics of Style: Rural Portraiture in the Hudson River Valley in the Second Quarter of the Nineteenth Century" (master's thesis, 1979, Winterthur Museum, Winterthur, Del.); Priddy, *American Fancy*, 99–133.

32. Hollander, *American Radiance*, 394–95; Joseph Davis, Sylvanus C. Foss, and Mary Jane Foss, probably Stratford, New Hampshire, 1836, collection of the American Folk Art Museum, New York; illustrated in Priddy, *American Fancy*, xxi, and Traditional Fine Arts Organization, Resource Library, available at http://www.tfaoi.com/aa/4aa/4aa504.htm (accessed 25 June 2009); also see Betsy Krieg Salm, *Women's Painted Furniture, 1790–1830* (Hanover, N.H., 2010).

33. Priddy, *American Fancy*, 9, 99, 115, 117; Frank O. Spinney, "Joseph H. Davis, New Hampshire Artist of the 1830s," *Antiques* 44 (October 1943): 177; Gail Savage, Norbert H. Savage, and Esther Sparks, *Three New England Watercolor Painters* (Chicago, 1974).

34. Porter, *Select Collection*, 28–30.

35. Porter ad, "Landscape Scenery Painting," *Gazette*, 20 November 1822, quoted in Priddy, *American Fancy*, 126; Hollander, *American Anthem*, 312.

36. Jacob Eichholtz, "Account Book," 1804–6, 1809–17, Historical Society of Pennsylvania, Philadelphia; Milley, "Jacob Eichholtz," 19; Rebecca Beal, *Jacob Eichholtz, 1776–1842, Portrait Painter of Pennsylvania* (Philadelphia, 1969), 157; John J. Snyder, "Federal Furniture of Lancaster Borough/City," *Journal of the Lancaster County Historical Society* 101, special edn. (Spring 1999): 20–21; Richman, *Pennsylvania German Arts*, 123.

37. Joseph Negus to Nathan Negus, 28 December 1819, in Agnes Dods, "Nathan and Joseph Negus, Itinerant Painters," *Antiques* 76 (November 1959): 435–37; see Monica Anke Koenig, "'Every thing with us will be uncertain': A New Look at the Experience of Nathan Negus" (unpublished paper, Historic Deerfield Summer Fellowship Program, Historic Deerfield, 1991); Sloat, *Meet Your Neighbors*, 114–18; Nathan Negus, Memorandum Books, Fuller/Negus Papers, Pocumtuck Valley Memorial Association Library, Deerfield, Mass.

38. Juliette Tomlinson, ed., *The Paintings and the Journal of Joseph Whiting Stock* (Middletown, Conn., 1976), 37. Stock's prices varied between five and ten dollars. For Greenwood, see Ethan Allen Greenwood, Diaries, 1809, Ethan Allen Papers, 1801–39, Manuscript Collec-

tion, American Antiquarian Society, Worcester, Mass.; Georgia B. Bumgardner, "The Early Career of Ethan Allen Greenwood," in *Itinerancy in New England and New York: Dublin Seminar for New England Folklife 1984*, ed. Peter Benes (Boston, 1986), 212–25.

39. See *Scientific American*, 6 September 1884; advertisement in Lipman, *Rufus Porter*, 5. See Rumford, *American Folk Portraits*, 169–72, for details of Porter's production of portraits. See Alice Carrick, *Shades of Our Ancestors* (New York, 1928), and Ellen Miles, *Saint-Memin and the Neoclassical Profile Portrait in America* (Washington, D.C., 1994), on silhouettists. One prodigious silhouette maker claimed a lifetime total of thirty thousand likenesses (Rumford, 107); Accession Files, Abby Aldrich Rockefeller Folk Art Museum Collections (AARFAC), Williamsburg, Virginia.

40. See Lipman, *Rufus Porter*, 89–158, on his farmhouse frescoes; also his own series of articles on "The Art of Painting," published in forty-nine articles between 11 September 1845 and 28 August 1847 in *Scientific American*.

41. Mary Black, "Rediscovery: Erastus Salisbury Field," *American Art Journal* 59 (1966): 50; Rumford, *American Folk Portraits*, 93–99; Mary Black, *Erastus Salisbury Field, 1805–1900* (Williamsburg, Va., 1963); Laura C. Luckey, "Family Portraits in the Museum of Fine Arts, Boston," *Antiques* 110 (November 1976): 1,008; Thomas N. Maytham, "Two Faces of New England Portrait Painting: Erastus Field and Henry Darby," *Bulletin of the Museum of Fine Arts* (Boston) 61, no. 323 (1963): 34.

42. George William Sheldon, *Recent Ideals in American Art* (New York, 1890), 57–58, quoted in Colleen Cowles Heslip, "Between the Rivers: The Rise and Fall of the Artisan Painter," in Heslip, *Between the Rivers* 23.

43. "Painting," *Fitchburg Gazette*, 14 February 1832.

44. Linda Muehlig, *Masterworks of American Painting and Sculpture from the Smith College Museum of Art* (New York, 1999), 49–51; "The Erastus Salisbury Field Paintings," Historic Deerfield Acquisitions, 1989; John Montague Smith, *History of the Town of Sunderland, Massachusetts* (Greenfield, Mass., 1899), 163, 330–37; Frederick Clifton Pierce, *Field Genealogy, being the Record of all the Field Family in America* (Chicago, 1901), 1: 513; Reginald F. French, "Erastus Salisbury Field, 1805–1900," *Connecticut Historical Society Bulletin* 28 (October 1963): 97–135.

45. Dorinda Evans, *The Genius of Gilbert Stuart* (Princeton, N.J., 1999), 90–95; Dunlap, *Rise and Progress of the Arts*, 2: pt. 1, 230; Beal, *Jacob Eichholtz*, xiv; Milley, "Jacob Eichholtz," 77–78, 92–93; Joyce Appleby, *Inheriting the Revolution: The First Generation of Americans* (Cambridge, Mass., 2001).

46. Black, *Erastus Salisbury Field*, 18.

47. Sloat, *Meet Your Neighbors*, 136–37, 101–2; For Matthew Prior see Rumsford, *American Folk Portraits*, 176–82; Nina Fletcher Little, "William Matthew Prior, Traveling Artist, and His In-Laws, the Painting Hamblens," *Antiques* 52 (January 1948): 44–48; Henry Joyce and Sloane Stephens, *American Folk Art at the Shelburne Museum* (Shelburne, Vt., 2001), 47–48; D'Ambrosio, *Folk Art's Many Faces*, 133–40.

48. Deborah Chotner, *American Native Paintings* (Washington, D.C., 1992), 59; Ruth Piwonka, *Painted by Ira C. Goodell: A Catalogue and Checklist of Portraits Done in Columbia County and Elsewhere by Ira C. Goodell* (1800–ca. 1875) (Kinderhook, N.Y., 1979).

49. Elizabeth R. Mankin, "Zedekiah Belknap," *Antiques* 110 (November 1976): 1,056–70; Sloat, *Meet Your Neighbors*, 90, 114–18; Herding, *My Egotistigraphy*, 31–34; Suzanne L Flynt, *The Fullers: A Family of Artists* (Deerfield, Mass., 1997); Nathan Negus, Memorandum Books.

50. For Bartlett self-portrait, see Rumford, *American Folk Portraits*, 47, and AARFAC files; Elizabeth Kornhauser, "'Staring Likenesses': Portraiture in Rural New England, 1800–

1850," in Sloat, *Meet Your Neighbors*, 27; see Negus self-portrait in *Meet Your Neighbors*, 115, and Prior, Plate 4; Joyce Appleby, *Inheriting the Revolution: The First Generation of Americans* (Cambridge, Mass., 2000).

51. Eichholtz, Account Book; Reynolds, *Discourses on Art*, 96; John Neal, *Observations on American Art: Selections from the Writings of John Neal*, comp. Harold E. Dickson (State College, Penn., 1943), 43; Milley, "Jacob Eichholtz," 42; David Jaffee, "Accounting for Jacob Eichholtz," in Thomas Ryan, *Jacob Eichholtz* (Lancaster, Pa., 2003), 29–55.

52. *Lancaster Intelligencer and Weekly Advertiser,* 5 December 1812; Eichholtz, Account Book; Milley, "Jacob Eichholtz," 85–86, 98, 95–97; Beal, *Eichholtz*, 81, 133, 255.

53. Taintor: Sloat, *Meet Your Neighbors*, 132–33; Carrie Barratt, "American Folk Art: Portraiture," available at http://www.metmuseum.org/explore/AmericanFolk/Folk12.htm (accessed 25 June 2009).

54. Rumford, *American Folk Portraits*, 152–54; Hollander, *Revisiting Ammi Phillips*, 19 AARFAC accession files for Dorr portraits.

55. Nelson, "Early American Primitives," 457; Vlach, *Plain Painters*.

56. Sloat, *Meet Your Neighbors*, 72–73.

57. Rumford, *American Folk Portraits*, 93–98; Bullard and Field Accession Files, AARFAC; Black, *Erastus Salisbury Field*, 20.

58. For Bassetts, see Sloat, *Meet Your Neighbors*, 75–76 (Bassetts), 41 (Hurlbut); Black, *Erastus Salisbury Field*, 24–26; Muehlig, *Masterworks of American Painting*, 49–51.

59. For Hubbards see Black, *Erastus Salisbury Field*, 24–26; "The Erastus Salisbury Field Paintings," *Historic Deerfield Acquisitions 1989*; Chotner, *American Native Paintings*, 538–39.

60. Black, *Erastus Salisbury Field*, 26–28; Joyce and Stephens, *American Folk Art at Shelburne*, 43; Hollander, *American Radiance*, 398; Rumford, *American Folk Portraits*, 93–99; *Sotheby's Fine Americana*, New York, 28–31 January 1993, Lot 672–673.

61. Black, *Erastus Salisbury Field*, 28–29; Ward, *American Folk*, 22–23; Thomas N. Maytham, "Two Faces of New England Portrait Painting: Erastus Field and Henry Darby," *Bulletin, Museum of Fine Arts* (Boston) 61, no. 323 (1963), 34; Clarissa Cook to Hannah R. Gillespie, 19 March 1829, in Accession Files, Museum of Fine Arts, Boston.

62. Ruth Piwonka and Roderic H. Blackburn, *A Visible Heritage: Columbia County New York: A History in Art and Architecture* (Kinderhook, N.Y., 1996), 69–70.

63. Horatio Gates Spafford, *A Gazetteer of the State of New York* (Albany, 1824), quoted in Mesick-Cohen-Waite Architects, *The James Vanderpoel House: Historic Structure Report* (Kinderhook, N.Y., 1989), deposited in the Columbia County Historical Society, Kinderhook, New York; Ruth Piwonka and Roderic H. Blackburn, *Ammi Phillips in Columbia County* (Kinderhook, N.Y., 1975).

64. Edward A. Collier, *A History of Old Kinderhook* (New York, 1914), 243; also Elizabeth Louisa Gebhard, *The Parsonage Between the Two Manors: Annals of Clover-Reach* (Hudson, N.Y., 1909); Franklin Ellis, *History of Columbia County, New York* (Philadelphia, 1876); Elizabeth W. Olmstead, ed., *Selections from the Correspondence and Diaries of John Olmstead 1826–1838* (Buffalo, N.Y., 1968); *Rural Repository*, 1824–51, Hudson, New York; Peter H. Stott, *Looking for Work: Industrial Archeology in Columbia County, New York* (Kinderhook, N.Y., 2007), 218–20.

65. *James Vanderpoel House: Historic Structure Report*; Historic Landscape Report, *James Vanderpoel House Property* (Kinderhook, N.Y., 1995); Mesick-Cohen-Waite Architects, *The James Vanderpoel House.*

66. Russell Dorr files, Columbia County Historical Society, Kinderhook,.

67. Tammis K. Groft and Mary Alice Mackay, *Albany Institute of History and Art: 200 Years of Collecting* (New York, 1998), 66–67.

68. Piwonka and Blackburn, *A Visible Heritage*, 129, for Johnson portrait of Sherman and Lydia Grisold, ca. 1837; Ruth Piwonka and Roderick H. Blackburn, *James E. Johnson: Rural Artist, a Catalogue of an Exhibition of Portraits by James E. Johnson, 1810–1858 of Columbia County, N.Y.* (Kinderhook, N.Y., 1975); Piwonka, *Painted by Ira C. Goodell*; Agnes Halsey Jones, *Rediscovered Artists of Upstate New York, 1700–1785* (Utica, N.Y., 1958); Goodell files, Columbia County Historical Society.

69. William B. Stoddard, 31 January 1835, *Rural Repository*, in Piwonka, *Painted by Ira C. Goodell*, 3.

70. Wendy Cooper, *Classical Taste in America* (New York, 1996), 212–14.

71. Jack Larkin, "The Faces of Change: Images of Self and Society in New England, 1790–1850," in Sloat, *Meet Your Neighbors*, 11; Louis Legrand Noble, *The Life and Works of Thomas Cole* (Cambridge, Mass., 1964), 196.

CHAPTER 7. THE INDUSTRIAL IMAGE

1. Dale Johnson, "Deacon Robert Peckham: Delineator of the 'Human Face Divine,'" *American Art Journal* 10 (January 1979): 31–36; Laura Luckey, "The Portraits of Robert Peckham," *Antiques* 134 (September 1988): 552–57; David Krashes, "Robert Peckham: Unsung Rural Master," *Folk Art* 21 (Spring 1996): 38–45; Ann Howard, "Deacon Peckham's World of Art: Notes on Robert Peckham (paper on file, n.d., Westminster Historical Society, Westminster, Mass.); Painter's Files, Abby Aldrich Rockefeller Folk Art Center, Williamsburg, Va.

2. Stephen Farnum Peckham, *Peckham Genealogy* (New York, 1922), 267–69, 315–17; William S. Heywood, *History of Westminster, Massachusetts* (Lowell, Mass., 1876); Ethan Allen Greenwood, Diaries, 1809, Ethan Allen Greenwood Papers, 1801–1839, Manuscript Collection, American Antiquarian Society, Worcester, Mass.; Georgia B. Bumgardner, "The Early Career of Ethan Allen Greenwood," in *Itinerancy in New England and New York: Dublin Seminar for New England Folklife 1984*, ed. Peter Benes (Boston, 1986), 212–25.

3. Luckey, "Portraits of Robert Peckham," 555; Carol Troyen, *The Boston Tradition: American Paintings from the Museum of Fine Arts, Boston* (New York, 1980), 90; Laura Luckey, "New Discoveries in American Art: An Early Family Portrait by Robert Peckham," *American Art Journal* 12 (Autumn 1980): 85–86; curatorial files, Museum of Fine Arts, Boston; *Hampshire Gazette*, 17 May 1815, quoted in D'Ambrosio, *Folk Art's Many Faces*, 122–23; Worcester *Massachusetts Spy*, 29 July 1829 and 19 March 1834; Peckham-Sawyer curatorial files, Museum of Fine Arts, Boston.

4. D'Ambrosio, *Folk Art's Many Faces*, 122–25; Christopher Columbus Baldwin, *Diary of Christopher Columbus Baldwin* (Worcester, Mass., 1901), 282; Whittier correspondence, Houghton Library, Harvard University, Cambridge, Mass., quoted in Luckey, "Portraits of Robert Peckham," 555–56.

5. Howard, "Deacon Peckham's World of Art"; Celia Bragdon, "Deacon Robert Peckham of Westminster, Massachusetts, His Life and Work" (paper, 1973, Westminster Historical Society, Westminster, Mass.); Robert Peckham letters, Fruitlands Museum, Harvard, Mass.; Peckham, *Peckham Genealogy*, 267–68; Westminster resident, quoted in Clara Endicott Sears, *Some American Primitives: A Study of New England Faces and Folk Portraits* (Boston, 1941), 82; Robert Peckham, *Historical Poem to Be Read at the Dedication of the Soldier's Monument in Westminster, Mass., July 4th, 1868* (Fitchburg, Mass., 1868).

6. Johnson, "Deacon Robert Peckham"; David Krashes, "Robert Peckham: Portrait Painter of Massachusetts," *Maine Antiques Digest* 15 (January 1985): 22D–24D; Luckey, "Portraits of Robert Peckham"; Rumford, *American Folk Portraits*, 371–73; Walter Heywood obituary, *Gardner News*, 7 August 1880, Rosa H. Brown, 23 August 1923; Rosa Heywood Painting files and Robert Peckham Painters Files, Abby Aldrich Rockefeller Folk Art Center, Williams-

burg, Va.; "By Popular Demand, vote results," exhibition, 2000–2001, courtesy of Barbara Luck, curator of paintings, AARFAC.

7. Deborah Chotner, *American Naïve Paintings from the National Gallery of Art* (Washington, D.C., 1985), 493–95; Inez McClintock and Marshall McClintock, *Toys in America* (Washington, D.C., 1961), 147–51; Sandra Brant, *Small Folk: A Celebration of Childhood in America* (New York, 1980), 128–29; Hollander, *American Anthem*, 406; Sears, *Some American Primitives*, 84; Luckey, "Portraits of Robert Peckham"; Johnson, "Deacon Robert Peckham," 30–31; Krashes, "Robert Peckham," *Antiques*; Elizabeth Donaghy Garrett, *At Home: The American Family, 1750–1870* (New York, 1990), 54. For Raymond Children, see Painting Files, American Wing, Metropolitan Museum of Art, New York; Museum of Fine Arts, Boston, Mass.; John Caldwell and Oswaldo Rodriguez Roque, *American Paintings in the Metropolitan Museum of Art* (New York, 1994), 361–63.

8. Grant Romer, "The Mirror with a Memory: The Daguerreotype as a Portrait Medium," in *Face to Face: M. W. Hopkins and Noah North*, ed. Jacquelyn Oak (Lexington, Mass., 1988), 29–36; Shirley Teresa Wajda, "'Social Currency': A Domestic History of the Portrait Photograph in the United States, 1839–1889" (Ph.D. diss., University of Pennsylvania, 1992); Alan Trachtenberg, *Reading American Photographs: Images as History, Mathew Brady to Walker Evans* (New York, 1989). See also Robert Taft, *Photography and the American Scene: A Social History, 1839–1889* (New York, 1938); Floyd Rinhart and Marion Rinhart, *The American Daguerreotype* (Athens, Ga., 1981); Richard Rudisill, *Mirror Image: The Influence of the Daguerreotype on American Society* (Albuquerque, N.Mex., 1971); John Tagg, *The Burden of Representation: Essays on Photographies and Histories* (Amherst, Mass., 1988).

9. Grant B. Romer, "'A High Reputation with All True Artists and Connoisseurs': The Daguerreian Careers of A. S. Southworth and J. J. Hawes," in *Young America: The Daguerreotypes of Southworth and Hawes*, ed. Grant Romer and Brian Wallis (Rochester, N.Y., 2005), 21; Rudisill, *Mirror Image*, 42–61; [Nathaniel P. Willis], "The Pencil of Nature," *Corsair* 1 (13 April 1839): 71–72; Samuel Morse, letter in Samuel Irenaeus Prime, *The Life of Samuel F. B. Morse* (New York, 1875), 401.

10. A. S. Southworth to Nancy Southworth, 21 May 1840, Southworth & Hawes Papers, Box 1, George Eastman House, Rochester, N.Y.; Romer, "Daguerreian Careers," 21; Charles Leroy Moore, "Two Partners in Boston: The Careers and Daguerreian Artistry of Albert Southworth and Josiah Hawes" (Ph.D. diss., University of Michigan, 1975), 25; Albert Sands Southworth, "An Address to the National Photographic Association," *Philadelphia Photographer* 8 (October 1871): 315–23, reprinted in *Secrets of the Dark Chamber: The Art of the American Daguerreotype*, available at http://americanart.si.edu/helios/secrets/darkchamberno frame.html?/helios /secrets/text_address.html (accessed 25 June 2009).

11. Romer, "Daguerreian Careers," 22–24; Rinhart and Rinhart, *American Daguerreotype*, 31–42; Rudisill, *Mirror Image*, 58–68.

12. Josiah B. Millet, ed., *George Fuller: His Life and Works* (Boston, 1886), 14.

13. Millet, *George Fuller: His Life and Works*, 14.

14. J. J. Hawes, "Stray Leaves from the Diary of the Oldest Professional Photographer in the World," *Photo-Era* 16 (February 1906): 104–7, available at http://americanart.si.edu/helios/secrets/darkchamber-noframe.html ?/helios/secr ets/text_stray.html (accessed June 25, 2009); Moore, "Two Partners in Boston," 157; Romer, "Daguerreian Careers," 24.

15. J. Gurney, quoted in "Photographic Section of the American Institute," *Anthony's Photographic Bulletin* 17 (12 May, 1886): 312; Rudisill, *Mirror Image*, 61.

16. *Gazette and Mercury* (Greenfield, Mass.), March 1840, quoted in Sloat, *Meet Your Neighbors*, 80; A. S. Southworth to Nancy Southworth, 30 September 1841, Southworth and Hawes Papers; Moore, "Two Partners in Boston," 25; Romer, "Daguerreian Careers," 24–25.

17. A. S. Southworth to Nancy Southworth, April 1841, quoted in Romer, "Daguerreian Careers," 26–27.

18. Nathaniel Hawthorne, *The House of the Seven Gables* (New York, 1990), 156.

19. W. H. Sherman, "The Rise and Fall of the Daguerreotype (As Seen by a Country Operator)," *Photographic Times* (30 January 1891), reprinted in *Daguerreian Annual 1997*, 211–14.

20. Anson Clark to Roland White, letter, 7 September 1841, Anson Clark Collection, Stockbridge Public Library, Stockbridge, Mass.; Richard Bolt, "Anson and Edwin H. Clark: Pioneering Daguerreotypists of Western Massachusetts," *Daguerreian Annual 1991*, 79–90.

21. John Lawton to Southworth, 11 June and 3 November 1841, Nashua, N.H.; Garner to Southworth, 28 September 1844, Chicopee, Mass.; Dolly Burr, 9 April 1845, Ashburnham, Mass., all in Southworth and Hawes Papers.

22. *Gazette and Courier* (Greenfield, Mass.), November 1843 and January 1844, quoted in Sloat, *Meet Your Neighbors*, 80; Beaumont Newhall, *The Daguerreotype in America* (1961; reprint, New York, 1976), 69–70.

23. Ambrose Andrews, letter to Mrs. Lydia Partridge, 25 June 1846, Watson Letterbook, Thomas J. Watson Library, Metropolitan Museum of Art, New York.

24. Juliette Tomlinson, ed., *The Paintings and the Journal of Joseph Whiting Stock* (Middletown, Conn., 1976); Michael R. Payne and Suzanne Rudnick Payne, "Isaac Augustus Wetherby: The Business of an American Folk Art Portrait Painter," *Folk Art* 32 (Winter 2007): 62; Black, *Erastus Salisbury Field*, 35; Diane E. Forsberg, "Erastus Salisbury Field: Mezzographs and Other Experiments with Photography in Portrait Painting," and Lauren B. Hewes, "Horace Bundy: Portraits Painted from Daguerreotypes," both in *Painting and Portrait Making in the American Northeast*, ed. Peter Benes (Boston, 1995), 235–254; Oak, *Face to Face*; Sloat, *Meet Your Neighbors*, 138; Randolph J. Ploog, "The Account Books of Isaac Augustus Wetherby: Portrait Painter/Photographer," *History of Photography* 14 (January–March 1990): 77–85; Isaac Augustus Wetherby, Daybooks, 2 vols., photocopy, New-York Historical Society, New York.

25. Sam F. Simpson, "Daguerreotyping on the Mississippi," *Photographic and Fine Art Journal* 8 (August 1855): 252–53; J. R. Gorgas, *St. Louis and Canadian Photographer* 23 (July 1899): 327.

26. "Letters from an Itinerant Daguerreotypist of Western New York," ed. Grant Romer, *Image* 27 (March 1984): 12–19. For other itinerants' accounts, see Thomas Kailbourn and Graham Garrett, "Oliver B. Evans: Daguerreian Artist of the Niagara Frontier," *Daguerreian Annual 1992*: 11–17; Jim Foster, "The Vexations of E. M. Wilson, Itinerant Daguerreotypist," *Daguerreian Annual 1992*: 126–27; "The Itinerant Artist," *Daguerreian Journal* (3 December 1851): 82–83; "The Traveling Photographer (Image)," *Harper's Weekly* (16 December 1871): Supplement, 1185; H. M. Holloway, "Isaac Augustus Wetherby (1819–1904) and His Account Books," *New-York Historical Society Quarterly Bulletin* 25 (April 1941): 55–69.

27. Abraham Bogardus, *Photographic Times* 15 (11 September 1885): 521, quoted in Trachtenberg, *Reading American Photographs*, 13; Trachtenberg, "Photography: The Emergence of a Keyword," in *Photography in Nineteenth-Century America*, ed. Martha Sandweiss (New York, 1991), 16–47; Taft, *Photography*, 48; T. S. Arthur, "American Characteristics: No. V. The Daguerreotypist," *Godey's Lady's Book* 38 (May 1849): 352–53; Hawthorne, *House of the Seven Gables*, 85; Cathy N. Davidson, "Portraits of the Dead: Sherman, Daguerre, Hawthorne," *South Atlantic Quarterly* 89 (Fall 1990): 667–701.

28. L. C. Champney to Southworth and Hawes, Letter, 9 March 1843, Box 1, Southworth & Hawes Collection; Sarah Holland to Southworth, 16 January 1846, Fairless, Vt.,

Southworth and Hawes Papers; "Mr. George and Jas. Perry's System of Daguerreotyping as Given by Mr. Jas. C. Spencer—Daguerreian Atelier," Ms. Notebook, Kingston, N.Y., 9 November 1845, George Eastman House, as quoted in Romer, "The Mirror with a Memory," 33; H. J. Rodgers, *Twenty-Three Years Under a Sky-Light, a Life and Experiences of a Photographer* (Hartford, Conn., 1872), 219.

29. Abraham Bogardus, *Anthony's Photographic Bulletin* 15 (1884): 62, quoted in William Welling, *Photography in America* (New York, 1978), 57–58; on Carpenter: Sloat, *Meet Your Neighbors*, 80–81, and Meet Your Neighbors Exhibition Files, Old Sturbridge Village Curatorial Department, Sturbridge, Mass.; Lucy Cutler Kellogg, *History of the Town of Bernardston, Franklin County, Massachusetts, 1736–1900* (Greenfield, Mass., 1902), 265–66; Romer, "The Mirror with a Memory"; Julian Wolff, "Daguerreotypes as Folk Art," *Clarion* 1 (Fall 1986): 18–24. Also, see "Daguerreotypes," *Litell's Living Age* 9 (20 June 1846): 551–52.

30. James F. Ryder, *Voightlander and I, In Pursuit of Shadow Catching* (Cleveland, 1902).

31. Ryder, *Voightlander and I*, 13–20. On Ryder, see Thomas H. Pauly, "In Search of 'The Spirit of '76,'" in *Recycling the Past: Popular Uses of American History*, ed. Leila Zenderland (Philadelphia, 1978), 28–49.

32. Ryder, *Voightlander and I*, 20, 22, 28.

33. Ibid., 28–32.

34. Ibid., 85, 90, 111–12.

35. Barbara McCandless, "The Portrait Studio and the Celebrity: Promoting the Art," in Sandweiss, *Photography in Nineteenth-Century America*, 53–63; Reese Jenkins, *Images and Enterprise: Technology and the American Photographic Industry 1839 to 1925* (Baltimore, 1975); M. Susan Barger and William B. White, *The Daguerreotype: Nineteenth-Century Technology and Modern Science* (Washington, D.C., 1991), 46–54; Rinhart and Rinhart, *American Daguerreotype*, 90–100; "Letter from an Old Artist," *Daguerreian Journal* 1 (November 1850): 44–45.

36. Marcus Root, "Some Thoughts on the Fitting Up of Daguerreian Rooms," *Photographic Art Journal* 5 (June 1853): 361–63; S. D. Humphrey, "Daguerreotyping in New York," *Daguerreian Journal* 1 (15 November 1850): 49; C. Edwards Lester, "M. B. Brady and the Photographic Art," *Photographic Art Journal* 1 (January 1851): 37; "Photography in the United States," *Photographic Art Journal* 5 (June 1853): 334–43.

37. Marcus Root, "Some Thoughts"; Editor, Knowledge of the Art," *Photographic Art Journal* 1 (January 1851): 49–50.

38. "The True Artist," *Photographic Art Journal* 2 (August 1851), available at http://americanart.si.edu/helios/secrets/darkchamber-noframe.html ?/helios/secr ets/text_trueartist.html (accessed December 20, 2009); Marcus Root, *The Camera and the Pencil, or The Heliographic Art* (Philadelphia, 1864), 99; J. H. Fitzgibbon, "Daguerreotyping," *Photographic Art Journal* 2 (August 1851): 91–93; Albert S. Southworth, "An Address to the National Photographic Association of the U.S.," *Philadelphia Photographer* 8 (October 1871): 315–23; Marcus Root, "Qualifications of a First-Rate Daguerreotypist," *Photographic Art Journal* 6 (August 1853): 112–15; and Gabriel Harrison, "The Dignity of Our Art," *Photographic Art Journal* 3 (April 1852): 230–32.

39. J. H. Fitzgibbon, "Daguerreotyping," *Daguerreian Journal* 2 (1 August 1857): 167–69; S. D. Humphrey, *American Hand Book of the Daguerreotype* (1858), cited in Wajda, "Social Currency," 201; Humphrey, "The Daguerrean Art: Its Present State and Future Prospects," *Photographic Art Journal* 2 (August 1851): 100; *Daguerreian Journal* 2 (August 1851): 209; Albert S. Southworth, "Suggestions to Ladies Who Sit for Daguerreotypists," *Lady's Almanac* (1854 and 1855), available at http://americanart.si.edu/helios/secrets/darkchamber-noframe.html?/ helios/secr ets/text_ladies.html(accessed December 20, 2009); "Photographic Re-Unions," *Photographic Art Journal* 1 (February 1851): 107–8.

40. For Brady, see McCandless, "The Portrait Studio and the Celebrity," 54; John Werge, *The Evolution of Photography* (London, 1890), 196–202.

41. Letter, John Toole to Jane Toole, 15–19 August 1857, reprinted in William B. O'Neal, *Primitive into Painter: Life and Letters of John Toole* (Charlottesville, 1960), 36–37.

42. "Formula and Lesson Book"; letter from J. E. Mayall to George Pyle, 6 June 1846; receipt from Mayall to Pyle for supplies, 1 April 1846; all in Francis C. Pyle Collection, Chester County Historical Society. Pamela C. Powell, *Reflected Light: A Century of Photography in Chester County* (West Chester, Pa., 1988), 17–18. I am grateful to Pamela Powell, curator of photography at the Chester County Historical Society, for introducing me to the Pyle collection and sharing research materials, such as a detailed chronology of Pyle's life. See also Leonie Reynolds and Arthur Gill, "The Mayall Story," *History of Photography* 9 (April–June 1985): 89–101.

43. George Pyle, Account Book; letter from Levi Scarlet to George Pyle, 19 August 1847; Francis Pyle Collection. Powell, *Reflected Light*, 18–20; John W. Bear, *The Life and Travels of John W. Bear, "The Buckeye Blacksmith"* (Baltimore, 1873).

44. Letter from George Pyle to Magdeline Pyle, 11 August 1849; Francis Pyle Collection. *Register and Examiner* (West Chester), 16 July 1850, Inventory of Good and Chattels of George Pyle, 1871, quoted in Powell, *Reflected Light*, 20; "George Pyle's Journal," typescript, Chester County Historical Society, West Chester, Pa.; broadside and tin shop sign in Chester County Historical Society Collections, West Chester, Pa.

45. Ambrose Andrews, letter to his sister, Mrs. Sarah Blackmer, 14 April 1853; Andrews, letter to his niece Abigail Andrews, September 29, 1855; Ambrose Andrews Letterbook, 1844–56; Thomas J. Watson Library, Metropolitan Museum of Art, New York.

46. Sherman, "Rise and Fall of the Daguerreotype," 212; Pyle Inventory quote in Powell, *Reflected Light*, 22.

47. T. S. Arthur, "The Daguerreotypist," 352–55; Wajda, "Social Currency," 288–90; Jackson Lears, "Beyond Veblen: Consumer Culture in America," in *Consuming Visions: Accumulation and Display of Goods in America, 1880–1920*, ed. Simon Bronner (New York, 1989), 73–98.

48. Chauncey Jerome, *History of the American Clock Business for the Past Sixty Years* (New Haven, 1860) 53, 56; Chris Bailey, *From Rags to Riches to Rags: The Story of Chauncey Jerome*, National Watch and Clock Collectors Bulletin Supplement 15 (Spring 1986): 145.

49. Jerome, *American Clock Business*, 55; Philip Barnes to Rensseleaer Upson, letter, 26 January 1838, Upson Papers, Connecticut State Library, reprinted in Chris H. Bailey, *Two Hundred Years of American Clocks and Watches* (Englewood Cliffs, N.J., 1975), 146; Hiram Camp, "Sketch of the Clockmaking Business" (1893), Connecticut Historical Society, Hartford, Conn.

50. Jerome, *American Clock Business*, 56–57; Bailey, *Two Hundred Years of American Clocks*, 128–30; Bailey, *From Rags to Riches to Rags*, 25; David S. Hounshell, *From the American System to Mass Production 1800–1932* (Baltimore, 1984), 57–60; Kenneth D. Roberts, *The Contributions of Joseph Ives to Connecticut Clock Technology, 1810–1862* (Hartford, Conn., 1970).

51. Jerome, *American Clock Business*, 57–58; Bailey, *Two Hundred Years of American Clocks*, 128–30; Bailey, *From Rags to Riches to Rags*, 56; Camp, "Sketch of Clockmaking Business."

52. John P. Bigelow, *Statistical Tables Exhibiting the Condition of Certain Branches of Industry in Massachusetts* (Boston, 1838), 50; John Gorham Palfrey, *Statistics of the Condition and Products of Certain Branches of Industry in Massachusetts* (Boston, 1846), 103; Frances DeWitt, *Statistical Information Relating to Certain Branches of Industry in Massachusetts* (Boston, 1856), 491–92; Donna Baron, "Furniture Makers and Retailers in Worcester County,"

Antiques 193 (May 1993): 785; Storch Associates, "Historic Documentation Report for Gardner Heritage State Park," Gardner, Massachusetts, 19 February 1981 (in author's possession), 21.

53. Heywood-Wakefield Company, *A Century Completed* (Boston, 1926); Richard Greenwood, *The Five Heywood Brothers* (New York, 1951); Storch, "Gardner Heritage State Park Report"; also, see invoices for shipments by sea to San Francisco, 1833, and rail to New Bedford, 1852, Heywood Brothers & Co., Records, 1833–81, Downs Collection, Winterthur Museum.

54. For Hill Brothers, see Irving Bell, "They Painted Hills," *Historical New Hampshire* 3 (February 1946): 11–21; also see Heywood Brothers, Painted Bedstead with Canopy, ca. 1855, Museum of Fine Arts, Boston, acc. 1978.305 and curatorial files for an example of the Hill Brothers' work on an elaborate piece of cottage furniture said to have been made especially for Levi Heywood.

55. William Herrick, *History of the Town of Gardner, Worcester County, Mass.* (Gardner, Mass., 1871); Herrick, "Gardner" in *History of Worcester County, Massachusetts*, ed. D. Hamilton Hurd (Philadelphia, 1889); Esther G. Moore, *History of Gardner Massachusetts, 1785–1967* (Gardner, Mass., 1967), 53, 195.

56. Jerome, *American Clock Business*, 92; Murphy, "Establishment of the American Clock Industry," 175–81; Manufacture of Clocks in Connecticut," *Simonds Colonial Magazine* 6 (1845): 239; Camp, "Sketch of Clockmaking Business," 7.

57. "Manufacture of Clocks in Connecticut," 238; Jerome, *American Clock Business*, 92.

58. Jerome, *American Clock Business*, 92; John Joseph Murphy, "The Establishment of the American Clock Industry, "The Establishment of the American Clock Industry: A Study of Entrepreneurial History" (Ph.D. diss., Yale University, 1961), 197; Worcester County Records, vol. 169: 165–66, R. G. Dun Records, Harvard Business School, Cambridge, Mass.; Storch, "Historic Documentation Report for Gardner Heritage State Park"; Herrick, *History of Gardner*, 168.

59. Herrick, *History of Gardner*, 141–46; Storch, "Historic Documentation Report for Gardner Heritage State Park"; William A. Emerson, *Fitchburg, Massachusetts, Past and Present* (Fitchburg, Mass., 1887), 185; Doris Kirkpatrick, *The City and the River* (Fitchburg, Mass., 1971), 1: 177–78; William Bond Wheelwright, *Life and Times of Alvah Crocker* (Boston, 1923), 15–21.

60. Nancy Evans, *American Windsor Chairs* (New York, 1997), 108 (Ash), 490–94; Accession Files, OSV Library; 1820 Census of Manufactures, Worcester County, State of Massachusetts; *Freedom's Sentinel*, Athol, Mass., 18 December 1827; Thomas Sheraton's designs in his *Cabinet-Maker and Upholsterer's Drawing Book*.

61. Josiah P. Wilder Day Books, 1837–61, transcription, Charles S. Parsons, "Wilder Chairs," unpublished paper, February 1973, Parsons Papers, New Hampshire Historical Society, Concord, N.H.; Donna K. Baron, "Definition and Diaspora of Regional Style: The Worcester County Model," *American Furniture 1995* (Milwaukee, Wisc., 1995)," 167–90; NHHS, *Plain and Elegant, Rich and Common*, 116–17; Evans, *American Windsor Chairs*, 513–15; Accession Files, Winterthur Museum, Winterthur, Del.

62. Kenneth Zogry, *The Best the Country Affords: Vermont Furniture, 1765–1850* (Bennington, Vt., 1995), 29, 152.

63. Christopher Clark, "The Diary of an Apprentice Cabinetmaker: Edward Jenner Carpenter's 'Journal', 1844–45," edited with the assistance of Donald M. Scott, *Proceedings of the American Antiquarian Society* 98 (1988): 303–94.

64. John Stocker Knowlton, *Carl's Tour in Main Street* (Worcester, Mass., 1889), quoted in Donna Baron, Frank White, and Karen Blanchfield, "Cabinet Furniture and Chairs,

Cheap: Making and Selling Furniture in Central New England, 1790–1850," research paper, 1993, OSV Library; Jacob Felton, Daybook, 1836–38, Fitzwilliam, N.H., 1836–1838, OSV Library; Evans, *Windsor-Chair Making*, 320, 293; Heywood-Wakefield, *A Completed Century*, 7; Greenwood, *Five Heywood Brothers.*

65. Murphy, "Establishment of the American Clock Industry," 202–3.

66. Jerome, *American Clock Business*, 62–64; Bailey, *From Rags to Riches to Rags*, 66; Murphy, "Establishment of the American Clock Industry," 212–15.

67. Margaret Berwind Schiffler, *Furniture and Its Makers of Chester County, Pennsylvania* (Philadelphia, 1966), 133; Barry Allen Kessler, "Of Workshops and Warerooms: The Economic and Geographic Transformation of Furniture Making in Chester County, Pennsylvania, 1780–1850" (master's thesis, University of Delaware, 1987), 73; Chester County Historical Society, *Two Hundred Years of Chairs and Chairmaking: An Exhibition of Chairs from the Chester County Historical Society* (West Chester, Pa., 1987), 21.

68. Bristol Manufacturing Co. to Chauncey Jerome, letter, Bristol, 7 July 1842, 18: 246, quoted in Murphy, "Establishment of the American Clock Industry," 227; Camp, "Sketch of Clockmaking Business"; Jerome, *American Clock Business*, 97–105.

69. Jerome, *American Clock Business*, 79–82, 96; Bailey, *Two Hundred Years of American Clocks*, 151–52; Bailey, *From Rags to Riches to Rags*, 99–102; Murphy, "Establishment of the American Clock Industry," 238–49.

70. Murphy, "Establishment of the American Clock Industry," 245; Jerome, *American Clock Business*, 97–105, Bailey, *Two Hundred Years of American Clocks*, 166–84; Camp, "Sketch of Clockmaking Business," 7–8.

71. Myron O. Stachiw and Nora Pat Small, "Tradition and Transformation: Rural Society and Architectural Change in Nineteenth Century Central Massachusetts," in *Perspectives in Vernacular Architecture III*, ed. Thomas Carter and Bernard L. Herman (Columbia, Mo., 1989): 135–48; Myron O. Stachiw, "The World of Emerson Bixby: Work, Family and Community in 19th-Century Barre, Massachusetts," OSV Research Paper, 1984, OSV Library; John Worrell, Myron O. Stachiw, David M. Simmons, and Nora Pat Small, "Archaeology from the Ground Up: The Bixby House and Site," OSV Research Paper, May 1992, OSV Research Library.

72. Stachiw and Small, "Tradition and Transformation," 142–44; Worrell, Stachiw, Simmons, and Small, "Archaeology from the Ground Up," 28–38; Richard Bushman, *The Refinement of America: Persons, Houses, Cities* (New York, 1992), 252–55; Jack Larkin, "From 'Country Mediocrity' to 'Rural Improvement': Transforming the Slovenly Countryside in Central Massachusetts, 1775–1840," in *Everyday Life in the Early Republic*, ed. Catherine Hutchins (Winterthur, Del., 1994), 187.

73. Gail Emily Nessel, "The Goodale Family: Seven Generations of Continuity and Change in Marlborough, Massachusetts" (master's thesis, University of Delaware, 1985), 61; Goodale Family Papers, Old Sturbridge Village Research Library.

74. Lois W. Martin, "A Vermont Country Wedding in 1858," *Old-Time New England* 61 (October–November 1970), 55.

75. Newton Simeon Hubbard, "The Hubbard Homestead," manuscript, 1895, OSV Library files; Jack Larkin, "Transforming the Countryside," 187; portraits: for Hubbard portraits, see Sloat, *Meet Your Neighbors*, 105–6.

76. Catherine Kelly, *In the New England Fashion* (Ithaca, N.Y., 1999), 218; Snell Family Papers, Special Collections, Amherst College, Amherst, Mass., digital collections available at http://clio.fivecolleges.edu/amherst/snell/ (accessed 25 June 2009) (see Snell Portraits, Ebenezer and Sabra, Amherst Special Collections).

77. Izard, "Another Place in Time," 241–56.

78. Larkin, "Transforming the Countryside," 187–90; Bushman, *Refinement of America*, 228–30. For illustration of Ackeley and Edson tables, see Zogry, *Best the Country Affords*, 150–51.

79. Larkin, "Transforming the Countryside," 188–89; Jack Larkin, *The Reshaping of Everyday Life, 1790–1840* (New York, 1989), 136; Bushman, *Refinement of America*, 228–32; Garrett, *At Home*, 54–55; Jane Nylander, *Our Own Snug Fireside: Images of the New England Home, 1760–1860* (New Haven, 1994), 112–13; Bruegel, *Farm, Shop, Landing*, 177.

80. John F. Kasson, *Rudeness and Civility: Manners in Nineteenth Century America* (New York, 1991), 176; Katherine C. Arlen, *Culture and Comfort: People, Parlors, and Upholstery, 1850–1930* (Rochester, N.Y., 1988), 7; See also Nancy Dunlap Bercaw, "Solid Objects/Mutable Meanings: Fancywork and the Construction of Bourgeois Culture, 1840–1880," *Winterthur Portfolio* 26 (Winter 1991): 231–47.

81. Central New England Cabinetmakers, list compiled by Jane Nylander, Spring 1974 (author's possession and copies at the Winterthur Museum, Winterthur, Del.); inventories transcribed of Smyrna Glazier and Caleb Young. For Levi Heywood, see Federal Census, Population Schedules, Gardner, Massachusetts, 1850 (p. 71) and 1860 (p. 33), Massachusetts Archives, Boston.

82. Atwood Family Files, curatorial file, Museum of Fine Arts, Boston; Ward, *American Folk*, 25; Inge Hacker, "Discovery of a Prodigy: The Portrait of Reverend John Atwood and His Family by Henry F. Darby," and Thomas Maytham, "Two Faces of New England Portrait Painting," *Bulletin of the Museum of Fine Arts Boston* 61 no. 323 (1962): 23–29, 30–41; Mary Panzer, *Matthew Brady and the Image of History* (Washington, D.C., 1997), 80–81.

83. "Daguerreotyping in New York," *Daguerreian Journal* 3 (15 November 1851), 19; Trachtenberg, *Reading American Photographs*, 39–43; Katherine C. Grier, *Culture and Comfort*, 44–48.

84. See Joan L. Severa, *My Likeness Taken: Daguerreian Portraits in America* (Kent, Ohio, 2005).

85. Susan Stewart, *On Longing: Narratives of the Miniature, the Gigantic, the Souvenir, the Collection* (Baltimore, 1984), 69.

86. T. S. Arthur, "The Daguerreotypist," 352–55; Wajda, "Social Currency," 288–90; Jackson Lears, "Beyond Veblen."

87. See Jean Baudrillard, *Le Système des Objets* (Paris, 1980), 255–83, in Mark Poster, ed., *Jean Baudrillard: Selected Writings* (Berkeley, Calif., 1988).

88. Miles Orvell, *The Real Thing: Imitation and Authenticity in American Culture, 1880–1940* (Chapel Hill, 1989), 50; Mark Twain, *The Adventures of Huckleberry Finn*, (New York, 1918), 139–40.

EPILOGUE

1. Hiram Camp, "Sketch of Clock Making Business"; (1893), Connecticut Historical Society; Chris H. Bailey, *Two Hundred Years of American Clocks and Watches* (Englewood Cliffs, N.J., 1975), 150–52; Chauncey Jerome, *History of the American Clock Business, for the Past Sixty Years* (New Haven, 1860) 7–116; Chris Bailey, "From Rags to Riches: The Story of Chauncey Jerome," *National Watch and Clock Collectors Bulletin Supplement* 15 (Spring 1986), 73–74, 99–101.

2. James Parton, *Captains of Industry* (Boston, 1884), 33; Bailey, *From Rags to Riches to Rags*, 109–10; Jerome, *American Clock Business*.

3. Jack Larkin, "The Merriams of Brookfield: Printing in the Economy and Culture of Rural Massachusetts in the Early Nineteenth Century," *Proceedings of the American Antiquerion Society* 96 (1986); 39.

4. *The Story of the Merriam Family: George, Charles, Lewis and Homer, Printers, Publishers and Men of Progress* (Springfield, Mass., 1887), 6–9.

5. *Story of the Merriam Family*, 10, 14–16; G. & C. Merriam Company, *The House That Merriam-Webster Built* (Windham, Conn., 1940), 8–9; Robert Keith Leavitt, *Noah's Ark: New England's Yankees, and the Endless Quest, a Short History of the Original Webster Dictionaries, with Particular Reference to Their First Hundred Years as Publications of G. and C. Merriam Company* (Springfield, Mass., 1947).

6. Lipman, *Rufus Porter*, 27–39; "Rufus Porter, Founder of the Scientific American," *Scientific American*, 6 September 1884. For Porter murals that have been "discovered" in recent years on farmhouse walls, see Sam Hooper Samuels, "In the Steps of Rufus Porter, Yankee Original," *New York Times*, 7 August 2005.

7. Jean Lipman, *Rufus Porter: Yankee Pioneer* (New York, 1969, rev. ed. 1980), 82–86; Porter, "Claro Obscuro, or Light and Shade Painting on Walls," *Scientific American*, 9 April and 11 September 1845, 12 March 1846.

8. "Editorial Correspondence," *Scientific American*, 6 August 1846; Lipman, *Rufus Porter*, 39–47; Rufus Porter, *Aerial Navigation* (New York, 1849); *A Yankee Inventor's Flying Ship: Two Pamphlets*, ed. Rhoda R. Gilman (St. Paul, Minn., 1969).

9. Mary Black, *Erastus Salisbury Field: 1805–1900* (Williamsburg, Va., 1963), 30–34; John Caldwell and Oswaldo Rodriguez Roque, *American Paintings in the Metropolitan Museum of Art* (New York, 1994), 500–503.

10. Beatrix T. Rumford, *American Folk Portraits: Paintings and Drawings from the Abby Aldrich Rockefeller Folk Art Center* (New York, 1981), 100–102.

11. Black, *Erastus Salisbury Field*, 34–39; John Vlach, *Plain Painters: Making Sense of American Folkart* (Washington, D.C., 1988), 20–25.

12. Paul Staiti, "Ideology and Rhetoric in Erastus Salisbury Field's *The Historical Monument of the American Republic*," *Winterthur Portfolio* 27 (Spring 1992): 43; Black, *Erastus Salisbury Field*, 41.

13. *Greenfield Gazette*, 9 June 1900, quoted in Black, *Erastus Salisbury Field*, 57.

Index

Brigham, Paul, 67, 117

Bright, George, 119

Brightly, Professor (daguerreotypist), 293, 294, 297

Brinton, William, 14

Bristol (Conn.), town of, 151, 171, 179, 184, 186, 313

Britain: American Revolution and, 83; charters with American colonies, 7; consumer revolution and, 2, 3; Revolutionary crisis and, 32; "Yankee clocks" seized by customs officials, 311–12

Brookfield (Mass.), town of, 19, 76, 310, 329

Brown, Gawen, 28

Brown, Gilson, 197–98

Brown, Henton, 9, 10

Brown, J., 223, 236

Bruckner, Martin, 111

Bruegel, Martin, 187

Buckminster, David, 210

Buell, David, 89

Bull, Celestia, 149

Bullard, Eleazer, 259, 260

Bullard, Emeline Sheldon, 260, 261

Bullfinch, Charles, 270

Bullock family, 121

bureaus, 121, 122, 210, 213, 318, 319

Burnap, Daniel, 62, 63, 65–68, 117, 150

Burpee, Newton, 197

Bushman, Richard, 32, 319

Buttre, William, 195, 200

The Cabinet-maker and Upholsterer's Drawing Book of 1793 (Sheraton), 210, 211

The Cabinet-maker and Upholsterer's Guide (Hepplewhite), 114–15, 210

cabinetmakers, 18, 21, 22, 59, 115, 119; country-trained, 193; innovations of, 27; portraits of, 261; specialization and, 312; tools of, xiv; urban, 25. *See also* furniture

Cahill, Holger, 221

Calvinism, 4

camera obscura, 239, 244–45, 282

Camp, Hiram, 305, 313, 314

Campbell, Harriet, 222, 236

Canada, 89, 131, 139

candlesticks, 319

capitalism, 3, 56, 220, 327; paper money and, 137; reorganization of labor process, xv

Captain Samuel Chandler (Chandler), 41, 42

Carew, Polly, 87

Carey, Mathew, 153–56

Carlisle, David, 125–27

Carpenter, Edward, 310–11

Carpenter, Elijah, 293

Carpenter, William and Mary, 82

carpenters/carpentry, 21, 56, 192

carpets, 93, 213, 266, 281, 317, 319–20

Carson, Cary, 14

Carter and Andrews, 207–8

cartography, x, 107, 111, 124. *See also* maps

carvers/carving, 18, 27, 39

cash payments, 21, 30

Casper, Scott, 156

censuses, 135, 159, 195, 205, 303, 310

chairmakers/chairmaking, ix, 3, 18; caners, 18; centralization and consolidation of, 306–7, 309–12, 314; decentralized production, 198; Gaines family, 19–20; industrial revolution and, 189–92; of Northampton, 60–61; of plain and fancy chairs, 202–7, 214; regional elites as patrons, 37; value of real estate owned by, 320–21; women outworkers and, 200–202; workshops and manufactories, 193–95, *196*, 197–200

chairs, ix, 8, 16; Chapin workshop, 39–40; Chippendale, 8, 27, 36, 40; fancy, 202, 206, 214, 217, 273, 306; flag-seated, 193, *196*, 200; Hitchcock, 149, 213–17, *215*, 323; leather-bottomed, 8, 9, 45; market revolution and, 148; as parlor furnishings, 318; rocking, ix, 199, 234, 317, 318, 321; upholstered armchairs, 121; workmanship of habit and, 27. *See also* side chairs; Windsor chairs

Champlain, Eliza Way, 85, 88

Champlain, George, 87

Champney, L. C., 289, 292, 293, 302–3, 325

Chandler, Anna Paine, 41

Chandler, John, 11

Chandler, Joseph Goodhue, 252

Chandler, Mary Gleason, 40, 42

Chandler, Capt. Samuel, 41, *42*, 43

Chandler, Winthrop, 2, 18, 81, 83, 191; artisanal roots, 92; community norms and portraits of, 30; death of, 42; Devotion family portraits, x, 1, 7, 11, 33, 35–36, 87; elite clientele of, 3; family of, 40–42; fancy aesthetic and, 240; innovations in portraiture, 27; life and career, 9, 11–12; patrons of, 41–45; self-portrait, 41–42, *44*

Chapin, Eliphalet, 28–29, 37, 39–41

Charles Holt (Way), 85–86, *86*

Charlotte Temple (Rowson), 135

Cheney, Ashael, 117

Cheney, Benjamin, 29, 63–64, 117, 147, 150, 175

Cheney, Martin, 117–18

Cheney, Silas, 89, 115, 214

Cheney brothers, 28

cherrywood, 21, 28; chairs, 8, 36, 40; in clock-making, 175, 181

Chester, Caroline, 54

Chester, John, 29–30

Chester County (Penn.), 61–62, 109; daguerreotypists in, 302; furniture making, 203, 204, 312

chestnut wood, 28

chest-on-chests, 56, 57

chests of drawers ("case drawers"), 9, 23, 50, 62,
320; by Bliss and Horswill, 119–20, 120; by
Cumiston and Buckminster, 209; by Dunlap
family, 25, 26; fancy bow front, 213; by Kneeland and Adams, 119, 121; by Spooner, 208, 210,
plate 6; as status commodity, 36

Children in Red series (Phillips), 222

*Child's Assistant to a Knowledge of the Geography
and History of Vermont* (Hall), 136–37

The Child's book of nature, "Dodo" illustration
from, 207, 208

china, 3, 16

Chin-Sung, 231–32

Chippendale, Thomas, 18

Chronology (Prince), 7

*Chronology Delineated / To Illustrate the History
of Monarchical Revolutions* (Eddy and Wilson),
134

civil society, 98

Civil War, 279, 313, 334

Clarissa Gallond Cook (Field), 262–63, 265

Clark, Anson, 286–88, 287, 289

Clark, Christopher, 227, 310

Clark, Edwin, 286

Clark, Heman, 174

Clark, Nathaniel, 160–61

Claypoole, Anna, 86, 87

Clemens, Paul, 187

clergymen, xiii, 6, 51, 154, 227, 310

clockmakers/clockmaking, ix, 3, 9, 21, 62–63;
apprenticeship and, 63–65; centralization and
consolidation of, 307–9, 312–14; Cheney family,
63–64, 117–18, 150, 152; in Connecticut Valley,
23; English, 25; innovations of, 27; in Litchfield,
89; machinery used by, 64; mass manufacture,
168–72, 174–79; materials used, 28, 29; regional
elites as patrons, 37; reinvention of clockmaking, 150–53; steps in manufacturing, 64–65;
Torrington as center of, 180; urban-based distribution system, 311–12; Village Enlightenment
and, 49, 79; Willard family, 118, 170–71; wood
varieties used by, 22

clock peddlers, 148, 151, 153, 171, 228; difficulties
encountered by, 158–59, 183–86; distribution
system and, 182–83; shelf clocks and, 173; tinware peddling and, 182; working on credit, 160,
161. *See also* peddlers

clocks, ix, 3, 117, 182; banjo clocks, 170–71, 171; box
clocks, 146, 147, 174; Enlightenment and, 49;
innovation in manufacture, 28; London tall
clocks, 9, 10; marketing of, 148, 179–87;
musical, 104, 104, 118, 119; pillar-and-scroll top
case, 174, 179. *See also* shelf clocks; tall clocks

clocks, brass, 28, 64, 67, 213, 327; arrival of cheaper
clocks, 174, 304–6, 305; as expensive items, 150,
174; scale of production, 308

clocks, wooden, 63, 89, 213, 319; brass clocks
favored over, 184, 311; hood of, 28, 29; as inexpensive items, 304; one-day, 304; painted dials
of, 151; prices, 187; scale of production, 171, 308;
Terry's revolutionized manufacture of, 170, 172,
304; ubiquity of, 186, 187; wheels, 181

Cogswell, Mason Fitch, 83

Cole, Thomas, 273

Collier, Thomas, 89

Colt, Samuel, 330

Colton, Elihu, 66, 67

Columbian (newspaper), 87

Columbiaville Manufacturing Society, 269

Comee, James, 191, 193, 195, 210

commercialization, x, 145; itinerants at center of,
157; mapmaking and, 130; portrait painters and,
226; social hierarchy dissolved by, 150; Victorian parlor culture and, 324

Committees of Correspondence, 34, 81

commodities, cultural, ix, xii, 48, 124, 326; cartographic, 109; fetishism of commodities, xv;
scarce, 281, 326; transformative power of, 162;
transportation improvements and, 124–25; of
Victorian parlor, x; Weems's popular biographies, 156

Common Sense (Paine), 33, 35

Condy, Jeremy, 32

Congregational church, 3, 35, 230, 278, 328

Congress, U.S., 33, 34, 126

Connecticut, 4, 11; in American Revolution, 41;
architecture, 93; clockmaking in, 28, 66,
147–48, 150, 152, 180–81; female academies, 86;
itinerant preaching banned by, 5; libraries, 8;
native woods of, 21; portrait painting in, 79;
probate inventories, 9; rural elite (village
gentry), 43, 84; state prison in Wethersfield,
205, 215; tin industry, 161–62

Connecticut Courant (newspaper), 32–33, 66, 121

Connecticut Land Company, 96

Connecticut River Valley, x, 18, 37, 98, 131, 190;
clockmakers in, 28; Enlightenment in, 49;
globe making in, 106; town settlement in, 124

Connecticut Valley doorway, 23

connoisseurship, 39

consumerism/consumer culture, ix, 157, 324; consumer revolution, 1–3, 12–14, 16, 45; cultural revolution and, 239–40; dangers of, in popular images, 164, *165*, 166, 168; gathering momentum of, 237–38; peddlers and, 187; portrait painters and, 226, 238

Continental Congress, 34, 88

Cook, Clarissa Gallond, 262–63, *263*, 266

Cook, Capt. James, 107, 109, 141, 142, 145, 242

Cook, Louisa Gallond, 262, 263, *264*, 265–66

Cook, Nathaniel, 262, 264, *265*

Cook, William Lauriston, 262, 264

Cooke Jr., Edward, 27

Cook's Voyages, 80

Cooper, William, 77

coopering, 19

Cooperstown (N.Y.), town of, 69, 73, 77

Copley, John Singleton, 11, 28, 81, 117, 286; community norms and portraits of, 30; Earl and, 83; life and career, 12; on plight of American painters, 88; portraits in patrician houses, 16–17; Tilley portrait, 35

Corbit-Sharp House, *15*, 17

cordwainers. *See* shoemakers/shoemaking

A Correct Map of the State of Vermont (Whitelaw and Wilson), 132, *133*, *134*, 135

Cosgrove, Denis, 107

cosmopolitanism, 45, 50; cabinetmaking and, 209–13; clockmakers and, 117; geographical expansion of, 95; globe makers and, 108; home furnishings and, 318; Philadelphia cultural institutions, 235; printing trade and, 73, 76, 77; Village Enlightenment and, 55, 106; of Walpole literati, 124, 129

counterfeiting, 137, 288, *288*

Country Builder's Assistant (Benjamin), 112

"The Country Lovers, or Jonathan Jolthead's Courtship with Miss Sally Snapper" (Fessenden), 128–29

Cowee, John, 205

Cowee, William, 278

Crafts, Ebenezer, 69

craftsmen, xi, 2, 17, 187; cosmopolitan links of, 50; dynamic tradition of, 28–29; farmer-craftsmen, 3, 19, 23, 192; gentility and, 259; middle-class identity and, 227; part-time, 20; quality of workmanship, 27–28; in rural commercial centers, 118; variety of, 59; Village Enlightenment and, 49, 55; wood varieties used by, 21–22

Crandall family, 281

Cranston, Joel, 53, 99, 100

credit, 80, 217; absence of, 78; clock-factory workers and, 179; in clockmaking, 181; credit agencies, 309; peddlers working on, 160, 161, 184

Crocker, Alvah, 309

Cumister and Buckminster firm, 210

Daggett, David, 4

Daguerre, Louis-Jacques-Mandé, 276, 282, 283

daguerreotypes, ix, xi, xiii, 318; arrival in America, 282–96; as challenge to painters, 279; invention of, 276; portraits, 159, *160*, *293*, *294*, *302*, plate 10; professionalization of, 296–303; saloons and "floating galleries," 289–92, *290*, *291*; Victorian parlor culture and, 322–24, 327; Wright's Lumber Mill employees, *274*, 275, 276

Daguerrian Journal, 296, 297

Daniel Boardman (Earl), 90, *91*

Darby, Henry F., 321–22

Darlington, Amos, Jr., 203, 204

Darlington, Amos, Sr., 62

Darnton, Robert, 101

Dartmouth College, 87, 107, 108, 117, 118; engraving of buildings of, 138; Federalist literati and, 128

Davis, Joseph H., 240

The Death of General Warren at the Battle of Bunker Hill (Trumbull), 334

debating societies, 97

Declaration of Independence, 88

decoration: fancy aesthetic, 238–48; "folk" motifs, 36; neoclassical, 49; painted imitation of expensive woods, 151; in portraits, *233*, *234*; rococo, 37

Deerfield (Mass.), town of, 72, 97

Deerfield Academy, 69–70, 97

Definitions and Elementary Observations in Astronomy; also, Problems on the Globes (Gummere), 110

Delaware, 16, 318

Deming, Simeon, 114, 115, 116

democracy and democratization, 128, 129; folk art and, 220–21; portraiture and, 303; social hierarchy dissolved by, 150

Dennie, Joseph, 123–24, 126–28, 130

Dennie, Mary Green, 123

Derby, Philander, 307

desks, 8–9, 105, *105*, 108

Devotion, Rev. Ebenezer, 1–4, 30; American Revolution and, 12; Atlantic world of printing trade and, 30; Chandler portrait of, *xvi*, 1; death of, 33; Great Awakening and, 4–7; local craftsmen and, 45; possessions of, x, 7–9, 13, 32, 36, 147; social world of, 149–50

Devotion, Ebenezer, Jr., x, 1–2, 45; children of, 87; life and career, 33–35; local craftsmen and, 3; portrait of, *xvi*, 1, 35–36; possessions, 36–40

prices, xiv, 30; books, 154–55; clocks, 150–51, 174, 185–87; daguerreotypes, 299; furniture, 115; globes, 142; maps, 138; portraits, 92, 94, 225–26, 236, 251

printers/printing, x, 18, 101; Atlantic world of, 30–33; British copyright restrictions, 31; consolidation of urban publishing, 328; globes and, 107; labor process, 22; rural consumers of print culture, 96–97; shops, 23; urban markets and, 78; Village Enlightenment and, 73–79; in Walpole, N.H., 125–26. *See also* books/book trade

Prior, William Matthew, 251–52, 254, 258

prison labor, 205, 215

Profile of a Lady with Ruff (Porter), 247

"The Progress of Science" (Lord), 55

Protestantism, evangelical, 154

Providence, city of, 31, 34, 59, 125, 205, 311

Psalms and Hymns (Watts), 77–78

Puffer, Sarah (Mrs. Newton Hubbard), 317

Putnam, Elijah, 194, 205

"putting-out" systems, 80, 193

Pye, David, 26–27, 178

Pyle, George, 300–303

Quakers, 109, 110, 269

"Qualifications of a First-Class Daguerreotypist" (Root), 297–98

Queen Anne style, 18–19

railroad transport, 203, 272, 309

Rainer, Joseph, 161

Raven, James, 31

The Reasonableness and Certainty of the Christian Religion (Jenkins), 7

Reed, Elbridge Gerry, 199–200

Reeve, Tapping, 68–70, 116

Rembrandt van Rijn, 297, 298

republican culture/ideology, xii, 47; cultivation of knowledge and, 97; female reason and, 54; literati's distrust of mobocracy, 127–28; neoclassical style and, 114; in ornamental design, 174; "Republican motherhood," 71

Reverend Ebenezer Devotion (Chandler), *xvi*, 1

The Reverend John Atwood and His Family (Darby), *321*, 321–22

Reynolds, Sir Joshua, 28, 81, 83, 228, 234; *Discourses on Art*, 254–55; guide to young artists, 297

Ridgely, Nicholas, 16

rifles, manufacture of, 174–75, 330

Ristow, Walter, 131

Rivington, James, 32

road networks, 125, 214

The Robbers (Schiller), 54

Roberts, Candace, 151–52

Roberts, Gideon, 151, 171–72, 182

Robinson, Lewis, 134, 138–39, 161, 352 n.61

rococo style, 37–39, 66, *67*, 130–31

Roger Sherman (Earl), 81, *82*

Roman Republic, ancient, 114

Root, Marcus, 297

Rorabaugh, William, 68

Rosa Heywood (Peckham), *274, 275*, 279–80, plate 9

Rowson, Susanna, 135

Roxbury (Mass.), town of, 11, 98, 170

The Rural Repository (journal), 272

Russell, Lady Caroline, 28

Ryder, James, 293–95, 325

St. George, Robert, 18

Sarah Pierce's Female Academy, 69–71

Savage, Edward, 117, 277

A Saving Interest in Christ (devotional tract), 11

Sawyer, Ruth (née Peckham), 277

sawyers, 206

Scarlet, Levi, 301

schools and schooling, 53, 68–73, 97, 109–10, 239. *See also* academies

Schuyler, Catherine Van Rensselaer, 83

sciences, 55, 107, 238

Scientific American magazine, 239, 330

Scotch-Irish settlers, 24, 25

Sedgwick, Catharine Maria, 53–54

Select and Original Dialogues, Orations and Single Pieces, designed for the Use of Schools (Robinson), 134, 138

A Select Collection of Valuable and Curious Arts (Porter), 238, 239, 241, 247, 255, 330

self-improvement, 47, 49, 51, 238, 248

Seymour, Thomas, 210

Shays's Rebellion, 211

Sheldon, Charlotte, 54

Sheldon, Lucy, 71

shelf clocks, ix, xi, 118; invention of, 172–74; in paintings and travelers' accounts, 187; peddling system and, 182; by Terry, 147–50, *148*; Victorian parlor culture and, 323

Sheppard, Sarah R., 110, plate 3

Sheraton, Thomas, 210, 211

Sherman, H. W., 286, 303

Sherman, Roger, 81, 88, 92

shoemakers/shoemaking, 19, 59, 100, 106, 108, 109

shopping, 312

Sibley, Solomon, 56, 60, 192

sideboards, xi, 36, 121; by Hayes, 13; neoclassical, 103–4, 111–12, *112, 113*, 114–16, 273 side chairs: by Brown, *197*, 197–98; Chippendale, 36; diamond-splat, *40*, 41; by Gaines, *20*; in portraits, 1; by Pratt, 198, *199*; rococo, *40*, 41; Victorian, 306, *307*

silhouettes, 226, 246, 276, 281, 367 n.39

silversmiths, 119

Smith, Ann Y., 89, 216–17

Smith, Chloe, 96

Smith, Margaret Bayard, 54, 342 n.15

Smith, Noah, 96

Smith, William Henry, and family, 332–33, *333*

The Smith Family (Field), 332–33, *333*

Snell, Ebenezer Strong, 318

Snelling, Henry Hunt, 296

social hierarchy, xiii, 150, 277; class mobility, 158; emergence of new hierarchy, 327; Victorian parlor culture and, 320

Society of Social Enquirers, 47, 48, 51, 97, 98, 100

Society of the Cincinnati, 92

sofas, 211, 213, 318

Some Thoughts Concerning Education (Locke), 35

Sons of Liberty, 4

Southworth, A. S., 282–83, 285–86, 289, 292, 302

Southworth & Hawes firm, 286, 288

specialization, 181, 195, 196, 312

Spooner, Alden, 195, 210–11, 213

Sprats, William, 93

Springfield (Mass.), town of, 78, 175, 329, 330

Staël, Madame de, 54

stagecoaches, 125

Staiti, Paul, 12, 334

Stamp Act crisis, 6

status, goods as signs of, 14, 16, 181

steam power, 203, 308, 310

Sterling (Mass.), town of, 189–93, 200, 217, 258, 310, 326; chairmaking workshops, 193, 195, 197–98; scale of production in, 203, 306

Stiles, Ezra, 33, 131

Stock, Joseph Whiting, 237, 244, 289

Stoddard, William, 272

storekeepers, 21, 80, 179; hatmaking industry and, 212; Heywood family, 205; as middlemen suppliers, 201; peddlers and, 157, 162–64, 184

stoves, 318, 319

Stowe, Harriet Beecher, 72

Strahan, William, 106

Straw, Thomas Ackely, 319

Stuart, Benjamin, 199

Stuart, Gilbert, 235, 250–51, 255, 272, 298

Styles, John, xv

subcontractors, independent, 313

Sully, Thomas, 235, 250, 251

surveyors, 21, 53, 131

Sweeney, Kevin, 14, 43, 114

tables, 9, 16, 213, 318; card tables, 121, 122; center tables in parlors, 317; circular, 319; Empire, 281; owned by portrait sitters, 45; Pembroke, 36, 115, 116

Taintor, Delia Ellsworth, 256

Taintor, Griswold, 256

The Talcott Family (Goldsmith), *233*, 233–34

tall clocks, 25, 27, 118; musical, 104, *104*, 118; by Terry, 168, *169*; Victorian parlor culture and, 323

Tallmadge, Benjamin, 89, 92, 116

Tallmadge, Mary Floyd, 92

taste, xiv–xv, 255, 272, 297, 326

Taylor, Rev. Nathaniel, 90

tea equipment, 9, 13, 14, 16, 17

technology, xv, 174, 178, 292

temperance, 74, 97, 279

Ten Broeck family, 223

Terry, Eli, ix, 68, 147–49, 182, 217, 273; "American System of Manufactures" and, 174; domestic interiors transformed by, 317; invention of shelf clock, 172–74; marketing of clocks and, 181–83; mass production of clocks, 175–78, *176*, *177*; reinvention of clockmaking and, 150–53; success as clockmaker, 168–72, 179, 187, 304

Terry, Eli, Jr., 182, 183, 185

Terry, Henry, 150, 168, 173, 177

Terry & Barnum Manufacturing Company, 327

textile industry, 2, 19, 189

Thomas, Isaiah, 71, 73, 76, 191; American Revolution and, 33; on printers in colonial period, 31; Walpole as print center and, 125–26

Thomas, Robert, 73–76, 96, 101, 344 n.50

Thomas, Seth, 168, 171, 174; business partnership with Terry, 173; clockmaking tools of, 178; death of, 314; new brass clocks and, 306; shop of, 172

Thompson, Zadock, 135–36

Thonet, Francis, 307

Throop, George, 234

Timothy Doty and Family (Peckham), 211–13, *212*

tinsmiths/tinware, 160–62, 179

Tocqueville, Alexis de, 97, 227, 329

Tontine Building (Windsor, Vt.), 112, 123

Toole, John, 300, 325

tools/toolmakers, 19, 21, 22; for clockmaking, 175, 178; lathes, 248

A Topographical Map of the State of Vermont (Blodget), 131

Tracy family, 120

Transcendentalists, 158

transportation, improvements in, 124–25, 310

Trent, Robert, 9, 39